Entertain Us

THE RISE OF
NIRVANA

GILLIAN G. GAAR

Entertain Us

THE RISE OF
NIRVANA

Entertain Us
THE RISE OF NIRVANA

by Gillian G. Gaar

A Jawbone book
First edition 2012
Published in the UK and the USA by Jawbone Press
2a Union Court,
20–22 Union Road,
London SW4 6JP,
England
www.jawbonepress.com

ISBN 978-1-906002-89-3

EDITOR Thomas Jerome Seabrook
DESIGN Paul Cooper Design

Printed by Regent Publishing Services Limited, China

1 2 3 4 5 16 15 14 13 12

FAR LEFT ABOVE: **Nirvana's first performance in Olympia, May 1 1987, when the band was known as Skid Row. Allison Wolfe, later of Bratmobile, said of the show: "I remember feeling like something big was happening."**

LEFT ABOVE: **Kurt at a show in Seattle, October 28 1988, when Nirvana opened for the Butthole Surfers.**

LEFT BELOW AND THIS PAGE: **Nirvana's first photo session, for the 'Love Buzz' single, with photographer Alice Wheeler, summer 1988. "I shot as much film as I possibly could," Alice said of the session, for which she was paid $25.**

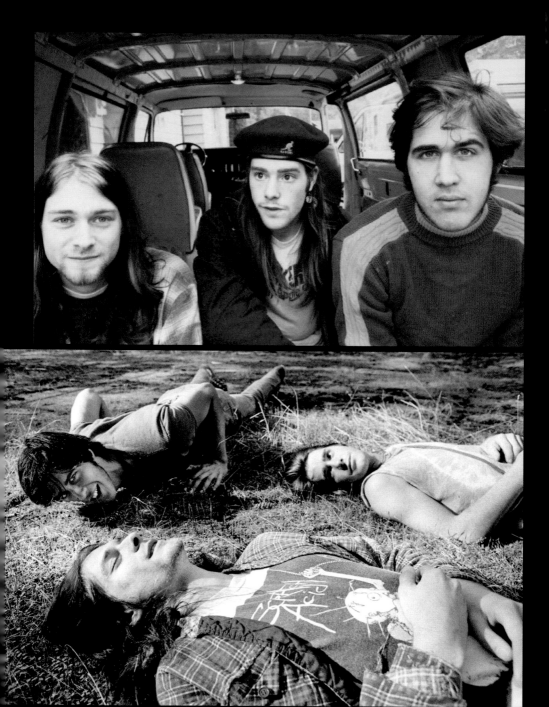

LEFT ABOVE: **Preparing to hit the road again, fall 1988. This picture was taken by Tracy Marander, Kurt's girlfriend, who photographed many of the band's early shows and shot the cover for Nirvana's first album, *Bleach*.**
LEFT BELOW: **Charles Peterson's first photo session with Nirvana, fall 1988. "They were shy but sweet," he recalled.**
THIS PAGE: **Nirvana at the University of Washington, Seattle, February 25 1989, with Jason Everman in the line-up.**

LEFT ABOVE: **A picture taken during this Seattle show on August 26 1989 became a cover shot on the December 1989 issue of** *The Rocket*. **It was the first time Nirvana had a magazine cover all to themselves.**

LEFT BELOW: **Nirvana at Seattle's Annex Theatre, April 7 1989. The crowd passed Kurt over their heads during the song 'Blew.'**

THIS PAGE: **Nirvana became friends with photographer J.J. Gonson when they played in Jamaica Plain, Massachusetts, on July 15 1989. Kurt drank Strawberry Quik as he said it helped his stomach.**

ABOVE AND RIGHT BELOW: **A return show at the University of Washington, Seattle, January 6 1990. The band trashed their gear to such an extent they were banned from doing any future shows at the venue.**
LEFT: **When Nirvana returned to Massachusetts in the spring of 1990, Kurt gave photographer J.J. Gonson a tape of the new songs they'd just recorded with Butch Vig in Madison. "They were amazing," she said.**
RIGHT ABOVE: **Nirvana at Man Ray, Cambridge, Massachusetts, April 18 1990.**

ABOVE: **Two shots of Nirvana at the Motor Sports International Garage, Seattle, on September 22 1990 – one of the most chaotic shows of their career. Kurt switched guitars at the end, smashing a guitar he only played for one song.**
LEFT: **Dave Grohl, seen here playing with Mission Impossible, played with a number of bands in the Washington DC hardcore scene before joining Nirvana.**
RIGHT: **Nirvana's final line-up, on the day they were interviewed by Dawn Anderson's magazine** *Backlash* **in 1991. "We get complete, 100 per cent creative control," Kurt told her of the band's newly signed contract.**

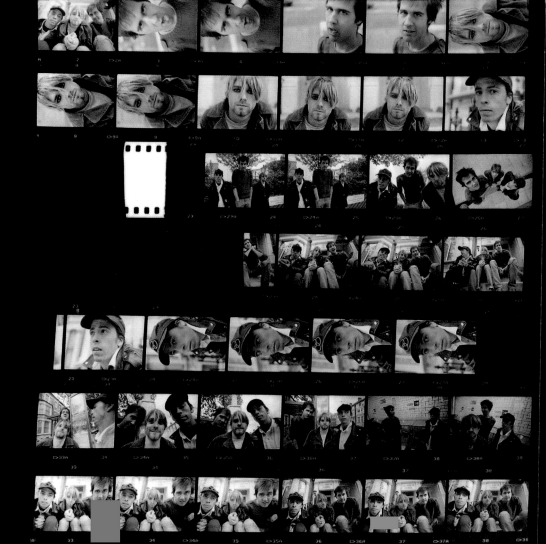

Here We Are Now

"I just thought that was a nice little title."
KURT ON 'SMELLS LIKE TEEN SPIRIT,' 1992

One day in the spring of 1991 – early April, perhaps, or maybe March – Kurt Cobain brought in a new riff to a Nirvana rehearsal, a riff that *Spin* magazine would later call "the most culturally important nine seconds of the 90s." Nirvana's rehearsals often began with lengthy jams ("A big part of the rehearsal experience was working on different things and experimenting," says Krist Novoselic), and the band jammed on this particular riff for some time – "the better part of an hour," according to one account.

"That song came out of nowhere," Krist says. "He just had that four-note riff." Neither Krist nor Dave Grohl regarded the song as anything special; Kurt later recalled that when he first played the riff to his bandmates, Krist had remarked: "That is so ridiculous." And Nirvana frequently jammed on riffs that were catchy enough during rehearsal and then forgotten forever. But this riff stuck, and the band found themselves returning to it again and again. "The simple guitar lines were so memorable," Dave later explained. Eventually, it began to evolve into a song.

"We were playing it for a while, and then we just stopped," Krist says. "And either I or Dave went: why don't we do this part slow? So we started playing it slow. And Kurt started to experiment a little bit and he did a verse melody; what he was doing before was pretty much the big chorus. And then we just put it together. It was that dynamic – like loud, quiet, loud, quiet. There was a little bridge, and a solo. It came together pretty fast."

Although the lyrics were not yet finalized, Kurt had just the title for the new song. It was a phrase his friend Kathleen Hanna, from the riot grrrl band Bikini Kill, had scrawled on his bedroom wall the previous August. The two had spent a particularly memorable evening together in Olympia, Washington, where they both lived, drinking and spray-painting graffiti on a local 'teen pregnancy center' that purported to offer non-judgmental advice to pregnant teens but in fact sternly counseled its clients against abortion (according to Kathleen, she'd sprayed 'fake abortion clinic' on the building, while Kurt had opted for 'God is gay'). They went to a bar and continued drinking, then ended up back at Kurt's apartment. Eventually, Kathleen picked up a Sharpie marker and wrote all over the wall before passing out, pen still in hand. Six months later, Kurt called her up with a surprising request.

"There's this thing you wrote on my wall and it was actually kind of cool," he said. "And I want to use it as a lyric in one of my songs." Kathleen agreed, even as she wondered: "How the fuck is he going to use 'Kurt smells like teen spirit' as a lyric?"

To Kurt, the phrase reflected the discussions he'd been having with Kathleen that night about teen revolution. "I thought she was saying that I was a person who could inspire," he said. But there was another underlying meaning to what Kathleen had written, something that was meant as a bit of a tease: Kurt's girlfriend at the time was Kathleen's bandmate in Bikini Kill, Tobi Vail, and the deodorant she used was named Teen Spirit. (Kurt always claimed not to have known of the deodorant's existence – using deodorant wasn't very punk rock.) In any event, 'Smells Like Teen Spirit' wasn't used as a lyric, but as the song's title.

Even before the lyrics were completed, Nirvana debuted the song live, at a show on April 17 1991 (a Wednesday) at Seattle's OK Hotel. This wasn't unusual. Throughout the band's history, they performed songs before Kurt had finished tinkering with them; sometimes a lyric wasn't completed until minutes before a song was recorded. An ad in

The Rocket, Seattle's music monthly, has the bands Leviathan, Deadly Effect, and Outrage originally booked to play that night. But that show was apparently cancelled, and a more alt-rock bill put together in its place, including not only Nirvana as the headliner, but also Bikini Kill and another Olympia band, Fitz Of Depression.

Stories of how the show came together are contradictory. One account has it that the show was arranged so Nirvana could earn enough money to buy gas for their upcoming trip to Los Angeles, where they were scheduled to record their major-label debut the next month. Another version says the show was set up as a benefit for Fitz singer Mikey Dees (aka Mikey Nelson), who had a number of outstanding traffic tickets, although Dees denies this. (Perhaps the confusion comes from Krist saying during Nirvana's set that Fitz had been pulled over on their way to the gig for driving a van with expired license tags and hit with a hefty fine.) Rich Jensen, who'd seen Nirvana from their early days in Olympia and was now working for their former label, Sub Pop, also describes the show as "unannounced": "We only heard about it that afternoon," he says. The fact that there's a poster advertising the gig – depicting a woman scrubbing out a sink with great industriousness – shows that there was at least some advance word, although Dave's comment during the band's set – "Thanks for coming out at such short notice" – suggests it was something of a last-minute show.

By the spring of 1991, Nirvana was a big draw, and the small club was filled to capacity; on being told the show was sold out, Rich had to bribe a bouncer to get inside. Another reason the show was packed was undoubtedly because Nirvana hadn't played in Seattle for five months, having devoted most of their time of late to woodshedding in preparation for recording their album. Nirvana was one of an increasing number of Pacific Northwest bands to have been picked up by the majors in recent years. In 1989, Soundgarden, another former Sub Pop act, released *Louder Than Love* on A&M; Alice In Chains debuted on Columbia with 1990's *Facelift*; Screaming Trees, who'd also recorded for Sub Pop, had recently released their major-label debut, *Uncle Anesthesia*, on Epic.

"Record companies are flocking to the Great Northwest, signing bands like crazy and hoping to find the Next Big Thing," *Rolling Stone* had written in 1990, although the article had gone on to note: "One has to wonder whether such key [Sub Pop] artists as Mudhoney or Nirvana could cross over into the Nineties mainstream without seriously compromising their sound." Nirvana was going to get the chance to find out when they left for LA to record their album for DGC, a subsidiary of Geffen Records. Kurt acknowledged this at the start of the show, wryly telling the audience: "Hello. We're major label corporate rock sellouts." The crowd whooped in response.

The 20-song set included such longtime Nirvana staples as 'Love Buzz,' 'Floyd The Barber,' and 'School'; newer material like 'Sliver,' their most recent single; a few covers (Devo's 'Turnaround,' The Wipers' 'D-7,' and an improvised 'Wild Thing'); and 'Verse Chorus Verse,' a melancholy pop song they'd never play live again. Fortuitously, the show was captured for posterity, as so many key moments in the band's career had been (remarkably, recordings exist of the band's very first and very last shows), as there were a number of cameras in attendance. Alan Pruzan was part of a three-camera crew, shooting from one side of the stage, with another camera on the other side, and one at the rear, and he also noted two women, not with his crew, shooting from the stage. "I shot as well as I could," he says. "It was pretty difficult. There was a lot of moving around. The thing that was funniest to me is that nobody bothered to adjust the stage lights, so they were primarily focused on the row of bouncer guys that were hired to keep people off the stage. So they were very well lit, but the band-members weren't so well lit."

Footage of the show that has since surfaced reveals a packed house with a crowd-surfer seen nearly every time a camera pans over the audience; the audience's constant heaving back and forth jostles the cameras as well. "There was already a frat boy kind of aspect to a

Seattle grunge-rock show," Alan says. "There was a period where that wasn't happening at all, but then there'd be the guy that would jump up on stage and be like: Nirrrvannaa! Fuck yeah! and all that kind of stuff. And that was happening a little bit at that show. You could certainly see it on the tape." After 'Negative Creep,' one of the stage invaders escaped with the microphone, causing Dave to implore: "Hey, can we have our microphone back so we can play some more songs?"

At the set's conclusion, Kurt launched into the opening riff of 'Teen Spirit,' Krist and Dave joining him after a few bars. When this clip was officially released as part of the Nirvana boxed set *With The Lights Out*, a line of dialogue is dubbed in with Kurt introducing the song by name, but in the original footage, there's no introduction: he simply starts playing the riff. After the commanding opening, the band scales back instrumentally during the verses, with Dave keeping up the beat, Krist providing most of the musical backing with his bass line, and Kurt simply playing a repeated two note interval after each line of the verse, gradually building up to the explosive chorus. For Sub Pop co-founder Jonathan Poneman, it was a moment akin to his reaction on hearing Nirvana's first demo tape back in 1988. "When it started, I remember thinking: wow, this is a good song," he told author Everett True in his book *Nirvana: The True Story*. "And then it came to the chorus and it was like time stopped still for a second. Everyone was like: this has got to be one of the greatest choruses I've ever heard in my life."

At this stage, the song only had one verse that Kurt repeated three times; none of its lyrics would be in the final version. A few key phrases would remain – the "hello"/"how low" wordplay that leads into the chorus, and another line that Kurt took from a joke he used to break the ice when arriving at a party. "A lot of times, when you're standing around with people in a room, it's really boring and uncomfortable," he explained to *Rolling Stone*. "So it was: well, here we are, entertain us. You invited us here."

But musically, this early version largely resembled the song that would reach the Top Ten in just six months time. The quiet verse/loud chorus dynamic – which Nirvana readily acknowledged was borrowed from the Pixies – creates a beguiling tension that finds its final release in the song's climax, as Kurt screams out *"A denial!"* over and over until it sounds like his throat is completely shredded. (In fact, years of such screaming had toughened his vocal cords.)

The crowd's enthusiastic response to 'Teen Spirit' surprised Dave, who thought to himself: "Hmm, that was kind of cool. A new song that nobody knows, and they're all bouncing around!" When the applause died down, Kurt joked: "This is our rock star encore right now, but we're not gonna go to the back room, we're just gonna stand up here for a minute, OK?" The band took a short break before going on to play another four songs. After the show, Stuart Hallerman, Soundgarden's sound engineer and a local studio owner, asked Krist: "You guys going to record that song for your record?"

"Yeah," Krist replied.

"Well, you should," Stuart told him. "It's a good song."

Around the same time, Nirvana recorded 'Teen Spirit' on a cassette they made for their producer, Butch Vig, to give him an idea of the songs they might want to record for the album that would eventually be called *Nevermind*. "They recorded on this boom box, and it distorted so badly that I could barely make out what they were playing," says Butch. "I couldn't understand anything that was going on, except that I could hear a little bit of the 'hello, hello' part in 'Teen Spirit' and the intro riff on 'Come As You Are.' As soon as Dave would start playing, it was so distorted it was like: *PAHHHAH*. He plays louder and harder than anybody I've ever met. So it was kind of hard for me to get a sense of what was going on."

Butch got a better idea when the band arrived in Los Angeles and rehearsed for a few days before entering the studio. "I didn't want them to play too much, 'cause I didn't want them to burn out on the songs," he explains. "But I remember, after hearing 'Teen Spirit,' I was so into the song I had them play it as much as possible. The song was amazing."

Kurt still hadn't finished the song. "There were a couple lines he was still working on," Butch says. "Plus the melody. I remember him sitting down with the acoustic, and he had a couple variations of the melody. He did ask me about them and they were all really good. The first one was a little more monotone-y; the one that we ended up going with flowed more, moved around a lot more. And over the chord progressions of the verse, it sounded more interesting, because then the second part – the 'hello, hello' part – gets more monotone-y, so I just thought it was a stronger arrangement because the melody moved a lot more right at the get-go of the verse, then sort of honed in to a drone-y buzz till the end of the chorus."

Kurt had been working on the lyrics for weeks; in his Cobain biography *Heavier Than Heaven*, Charles R. Cross says there were "about a dozen" drafts of the song's lyrics, four pages of which appear in *Journals*, which reproduces select pages from Kurt's personal notebooks. The final lyric is a series of contrasts and contradictions: the defeatist posture of the verses (each of which has a negative word like "lose," "worse," or "hard") as compared with the more upbeat spirits of the chorus; the "mulatto"/"albino", "mosquito"/"libido" lyrical pairings; and most strikingly the bold admission of being "worse at what I do best." It's the closest look one gets at the singer's psyche, an admission of loss even in the midst of success (perhaps also a reflection of his feelings about his eventual break up with Tobi Vail). The rest of the time, Kurt seems to be shrugging off too much scrutiny, ending the third verse almost dismissively: "Whatever. Never mind."

The meaning of the lyrics would be endlessly debated after 'Teen Spirit' became a hit, which was also part of its appeal; because of the lyrical ambiguity, the song was open to numerous interpretations. In the DGC press release to accompany *Nevermind*'s release, Kurt pointed to the song's theme of disaffection, describing the song as being about "my generation's apathy. I'm disgusted with it." Quick to avoid alienating his audience, he added: "I'm disgusted with my own apathy too, for being spineless and not always standing up against racism, sexism, and all those other isms the counterculture has been thinking about for years." He was less self-conscious in his first interviews for the album, telling *Pulse*: "It's a typical teenage aggression song. It has revolutionary themes, but I don't really mean it in a militant [light]. The generation's apathy is getting out of hand. [I'm] pleading to the kids: wake up!"

Neither Dave nor Krist felt the song had much of a deep meaning. "Seeing Kurt write the lyrics to a song five minutes before he first sings them, you just kind of find it a little bit hard to believe that the song has a lot to say about something," Dave explained to Michael Azerrad, author of *Come As You Are: The Story Of Nirvana*. "I've always felt that the song was an observation of a culture mired in boredom amidst relative luxury," Krist wrote in his memoir/manifesto *Of Grunge And Government: Let's Fix This Broken Democracy!* "In other words, many have the means to make their way but choose not to do so. The lyrics don't convey a literal message guiding people toward a sense of liberation. It's simply a comment on a condition."

"Sometimes Kurt's lyrics were nonsensical to me," Krist says. "I don't know what they meant. But I thought he always wanted to do that: be kind of cryptic, and just kind of play with words instead of be overly political. Just more kind of poetry."

'Teen Spirit' had already proved its strength in live performance; it was Butch Vig's job to create a recording that had the same unbridled passion. Already excited about the song, he worked to make 'Teen Spirit' sound as compelling in the studio as it did when he listened to it at rehearsals. He achieved this by having the band do more overdubbing than they had previously done in the studio, telling them: "When you guys play live, it's just so incredibly loud and intense – it's larger than life and I'm trying to use some of these things I know in the studio to make you guys come across that way."

Butch took particular care in layering the guitar sounds. "Kurt wanted to play it live all the way through," he says. "And I wanted to really be able to focus on the sounds on each section, instead of him just stepping on a pedal and changing it. I was trying to make the parts really defined, having the clean guitar in the intro, then the heavy guitar, then the effected, sort of watery guitar in the verse. It took a while, because Kurt was used to playing it live; it took him a second to get his timing. I think we probably spent the better part of a day doing the guitar overdubs. I was actually kind of amazed that he seemed to be relatively patient that day, because a lot of times if he couldn't get something in a couple of takes, he would just lose interest and want to move on to something else." Kurt also balked when Butch wanted him to double-track his vocals, until the producer, knowing Kurt was a huge Beatles fan, told him John Lennon had done the same. "He'd think about it for a second and go: OK, I'll do it."

Butch also shortened the song's chorus, but made few other changes to the basic arrangement. "Just some suggestions for fills that Dave was doing coming out of the choruses and getting into the verses and things," he says. "Nothing major, like: boy, you need a new bridge, or this chord doesn't work so right with the chorus. All the parts were there to begin with. It was just trying to make it all flow really well."

The final recorded version emphasizes the dynamic texture of the song and skillfully captures its bristling energy. The opening, with Kurt strumming the main riff, is stark, setting the listener up for the powerful impact the full band makes when they come crashing in after a few measures, making it obvious why this is a riff a group of musicians could easily jam on for hours. The verses steadily increase in intensity, from a quiet beginning, rising to the moderate "hello"/"how low" section, up to the raging chorus, when the band plays all out. At the song's end, after the last time through the chorus, the band pushes themselves even harder, Kurt's repeated cries of *"A denial!"* ringing out with unmistakable fury, although it's never clear what's driving his frustration or what it is he's raging against. It's a question that's left hanging, unanswered, as Kurt's voice and guitar finally mesh together at the song's end, and the final chord slowly dies away.

It's Kurt's voice that gives the song its character, and stamps it most firmly with his personality. His almost languorous drawl during the verses (which was much parodied by 'Weird Al' Yankovic in his song 'Smells Like Nirvana') is as enigmatic as the lyrics; he could be world-weary, introspective, or disinterested. But his full-throated delivery in the choruses is scorching, tapping into an unexpected well of emotion. "He was an amazing singer," says Butch. "There's sort of a toughness and a fragility at the same time that you don't hear in very many people – almost sort of a feminine side, and a vulnerable side. I think people can hear that."

When Butch played a rough mix for the band, even they seemed surprised at how strong it was. "Butch is like: hey, listen to this song," says Krist. "And he played it and it was just like: whoa, this song really rocks! The stars were aligned or something. The performance showed the power of the band – everybody was right on. And it was amazing. That song started to stick out."

"I remember we finished the record and I would just play 'Teen Spirit' over and over in the car," says Butch. "It just sounded so amazing; everything was just coming straight out of the speakers at you. I knew that was going to be one of the key tracks on the record – not knowing how big that song was going to become, but I knew it was going to be something powerful."

No one expected 'Smells Like Teen Spirit' to be a hit – not the band, their producer, their management, their label. "I thought 'Teen Spirit' was another good song, and it might get on [MTV's alternative-rock program] *120 Minutes* and allow us to tour with Sonic Youth or maybe headline Brixton Academy," Dave told his biographer, Paul Brannigan, in *This Is A Call*. "But no one thought it was a hit single because a hit single was just unimaginable. There was no world domination ambition. Because that just couldn't happen. That wasn't *allowed* to happen."

'Teen Spirit' was meant to be the song that opened the door for subsequent, more accessible singles from *Nevermind*. Instead, as Butch puts it, "it lit a match and started a fire." The song, the end result of the countless hours Kurt spent writing and re-writing lyrics and poetry; the range of musical influences the band-members had (Kurt was fond of describing Nirvana's music as "The Knack and the Bay City Rollers being molested by Black Flag and Black Sabbath"); and the hard work that Nirvana had put in over the four-plus years they'd been together, had proved to be irresistible. This, as *The Rocket* proudly noted in a profile of the band when *Nevermind* was released, was "music so simple and so true it gives you an unreachable sense of near-bursting." Six months after 'Teen Spirit' was written, and four months after it was recorded, it was being heard on an ever-growing number of radio and television stations, not just in America but around the world.

It should have been a moment of triumph for the band. Kurt had longed for this moment since he was a child, bragging to his friends that he was destined to be a rock star. By the fall of 1990, his confidence was such that he told his UK publicist his next singles were guaranteed to be Top Ten hits. But by the time 'Teen Spirit' reached the Top Ten, and *Nevermind* was on the verge of topping the US charts, success had become an unexpected burden. As 'Teen Spirit' became a generational anthem, Kurt quickly became tired of explaining what it 'really' meant, and eventually began to distance himself from the song, insisting he wrote others that were just as good. Nor was he comfortable in his new role as the heralded voice of a generation.

"I'm a spokesman for *myself*," he insisted in the first *Rolling Stone* cover story on the band. "It just so happens that there's a bunch of people that are concerned with what I have to say. I find that frightening at times because I'm just as confused as most people. I don't have the answers for anything. I don't want to be a fucking spokesperson." His unhappiness led to his becoming mired in heroin addiction, and he increasingly withdrew from the world, eventually taking his own life in April 1994.

And so in a sense 'Smells Like Teen Spirit' was the beginning of the end for Nirvana. It was the song that changed everything for the band, for the better and for the worse. Yet there is more to Nirvana's story than simple tragedy. *Nevermind* altered the cultural landscape; despite coming out early in the decade, it was still being acclaimed as one of the best albums of the 90s as the new century began, and 'Teen Spirit' was equally lionized.

"It was so much more than a hit album," says Mark Kates, DGC's head of promotion. "It was a moment in time. It's been played on the radio every day since we sent out that first single. It has! There was something that was accomplished by that song, and by that album, in terms of reaching people in a way that was completely unimaginable. And somehow Kurt's pain reached everyone else that had his pain – seemingly so, because there's really no other explanation for it being that big. Obviously, yeah, it's a catchy song, but, you know, so was [Lady Gaga's] 'Poker Face' and I don't think that's going to have the same resonance 20 years later. So I think it's a combination of: the timing was great, and there's the emotional aspect – which is, I do think, the most important thing, that it just reached people in an inexplicable, deep way. And, you know, I think that's just what it is: it's a catchy song, an amazing video, and one of the best albums ever made."

'Smells Like Teen Spirit' remains Nirvana' best-known work – "that one song that personifies the band," as Dave later put it. But the journey to becoming an international sensation wasn't an easy one. There were innumerable obstacles along the way, and more than a few times when the band could simply have fallen apart. But Kurt in particular had a determination – a single-minded focus – that kept Nirvana on an upward trajectory as they rose from the confines of a small, obscure town in Washington State.

CHAPTER 1

In The Pines

"See those trees against the sky / Northwest breezes blowing by / Life's so full of good things / Life's so good!"

RADIO JINGLE FOR ABERDEEN FEDERAL SAVINGS & LOAN

On February 20 1987, when Kurt Donald Cobain turned 20 years old, he was finally at a point where his life had a sense of direction. Since dropping out of high school in the spring of 1985, he'd drifted along aimlessly, briefly working various menial jobs but more often unemployed, going through periods of homelessness, crashing at the homes of various friends. The only reason he was now living in a home so small his friend Krist Novoselic referred to it as "a little half-house," was because his mother had loaned him the money to put down a deposit and pay the first month's rent.

Kurt had long yearned to be in a rock band, but his previous endeavors had failed to generate much interest. Now that he had a place of his own – or mostly his own, since he actually shared the house with Matt Lukin of the Melvins – he and Krist were determined to get a band going. They had roped in another friend from the Melvins circle – a drummer named Aaron Burckhard – and had begun rehearsing. Within a month of Kurt's 20th birthday, the as-yet-unnamed band would play their first show. After years of false starts, Kurt's career as a musician was finally getting off the ground.

It was a dream he'd had ever since he was a child, later telling his biographer, Michael Azerrad, that at age seven he "thought for sure I could be a rock star … I thought the United States was about as big as my backyard, so it would be no problem to drive all over the place and play in a rock band and be on the cover of magazines and stuff." Aberdeen, Washington, seemed an unlikely place for such dreams to come true. It had been founded in 1884, when logging was the predominant industry there and in the adjacent towns of Hoquiam and Cosmopolis, all of which were nestled around a series of rivers that fed into Grays Harbor. Aberdeen's population peaked in 1930 at just below 22,000, but the Great Depression hit the area hard, and the number of residents dropped steadily over the subsequent decades. Aberdeen still had a population of 19,000 when Cobain was born there on February 20 1967, but the timber industry was falling into decline, and the town's boom days were long since over.

A half hour's drive from the Pacific Coast, and 100 miles from the nearest large city, Seattle (also the largest city in Washington State), life in Aberdeen – a town just three miles long and four miles wide – was isolated. "It's just a little bit behind the times," says Jeff Burlingame, who grew up in Aberdeen and was later a journalist for the local newspaper, the *Daily World*. "It was a small town life, pretty much. There were a few things you could do: you could be real athletic, you could be creative and be shunned, or you could be into music and be shunned. It was a slower-paced life, and there just wasn't as much culture. Kurt was one of those guys that was looking for culture, and it just wasn't there." Aberdeen was a place stuck in the past rather than looking toward the future.

As a child, Kurt nonetheless stood out among others his age due to his keen interest in art and music – something his parents, Don and Wendy, encouraged. By the age of two, a children's harmonica and drum were among his favorite toys, and his aunt Mari Earl (Wendy's sister) taped him on a Sony reel-to-reel deck as he sang 'Hey Jude' and the theme from *The Monkees* TV show at the same age. "I was so in love with The Beatles," he told Everett True. "I would dress up like John Lennon and pretend to play guitar, and hold mini-Beatles concerts for my family when they came over." At age four, following a trip to the park, Mari watched as her young nephew went to the piano and banged out a rudimentary song about the trip. "I was just amazed," she told Charles Cross. "I should have plugged in the tape recorder – it was probably his first song." Kurt's sister Kim, three years younger than her brother, recalls Kurt being able to pick out a song's melody on the piano after hearing it on the radio.

Kurt was also an avid visual artist. The book *Cobain Unseen* has a photo of him in front of an easel apparently about to copy a comic book cover, and when he was older he shot short films on a Super-8 camera, some of them featuring clay figures he'd sculpted himself. But eventually music began to occupy more of his time. He'd been given a Mickey Mouse drum set at Christmas just before his eighth birthday, and played drums in the school band. Then, in 1981, he asked for and received a cheap second-hand guitar for his 14th birthday. By then he'd moved on from the pop of The Beatles and The Monkees to 70s hard-rock acts like Led Zeppelin, Black Sabbath, Aerosmith, and Kiss, although his rock tastes were still balanced by pop. He also became a fan of new wave after seeing The B-52's on *Saturday Night Live*, and Devo would become another favorite.

When he finally acquired a guitar, Kurt briefly took lessons from Warren Mason, who worked at Rosevear's Music Center in Aberdeen. Mason also upgraded his instrument, getting him an Ibanez. "His main goal was to learn 'Stairway To Heaven,'" Mason later recalled. Among the other songs Kurt learned to play were AC/DC's 'Back In Black,' Queen's 'Another One Bites The Dust,' and The Cars' 'My Best Friend's Girl' (which Nirvana would play at their very last show, on March 1 1994 in Munich), all indicative of his listening tastes at the time. The lessons quickly fueled his own burgeoning musical creativity. Realizing that "with power chords, you could play just about anything," he soon began writing his own songs. "I didn't think it was important to learn other songs," he said, "because I just knew I wanted to start a band."

Music also provided an escape from a troubled home life. Kurt's parents had divorced when he was nine years old; for a time, he lived with his mother and sister in Aberdeen, then moved in with his father, who'd moved to the town of Montesano, 11 miles east. But as each parent took up with a new partner, and Kurt reached his teens, he became withdrawn and argumentative, eventually leaving each household and being passed around among other relatives in the area. By the end of his high school years, he'd moved on to staying with friends, or wherever else he could.

His musical tastes were also beginning to veer toward punk rock. Kurt had become intrigued by punk after reading about the Sex Pistols' shambolic 1978 American tour in *Creem* magazine, later telling writer Jon Savage he'd "fantasize about how amazing it would be to hear their music and be a part of it." As it happened, New York punkers the Ramones had actually played Aberdeen on May 3 1977 at the Rocker Tavern, a bar that hosted local acts and the touring bands that occasionally dropped in between dates in Seattle and Portland, Oregon, the next largest city to the south. "Owning a live music/liquor venue in a town like Aberdeen is always an adventure," the club's owner, Stan Foreman, later noted. "It appealed to a crowd that worked hard in the mills and timber industry and played hard on the weekends."

The Ramones were an unusual choice for a venue more likely to feature mainstream touring acts like Foghat or The Guess Who. "I heard the Ramones were coming, and I think there was me and one other guy in high school who even knew who they were," says Kurdt Vanderhoof, then an aspiring guitarist. "I couldn't believe the Ramones were playing! I went down there and I couldn't get in – I was 16, I couldn't get into the bar – but I wanted to hear it. So I just hung out outside. A couple of people I knew – older brothers of some of my friends – they did get in, and they were all like: those guys suck, they were stupid!"

It was a prevalent attitude in the region, and aside from that one occasion, no other punk groups made it into Aberdeen. So Kurt was left to play what he imagined punk might sound like, telling Azerrad his early songwriting efforts were "three chords and a lot of screaming … like Led Zeppelin, but it was raunchy and I was trying to make it as aggressive and mean as I could." It was a deprivation that actually worked to Kurt's advantage, forcing him to develop his own creativity instead of simply absorbing outside influences.

By the end of 1982, Kurt had made enough progress with his songwriting that he wanted to take the next step and make a recording. During Christmas break that year he made his first known home demos at his aunt Mari's Seattle home. Mari had begun playing guitar at age 11, and made her first public appearances at local venues where her brother Chuck's band, The Beachcombers, was playing. She later formed a four-piece band that would play in Elks and Moose lodges, as well as hotel lounges in the region. She married and moved to the Seattle area in 1979, and for a time continued performing as a solo artist.

A shared interest in music naturally drew Kurt and Mari together, and when Kurt got his first guitar, he phoned his aunt to ask if guitar strings were put on alphabetically. When he arrived to make his demo, he was just as solicitous about learning to use her equipment. "He always was very, very careful," she says. "And whenever he ran into any problems with the equipment he would always ask me: Aunt Mari, could you help me with this?"

Kurt used Mari's four-track TEAC reel-to-reel deck; he also played guitar and a "funky little Sears bass" that his aunt owned (and which later sold at auction for $43,750). But when Mari offered him the use of her Roland Compu-Rhythm drum machine, Kurt firmly turned her down. "Oh, no way," he said. "I want to keep my music pure." Instead, he used his pink Samsonite overnight suitcase as a makeshift drum, borrowing wooden spoons from Mari's kitchen for drumsticks. In search of more unusual sounds for the recording, he also made use of a duck call that Mari had. "He just had to put some weird things in there," she recalled.

Although Kurt recorded his music in the room alone, Mari and her husband could hear it ringing throughout the house. "Most of what I remember about the songs was a lot of distortion on guitar, really, really heavy bass, and the clucky sound of the wooden spoons," she says. "And his voice, sounding like he was mumbling under a big fluffy comforter, with some passionate screams once in awhile." Kurt named the tape *Organized Confusion*, a phrase he also wrote on a T-shirt, but while he presumably made copies of the recording for his friends, none have surfaced to date. A month after the session, Kurt sent his aunt a letter, apologizing for making so much noise at her home. "I can't handle the thought of invading your braincells [sic] with my chainsaw music," he wrote. "I can't see how you could stand it the last time I was up there."

In the summer of 1983, Kurt made the surprising discovery that there was a real live punk-rock band in Montesano. The band was the Melvins, who had only been active for a few months, founded by Roger 'Buzz' Osborne. Buzz, who'd moved to Montesano at age 12 from the even smaller town of Morton, Washington, was initially a fan of hard-rock acts like Kiss, Aerosmith, Black Sabbath, and AC/DC, but had become interested in punk after some friends raved to him about a Clash show they'd seen in Seattle. Photos of acts like David Bowie and the Sex Pistols in *Creem* further piqued his interest. Unlike the many music fans who saw a clear divide between punk and hard rock/metal, Buzz was quick to pick up on the similarities between the genres. "The Sex Pistols album [*Never Mind The Bollocks*] just sounded like a logical extension of what I'd already been listening to," he explained. "Whether it was Ted Nugent or whatever, the vocals were different, but I didn't think the music sounded a whole lot different … and then I gradually got into more and more punk rock type stuff solely on my own."

Buzz had started playing guitar toward the end of his high-school years, teaching himself by listening to the few punk records he owned; he wouldn't own an electric guitar until after he graduated. He introduced a fellow student, Mike Dillard, to punk by playing him

Never Mind The Bollocks ("I was going: oh, my God, this is the greatest thing I've ever heard!" Mike recalled), and the two began jamming together, with Mike on drums. Mike then brought in his cousin, who owned a bass, and another classmate, Matt Lukin, as a second guitarist. But as Mike's cousin rarely showed up for jam sessions, Matt soon moved over to bass. The budding group began by playing covers of classic rock acts like The Who, Jimi Hendrix, and Cream, but quickly realized that if they wanted to have any kind of credibility they'd have to write songs of their own. "There was no future unless you were writing your own music," Buzz said. They also needed a name, and decided on the Melvins, the first name of the manager of the Montesano Thriftway where Buzz and Mike both worked. It was both an in-joke – neither Buzz or Mike liked their boss – and deliberately enigmatic, its simplicity offering no clue as to what the band's music might sound like. "We wanted a name that was like the Ramones," Buzz explained.

Kurt had been given a flyer by Buzz when he was at the Thriftway one Friday that read: 'The Them Festival. Tomorrow night in the parking lot behind Thriftway. Free live rock music.' Curious, he returned on Saturday to find the band set up in a park-and-ride lot behind the store. "We found this outdoor plug from a building next to the parking lot," said Mike. "We just dragged a big extension cord over there and plugged all the amps and stuff in and set up at about seven o'clock." At the time, the Melvins played at the breakneck pace typical of punk and hardcore. Their songs were rarely longer than two minutes, with each musician playing his instrument in an all out attack, topped by Buzz's abrasive vocals. Although the group's first official release came out in 1984, the 2005 CD *Mangled Demos From 1983* has recordings made during this period.

Kurt was enthralled by the band. "They played faster than I ever imagined music could be played and with more energy than my Iron Maiden records could provide," he wrote. "This was what I was looking for." He later told journalist Gina Arnold: "When I saw them play, it just blew me away. I was instantly a punk rocker." He immediately became one of the band's followers, a small group of like-minded friends who hung out at Melvins rehearsals in Montesano and were mockingly called 'Cling-Ons' by Buzz. (The 'Cling-On' nickname was first mentioned in *Come As You Are*, but future Melvins drummer Dale Crover later insisted, in journalist Mark Yarm's book *Everybody Loves Our Town*: "Whoever says we called the people who hung out with us the Cling-Ons is completely full of shit, because I never heard anybody described as Cling-Ons.") Kurt was already familiar with some of the band-members; he'd been on the same baseball team with Matt, and had Buzz in his art class. "He was always a good artist, drawing-wise," Buzz said of Kurt. "[He] would draw really amazing caricatures of the teacher having horrible things done to him."

Kurt's entrance into the Melvins circle proved to be an invaluable step in the development of his own career. He'd finally discovered a group of friends who were as serious about music as he was. The band set a further example in their determination to do something musically different, stepping outside the 'cover band' status of most local acts. And four out of Nirvana's eventual six drummers would have direct ties to the Melvins. "Nirvana changed the shape of music all over the world," Buzz later told Jeff Burlingame. "And if it wasn't for the Melvins, they never would have existed. Remember: No Melvins, no Nirvana."

Buzz's collection of punk records was also useful in introducing Kurt to music otherwise unobtainable in Aberdeen. Buzz had expanded his own knowledge of punk acts when he'd met Kurdt Vanderhoof in the fall of '83, when both briefly attended Grays Harbor Community College. Kurdt had returned to Aberdeen after a stint in The Lewd, a Seattle-based punk band who'd relocated to San Francisco. When The Lewd fell apart, Kurdt decided to go in a more heavy metal direction and tried forming a band he wanted to call Metal Church. But when his initial attempts to start the band failed to take off, he returned to Aberdeen. "I went back to Aberdeen just so I could live at my mom's," he says. "And I knew some musicians that could get into the metal thing. They couldn't get into the punk thing, but the metal thing, they could."

Kurdt was happy to share his punk record collection with Buzz, and even sang with the band at an early Melvins show. "I was apparently the only guy that knew all those songs they were doing," he says. "They were doing Ramones and Sex Pistols and all that kind of stuff." Buzz described Kurdt's record collection as "a really good education. I never would have found those records; none of that stuff was ever down there." Buzz also tracked down punk records via mail order, patiently waiting "weeks and weeks and weeks" for them to arrive. Another source was Tim Hayes, a friend who worked at DJ's Sound City at Aberdeen's Wishkah Mall (and later became the owner of Seattle indie record store Fallout Records), whose boss would let him take promos of non-mainstream acts the store wasn't interested in selling: Black Flag, The Stranglers, The Cramps, The Dead Boys. Buzz in turn made compilation tapes of the records, which he then passed out to his friends, introducing the small but passionate Grays Harbor punk community to numerous other groups they would otherwise not have heard. Kurt, for one, found himself drawn to "the psychotic, weird, dirgey bands like Butthole Surfers, not for straight hardcore jocks, like Minor Threat."

Also among the band's fans was a six-foot-seven teen named Krist Novoselic. (Novoselic had Anglicized his birth name to 'Chris' at this time, but later reverted to the original spelling. This book will refer to him as 'Krist' throughout.) Krist Anthony Novoselic was born on May 16 1965, to Krist and Maria Novoselic. Both of his parents were originally from Croatia, and emigrated to San Pedro, California, where they met and married in 1964. (Pronounced Novo-SELL-itch; 'Novoselic' translates to 'new villager' or 'newcomer.')

Krist was born in the nearby town of Compton and raised in Gardena, where the family grew to include another son, Robert, and a daughter, Diana. Krist had been "obsessed" with music since his childhood, listening to AM radio while watching his father work on the family Volkswagen. "My dad used to listen to Chuck Berry and The Rolling Stones and stuff," he says. "He listened to Dick Dale. My dad was always cranking four-track tapes. He had this garage, it was kind of his club house, and he would paint, work on cars, just kind of dink around – like what I like to do – and listen to music. So I listened to a lot of music." The Beatles were another big favorite. He was just as keen to find music shows on television, watching such programs as *American Bandstand*, *Soul Train*, and *Midnight Special*. By the 70s he too had moved on to hard-rock/metal acts like Black Sabbath, Aerosmith, Led Zeppelin, and Kiss. ("When I was really young, like ten years old, I had all their posters and stuff," he later admitted of the latter group, with what journalist Jerry McCulley recalled as "uncharacteristic sheepishness.")

In 1979, the Novoselics moved to Aberdeen, where Krist felt decidedly out of place. "I was now in a different social scene, where the kids dressed different," he later explained. "There weren't a lot of kids in school that I could relate to with music … Maybe I just had a little more sophisticated understanding of music. But I wasn't very happy and my parents noticed that. And they go: oh, let's send Krist to Croatia and see if that will work for him."

Krist spent a year in his parents' homeland, encountering a very different educational system than what he'd been used to at home. "School was very demanding," he recalled. "You had to study a lot. It seemed like the standards were a lot higher in their public education." Along with studying more orthodox subjects like history and math, there were classes like Civil Defense that touched on the harsh realities outside the schoolroom walls. "There were a couple times when the teacher brought this huge machine gun to class, and showed us how to disassemble it and put it back together."

With his shortwave radio, Krist was able to gain exposure to the punk and new wave music beamed to the continent by the BBC.

When he returned to Aberdeen in 1980, he began making music himself. As a child, he'd taken accordion lessons, and now his mother bought him a guitar. "It just seemed like I listened to so much rock'n'roll, I just thought I'd take it up. So I started playing guitar."

Krist still felt out of place among his classmates, but kept busy in other ways, taking vocational classes in addition to his high-school coursework, as well as after-school jobs. He'd also been conscientiously taping each week's broadcast of *Your Mother Won't Like It*, the punk/new-wave show that aired on Seattle station KZOK. He finally found people who shared his musical interests when a co-worker at Aberdeen's Taco Bell introduced him to Buzz and Matt, bringing Krist into the Melvins circle. Buzz was also impressed with Krist's taste in music. "I played Krist some music, and he was one of the few people who actually got it," he said. Krist had found others in Aberdeen more resistant to new music; one friend he tried to interest in punk brushed him off, saying: "Ah, that punk-rock stuff – all it is is: 'Want to fuck my mom! Want to fuck my mom!'"

With few places available to play locally, the Melvins started landing gigs out of town, first in Olympia, the state capital, an hour's drive east from Aberdeen. But when Mike began spending more time with his girlfriend than the band, Buzz decided he needed to be replaced, although he avoided firing his friend by asking Matt to tell Mike the band was breaking up. He then asked Krist if he knew any drummers, and Krist introduced him to Dale Crover, who had also jammed with Krist's brother Robert. Buzz had previously seen Dale playing in local cover bands, "doing Iron Maiden or some crap."

"That's really all there was," Dale explained. "If you wanted to be in a band, [you'd] play with people that wanted to do high-school dances. To do these shows, it was covers of the day." Dale was excited to be asked to join the Melvins because he knew the band played the occasional show out of town. For his part, Buzz was excited about Dale's powerful drumming. "He was more into heavy metal," he said. "And then we introduced him to the punk rock thing, and a thousand things really changed for us. We've got a top notch, number one great, amazing drummer, and that just pushed us through to what we ended up doing, which was music that's far more complicated, way more musical." A guitar player friend of Dale's, Larry Kallenbach, would also have a huge impact on the Melvins sound, teaching Buzz the drop-D tuning used on Black Sabbath's 'Into The Void,' with the low E-string tuned down a whole step to give the music a darker, heavier sound.

Once Dale joined the band, Melvins rehearsals moved to his parents' house in Aberdeen. Dale's older siblings had moved out, so there was plenty of room. "His parents were finished with raising kids and he got away with murder," said Buzz. "He was able to do whatever he wanted. The neighbors there – as long as we got done by 7pm, they didn't care. We practiced all the time." Kurt and Krist were regular attendees at the band's rehearsals. "They were open-minded weirdos," said Buzz. "As far as you can be in that environment. When there's not a lot of people that are thinking along the lines that you are, then you tend to gravitate toward the ones that are. We had a really dark sense of humor about everything. We would do all kinds of stupid things. One of our favorite things to do was to take want ads from newspapers that were six or seven months old and then call the people: are you guys selling that car? We thought stupid shit like that was hilarious." Another project was an idea for a magazine called *Sluts And Gore*, featuring "porno, biker[s], and gore." "We'd spend all this time making these stupid collages out of cutting up all these other porno mags, and [Kurt] would draw all these crazy pictures," Buzz recalled. "I wish I still had those; they were hilarious."

Krist was another happy recipient of Buzz's compilation tapes. "Buzz was kind of like this punk-rock evangelist," he remembered. "He would preach the gospel of punk rock." He was particularly impressed with the first album by San Francisco band Flipper, *Album* (aka *Generic Flipper*), although he admitted it took a few spins before he fully appreciated the band's raw sound. "[The] third time I heard it, it just blew me away," he said. "But at the same time *Generic Flipper* is nowhere on the radar screen … society doesn't recognize how important this is. Well, I recognized it, and Kurt sure did. He loved that record." (In late 2006, Krist would join Flipper for a two-year stint.)

One of the few opportunities for local bands to play a more professional venue than a house party came on May 4 1984, when the Melvins opened for Metal Church at Aberdeen's D&R Theatre. "That show went really, really well, surprisingly," Kurdt recalls. "We had a lot of people show up. It was just a time when everybody was kind of excited about what was going on in music, and we happened to have some kind of a reputation already. We had just done our first recordings, and we ended up on the *Northwest Metal Fest Compilation* record." Krist joined the Melvins during their set for a cover of Cream's 'Sunshine Of Your Love.' It was probably his first public performance.

Seeing other shows necessitated travel, usually up to Seattle. "Matt had this big Impala," Krist recalls. "It sat six comfortably: big bench in front, bench in back. We just cruised up there." They didn't just see punk shows; Buzz recalls seeing Van Halen as well as Black Flag. "I didn't see a lot of difference; I thought they were both equally good," he said. "But I appreciated the punk rock stuff more because it was more intimate and that's what drove me away from arena rock eventually. Punk rock spoke to me more, and the intimacy and the message and things of that nature. And then I realized – this was really a big eye opener – that the world is bigger than the world that I'd been in, and that there's a lot more cool things going on that the people that I was around had no idea about."

At the time, no clubs in Seattle regularly hosted punk shows, so concerts were held in a variety of unlikely venues, including the hall of one building originally built to cater to Seattle's Norwegian community (hence its original name, the Norway Center), and later rented by a conservation group called The Mountaineers. It was here that Kurt first saw Black Flag on April 27 1984, later claiming to have sold his record collection in order to buy a ticket. The tour was in support of Black Flag's *My War* album, which is especially notable for the three songs on side two ('Nothing Left Inside,' 'Three Nights,' and 'Scream'), on which the band moved from their usual fast pace to a slower grind. It was a stylistic change that Dale cites as the inspiration for the Melvins to pursue a similar direction.

The show made an equally strong impression on Kurt. "I just remember him saying: that's exactly what I want to do," Buzz later recalled. A picture of Kurt later published in *Spin* magazine revealed a flyer from the show, also mentioning support act Meat Puppets, posted on his bedroom wall. If you'd told the grinning boy in the photo, sitting on his unmade bed, holding a guitar plastered with stickers, that in a decade Meat Puppets would be opening for his own band, he wouldn't have believed you.

Music offered the one bright spot in Kurt's life; beyond that, his future prospects seemed increasingly dim. He dropped out of high school in the spring of 1985 and soon found himself working as a janitor at the very school he'd just left. Most of his janitorial jobs were short term, as were his living arrangements; he was evicted from one apartment, and asked to leave two other friends' homes when he overstayed his welcome. The only area in which he showed any sense of discipline was music. He jammed with the Melvins when he could, although there are conflicting stories about whether or not he was ever seriously considered as a potential fourth member. But he was a regular at all their shows, sometimes helping to carry in their gear in order to get in for free, and drawing a Kiss mural on the side of the band's van. He also played with anyone who was willing, although he had so far been unable to get a band together that moved beyond the practice room.

"We had several 'joke' bands, as we called them then, but our main focus was on the Melvins, who were starting to get an Olympia/Seattle-based following," says Greg Hokanson, another friend who hung out at Melvins rehearsals. The shortlived band that Kurt put together with Hokanson and Dale Crover certainly had a joke name – Fecal Matter – and only managed to play one show. The group made a few primitive recordings on a boom box, with some simple overdubbing, recording a backing track and then playing it on a stereo while Kurt sang into the boom box.

Hokanson recalls the band working through a number of covers: the Ramones song 'Carbona Not Glue,' the blues number 'Nobody's Fault But Mine' (which Led Zeppelin had recorded on *Presence*), songs by Jimi Hendrix and The Monkees, and "an Elvis song." Kurt also worked on original material. Another friend, Eric Shillinger, recalls them playing such songs as 'Venereal Girl,' a raunchy parody of Madonna's 'Material Girl'; 'Let's Roll, Diamond Dave,' ("Let's roll" being the catchphrase of a friend's father); and 'Quad,' which attacked the pretentiousness of a friend who put the numerals 'IV' after his last name. Another song of the period, 'Ode To Beau,' was a country & western number about a fellow student who'd killed himself.

Although Kurt didn't make the cut as a Melvin, Buzz was nonetheless impressed with his efforts to do something different. "I remember him showing me things and I thought: wow," he said. "There's a certain magic to putting two simple chords together in a way that sounds nice to someone. He had the ability to do that. Now, was he the greatest singer? No. Was he the greatest guitar player? No. But he has something that people who are better singers and better guitar players don't have – the ability to put something together in an interesting way. That kind of technical ability of being able to master full guitar playing and be an amazing singer has nothing to do with writing music, you know. Nothing."

In the spring of 1986, Kurt decided to more formally document Fecal Matter's work, and Matt drove him and Dale back to aunt Mari's house to record another demo. ("Since I wasn't as good a drummer as Dale I didn't do any recording with them," Hokanson explains.) This session was previously thought to have happened in December 1985, but Mari remembers it taking place around Easter. "They set up in my music room and they'd just crank it up!" she recalls. "It was loud. They would put down the music tracks first, then he'd put the headphones on and all you could hear was Kurt Cobain's voice screaming through the house! It was pretty wild. My husband and I, we'd just look at each other and smile and go: you think we should close the window so the neighbors don't hear? So they don't think we're beating him or something!" Mari also noted how Kurt had improved as a musician since his last visit. "He was much more confident in his vocals," she observed. "And he was more progressed in knowing what he wanted the thing to sound like."

Kurt and Dale recorded a total of 13 of Kurt's songs, with Kurt on guitar and vocals, Dale on bass and drums. They survive as the earliest known examples of Kurt's songwriting. The music clearly reveals his influences: fast, thrashing punk, and the slower chug of hard rock. Vocally, he's still searching for a style. Having not yet found that familiar, rasping drawl, he growls and shouts, he sings in a clipped British accent, he speaks in a mumbling drone, as in the verses of 'Downer,' a rumination on the blandness of society. ("I think I may have grown a bit as a lyricist since writing this," he later sardonically observed of the song.)

"It sounded *exactly* like Black Flag," Kurt later recalled of the Fecal Matter material. "Totally abrasive, fast, punk music. There were some Nirvana elements, some slower songs, even then. And some heavy, Black Sabbath-influenced stuff. I can't deny Black Sabbath. Or Black Flag."

Lyrically, the songs took broad, sarcastic swipes at mainstream society (one of them also attacked people for latching onto to punk simply because it's "trendy"), but Mari also noted a more disturbing thread when she looked at Kurt's notebook of lyrics while he and Dale were taking a break. "I was looking through the lyrics, and I found this one song that kind of bothered me a little bit because I remember the name of it being 'Seaside Suicide,'" she explained. "It just kind of left me with the feeling that possibly Kurt had tried to commit suicide or had wanted to or had had thoughts about it – something. That kind of bothered me. And yet, I never talked to him about it. How I wish I had, you know?" This song appears not to have been recorded at the session. Nor did Kurt discuss his songs with his aunt. "As far as really sharing his music with me, and asking what I thought, he really didn't do that," she says. "Kurt was very sensitive about the stuff that he wrote and he was very careful about who he let hear it. He didn't really like someone just poking fun at it. And being a songwriter myself, I can understand that."

One song in particular stands out: 'Spank Thru.' Of all the Fecal Matter songs, it veers the closest toward pop, with an atypically jangling guitar opening. Kurt's voice drones during the verses, going up an octave in the chorus, which he sings with a mock sincerity appropriate for a parody of a love song with references to masturbation. The song is the only one from the Fecal Matter session to be officially released thus far (on the 2005 compilation *Sliver: The Best Of The Box*), although a number of the other songs have surfaced on the collector's circuit in either partial or complete form. 'Spank Thru' and 'Downer' would later be re-recorded, and 'Annorexorcist' would also be performed live for a brief period, while lyrics from other numbers would resurface in the Nirvana songs 'If You Must' and 'Even In His Youth.'

Kurt named the tape *Illiteracy Will Prevail* and immediately dubbed off copies for his friends, with a handmade illustration on the J-card of a pile of excrement surrounded by flies. He spelled his name correctly on the inside of the J-card, but on the outside credited himself as 'Kurdt = Guitar/Mouth.' It was the first time he was known to have spelled his name in this fashion, and he was credited as 'Kurdt' on all future record releases until the 'Smells Like Teen Spirit' single, as well as in interviews and press releases. "I have no real reason," he later told Azerrad about the various name spellings he used over the years. "I just didn't bother spelling it correctly. I didn't care." Of course, there was already another Aberdonian who spelled his name the same way: Metal Church's Kurdt Vanderhoof.

Dale was later dismissive of the recording, telling writer Greg Prato, in *Grunge Is Dead*: "People talk about that demo like it's this unreleased thing that must be amazing. But not really. A crappy four-track demo." At the time, Buzz thought otherwise, as he wrote in a letter to Krist and his girlfriend Shelli Dilly, who had moved to Arizona in early 1986: "Ko-bain and Dale went up to his aunt's house and made a tape of some of Kurt's songs. I was pretty impressed. Some of his songs are *real* killer!, despite the poor sound quality. It seems good, but could've been better with a little more time. Nevertheless it's still a *great* demo. I think he could have some kind of future in music if he keeps at it." The letter was dated April 16 1986 – more proof that the session happened in 1986, not 1985. Had the session been in December 1985, Kurt would undoubtedly have given Krist a tape then. And the letter makes it clear Buzz is talking about a recent event, not something from four months ago, when Krist was still living in Aberdeen. Kurt's aunt says the session happened around Easter, which in 1986 was on March 30 – two-and-a-half weeks before Buzz wrote his letter.

Kurt continued practicing the Fecal Matter songs with Buzz and Mike Dillard, but the project quickly fell apart. Instead, Kurt ended up making his public debut in a one-off trio called Brown Towel (a name misspelled as 'Brown Cow' on some posters) on May 3 1986, at GESCCO (Greater Evergreen Student Community Cooperative Organization), a venue affiliated with The Evergreen State College in Olympia. Kurt recited his lyrics and poetry as Buzz and Dale backed him. Although he later confessed that his nervousness made him get "totally wasted" on wine before the performance, he acquitted himself well, "just jumping around the stage reading, singing, and screaming," as Dale later put it – a fair description of Kurt's performing style in Nirvana as well. "I had a splendid time," Kurt later told the fanzine *Matt Lukin's Legs* about the gig, describing the music as "Buzz's Minutemen-styled tunes."

The show also helped distinguish Kurt from the other Melvins followers. Slim Moon and Dylan Carlson, who both lived in Olympia and were then in the band Nisqually Delta Podunk Nightmare, had previously seen Kurt at shows and parties. At one such gathering, as Slim and Dylan were outside talking about abrasive punk band Big Black, Kurt had coolly announced "I like Big Black" as he walked by. "And he said it in this voice, like it was so loaded with meaning," Slim remembered. "It was like: I know you think I'm just a redneck who hangs out with the Melvins, but I know about Big Black. … It was, like, this challenge. Like: I'm not who you think I am. There's more to me than you think, than what you've written me off as." (Kurt would later attend Big Black's final show, at the Georgetown Steamplant in Seattle on August 11 1987; the band's singer and guitarist, Steve Albini, would later produce Nirvana's *In Utero*.) Now, at the Melvins show, they were surprised to find Kurt had talent in his own right; afterward, Dylan went up to Kurt and told him it was one of the best performances he'd ever seen.

Although Kurt's attempts to take his music further were still stymied by his inability to find any compatible musical collaborators, he was now nonetheless focused on pursuing a musical career, having gone so far as to ask his aunt Mari for advice on how to put together a demo and dealing with song publishers. She sent him a copy of *Making It With Music: Kenny Rogers' Guide To The Music Business*. "That says to me, and should say to others, that he was definitely looking to get into the music business and that was the direction he was heading at that particular time of his life," she later recalled. "So many people think that Kurt was like: oh no, I don't care if I'm ever famous. I don't believe that at all. I don't believe that for a moment. I think, in every musician, there's a part of us that wants to be up on that big stage and wants to be on MTV. And he definitely had stuff inside of him that he felt was worthy of getting out there and making it. He thought he could do it, and so I sent him that book."

Kurt would finally find the musical partner he'd been looking for in Krist Novoselic, who returned to Aberdeen in the latter half of

1986, having spent only a few months in Phoenix. (There were fewer job opportunities than expected, and Krist and Shelli found Arizona too hot and plagued by "all those Republicans.") Kurt and Krist had previously jammed together as teenagers and were both in a Melvins side-project band called the Stiff Woodies, a name inspired by the name of a Seattle punk band, Limp Richerds. (Krist's stage name in the group was 'Phil Atio.') "That band was just like a revolving door, just messing around," says Krist. "Just having fun and drinking alcohol and jumping around and screaming. Making noise." Kurt played both guitar and drums in the group, and Krist occasionally took a turn as a singer. A surviving recording of a session at KAOS, Evergreen's radio station, has him handling the lead vocal on the uptempo 'Breakdance Boogie,' enthusiastically urging the listener to "Party down! Party up!"

At the time, Krist's musical ambitions were less serious than Kurt's. "I was having fun, having kicks," he says. "I always wanted to be in a band, but there was nobody I could be in a band with." Now that he'd returned to Aberdeen, Kurt gave Krist a copy of the Fecal Matter tape. "I was dinking around the house listening to it, and I said: hey, this is really good," he recalls. "I really liked it. I thought it was cool; it was good melodies and interesting." He was especially impressed with 'Spank Thru.' "It's a well put together song. It's got a hook. It's kind of unique. It sounds different. And I went: yeah, let's do it."

"We kind of found each other," Krist says of his musical alliance with Kurt. "Just out of necessity. Just to play music together. Of all the people that were hanging out with the Melvins, there was just something. We were drawn to each other. It made sense." The hard times were far from over, but the band that would become Nirvana was on its way.

CHAPTER 2

First Steps

"It made me feel special. It was exciting to be a 'subversive' type of person in a town where there wasn't anyone like that."

KURT TO *ALTERNATIVE PRESS*, 1991

In September 1986, Kurt moved into a small house at 1000½ East 2nd Street in Aberdeen, universally referred to as 'the shack' due to its dilapidated condition. It quickly became as much of a hangout for their friends as Dale Crover's home had been, with the added benefit of having no parental figures around. Krist was already Kurt's most frequent jamming partner, but it took them a while to find another member for their nascent group. They rehearsed with one friend, Bob McFadden, upstairs at Maria's Hair Design, the beauty parlor owned by Krist's mother. Other musicians came and went, as the two constantly rejigged the line-up, including who played which instrument; sometimes Kurt and Krist switched from their usual guitar and bass roles to drums and guitar, respectively ("Kurt was really good on drums," Krist recalls). They also toyed with the idea of putting together a Creedence Clearwater Revival covers band, but like many of their ideas it came to nothing. "That was a ploy to make money," Krist explains. "Play in a tavern, like a bar band, but we thought we'd play cool songs. It was just something to do to screw around on the side. We played once or twice and got bored with it."

They finally approached Aaron Burckhard, a drummer they'd met at Melvins practices. According to Matt Lukin, he and Buzz had briefly considered Aaron as Mike Dillard's replacement in the Melvins, but decided against it, in part because of Aaron's moustache – the bane of punk rockers. "Having a big, bushy Tom Selleck moustache just meant you were trying to be something you weren't," Matt explained. Aaron, older than both Kurt and Krist, had grown up in West Seattle and moved to Aberdeen in his mid-teens, where he played in a local band called Soon. Aaron lived behind Dale Crover's house, across an alley dubbed Swagger Alley. "I used to go over and watch the Melvins practice a lot," he says. "Every time they practiced I was over there. It was just something to do. I was amazed at how loud they were."

Aaron was also hanging out at Kurt's shack. "We used to party in there!" he says. "We used to drink Schmidt beer and smoke pot all day and play music. Kurt didn't have a refrigerator or a stove. All he had was a little toaster oven. And in his room, he had a framed picture of Bobby Sherman up on his wall. I never really understood that, so that was pretty weird."

Despite being a staunch metal-head – "I was into Mötley Crüe and AC/DC and Kurt was more into the punk scene," he says – Aaron agreed to join the fledging band. "I'd heard that Kurt was a guitar player and that Krist was a bass player," he says. "I never heard 'em play before. The day that I joined the band, I didn't have no drums, so we went out to a friend's house and he set me up with some drums, and we went over to Kurt's house and practiced that same night."

It was an early indication of Kurt's single-minded focus on rehearsal. "Kurt was just a stickler for practicing," Aaron says. "We practiced a lot, every day, for hours. Once Kurt got off work, it was practice non-stop. It was pretty crazy. Sometimes we'd play the same song over and over until Kurt got it right, you know?"

"We would play the set and then I would just start playing the songs again right away without ever looking up to see if those guys wanted to play them again," Kurt later told Azerrad. "I'd just whip them into shape."

Although the band would warm up with Led Zeppelin covers, from the outset they concentrated on original material. The songs were all Kurt's, although he tried to downplay his dominant role, telling one journalist: "I don't like to be considered the songwriter … but I do come up with the basics." It was a songwriting pattern that would continue throughout Nirvana's career, with the germ of a song idea generally coming from Kurt.

"He was the lead songwriter," Krist confirms. "He had the idea – like he had riffs and a vocal line he'd be hammering out; he'd be holed up somewhere by himself, hammer things out, and then he would just start busting 'em out at rehearsal. Sometimes it was just a riff and a vocal melody; sometimes it was a couple riffs, more like a song. Then it depended on what everybody else's input was. The drummer's really important. The drums kind of set a tone, a beat, that tells you what kind of personality the song's going to have. And I'd put my spin on it. I'd get a hit off the song and try to do something interesting, instead of just follow the guitar; I'd just go for things, or come up with another part, like a bridge part or something. He'd just have the one riff and melody, and I'd just bust something out. And then we'd all jump onboard to that. And then next thing you know that'd be another part of the song. A lot of it was unsaid; the band just cranked it out. But it definitely had a leader. Kurt knew what he wanted to do."

Three songs from the Fecal Matter tape were rehearsed: 'Spank Thru,' 'Downer,' and 'Annorexorcist.' Krist dismisses the latter number as "grotesque punk rock"; it was the melodic pull of songs like 'Spank Thru' that were of greater interest for him. And for all Kurt's later disparagement of 'Downer,' Krist felt it showed the band's versatility. "It's kind of like an alt-punk song," he says. "It shows the band right from the start wasn't a hardcore band or wasn't a rock band; the genre was kind of alt-punk. We tried to be original, to have a song that's unique and has its own personality. I know Kurt was listening to a lot of Scratch Acid and Butthole Surfers. Just songs with personality."

Kurt was also busy writing new material, drawing on the hours he spent "sitting around in my underwear, just picking out riffs, pieces of songs." "Kurt did so much work while the rest of us were off having our lives," says Ryan Aigner, who knew Kurt and Krist from school, and, living a block away from Kurt's shack, was a frequent visitor to rehearsals. "He sat in that house writing and listening to music, and plotting and planning everything that pertained to the music and to the band. And just being very, very creative all the time – not feeding himself, not shopping, not showering, not preening, not doing all the dozen things that normal people do; Kurt didn't bother with that. He had stacks and stacks of notebooks that were full of these ramblings that he would pluck lyrics out of for his songs. So when they would come to rehearsal, he was ready: he was locked and loaded. He spent a tremendous amount of time working at all hours. That's the way Kurt was."

New songs like 'Mexican Seafood' and 'Hairspray Queen' were very much influenced by the edgy punk of acts like Butthole Surfers and Scratch Acid; 'Hairspray Queen' also has a scratchy guitar line right out of the Gang Of Four/Au Pairs school. Krist describes such songs as "real alt-rock, really original, trying to be brainy or trying to be interesting, you know what I mean? And 'Mexican Seafood,' it's actually kind of funk; that song takes a few hard turns. It's a very rhythmic song. It's alt-rock, not just straight-ahead big riff rock." Both songs are lyrically busy. 'Mexican Seafood' draws on Kurt's interest (some would say obsession) with bodily functions, in this case apparently referring to the after effects of venereal infection, while 'Hairspray Queen' is more free associative, particularly in the wordplay of "mind" and "mine."

Kurt professed to spend little time on his lyrics. "I don't consider lyrics a big deal at all," he said in 1989. "As long as it has a good melody line, a hook and live energy is far more important." "I remember Kurt explaining to me one day how he wrote vocal lines," says Ryan. "He said: I don't even do words, I sort of write the vocal melody with consonants and vowels and just go: blah blah blah blah

blah. After he got it all phrased out, he would go through his notebooks and begin plugging words in to see how they fit. And as the song began to take shape, he'd start playing around with the words again, to see how you could twist them into meaning something. To him, making the words mean something was the last thing. And then the words would change. You would go to a show at the Community World Theater [in Tacoma], and then a show at the Squid Row [in Seattle], and the same song would be different. Because quite honestly he didn't remember the words."

But there certainly was 'big riff rock' as well, as evidenced by new songs like 'Pen Cap Chew' and 'Aero Zeppelin.' "That was a joke," says Krist of the latter song. "That was a riff-o-rama, a bunch of riffs put together." Both 'Aero Zeppelin' and 'If You Must' also offer something of a critique of the music business. 'If You Must' is in part concerned with the pressure of having to write a song, while 'Aero Zeppelin' ridicules the mindless fans who blindly follow any act if it's been properly "branded." It was the kind of commentary that might be expected from the latter-day Kurt Cobain who routinely disparaged rock stardom, but was surprising for a band whose performances had so far been limited to practices in a tiny living room.

That was about to change. The unnamed band's first attempt to play somewhere else besides Kurt's house – a party in Olympia – was over before it even began when the expectant trio arrived at their destination to find a next door neighbor already complaining about the noise. "I loaded up Krist's bass stuff in my car, and Krist rode with Kurt," Aaron recalls. "We all met up at this house party, and there was just a mass of people. But as we were going in, some old lady next door was screaming: I called the cops! I called the cops! You'll be shut down! So we all get in the house, and they had all the band stuff in there, but we couldn't play." The musicians returned home in defeat.

Soon after that, in March, Ryan helped set up a date at another house party. "I inserted myself into this thing," he says. "I was very industrious." Ryan was friends with a guitarist named Tony Poukkula,

a former roommate of his, who'd also been in a local band called
Black Ice. Tony was now living in Raymond, a small town 29 miles
south of Aberdeen, with his friend Jeff Franks, who was a drummer.
"There was a good music community back then," says Tony. "One day
I would be jamming with Dale Crover, the next day Metal Church
would be dropping by our practice pad to show us their new demo."

Hoping to find a place for his friends to play other than the
shack, Ryan approached Tony about having them play at his home.
"Sure, bring 'em down," Tony said. "Always having a party here,
there's always some beer, have them come over."

"So the next week I'm up in Aberdeen and I'm saying we should
do this," says Ryan. "It probably took a week or two to convince them.
It was one of those deals where I said: look, I'll get the van. I'll haul
the gear. I've got the money, I'll put the gas in the tank. All you've
gotta do is just show up. They didn't know these people, so they were
self-conscious about it. I said: well, it's Tony, you remember Tony. He's
a nice guy. It'll be fine. We'll have fun. Get a case of beer; turn it into
a party. So basically that's how it all happened – I just pushed it by
financing the whole thing."

A Saturday night date was finally agreed on – author Jeff
Burlingame cites March 7 in his Kurt biography – and Ryan, who
worked as a carpet layer for Benny's Quality Floors, borrowed the
company van to drive the group, which also included Kurt's girlfriend
Tracy Marander and Krist's girlfriend Shelli, over to Raymond. "It
was our first show, obviously we was all excited about playing," says
Aaron, who was also pleased he'd able to use the host's drum kit.
"Tony had a mint drum set so I was like: cool, cool, we don't have to
load my crappy set!" Nonetheless, he admits to feeling somewhat
intimidated by the partygoers. "We called them socs – high class, just
better-than-us kind of people," he says, referring to the terminology
used in S.E. Hinton's classic novel of teen alienation, *The Outsiders*,
which pitted the middle-class 'socs' (pronounced 'so-shez,' as in
'social') against the working-class 'greasers.'

The rest of the group also felt a bit out of place, as the party attendees were far from the punk rockers they were used to hanging out with in Aberdeen, even though they'd been classmates of Tony's. ("Their coming down to Raymond was just a bunch of old friends of mine coming to my house to play some music," he says.) "Part of it was our own fault, because we dressed like bums," Ryan recalls. "Tracy was from Olympia and she would wear kind of bizarre clothing. Kurt would wear kind of ratty clothing. Krist, who was able to socialize very well, would wear kind of weird, quirky clothes. Shelli's dressed all in black. And I'm wearing the black leather jacket, denim jeans with gigantic, gaping thrashed holes. My pants looked like that because I was a carpet layer, and then it was cold, so you'd wear long johns; they were probably dirty. And we wouldn't wash our hair, so it would stick up and be greasy. We would go to a show in Tacoma or Olympia or Seattle, that's how all the kids looked. But when we would show up socially somewhere in Aberdeen or Hoquiam, that's not the way the kids looked.

"So we walk into the room, and we've got an attitude. We've got a scowl on our face. We're not really sure we want to be there. If you've ever been in one of those situations where you walk into a room and you go: hey, no one told me it wasn't a costume party! – that's the way it was. And we feel awkward. We're waiting for someone to walk up to us and say: hey, you guys got here! We've been waiting for you all night! But that never happened."

Nonetheless, Jeff Franks made sure to record the show on a Sony Walkman, thus preserving Nirvana's first non-rehearsal show. "We were always recording our sessions," says Tony. "Most of the time with a four-track. But this time I think Jeff had his little stereo Sony Walkman recorder running just out of habit. I remember standing in our kitchen and him opening his jacket revealing the recorder with the stereo mic clipped to his collar." Because Tony and Jeff were used to jamming with people who came by their house, they'd assumed that would be case the tonight. But when Tony picked up his guitar, he says it "quickly became apparent that Jeff and I were not going to be able to play. Ryan came over to me and said they're not much for jamming with others, so I set my guitar down, grabbed a beer, and enjoyed the show."

The band warms up with 'Downer,' which had progressed markedly since its appearance on the Fecal Matter tape, most noticeably in the faster tempo. After a break, Kurt indulges in a lengthy bit of feedback before finally launching into 'Aero Zeppelin.' It's the first time we hear the drawling vocal style that would become very much a part of Nirvana's sound, although here the pounding riffs emulating the bands name-checked in the song's title take precedence. Even accounting for the extended intro, the song runs almost six minutes; it would later be tightened up to just under five minutes. ("One thing that Kurt would do is when he arranged a tune he'd tend to drive the riff into the ground," Krist later explained. "And so I would come in and say: well, we need to do that riff half as long.")

There's little response from the audience, who can be heard chatting amiably between songs, and the pauses in the recording make the event seem less of a continuous show than a party occasionally interrupted by a few songs – the band are hardly the focal point. Nonetheless, they persevere, going into 'If You Must,' with Kurt's keening vocal matched by the instrumental drone that was also key to Nirvana's sound, and when Kurt goes up an octave during the bridge, the song surges with power.

After another break, the group goes into a cover, prompted by Krist's constant noodling on the opening riff of Led Zeppelin's 'Heartbreaker.' Kurt eventually joins in, providing the crowd with a taste of something more conventional, even though Krist's over-the-top vocal suggests that, for the band at least, there was also an element of parody. Kurt gamely obliges requests for a solo, then segues into Zeppelin's 'How Many More Times,' with Krist and Aaron soon joining in.

Now gaining some momentum, the band positively races through

'Mexican Seafood.' Then comes the grind of 'Pen Cap Chew' – surely heavy enough for any Zeppelin fan – followed by a somewhat ragged 'Spank Thru,' which Kurt introduces as 'Breaking The Law,' and which comes to a stuttering halt, causing someone to guffaw: "They fucked up!" It takes a few minutes for the band to start the next number, making two attempts at starting 'Hairspray Queen' before they're able to get past the opening and finally turn in a solid yet thrash-heavy version, with Aaron's cymbals very much to the forefront. The recording cuts off after a request for 'Stairway To Heaven.'

"We were really drunk," Kurt later remembered of the show, "so we started making spectacles of ourselves." Krist had been particularly high-spirited during the set, jumping on the console TV, then leaping through the living room window and running back inside the house via the kitchen. "Instead of just playing our show, we thought, why not have an event?" he recalled to Charles Cross. "It was an *event*." Tracy and Shelli eventually decided to act up as well, caressing Krist's bare chest: "just to be goofy, because everyone seemed like they were uptight," Tracy said. "We were trying to be as outrageous as we could." Kurt was especially pleased that a "mock-lesbian scene" between Tracy and Shelli "really started freaking out the rednecks!"

"I just remember getting drunk," says Aaron. "I don't think we had a setlist. I think we wrote down like four songs that we knew, and the rest were just songs we were still practicing, but we played 'em anyways, you know? And Krist found some of that fake vampire blood shit and put it all over himself and kept jumping through the living room window and running around back into the kitchen. So it was pretty crazy." Ryan recalls Kurt simply walking off when he got tired of playing; Ryan then joined the other musicians jamming on Flipper's 'Sex Bomb' as the party guests retreated to the kitchen.

The visitors' attempts at being 'outrageous' eventually began to get out of control, as Ryan realized when Tony came over to speak to him. "Hey, you know, things are getting a little out of hand," Tony said. "Maybe you guys should leave." "Really?" Ryan asked. "What do you mean?" "Well," Tony replied, "Krist is out there pissing on everybody's cars."

"We were in the doorway between the living room and the kitchen when this happened," says Ryan, "and I remember peering out the window above the sink, looking up, and there's Krist. They had this big light outside; you could see the rain coming down, and Krist has got his shirt off, he's standing on top of the van, and he's peeing. And I'm going: oh Jesus fucking Christ! I go outside, and people are going: why is he doing that? What the fuck? What's the matter with you guys? And I'm going: I'm sorry, it's all right."

Ryan's attempt at damage control was further hampered when he ran into Kurt talking to a young woman by the back door. "She had one of those really done-up hairdos," he says. "And Kurt's reciting the words to 'Hairspray Queen' and he was saying these obscenities to her. And I was just like: what are you telling her? And he says: well, she asked me what the lyrics to 'Hairspray Queen' were. And I go: Kurt, those aren't the words to that song! And he goes: well, I know, but she doesn't know, so fuck her. And I was like: why are you guys doing this – this is exactly what I was worried about you doing, you guys acting like a bunch of fucking kids."

And yet, that was partly the point. "Because they'd actually offended people, the whole event had become a success," Ryan continues. "There were really two ways it could have gone. It could have gone really great, where everyone went: wow, you guys are the next big thing, where have you been all our lives? Or they could be run out of town. And since they weren't greeted with praise, and were run out of town, that constituted a success: yeah, we offended them, and that's what we wanted to do, because we're punk rock." Aaron concurred with that assessment. "The show was fun, but we didn't know how we went over, really," he says. "But it sounded all right to us, you know. I guess we didn't care what other people thought."

"It took us a while to get packed up, to get everybody corralled, and I was pretty loaded," Ryan admits. "After the anxiety of getting out of there, and being like: OK, we're on the road, we're going home, nobody's hurt, I think we've got everybody. I sort of had the adrenalin kind of wane and I realized: holy shit, I'm really drunk! And about that time we were coming out of Raymond, going up the hill to go over the pass there, and I remember people saying: your driving's not so hot. I pulled over and Aaron took over driving. I don't really remember much of the way home." In all the excitement, the band-members remained unaware that their very first show had been recorded, and none of the members ever received a copy of the tape. Seventeen years later, 'Heartbreaker' would be the opening track on Nirvana's *With The Lights Out* boxed set.

After the Raymond show, Krist introduced a song to the group that would become an integral part of the setlist for the next six years: 'Love Buzz.' The song was originally recorded by the Dutch band Shocking Blue, who enjoyed an English-language US/UK hit with 'Venus' in early 1970. Krist found the song on a self-titled American compilation of the band's work that had been given to him by a friend who'd picked it up at Dill's Second Hand Store in Aberdeen. "The whole beauty behind Dill's was that everything was a buck," says Ryan. "It didn't matter what it was, every record was a dollar. And so if you found a gem, you really had something because you were only going to pay a dollar for it."

"I put the record on as I was getting ready for work and I thought: God, this is a great record," Krist recalls. "And that song came on and I was like: this is a really cool song!" When Kurt came over to visit the next day, Krist wasted no time in playing him the record. "Check this song out!" he said. "Isn't it cool?" Kurt agreed, and suggested the band do a cover of it, although they didn't bother telling Aaron it wasn't an original number. "We played that song for six months before I even knew it was a cover song," Aaron says. "I mean, it's not like we sat down and Kurt put it on and said: this is the way it goes. I just figured Kurt wrote a new song."

In fact, there are few similarities between their version and Shocking Blue's original. The Eastern flavor of the Shocking Blue version comes through strongly in its use of sitar; the song was also taken at a moderate tempo and has a harsher feel due to the stentorian lead vocal of Mariska Veres, who sounded not unlike Grace Slick. Kurt only learned the song's first verse and chorus, changing "king of my dreams" to "queen of my heart"; intriguingly, he also changes "hear my love buzz" to "feel my love buzz." Despite the lack of sitar, the guitar and bass nonetheless manage to create a suitable Eastern-sounding drone, with the song's instrumental break allowing Kurt to indulge himself by creating squalling feedback. "The whole idea of a cover is to have some fun," he explained to *Melody Maker*. "We've never tried to do a straight copy and we've never bothered to pull a song apart in order to learn it properly, we'd rather just get on and do it." Krist agrees. "We never tried to 'cover' the song; we kind of did our own version of it," he says. "It took on a life of its own."

Kurt found another song for the band to play, 'White Lace And Strange' by Philadelphia trio Thunder & Roses (once again, Aaron was unaware that the song was a cover). The song was the opening track on the band's sole album, 1969's *King Of The Black Sunrise*. "It just sounded like Cream or something," says Krist. "Because it was so straight ahead. We didn't have a whole heck of a lot of songs in our repertoire, so we'd throw in a few covers. And we weren't going to do metal covers, we thought we'd do something obscure. We liked to have fun too, you know." Nirvana's version of the song was a good deal more rollicking than the earnest original, and taken at a much faster clip. They make no attempt to replicate the chorus harmonies, and the song's instrumental break is scaled back to a brief 30 seconds. It's the kind of song a band kicks into when they're taking a break from more serious work.

A more important addition to the set was a new original number,

'Floyd The Barber.' In contrast to more complex numbers like 'Beeswax' or 'Mexican Seafood' – songs written only a few months previously – 'Floyd The Barber' is positively stark in its simplicity, and thus packs more of an emotional punch. The song takes the genteel setting of Mayberry, the fictional small town in the 60s sitcom *The Andy Griffith Show,* and laces it with black humor, as the luckless protagonist who visits Floyd Lawson's barber shop finds himself strapped to the chair, sexually assaulted, and slashed with razors by the show's characters. Like David Lynch's depictions of small town life in *Blue Velvet* and *Twin Peaks*, the song delights in exposing the dark undercurrents swirling beneath a seemingly idyllic setting. It would become one of the most durable songs in Nirvana's repertoire.

The band's first non-party show came on April 18 1987, when they played the Community World Theater in Tacoma, a blue-collar city 80 miles from Aberdeen. The theater was a former movie house, and the band's show was arranged through Kurt's girlfriend, Tracy, who knew the booker, Jim May. Needing some kind of name for the show, the group settled on Skid Row; Kurt wrote the name in big block letters on the pink suitcase he'd used as a drum on his *Organized Confusion* demo and that he was now carrying guitar parts and cables in.

The Community World would be their regular venue for the next year. "They were crazy shows," says Aaron. "I just remember it being cold. It was always cold in the theater, and Krist was always wrapped in a blanket. But they were fun." The shows never drew a big crowd, but helped the fledging band develop a following, with Ryan loyally driving his friends to the shows. "I generally provided vehicles, particularly early on, because I was a carpet layer, and we had carpet vans that were readily available," he explains. "I would lie to my boss and tell him a friend of mine was moving or whatever, and can I borrow the van for the night. I wouldn't tell him that I was driving halfway across the state hauling a rock band and there's probably a bunch of beer involved. I didn't tell him things like that." One of the other bands on the bill was Nisqually Delta Podunk Nightmare, with

Slim Moon and Dylan Carlson, who had each been favorably impressed by Kurt's one-off performance with the Melvins the previous year. They gave Skid Row the thumbs-up as well. "You could definitely tell [Kurt] was into Gang Of Four at that time," Dylan observed. "A lot more complex rhythm. A herky-jerky kind of sound." Slim recalled Kurt being "very glammed out. He wore platform boots and this crazy outfit and all the songs seemed like a riff just played over and over and over again. But his singing was very engaging ... I thought they were pretty cool."

Skid Row's performance was strong enough that it led to the band's first show in Olympia, a town that would have a huge impact on the band's, and especially Kurt's, musical development. Olympia was home to The Evergreen State College, a non-traditional institution where students designed their own program of study and received evaluations instead of grades. Evergreen encouraged innovation and progressive thinking among its student body, and attracted people interested in taking an active role in shaping their own education, with the result that Olympia had a much richer streak of unconventionality than was usual in a college town. "They would allow outsiders to come there and throw wild parties," Buzz Osborne recalled. "Any town that has something like that will have alternative culture as well, you know. A town that doesn't have it, it's not going to have punk-rock shows. It's not going to have people from the outside coming in, bringing their ideas, and wanting to do things along those lines for like-minded people. Olympia's had that solely as a result of that college."

Evergreen's radio station, KAOS, became one of the foremost alternative stations in the country after John Foster, originally hired as the station's record librarian, changed the station format in the late 70s to one mandating that 80 per cent of the music broadcast had to be on an independent label. "KAOS radio was one of the few stations in the country – in fact, I think it might have been the only station in the country – that had an independent music policy," said Bruce

Pavitt, an Evergreen student and music fan who was excited by the wide range of music the station aired. Bruce was originally from Park Forest, a suburb of Chicago, and after two years at Blackburn College in Carlinville, Illinois, had transferred to Evergreen, where, he liked to say, he majored in punk rock.

Bruce was inspired not only by John's work at KAOS but also by the magazine he co-founded, *OP*, which initially appeared as an insert in the KAOS program guide (its first standalone issue was published in August 1979). *OP* covered independent artists from A to Z – quite literally, with each issue writing about artists whose names started with A, then B, then C, right on through the rest of the alphabet (accordingly, the magazine's run ended after 26 issues). In addition to being a KAOS DJ and a member of two bands, Tiny Holes and War With Elevators, Bruce also interned at *OP*, and before long decided to put out his own publication. In 1980, he published the first issue of a zine he called *Subterranean Pop*; by issue three, the name was shortened to *Sub Pop*.

"The *Sub Pop* fanzines featured record reviews, organized regionally, which was unique," says Bruce. "It was the only magazine in the country solely devoted to US indies. No real band features, per se, although I did include original photos by bands such as X and The Lounge Lizards, as well as The Blackouts and The Beakers from Seattle. *Sub Pop* covered a lot of records from more obscure regional scenes, and always provided addresses. Pre-internet, it was an excellent information source for obscure indie discs." As the editorial in the third issue put it: "We have to decentralize our society and encourage local art and things and music."

Bruce published nine issues of *Subterranean Pop/Sub Pop* between 1979 and 1983. Issues five, seven, and nine were "cassette zines" – essentially compilation tapes. "I was writing about a lot of music that people really had a hard time getting access to, so releasing cassettes of demo tapes from some of these groups seemed to make sense," he explains. The cassettes not only featured acts from the Northwest

(Seattle's Little Bears From Bangkok; Portland, Oregon's Neo Boys; Vancouver, B.C.'s 54/40), but around the country as well (Jad Fair from Maryland/Washington DC; Get Smart! from Lawrence, Kansas; The Nashville Scorchers). With a canny eye toward marketing, Bruce tapped a fellow Evergreen student, Charles Burns, to illustrate the cassette J-cards, aware that the black and white artwork would more readily capture attention when reproduced in a magazine (cartoonist/author Lynda Barry, another Evergreen student, had provided the cover illustration for *Subterranean Pop #2*). Tapes were sold for $4 apiece on generic tape or $5 for a higher-quality normal bias cassette. "I paid my rent and electric bill for a year just off these cassettes," Bruce later said.

Bruce's work in turn inspired another Evergreen student and music fan, Calvin Johnson, who also DJ'd at KAOS and wrote for *OP*, in addition to contributing to *Sub Pop*, both as a writer and artist: he appeared on *Sub Pop 5* as a member of The Cool Rays (his first recorded appearance) and on *Sub Pop 9* in the group Laura, Heather & Calvin. Noting the success Bruce had with his inexpensively produced cassettes, Calvin decided to launch his own label, K Records (the 'K' stood for 'knowledge,' he explained), with the first release being the tape *Survival Of The Coolest* by Olympia band Supreme Cool Beings in 1982. K's 1984 compilation tape, *Let's Together*, featured the first Melvins recording. The same year also saw the release of K's first vinyl record, the single 'Our Secret'/'What's Important' by Calvin's latest band, Beat Happening, produced by Greg Sage of Portland band the Wipers.

All of this made Olympia a fertile and welcoming environment for a developing band. Slim was booking a May 1 show at GESCCO, which was to feature his own band, Nisqually Delta Podunk Nightmare, and another Olympia act, Danger Mouse, with a cover charge of $2.50. Having enjoyed Skid Row's show the previous month, he asked if they'd like to play as well. The set almost didn't happen; right before the band went on stage, an inebriated Krist was deemed too drunk to go on. But the band was finally allowed to play, due to the fact that it was GESCCO's closing night. Allison Wolfe, who later formed the band Bratmobile, was in the audience. "It was great," she said. "I remember feeling like something big was happening. Even though no one was there, that band was the perfect blend of 70s punk, but it also had this Zeppelin feel to it."

The resulting performance also led to the band's first radio appearance. Evergreen students John Goodmanson and Donna Dresch were in Danger Mouse, and John in particular was fascinated by Skid Row's antics. He recalls the standout being when Kurt would "jump up in the air and do the splits" while wearing "these weird, really tall clogs" – likely the same platform shoes Slim Moon had noticed Kurt wearing during Skid Row's Community World Theater performance (and which Kurt had purchased at Dill's Second Hand Store). "That was quite a performance-like rock moment. He also played with a delay pedal, which was not punk rock. And I did as well, so we kind of bonded on that geek-out level. I remember after they played, Donna getting mad at me. She was like: you like them better than us, don't you? And I was like: mm-hmm! I was super into them. I really dug their whole trip. It seemed so fresh and exciting. I was a big fan of older-school punk-rock stuff, like Social Distortion and stuff like that, but I liked the 70s punk stuff too, and it seemed like a really potent combination of that."

John and Donna each hosted radio shows which ran back-to-back on KAOS: *The Toy Train Crash Backside Bone Beefcake Show* and *Out Of Order*. ("I was like 19 – how embarrassing!" says John of his show's name. "But that's what it was called.") The shows also featured live sets by local bands and other acts passing through town, and right after the GESCCO show John made arrangements for Skid Row to appear. The show's exact date is uncertain. John says the shows were broadcast on Monday nights, but a cassette tape labeled 'Out Of Order' pictured in the book *Cobain Unseen* has a date of May 6 1987 (a Wednesday).

"It was a good break for us to do that," says Krist. According to Ryan, Kurt certainly saw it as a step up. "I think it was sort of the legitimacy of the show," he says. "I know Kurt really didn't want to play in Raymond. He wasn't really happy about that. Kind of a constant theme throughout Kurt's career, to me, was that he was a little bit critical of his audience. He wanted to respect his audience, and his audience needed to be a certain caliber of character. And if he didn't like who was listening to him, it disturbed him. And I think that may have had something to do with the quality of the performance in Raymond. He didn't like what was going on there. It wasn't worthy. He was a little bit of a snob in that way. And KAOS was an entirely different thing. KAOS was exactly the kind of audience that he wanted."

Despite striking him as "tough kids from Aberdeen," John found Skid Row easy to work with. "Krist was always a sweetheart," he says. "Kurt was pretty quiet. The drummer was this metal dude. He had a funny moustache. He was way more macho than anybody else. But they didn't seem intimidated. 'Cause it's so low key at KAOS, it's super casual. It's goofy community radio stuff. There was just a little six-channel mono mixer; there wasn't much of anything there to even do a soundcheck with."

John decided to record the show on tape. "I was just super into it, which was why I committed it to the two-track machine, and even recording at high speed, which, for somebody as broke as me at the time, was a big deal," he says. "Then I'd have it and I could play songs later on, on other radio shows." It would be the second known recording of the band. "The tape I made was from the production room, which was where the nice reel-to-reel machines were," John explains. "So it's not a tape of the air feed. I would go in there and get everything ready and then go in with the band, and Donna would be doing the radio show. We had four hours, so she would be doing an hour of regular radio and telling people what was coming up, and then in hour two we'd cut over to the band live in the studio."

There was no way to easily communicate with a band while they were performing, however. "On the tape you can hear some confusion," says John. "Like: are we done yet? What, you want us to play? It was really like: they're in a ten-by-ten concrete room, and somebody's poking their head in the room going: c'mon guys, let's play another song. And that's all way off mic, super quiet, then the band has to talk about what song to play, and then they play it. Those big gaps in between songs are college-radio-style dead air. Everything's turned way down, because everybody's screaming, and there are no compressors at a college radio station. So there's no way to easily get a microphone level up to just talking in between songs, so everything dies down and it's really quiet. I turned up the vocal channel really loud to try and hear somebody talking about the next song, and then the first note of the next song would be incredibly loud."

According to Aaron, Kurt chose the songs for the performance. "He made the setlist, although we probably had a little bit of a say in it," he says. "It was mostly all Kurt's project. You know: these are the songs we're doing. We just agreed." The set gets off to a good start with 'Love Buzz,' already recognized as one of the group's strongest numbers (or maybe the fact that it was a new addition to the setlist made it something of a novelty). The cascading guitar intro sounds much the same as it would when the band professionally recorded it little more than a year later, although at this stage the lyrics have been distilled to the first line of the first verse, and the sole line in the chorus, with Kurt taking great delight in shrieking out the word "*buzz!*" The song's two instrumental breaks allow for the usual playful guitar improvisation – the second break is especially twisted – but it's Kurt's voice that makes the strongest impression. On 'Love Buzz' in particular, Kurt's drawling vocal walks a thin line between parody and seriousness – the kind of technique that Queen's Freddie Mercury was the master of.

"Are we still on? What's with all the hubbub?" Kurt asks before launching into 'Floyd The Barber.' 'Floyd' is taken a tad slower than it would be in its final version, making it somewhat plodding here, although Kurt's glee in delivering the sinister lyric is obvious. 'Downer' is faster than the Fecal Matter version, but again not yet as fast it would be. In contrast to the earnestness of 'Downer,' 'Mexican Seafood' swings with raucous fun, even though Kurt's vocals are buried in the barrage of sound.

There's another brief pause with Kurt again asking: "What? Are we still on?" before the suggestion is made to perform 'White Lace And Strange,' which the band had first played at the GESCCO show. The song races along with gusto; indeed, the band invests noticeably more energy into this song than they do their original songs. Part of this was undoubtedly due to a lack of self-consciousness; because the song was a throwaway, there was no need to take it seriously. Thus the band relaxed and turned in a highly spirited performance of a song they'd never play live again.

'Spank Thru' continued the mixing of musical genres: along with the hard rock of 'Floyd The Barber' and the arty punk of 'Mexican Seafood,' 'Spank Thru' was fairly unadulterated hard pop, albeit undercut by Kurt's over-the-top vocals, his drawl alternating with a stretched-out scream. The pace instantly changes with the charging guitar intro of 'Annorexorcist.' But while the verses are trademark heavy-metal riffage, and most of Kurt's delivery akin to the yelping of 'Mexican Seafood,' during the bridge the music suddenly takes a Melvins-like swing into something slower, and that melodic, hypnotic drone so much a part of Nirvana's sound is instantly recognizable. After a few tantalizing seconds, however, the song heads back just as suddenly into more frantic terrain.

'Hairspray Queen' sounds more confident in comparison to the Raymond show, Kurt switching between the harsh/softer vocal delivery with ease, although his energy flags a bit over the course of the song. This is even more evident in 'Pen Cap Chew,' with Kurt not even bothering to sing all the lyrics at times, instead screaming or moaning out nonsense syllables. "That's it," Kurt announces at the end of the song, but in fact there was one more number, which unusually only featured bass and drums, with Kurt free associating a lyric (perhaps not dissimilar to the material he'd performed with Buzz and Dale at GESCCO the previous year). A bootlegger entitled the piece 'Help Me, I'm Hungry' after a line in the song, which is how it was titled when it was later released on the *With The Lights Out* boxed set. ('White Lace And Strange' and 'Annorexorcist' also appear on the box; although the latter title was spelled with one 'n' on *WTLO*, the band's setlist indicate that it was actually spelled with two.) Today, the track is known in trading circles as 'Vendetagainst,' a deduction made from the fact that the phrase appears both as a lyric in the song and on an early Nirvana setlist.

"The very next day we showed up for practice and Kurt had this easel with a big sheet of paper on it," Aaron recalls. "He drew a big picture of a pen with its cap all chewed up. That was our new name: we were Pen Cap Chew. That was kind of a weird transformation. I don't know where he got it from." Kurt also wrote the new name on his pink suitcase. "We had a new name every week – we'd get kind of bored of them," Krist explains. In Aaron's recollection, when Kurt received a copy of the KAOS show, he gave the recording a playful name: *A Is For Aaron Who Fell Down The Stairs And Shit His Dress*, drawing an accompanying illustration of a stick figure falling down the stairs.

A rehearsal tape from this period survives and has two more new numbers in their only known performances. One was later entitled 'Mrs Butterworth' when included on *With The Lights Out*. It's an uptempo, driving number that suddenly lurches into comedy in the middle during a spoken-word section – the only such section in any Nirvana song – in which Kurt imagines himself selling trinkets at a flea market (an idea he'd return to later). The other number begins with a repetitive two-note drone, which Kurt then imitates, the guitar line later spiraling up and down like a ball slowly going up in the air only to come back to earth. Largely instrumental, it may have been more of a jam than a proper song, and in any case, neither it nor 'Mrs Butterworth' were taken any further.

The band's next known show, at the Community World Theater on June 27, was indeed under the name Pen Cap Chew. After that their momentum stalled. The band's only other confirmed show of the year was on August 9 1987, again at the Community World Theater, this time as Bliss. Part of the problem was logistical. After the KAOS show, Kurt moved in with Tracy in Olympia; Krist and Shelli moved to Tacoma; and Aaron remained in Aberdeen. With the band-members now living in three different places, they had to make a considerable effort to practice together, and with no regular venues other than the Community World Theater interested in having them perform, there was no great incentive to make that effort. "Everything just kind of fell apart," says Krist. Not until 1992, in the first flush of Nirvana's mainstream success, would every member of the band again be living in the same city.

CHAPTER 3

Bright Lights, Big City

"Only by supporting new ideas by local artists, bands, and records can the US expect any kind of dynamic social/cultural change in the 1980s. We need diverse, regionalized, localized approaches to all forms of art, music, and politics."

BRUCE PAVITT IN *SUBTERRANEAN POP #1*, 1980

As Kurt and Krist struggled to get their band off the ground, the Seattle music scene was going through its own growing pains. With a population in the late 80s of around 500,000 people, Seattle was Washington State's largest city, and best known at the time as the home of the aircraft manufacturer Boeing (the company's founder, William Boeing, had previously worked in the logging industry in Grays Harbor, serving as president of the Greenwood Logging Company). In 1987, Starbucks had just opened its first store outside the city. The personal computer boom that would make Microsoft a household word was some years away; Amazon and *Frasier* (not to mention *Twin Peaks*) had yet to be conceived.

If Aberdeen and Hoquiam were seen as provincial backwaters to Seattle's residents, that mirrored how Seattle, and indeed the Pacific Northwest as a whole, was perceived by the rest of the country. Only a handful of musical acts had made much of an impact outside the region; the Pacific Northwest was where performers came from, not where they stayed. The list of those who had ties to the area and went on to greater success elsewhere was impressive: Bing Crosby, born in Tacoma, and raised in Spokane (on the Eastern side of the state); Ray Charles, who spent his formative musical years in Seattle, during which time he befriended a Garfield High School student named Quincy Jones; and Jimi Hendrix, who also attended Garfield High. Heart, initially based in Seattle's suburbs, found success only after relocating to British Columbia, Canada, and then (unusually) moved back to Seattle for the rest of their career.

From the late 50s to the mid 60s, only a handful of acts from the region went on to enjoy some measure of success, including Olympia vocal group The Fleetwoods ('Come Softly To Me,' 'Mr. Blue'), and Tacoma acts The Ventures ('Walk Don't Run'), and The Wailers, aka The Fabulous Wailers ('Tall Cool One'). The Wailers were the first Northwest act to release a cover of Richard Berry's 'Louie Louie' in 1960, transforming what had originally been a Latin-flavored rhythm & blues number into a garage-rock classic. The Wailers' version also provided a template for the first hit version of the song, released by Portland, Oregon-based band The Kingsmen in 1963 (Don Gallucci, who played electric piano for the group, would carry garage rock's legacy into the next generation, producing The Stooges' 1970 album *Fun House*). The song became such an anthem for the region that there was a serious, albeit ultimately unsuccessful, attempt to make it the official Washington State song in 1985.

The Pacific Northwest's identification with 'Louie Louie' reflected the area's love of garage rock, as epitomized by another Tacoma act, The Sonics. During their 60s heyday, the five-piece group recorded wild, unhinged numbers like 'Psycho,' 'Strychnine,' and their signature song, 'The Witch,' that pushed garage rock into more raucous territory; in the words of Jack White of The White Stripes, it was "punk long before punk." Although The Sonics remained a cult act, innumerable punk and alternative rock bands would later cite them as an influence. The Northwest was also home to a thriving metal scene, with metal acts being more readily signed to a major label than punk or alternative bands. Most only found moderate success, the most notable exception being Queensrÿche, who signed to EMI in 1983, releasing their breakthrough album, *Operation: Mindcrime* in 1988.

Seattle's punk and new-wave acts of the late 70s and early 80s also achieved no more than regional interest, and bands still tended to leave the Northwest in search of more opportunities. Cult act The Screamers, who'd been dubbed 'techno-punk' as the band featured keyboards and drums but no guitars in their line-up, relocated to Los Angeles; the moody Blackouts moved to Boston and then San Francisco (three members of the band, Paul and Roland Barker and William Rieflin, later joined Ministry); singer-songwriter Penelope Houston also moved to the Bay Area, where she formed The Avengers; and trash-rock band The Mentors moved to LA, going on to greater infamy when the lyrics to their song 'Golden Showers' were read aloud at a hearing on record labeling and song lyrics before a congressional Committee on Commerce, Science, and Transportation in 1985.

"It was a much more provincial place, Seattle, in those days," says Kurt Danielson, a member of the bands Bundle Of Hiss and TAD. "And geographically isolated, more so than today, because of no internet. And bands – international touring bands – tended to avoid Seattle because of routing issues. Oftentimes Seattle was a bit out of the way. If you played Vancouver or Portland, you didn't need to play Seattle as well. Some bands avoided the whole Northwest, because it wasn't economically feasible to go out of your way to get here. Because of issues like that, Seattle seemed to get sort of edged out more often than not back in those days."

The music scene also tended to be derivative. "We had our indigenous music, but it was heavily influenced by the post-punk stuff coming out of England," says Danielson. "It didn't have a sense of coming from the heart. It was manufactured, to an extent. Because you had all these bands like 3 Swimmers or The Blackouts that were heavily influenced by Gang Of Four and that kind of post-punk ethos or aesthetic."

"In the early 80s, Seattle was like a million second cities," producer/musician Steve Fisk says in the film *Hype!* "It had a fake

Talking Heads, it had a fake Pere Ubu, it had a fake Killing Joke, it had all the fake Ramones you could shake a stick at, and people from Bellevue [a neighboring city] singing with English accents." Steve's point is aptly illustrated by the bands on the compilations *Seattle Syndrome Vol. 1* and *Vol. 2*, which were released in 1981 and 1983 respectively. The albums feature contributions from The Blackouts and 3 Swimmers in addition to girl-group covers act The Dynette Set, punk bands The Fartz and The Refuzors, and future Guns N' Roses bassist Duff McKagan playing drums on The Fastbacks' power-poppy 'Someone Else's Room.'

There was nonetheless sufficient interest to support a magazine that focused on the local music scene. October 1979 saw the publication of the first issue of *The Rocket*, a monthly music paper founder by staffers of the alternative weekly *The Seattle Sun* who had become fed up with the *Sun*'s editorial agenda. (According to *Rocket* founding editor Robert Ferringo, the breaking point came when the *Sun*'s editor suggested doing a cover story on the topic 'What Ever Happened To Macramé?') "We believe the local music scene to be vibrating with life, multi-faceted, and responsive to a wide range of audiences," the paper's first editorial stated. "We will cover national acts like The Cars, but remain committed to supporting local music." For all the subsequent criticism about what the paper did – and did not – cover, *The Rocket* became a clearinghouse of information for the local music scene, offering more comprehensive club listings and reviews of independent releases than were available in the mainstream dailies (of which there were two in Seattle at the time, *The Seattle Times* and *The Seattle Post-Intelligencer*). 'Musicians wanted' classified ads were also free, providing another invaluable service. Future Kurt Cobain biographer Charles R. Cross became the magazine's owner and editor in 1986.

The Rocket's first cover was a picture of Harry Kool, a local record producer, sitting in the control room of Triangle Studios, located in Seattle's Ballard neighborhood, then home to the city's sizeable

Scandinavian population. Just over five years later, under a new name, the studio would become the recording base for a new crop of bands that would have an impact that reached far beyond the Northwest. But for the first half of the 80s, Seattle music seemed stuck in the doldrums. A 1984 article in *The Rocket* posed the question 'Who's Killing Seattle Rock And Roll?' The article pointed to various factors, including a sagging economy, the tendency of original artists to leave Seattle for LA or the East Coast, and the lack of all-ages venues. The article tried to end on a positive note, which turned out to be unexpectedly prescient: "What this town really needs is one band to blow us all away. Just one band that can play some new music that captures the imagination of the town, that would turn everything around … There's somebody out there right now who could do it." But the dearth of live clubs open to bands playing original material remained an on-going problem. The pickings were so slim that in *The Rocket*'s year-end listings for 1984, the winner of the 'Best Venue' category was 'your living room.' "The 1984 music scene in Seattle was slow death," the accompanying article concluded. "We were boring, you were too. Admit it." A poster stapled on telephone poles around the city at the time was equally blunt. Its four words, clipped from different magazines, told the story as starkly as a ransom note: "Seattle Scene Found Dead."

In 1983, Bruce Pavitt moved to Seattle after graduating from Evergreen. He wasted no time in immersing himself in the city's music scene, DJ'ing at a shortlived all-ages club called the Metropolis in the city's historic Pioneer Square district and working at an independent record store, Bomb Shelter Records. While at Bomb Shelter, he oversaw the release of the debut EP by The U-Men, on the store's own Bomb Shelter label, set up specifically to release the record. The U-Men were Seattle's premiere underground group of the early 80s. Whereas other bands of the era were more likely to give a punk spin to 50s rockabilly, The U-Men applied their punk touch to 60s garage rock, which gave their music a darker – and at times more sinister – cast, especially when topped by lead singer John Bigley's raspy, growling, off-kilter vocals. They passed into legend when they capped a performance at Seattle's annual Bumbershoot arts festival in 1985 by setting the moat in front of their outdoor stage on fire.

Bruce then moved on to Yesco Audio Environments, a company that produced tapes of background music used by stores and offices. In 1987, the company merged with the corporation better known for manufacturing such background music (usually easy-listening re-recordings of popular songs): Muzak. Although it was a menial job – the work involved duplicating tapes or cleaning tape cartridge boxes – working at Yesco put Bruce in contact with a number of aspiring musicians who had gravitated toward the company as their day job, an irony Bruce fully appreciated. He also became a DJ at the University of Washington's (UW) radio station KCMU, where non-students were allowed to volunteer, and in April 1983 began writing a regular column at *The Rocket*. Both the radio show and the *Rocket* column used the name Sub Pop.

Bruce's February 1986 *Rocket* column had a brief review of the debut release by a local band called Green River, the EP *Come On Down*, which, Bruce wrote, "flames like hell ... A fat nod to The Stooges' *Fun House*. HEAVY." Green River had formed in 1984, and comprised Mark Arm (who also worked at Yesco and DJ'd at KCMU) on guitar and vocals, Steve Turner on guitar, Jeff Ament (originally from Montana, where he played in the punk band Deranged Diction) on bass, and Alex Shumway (aka Alex Vincent) on drums; Stone Gossard was later brought in on guitar so that Mark could concentrate on his vocals. Green River were one of a number of new Seattle bands who melded together punk, heavy metal, and hard rock in a style that had yet to be named. In the late 70s and early 80s, punk and metal had been warring camps – both figuratively and often literally – but this new generation was far less doctrinaire about their musical tastes. The band's name also reflected the sarcastic, twisted humor of the scene. While partly a reference to the classic rock of Creedence Clearwater Revival, it also referred to the name given to a serial killer then terrorizing the greater Seattle area, who had left a few of his victims in the river of the same name located just outside the Seattle city limits (the killer, Gary Ridgway, was eventually arrested in 2001).

Another local band, Soundgarden, were also treading new musical ground. The band was formed in 1984 by guitarist Kim Thayil, bassist Hiro Yamamoto, and Chris Cornell, who originally sang and played drums, then moved down front as lead singer (also occasionally playing guitar) with the arrival of drummer Scott Sundquist. Kim and Hiro had both attended high school with Bruce Pavitt back in Illinois. Kim (who was originally born in Seattle, but had left the area at age five with his parents) had also played in a band with Bruce's brother, and was a DJ at KCMU. Like Green River, the band's music didn't readily fit into any one category; while Cornell's tendency to sing in his upper range led to inevitable comparisons with Led Zeppelin, the music had a decided alternative edge. The band's ethereal name was taken from the sculpture 'A Sound Garden' in a local park, which moved in the wind and made an eerie wailing sound. "We liked 'Soundgarden' because it wasn't real obvious," said Kim. "It sounds like Pure Joy or Rain Parade. It fools people."

Green River and Soundgarden had an immediate influence on others in the music scene. "I saw Green River as an attempt to explore noise for its own sake, a soulful approach to guitar-based rock like The Stooges, as opposed to a more restrained, more consciously artistic or nihilistic New York/Manchester/London-influenced aesthetic," says Kurt Danielson. "It was a very inspiring time. It was like there was an airborne disease – like a bacteria that was floating around – and if you were susceptible to it, it could infect you. I was susceptible to it. I had this vision of a kind of music that was rooted in a post-punk aesthetic, right? And suddenly here comes this bacterium. It invades my system, and it transforms my thinking on how this music should sound. And suddenly it was very exciting; you didn't know where it might go. You had pockets of interesting music that posed a possible answer, or a possible definition for the future – there were options all of a sudden. Maybe they weren't very clear options, maybe they weren't even attractive, but they were options nonetheless, and there was a sense that there was a multiple number of choices you could make in music, not just one or two, as seen before."

Green River and Soundgarden had also caught the attention of Chris Hanzsek, who, inspired by the *Seattle Syndrome* compilations, had moved to Seattle from Boston with his girlfriend, Tina Casale, in 1983, with plans to open a recording studio. The two opened the first incarnation of Reciprocal Recording in January 1984, in Seattle's Interbay neighborhood. Green River were one of the first bands to work there, having recorded part of *Come On Down* at the studio. The EP was released by Long Island, New York-based Homestead Records in 1985, and was also supported by some out-of-state touring, a rarity for Northwest alternative bands at the time.

Hanzsek lost the lease on his studio after a year. While looking around for a new location, he and Casale also planned to start a record label, C/Z Records. At the suggestion of Mark Arm and Jeff Ament, the couple decided to launch C/Z with a compilation featuring current Seattle bands, eventually entitled *Deep Six*, referring both to the number of bands on the record and the overall heaviness of their music. Along with Green River, the participation of Soundgarden was a given, and Soundgarden's contributions, 'Heretic' and 'Tears To Forget,' marked the only recorded appearance of drummer Sundquist. The Melvins and The U-Men were also signed on. "They said: we'll record you if you come down to the studio," Buzz Osborne recalled of his band's participation. "And we didn't have any money for recording or anything, so that was great."

"The U-Men were not originally on the album," says Daniel House, then a member of Skin Yard. "The reason they were asked was because they were the only band that had anything out previously. So Chris and Tina figured that having a U-Men track on there would make a difference in being able to sell some records locally." Skin Yard – formed in 1984 with Daniel on bass, Jack Endino on guitar, Matt Cameron on drums, and Ben McMillan on vocals – weren't originally in consideration for *Deep Six* either, but when Daniel caught wind of the project, he persuaded Chris to include his band on the album. (By the time *Deep Six* was released, Matt Cameron had replaced Scott Sundquist in Soundgarden.) The final *Deep Six* band was glam-metal act Malfunkshun, based on Bainbridge Island, a 30-minute ferry ride from Seattle. The band was formed in 1981 by Kevin Wood and his brother Andrew, a flamboyant personality who billed himself as Landrew, The Love Child.

Deep Six was officially released on April 1 1986 (Jack Endino made a note in his journal that the bands were given personal copies of the record on February 10). In her review of the album in *The Rocket*, Dawn Anderson noted the varied musical influences the bands displayed, which she said resulted in "music that isn't punk-metal but a third sound distinct from either." By then, Dawn had seen most of the *Deep Six* bands live. "I don't know if I would've liked the record as much as I did if I hadn't," she says. "Because it wasn't the most immaculately produced album ever released." ("There are all sorts of rookie things going on with the recording," Hanzsek conceded. "Let's just call it 'muddled.'")

"I think it sort of lost something in translation if you didn't know what these bands were going for," Anderson continues. "I loved these new bands. I thought they were awesome. Green River, I thought they were just so fucking entertaining, and Mark Arm was always so funny. And also I just loved really, really loud obnoxious rock. And they delivered that!

"The first time I saw the Melvins and Soundgarden was when

they opened for Hüsker Dü. And there were a lot of really, really baffled people in the audience, because these were brand new bands nobody knew yet. Soundgarden was very extreme and punishing, maybe a little more intricate, maybe a little more unusual then the Melvins were at that time. The Melvins weren't doing their real slow sludgy stuff all the time yet, they were still doing some faster stuff. Matt Lukin was jumping around and doing all this posing, and he had all this hair – they were just so extreme and so shameless about being heavy that there were a lot of people shaking their heads, saying: are these guys joking? You know, all these scenesters going: do these guys even realize that they're funny? I was like: God, you guys have no clue. Because it didn't matter whether they knew they were funny or not. It really didn't matter. I think they did know, but I thought they were awesome either way."

Although only 2,000 copies of *Deep Six* were pressed, it took "a good three years" for the bulk of the records to sell. "There was no idea that any of the history that unfolded after that, would," says Daniel House. "They were just a bunch of unknown nobodies." The Melvins would soon record for C/Z again, resulting in their *Six Songs* EP (subsequently expanded and released as *8 Songs*, *10 Songs*, and finally *26 Songs*). The record continued the band's move toward the heavier, sludgier sound that would become their trademark. At the end of 1986 they would record their landmark *Gluey Porch Treatments* album, a glorious, grinding wash of thundering noise that provided further inspiration for the new Northwest bands. Kim Thayil and Mark Arm had already taken note of Buzz's drop-D tuning. "It makes things a little bit lower, a little bit heavier," Kim explained to Mark Yarm. "After that, I went ahead and wrote a number of songs in drop-D tuning – the first song I wrote with it was 'Nothing To Say.'" Buzz was unaware of the record's influence at time. "We didn't have a lot of people that were interested in that record, hardly anyone, you know?" he later said. "It's nice to know that I wasn't wrong. That stuff, it's timeless and it worked. It worked then and it works now."

However, *Gluey Porch Treatments* would be released not by C/Z but by the San Francisco-based label Alchemy Records (Buzz Osborne and Dale Crover would eventually relocate to San Francisco, leaving bassist Matt Lukin behind). And after breaking up with his girlfriend, Chris Hanzsek decided he was no longer interested in running a record label, so he sold C/Z to Daniel House. ("Skin Yard was unable to get successfully signed, which was really the motivation in the first place to go ahead and take the label over," says Daniel.)

Despite the low sales, *Deep Six* – which was re-released on CD in 1994 – was the first compilation to document the new sound that was coming from the Northwest. "The *Deep Six* album really did do a lot," says Dawn. "Because they put all these bands together on one album, and it gave you the feeling that something might be happening there." Faith Henschel, then the music director at KCMU, was also moved to put together compilation tapes of local bands that she then sent to record labels and agents in a further attempt to drum up interest in the scene. Henschel gave the tapes, which featured Soundgarden, Green River, and Skin Yard, along with other bands whose members would later surface in higher profile bands (Room Nine's Rod Rudzitis in Love Battery; H-Hour's Tad Doyle in TAD; Bundle Of Hiss' Dan Peters in Mudhoney), a bold, and some thought wildly improbable, title: *Bands That Will Make Money*.

The year 1986 also saw Bruce Pavitt taking the first steps into making Sub Pop a record label with the release of its first vinyl LP, the *Sub Pop 100* compilation. "The tapes had done fairly well, so transitioning to vinyl was pretty easy," Bruce explains. "Everything just flowed from wanting to share music with people." The album mirrored the musical mix on Bruce's *Sub Pop* tapes, featuring the Wipers, The U-Men, musician-producer Steve Fisk, Sonic Youth, Scratch Acid, and a brief spoken introduction by musician-producer Steve Albini. The album sold 5,000 copies, which at the time, Bruce said, "was like having a

Gold record in the indie scene." He used the profits to take an extended trip to Amsterdam.

Bruce's next project was to release a Green River record. "For one thing, I was friends with Mark," he explains. "This is a little-known secret, but I'm actually the person who convinced Homestead Records to put out *Come On Down*. The record stiffed and the band got dropped, but I still thought they were a brilliant band, especially live." He was also keen to work with Soundgarden, having recognized their potential. In 1989, he told me during an interview: "The singer has a commercial voice, but the band is unlike anything in the market. I think they're gonna shake up the rock world." But he didn't have sufficient funds to work on both projects, so Kim Thayil suggested he team up with another person interested in working with Soundgarden, Jonathan Poneman.

Jonathan, originally from Toledo, Ohio, had moved to Bellingham (a city 90 miles north of Seattle) with his girlfriend in the 70s. When the relationship ended, he moved to Seattle in September 1979. "My primary motivation was to get in a position in the music community where I would not be invisible," he says. He first became a musician, playing in local bands The Rockefellers and The Treeclimbers (subsequently dismissing the latter as "mid-80s twinkie pop"). He eventually became the host of *Audioasis*, a program on KCMU that spotlighted local acts, and also booked acts at the Rainbow Tavern, a venue just down the road from the UW, where he first saw Soundgarden. "It was one of the most riveting shows I'd ever seen," he says. "Because this was a band that effortlessly possessed the qualities of rock'n'roll that I always thought were important: an element of spontaneity, danger, intensity." The gig also convinced Jonathan to quit The Treeclimbers. "Seeing that show taught me exactly why I was never going to succeed as a musician in the manner in which I would want to," he says.

Bruce and Jonathan knew each other through KCMU, and Jonathan had also worked at Yesco. Kim thought the two could work well together. "Bruce had pretty good judgment in terms of cultural trends, fashion and stuff like that," he says. "That's his art and his vision – knowing what people will like, and how to make people like things. He had a lot of ideas – he just didn't have the money to work with them. And here Jonathan had money and was ready to put out a record with us. Jonathan was very confident in his own ability to get a record out there and have people notice it. We weren't as confident. We knew he could make a record, but we knew that Bruce could get it noticed. So I gave him Bruce's phone number and address."

Although the two men were initially resistant to the idea of working together, they soon realized that pooling their resources would help them both. "It was like an opportunity to step up, instead of trying to conjure a name for a record label," Jonathan says. "It made sense," agrees Bruce. "I had a PO Box and a logo and a few phone numbers for distributors, so I kind of had my foot out of the gate there. And Sub Pop at that time had no funding, per se; $12 every six months to pay for the PO box was about as deep as it went. So for Jon to step up and go: hey, I can help fund this – that was awesome." Jonathan invested the $15,000 he'd saved in savings bonds, and the two were now partners.

Sub Pop firmly established their regional focus in 1987, releasing Green River's *Dry As A Bone* EP and Soundgarden's 'Hunted Down'/'Nothing To Say' single and *Screaming Life* EP. "Washington has the hottest regional rock scene in America," Bruce said at the time, explaining Sub Pop's planned emphasis on Northwest acts. Jonathan concurred: "Regionalism in pop music, aside from being a romantic notion, is pragmatically a good base to spring from." The description of *Dry As A Bone* in Sub Pop's catalogue also introduced a new word that would come to be intrinsically linked with both the label, and the Northwest's music scene itself: "Gritty vocals, roaring Marshall amps. Ultra loose GRUNGE that destroyed the morals of a generation."

It was not the first time the term 'grunge' had been used to describe music; Lester Bangs, for one, had used it in articles about garage rockers Count Five. Its first known appearance in reference to a Seattle band had come in 1981, in a shortlived music paper called *Desperate Times* (which published a total of six issues). Mark Arm had sent in a joke letter to the paper attacking his pre-Green River band, which read in part: "I hate Mr Epp & The Calculations! Pure grunge! Pure noise! Pure shit!" signing the letter with his real name, Mark McLaughlin. At this point 'grunge' simply referred to how music sounded; eventually it would become a descriptive term of the music's style, thus creating a new genre, to Mark's amusement. "Grunge was an adjective; it was never meant to be a noun," he told Mark Yarm. "It was never meant to coin a movement, it was just to describe raw rock'n'roll."

The Green River and Soundgarden records also established several precedents for how Sub Pop's releases would be presented. Beginning with the Soundgarden records, initial pressings of a release would often be available in limited edition runs on colored vinyl (the *Screaming Life* EP on orange vinyl, the 'Hunted Down' single on blue vinyl) in a deliberate attempt to curry favor with record collectors. The outer packaging was equally important. Sub Pop regularly released EPs because the 12-inch cover size made a greater visual impact than a 7-inch single. The record covers also had a uniform look, as they featured the striking black and white photography of Charles Peterson.

Charles grew up in the Seattle suburb of Bothell and had begun shooting photographs as a child, developing them in a darkroom his grandparents had set up in their laundry room. By high school, he was shooting for the school newspaper and yearbook, despite the persecution he occasionally received as the school's only open punk rocker. "Imagine being harassed by the entire football team (egged on by the coaches) while trying to take their group photo: Punk rock faggot! We're gonna kill you!" he recalled. His photography teacher also dismissed his interest in shooting rock'n'roll bands as it wasn't a 'serious' subject. "My mother used to say that too: maybe you should stop with this rock'n'roll thing and start doing something else? I was like: no, mom, it'll pay off someday. It really will." Charles met Mark Arm in the dorms at the UW, and had shot pictures of Mark's first band, Mr Epp & The Calculations (named after a math teacher at Mark's high school). When Bruce was looking for artwork for Green River's EP, Mark suggested he look at Charles's photographs.

Charles and Bruce had a passing acquaintanceship, as both were DJs at KCMU. "I brought my pictures over and Bruce was just like: Wow! Yeah! Dude!" he recalls. "Just ecstatic over them. He was like: yeah, we can do this – I love your stuff!" It was not just the quality of Charles's work that impressed Bruce. He also liked how the pictures gave Seattle bands a visual identity to match their musical one. Charles shot acts from the very front of the stage, producing tightly framed pictures that captured the bands in action, with the audience frequently as prominent as the musicians, and used a blurred effect that readily conveyed a sense of the band in motion. "That was just using a flash and balancing what stage lighting was there with the shutter speed – a longer shutter speed, and then the flash captures the action," he explains. "It's not unique. It's not anything particularly special. I think it's more a matter of how far you go with it or how much you restrain it, depending on the situation, and using it to your best advantage. It's easy to get too crazy with it, and then it's just kind of like: yeah, whatever. You still have to capture the moment and maintain the composition for it to work."

It was a look that Bruce wanted to link with Sub Pop, telling Charles: "Let's have this as the vision for the label." "I will tell you here and now that seeing Charles's photos prior to putting out *Dry As A Bone* inspired me to start focusing on Seattle music," says Bruce. "Because I realized that a consistent visual representation could help the label develop. So Charles's photography was instrumental in inspiring me to try and focus on Seattle."

The records also had a uniform sound as they were all produced by Skin Yard's Jack Endino, who had become the in-house producer at the new Reciprocal Recording. Jack was born in Connecticut but moved to Bainbridge Island when he was in his teens. On graduating from the UW in 1980 with a degree in electrical engineering, he worked as a civilian engineer at the Puget Sound Naval Shipyard in nearby Bremerton. "I did that for two years and seven months and I decided I'd had enough of it," he says. "So I bailed and quit cold turkey and lived on my savings for a couple of years." Jack first moved to Belfair, a small town 70 miles southeast of Seattle, where he spent considerable time playing guitar and drums, learning how to record his efforts on a four-track tape deck.

On moving back to Seattle, Jack met Daniel House through a mutual friend; the two then formed Skin Yard in 1985. "Daniel introduced me to a lot of his friends, like the guys in Green River, and various other people," he says. "And Kim Thayil from Soundgarden lived about a quarter mile from my house. I started having a lot of people over, jamming in my basement, and I would always record them on my four-track. And pretty soon someone asked me to do a demo for them and I started making four-track demos. And then Green River asked me to help them with their first single ['Together We'll Never'/'Ain't Nothing To Do,' released in 1986 on the band's own Tasque Force label]. They wanted some help mixing it, so I helped them with that."

Jack was interested in finding a studio to work in, and learned that Chris Hanzsek was still looking for a new location for Reciprocal. "Someone I knew was getting out of the studio business, so their building was going to be vacant," he says. "And that was Triangle Studios, and they were right down the street from where I lived. So I said: hey, what would it take to assume the lease on this place? So Chris and I moved in." Jack and Chris were initially partners in the venture, but Jack soon decided he would rather concentrate on producing, and Chris bought out his interest.

At 900 square feet, Reciprocal wasn't much bigger than a one bedroom apartment. As the studio's previous name, Triangle Studios, suggests, the building was three sided, with the entrance in one point, the control room in another, and the bathroom in the third. "It was a small studio, great live drum sound," says Jennifer Finch, who recorded at Reciprocal as a member of L7. "Jack Endino was very mellow as a producer. I mean, he really just set up microphones and let the band play live." Jack even initially eschewed the formal title of 'producer'; his early Sub Pop records have the credit 'recorded by.' "Having a 'producer' was not indie-rock enough in 1988," he explains. "It was kind of suspect, ideologically. It even kind of made me cringe at the time. Remember, I'd only been working in a studio for two years or so. I didn't have the nerve to call myself a 'producer' yet, not for a couple more years – hence, 'recorded by.'"

Since Sub Pop's bands had already worked with Chris or Jack, Reciprocal naturally became the studio of choice for the label. "The first clients we got at Reciprocal were Green River and Soundgarden, almost immediately," says Jack. "So it sort of went on from there. I thought it was a cool little scene. Everybody went to everybody else's shows – that's been said many times, that there were a couple of clubs where most of the people in the audiences were the other musicians."

There was another element that was just as key to Sub Pop's releases as the sound of the records and the look of their packaging, something that would focus as much attention on the label as the bands: hype. "We're trying to capture the public's imagination, create the idea that there's all this music in Seattle," Jonathan told me in 1989, and both he and Bruce understood the importance of having a compelling narrative in capturing that attention. Anyone who took the time to study the spine of the *Sub Pop 100* cover would've read an audacious proclamation: "The new thing: the big thing: the God thing: a mighty multinational entertainment conglomerate based in the Pacific Northwest." It was an example of the kind of hyperbole that would become Sub Pop's stock in trade. The label's T-shirts would boast of their 'World Domination Regime,' while at the same time mocking the prevailing acquisitiveness of the 80s, epitomized by the prevailing yuppie culture in urban American centers of the period by producing other T-shirts that read 'Loser.' It was a way of talking up the label, but with a self-deprecating wink, thus avoiding sounding too egotistical. "Bruce and I were obviously indulging in what was to become the national pastime in the 90s – irony," says Jonathan.

There was no doubt about Bruce and Jonathan's ambitions for their label, however. Larry Reid, who managed The U-Men and operated various alternative art galleries in Seattle that doubled as performance spaces, remembered Bruce telling him "the Seattle music scene is going to take over the world!" at a U-Men show. "Under the circumstances, to make a preposterous statement like that – but he said it with conviction," said Reid. "He wasn't laughing." Other people in the scene readily connected with Bruce's passion for what he wanted to do. "Bruce was really excited about ideas," says Kurt Danielson. "If he heard something, or saw something, that excited him, his enthusiasm was very infectious. It was contagious, you know. It was fun working with him, because he had that kind of childlike enthusiasm that is so rewarding in artistic endeavors, and so rare. His enthusiasm was such that it knew no bounds – it brooked no opposition. And you know, the 'world domination' trip was kind of another demonstration of his enthusiasm. Obviously it was a joke in a sense. It was hubris in another – in being arrogant enough to claim world domination, you are bound to anger the gods, but on the other hand, it's good press, you know?"

Bruce and Jonathan's determination also made the bands feel like they were part of something destined to get bigger. One time, when Chris Cornell ran into Bruce at a show and commented on the number of good new bands there suddenly seemed to be in Seattle, he was surprised when Bruce put his arm around him and announced: "Seattle's gonna take over the world!" "It was a bit tongue-in-cheek, but it wasn't really," Cornell recalled. "He was serious about it. And that was the first time that I actually believed it and felt like someone did have a vision." "We were interested in working with Sub Pop because it was more exciting," says Kim Thayil. "I was confident that their taste in music was good, the bands were good – in fact everything about their style was interesting and unique. I thought it could be a huge phenomenon. I didn't think it *would* be, just that it *could* be."

In 1988, Sub Pop stepped up production, putting out 12 releases. The label also became a full-time endeavor for Bruce and Jon, who decided to quit their day jobs (Bruce stopped writing his *Rocket* column the same year). "It was a bold move," says Bruce. "It's when we really started to go into it professionally. Even though we weren't necessarily that professional in our execution, it was a pretty big leap for us. It sure felt good to quit my job at Muzak. It was a blessing that we both had really crappy jobs." The label's first office was located on the 11th floor of the Terminal Sales Building in downtown Seattle; although they moved into the building in March, they date the label's official launch to the date on their lease: April 1 1988 – two years after the release of *Deep Six*.

The label got off to a rocky start. By the end of May they'd gone through all of their money, and they only managed to stay afloat because the manufacturer who was printing the jackets of Green River's *Rehab Doll* EP agreed to fill the order before it had been paid in full. In August, when the telephone was on the verge of being disconnected, they sent the phone company a rubber check. "We did a few mildly dishonest things to stay in business," Bruce conceded. The company's perennial financial difficulties spawned their tongue-in-cheek motto: "Going out of business since 1988."

"They were flying by the seat of their pants completely, without business experience, or very little," says Kurt Danielson. "They just had some really passionate ideas about the music scene, and the need for there to be a platform, a label, to get that music out there. They were totally devoted to doing whatever it took, and because of this they would often say or do things that they couldn't really promise to bring to fruition. Because they wanted to so badly, they just did things on a shoelace, on the fly, and I don't know how often they came close to losing that first office space, or not being able to pay the phone bill, or not being able to pay for an ad here or an ad there. It was very, very much a day-by-day enterprise, and super-stressful for those guys."

Another initial problem was that while Bruce and Jon had planned on having Green River as one of their top acts, the band had broken up by the time *Rehab Doll* was released. Mark Arm felt the EP indicated the growing musical split within the band. "You listen to the riffs, and they're sort of like kind of Aerosmithy sort of riffs," he says. "And I'm just spewing angst and black humor over the top of it. It doesn't really mix very well." While in LA on their final tour in 1987, Green River had opened for Jane's Addiction. The band greatly impressed Jeff Ament and Stone Gossard in particular – "It was the first time I had seen an alternative music show where it was like the most reverential hard-rock crowd," Jeff later said. "Jane's Addiction showed us that you could do something totally different and make it work" – but it wasn't a musical direction Mark was interested in pursuing at all. Jeff, Stone, and Bruce Fairweather (another KCMU DJ, who had replaced Steve Turner in Green River), had already begun jamming with Andrew Wood on the side, and one day when Mark and Alex Shumway showed up for rehearsal, the other three told them what they'd been suspecting for some time: Green River was over. "I wasn't super happy with the way things were going, musically," says Mark. "But then I had a feeling like: OK, great, what do I do now? There was a show soon after at the OK Hotel. And Dan Peters was there. I was just totally hammered, and I went up to him and said: hey, guess what, Dan: Green River broke up. And then I vomited!"

"Frankly, I think Jon and I were a little shocked," says Bruce about hearing the news of Green River's demise. "We quit our day jobs, spent five thousand dollars on that Green River record, and as soon as we opened the doors it was like: here's your tape; we just broke up last night. Great!" "It was challenging to really launch the label with a band that's just broken up," says Jonathan. "But almost simultaneously, Mark announced that he was forming Mudhoney, and so we immediately took some money and put them in the studio." Mudhoney (who took their name from a Russ Meyer film) had Mark Arm on vocals, Steve Turner on guitar, and Dan Peters on drums; Matt Lukin, who'd moved to Seattle from Aberdeen, was on bass. The band would become the definitive Sub Pop band from their first release, the classic single 'Touch Me I'm Sick'/'Sweet Young Thing Ain't Sweet No More,' which was billed as "two incredible noise/grunge hits from this great new band" in the Sub Pop catalogue (with the first pressing on brown vinyl).

"Mudhoney are the royal heirs of mid-60s Northwest punk," Bruce notes with pride. Soon Green River's split was being cast in a more positive light. "I think it was a good thing that Green River broke up," Jonathan concludes. "They obviously all had different things that they needed to do." The other members of Green River, Jeff Ament and Stone Gossard, teamed up with Andrew Wood and Ragan Hagar as Lords Of The Wasteland; after Greg Gilmore replaced Hagar, and Green River's Bruce Fairweather joined the line-up, the band became Mother Love Bone. When Mother Love Bone broke up following Wood's death in 1990, Ament and Gossard formed Pearl Jam, and Fairweather joined Love Battery.

With the emergence of Sub Pop, C/Z, K, and other labels providing evidence of a healthy and growing music scene, one *Rocket* writer became convinced that the time was ripe for a publication that focused exclusively on the Northwest, and *Backlash*, billed as "Seattle's only local music magazine" made its debut in December 1987. The magazine's editor, Dawn Anderson, had previously published a shortlived publication called *Backfire*, which bravely bridged the punk/metal divide; the first issue featured stories on both Iron Maiden and Black Flag. Dawn was a regular *Rocket* contributor, but was looking for a fulltime writing position. After she was hired as the editor of the *Lake Union Review*, a neighborhood newspaper, she was able to convince her publisher to put out a music paper. "He didn't think it would work," she says. "But finally he said: well, if you can make the first issue break even, you can do it."

For most of its existence, *Backlash* was "100 per cent Northwest music and nothing else, mostly Seattle," she says. "And there was nobody else doing that. There was a lot of local music that wasn't really getting covered and part of that was the early grunge stuff, which no one was calling grunge back then, except maybe Jack Endino. So part of why *Backlash* started was to cover that. But we covered everything. We were really, really specific geographically, and really, really general musically – musically we were all over the place. We would write about [local rhythm & blues act] Duffy Bishop, but we also wrote about some rock stuff, and some punk stuff that really didn't get covered anywhere else at the time."

While *Backlash* would never come close to challenging *The Rocket* in terms of circulation, its presence was an indication of a steadily growing interest in the Northwest music scene. But for all Bruce and Jonathan's talk of world domination, there was still little indication that Northwest music acts would generate much enthusiasm outside the region. "It was a very surreal experience when your dreams manifest like that," says Bruce about the attention that Sub Pop, and the Pacific Northwest, subsequently enjoyed. "I kind of liken it to the following: imagine if somebody stepped up to you and said: within the next two years Anchorage, Alaska, is going to have the hottest music scene on the planet, do you want to give me some money? The odds against that were pretty high. And that's kind of where Seattle was at that time. It was a million-to-one shot."

CHAPTER 4

Underground Attitude

"I just can't believe that anyone would start a band just to make the scene and be cool and have chicks."
KURT TO *OPTION*, 1991

After several weeks without contact, Kurt finally reached out to Krist in Tacoma. "I got a letter from him," Krist recalls. "It was kind of a funny letter. I wish I still had it. It said: Let's get back to playing. No obligation. It was like he was sending me a form letter from some sales marketing firm, like: you've won something! No obligation. Well, some – he put that on there. And so we started getting back together. And then I really got into it, 'cause it was fun."

The musical bond was between Kurt and Krist; neither of them bothered to contact Aaron Burckhard about getting back together. "We got really serious and he wasn't that serious," Kurt later explained to journalist Gina Arnold. "So we had a lot of trouble starting out. It didn't seem like a real legitimate band, or as legitimate as we wanted it to be." Indeed, the first word in the 'Musicians Wanted' ad they placed in the October 1987 issue of *The Rocket* emphasized their newfound dedication:

> "SERIOUS DRUMMER WANTED. Underground attitude, Black Flag, Melvins, Zeppelin, Scratch Acid, Ethel Merman. Versatile as heck."

The ad, signed 'Kurdt,' proved unsuccessful, and as Kurt was keenly interested in making a more professional demo as soon as possible,

Dale Crover was drafted as a temporary drummer. Knowing Dale was committed to the Melvins, the musicians spent their time rehearsing in preparation for recording the demo instead of looking for gigs. "I would pick up Kurt in Olympia," says Krist, "and we would drive to Aberdeen and rehearse at Dale's mom's house. We had some intense rehearsals." Dale's forceful drumming gave the songs a greater power and depth, and it was not surprising that a new song written during this period, 'Paper Cuts,' displayed a clear Melvins influence. Ominous, heavy beats lead into the tortured tale of an Aberdeen couple who keep their children locked in a room. Whether the story was true or not, it was rife with dramatic possibilities, and it appealed to Kurt's bleak view of the world.

"'Paper Cuts' was awesome," says Krist. "That is like the quintessential grunge song. There's power, there's a cohesion – it's just like one riff – one note! What's the first song on *Black Sabbath Volume Four*? ['Wheels Of Confusion'/'The Straightener'] One note, make a riff out of it. And then it just busts out and it's just devastating, the progression, this riff. That's a great song." Another new song, 'Beeswax,' reprised the new-wave feel of 'Hairspray Queen,' especially in its opening descending guitar-line, as well as the off-kilter rawness of a band like Scratch Acid. The rambling, stream-of-consciousness lyrics also bring to mind the wordplay of 'Downer.'

Once Kurt felt the songs were sufficiently rehearsed, he called Reciprocal Recording in Seattle. He told Michael Azerrad he chose the studio because it was the least expensive, although others recall the choice being determined by the fact that Soundgarden's *Screaming Life* was recorded there. Jack Endino took the call, and when Kurt explained that he "wanted to record some songs really fast" and was working with Dale Crover, Jack was immediately interested. "Skin Yard played shows with the Melvins many times," he says. "And I thought that meant it's not going to be some shitty band, if Dale's playing with them. So I said yeah, come on up." (Ironically, when Aaron Burckhard's subsequent band Attica recorded with Endino, they used the same pitch in setting up their session, telling him: "We're friends of Nirvana. Our drummer used to be in the band.") Jack scheduled the session with 'Kurt Kovain' and his band on January 23: "He didn't tell me how to spell it. I just thought I heard him say 'Kovain.'"

Krist's friend Dwight Covey drove them to Seattle in his truck fitted with a camper on top. The three musicians arrived around noon and wasted no time, setting up and laying down the instrumental tracks with dispatch. "Did it all live," says Krist. "I don't think there are any punch-ins. I knocked my amp over. I played my bass through a Twin Reverb and then I pulled on it and knocked it over!" The only overdubbing came when Kurt recorded his vocals (Dale also added backing vocals to 'Downer' and 'Spank Thru'). "We ran through the songs instrumentally," says Jack, "and then Kurt said: OK, we'll do the vocals now. And he went through the vocals in one take – I just started at the top of the reel and pressed 'record,' he'd sing it and then go: OK, next! And I'd say OK and press 'record' again."

Recording began with 'If You Must.' Despite Kurt's dislike of the song (he later described it as "sickening and dumb"), it's especially compelling in this version. Kurt's high-pitched vocal in the first verse never sounded as eerie, making his move into a full-throated scream on the last word of the first verse, "attitude," all the more startling. With Dale pushing the band on drums, 'Downer' is distilled to a fast and furious 102 seconds, in stark contrast to the Fecal Matter version, which was more than twice as long. Kurt's rapid-fire vocal delivery gives the song an additional punishing edge, making 'Downer' the closest thing to hardcore that Nirvana ever recorded. But nowhere else did Dale's presence on drums transform a song as much as on 'Floyd The Barber.' His relentless pounding truly brings out the song's menacing quality, matched by Kurt's anguished vocal, and, indeed, the song was never improved on in subsequent recording sessions. "He's a powerhouse," Krist said of Dale Crover. "He's solid and straight-ahead when he needs to be, and at the same time he could be incredibly complex and inventive."

'Paper Cuts' features another remarkable vocal performance, veering from dreamy crooning to throat-shredding screeches and back again. "That's what makes the whole song – the vocals," says Krist. The performance of 'Spank Thru' is especially confident, Kurt's vocal again finding the perfect midway point between sincerity and parody. But he goes fully over the top in 'Hairspray Queen,' twisting his voice as much as his choppy guitar line. 'Aero Zeppelin' benefits from its shorter running time, but it's still a song that betrays its influences more than it reveals the writer's own voice. The same could also be said of 'Beeswax.'

Taken at a faster tempo, 'Mexican Seafood' becomes almost playful, despite the scatological lyrics. The brooding 'Pen Cap Chew,' the last song recorded, is considerably shorter than the KAOS version, although this was due in part to the fact that the song was too long to fit on the 33-minute tape reel; it was also given an early fade-out, as no one could afford to buy another reel. A rehearsal tape from this period shows that the group also rehearsed 'Annorexorcist' and a more new-wave-styled number, 'Erectum,' indicating they might also have recorded these songs, if they'd had enough money for another reel of tape.

Recording finished around 4pm, with the mixes done by 6pm; the band could stay no later as they had to leave for a show that night at the Community World Theater. Given the time frame, Jack worked quickly on the mixes, estimating he was only able to spend around 12 minutes per song. "They pretty much just let me do whatever I wanted with the mixes," he says "I think they just wanted a tape of some kind. They had no plans to make an album; they just wanted to get these songs down."

Jack gave the musicians a copy of the session on cassette, and asked if he could hold on to the eight-track master to make his own mix. "I just liked the songs," he explains. "I thought: this is really cool, I'd better make myself a copy of it. It was the best thing I'd heard in a while at the studio, so I really, really wanted a tape of it. I did that a lot, actually; if I liked something, I often made myself my own copy. I would have made a cassette off of their mix, but they were on their way out the door; they had to go soundcheck at the Community World.

"So I convinced them to leave the eight-track. I sort of had to beg for it. I said: why don't you leave this here so I can make myself a mix of it? Maybe some people I know would like to hear it. And they were like: yeah, fine, we'll get it later. So I made my own version of the mix after they left; I just put the eight-track back on and ran through it again and made myself a copy of it. All the settings were there, so I just went ahead and rolled it. It's a little different from the one that they took home, because I thought: I'm not in a hurry now, let me make a nice tape for myself." Due to Dale Crover's involvement, Jack called the tape the 'Dale Demo,' which is how the recording is known in collecting circles.

After being bootlegged extensively, most of the songs on the Dale Demo were later officially released, with the exception of 'Spank Thru': 'Floyd The Barber' and 'Paper Cuts' on the *Bleach* vinyl album; 'Downer' on the *Bleach* CD; 'Hairspray Queen' on the 1989 *Teriyaki Asthma* compilation EP; 'Beeswax' on the 1991 *Kill Rock Stars* compilation album; 'Beeswax,' 'Hairspray Queen,' 'Aero Zeppelin,' 'Mexican Seafood,' and 'Downer' on the 1992 rarities collection *Incesticide*; 'If You Must' and 'Pen Cap Chew' on *With The Lights Out*.

One reason it took such a long time for 'If You Must' to be officially released was Kurt's dislike of the song. "He hated that one almost immediately," says Jack. "I think it's a great song. It's very heavy, it's really ponderous, but it's got a verse, a chorus, a bridge – it's catchy, you can remember it. But Kurt, almost immediately – he was embarrassed about it. It was too heavy. Which is one of the reasons it's not on *Incesticide*, because Kurt just didn't like it anymore. He was just like that sometimes." It set up a pattern that would be repeated throughout his career. Kurt invariably found fault with all his subsequent recordings.

Jack still regrets that he wasn't given the chance to work on the tracks that did appear on *Incesticide*. "I wish I'd had a chance to remix them," he says. "Because literally what they did is they took the tape from the first day that I ever recorded them, when I mixed ten songs in an hour, and that's the tape that got put on *Incesticide*. It's always bummed me out, because in any given afternoon I could have made a better mix of all those songs than what's on *Incesticide*. Those songs could have sounded as good as *Bleach*, you know, such as it is. But that's just the way it went."

At the show at the Community World that night, the band, billed as Ted Ed Fred, played the songs they'd just recorded at Reciprocal, in the same order, although there was a break when Kurt's string broke during 'Hairspray Queen,' after which the band simply went on to the next song, 'Aero Zeppelin.' 'Pen Cap Chew' was followed by 'Annorexorcist,' a complete 'Hairspray Queen,' and 'Erectum,' which segued into a cover of Zeppelin's 'Moby Dick'; 'Downer,' 'Floyd The Barber,' and the 'Erectum'/'Moby Dick' medley were later released on *With The Lights Out*. ('Erectum' is misidentified as 'Raunchola' in the liner notes; the song's actual name is taken from the show's setlist.)

Eric Harder, a friend of the band, made a videotape of the show – the first known footage of Kurt and Krist in performance. Ironically, it's Dale Crover, seated and obscured by his drum kit, who's the most animated, his head bouncing up and down, sticks flailing in the air, while Kurt and Krist mostly stand in place, stage right and stage left respectively, only speaking to the audience when the guitar string breaks. Both the Dale Demo and the videotape capture early Nirvana at the point when the band was on the verge of change; it was the last time 'Downer' and 'Annorexorcist' were known to be performed live, and 'Mexican Seafood,' 'Hairspray Queen,' 'Aero Zeppelin,' 'Beeswax,' and 'Pen Cap Chew' would all be dropped from the band's repertoire in less than a year – "probably because they weren't very interesting," says Krist.

Back in Aberdeen the next day, Eric Harder filmed the musicians miming to songs from the demo at the RadioShack store where he worked. Brief snippets of the band going through 'If You Must' and 'Paper Cuts' were later shown on the television program *American Journal*; at one point Kurt executes a spectacular leap through the air, making a sliding landing on his knees, and cigarette smoke was blown across the camera lens in the hopes of adding some 'atmosphere.' Better production values might have resulted in a video that sent up consumer culture. Instead, the band looks like no more than what they are: a group of friends rehearsing in an electronics store, with 'party lights' winking desultorily on the shelves behind them.

Back in Seattle, Jack Endino had begun passing out copies of the demo. "I liked the band," he says. "I thought they were really good. I was excited and I wanted people to hear them." One of the first people to hear the demo was his then girlfriend, Dawn Anderson (the two later married, and subsequently divorced). "I heard it the day after it was recorded," she recalls. "Jack brought it over, and we listened to it together. The first thing that really grabbed me was 'Hairspray Queen' of all things, just because I was so into abrasive stuff back then. I loved its heaviness, but beyond the heaviness there was a real artfulness about it. It wasn't just hammering at you. There was really stuff going on. And I really liked Kurt's voice. It's hard to say anything without sounding like a complete cliché, but it was just so real, it was so gritty, and obviously sincere. You could tell he wasn't posturing."

A copy of the demo also made its way to Dawn's friend Shirley Carlson, a KCMU DJ who promptly got songs from the recording added to the station's playlist. More importantly, Jack also gave a copy to Jonathan Poneman. "I don't remember my exact words," says Jack. "I just said: hey, these scruffy guys from Aberdeen came in. Listen to this, this is pretty cool." Jonathan listened to the tape, and was immediately won over by the very song that Kurt so despised: 'If You

Must.' "It had this bridge in there, where he just did this – how do I put it? – *opening up*, and just let it out," he later recalled. "I just went: oh my God, this guy is really incredible! So I called him up, said I loved the tape, and that we should be making a record."

Jonathan's business partner was initially unconvinced. "I remember hearing that Pavitt didn't like the demo," says Jack. "He thought it was too rock. Pavitt did not like heavy rock. He did not like metal. He didn't like 'riff-rock' per-se – he hated that stuff. I remember I was doing sound at Green River's *Dry As A Bone* record-release show at [Seattle club] Scoundrel's Lair and I was playing a compilation tape with some Black Sabbath over the PA, and Bruce came up to me and wanted to know what it was. 'What's this cool tape you're playing?' It's like: Bruce, it's Black Sabbath. He had never listened to Black Sabbath. All he knew was 'Iron Man,' probably from the radio. He'd never listened to the other seven albums, or whatever it was. That was fairly revealing, you know? I was shocked. I couldn't believe anybody could have possibly grown up in the 70s and not heard Black Sabbath at some point."

Meanwhile, Kurt had been busy dubbing copies of the Dale Demo himself and sending them out to different labels, trying to spark some interest. He approached the alt-rock heavy hitters, including Alternative Tentacles, home of the Dead Kennedys, and SST, who released records by Black Flag, Meat Puppets, and Hüsker Dü. (SST founder Greg Ginn later told Charles Cross he found the demo derivative, "by-the-numbers alternative.") He was especially interested in being on Chicago-based Touch And Go (which, like Sub Pop, had started out as a 'zine), as he was a big fan of Scratch Acid, who recorded for the label (as did Steve Albini's band Big Black). He sent a number of tapes to Touch And Go, accompanied by letters offering to pay the recording and production costs for any potential release, but received no response, although Nirvana would eventually release a split single for the label in 1993, with The Jesus Lizard, featuring Scratch Acid's David Yow, on the flipside.

Of more immediate concern was the need to find a permanent drummer. Buzz Osborne had decided there wasn't much of a future for the Melvins in the Pacific Northwest, and planned to move to California (initially San Francisco, the band later relocating to Los Angeles). "The good old days weren't so good," he later remarked. "Ohhhh yeah, so much romance in poverty … us and Soundgarden and Malfunkshun would advertise for a month and get 40 people at the show. Yeah, that was great. Real character building. The best thing that ever happened to us was moving away from Seattle." Dale Crover had always been a temporary fill-in, but now that he was scheduled to leave, finding a new drummer became imperative.

Another Musicians Wanted ad was placed in *The Rocket* in March: "DRUMMER WANTED. Play hard, sometimes light, underground, versatile, fast, medium, slow, versatile, serious, heavy, versatile, dorky, nirvana, hungry." It was again unsuccessful (interestingly, no one has ever come forward later to say they answered one of Nirvana's ads). John Goodmanson recalls that George Romansic, his bandmate in Danger Mouse, auditioned for the spot. "He came back from that and he was like: yeah, they're saying they want to really simplify everything they do, and that's not really my thing. So he didn't take them up on it." In the end, Dale recommended another Aberdeen drummer, Dave Foster, as his replacement. The band immediately began rehearsing, with Dave asked to strip his kit from 12 pieces down to six. His only other instruction was "just hit 'em hard."

One of Dave's first shows with the band was a March 19 date at the Community World Theater, with Slim Moon's new band Lush also on the bill; when called back for an encore, the band obliged with a cover of Creedence Clearwater Revival's 'Bad Moon Rising,' the only known time they played the song. Kurt designed an elaborate poster for the gig, first reproduced in *Come As You Are*, unveiling the band's new name: Nirvana. (Given that the band had gone through numerous name changes, the poster also provided the helpful tagline "Also known as Skid Row, Ted Ed Fred, Pen Cap Chew, Bliss.")

Kurt had likely been thinking about the name for some time. Not only was it used in the *Rocket* ad, it also appears in the song 'Paper Cuts,' when he sings the word several times (though pronouncing it "nir-van-uh" instead of "nir-vah-nuh"). Asked about the name choice later, he told the fanzine *Matt Lukin's Legs*, with a touch of braggadocio: "We needed something rough that would still let the babes know we are eager to please." A later explanation given to *Submerge* was more down to earth: "There's no reason at all, it just sounded nice."

Sometime over the next month, Nirvana played their first show in Seattle. As with some of the other events during the band's early years, there is uncertainly as to exactly when that first show took place. Krist recalls it being at the Central Tavern, one of the few Seattle clubs to welcome bands playing original music. In an echo of their first aborted show at an Olympia party in 1987, Krist insists: "Nobody came. Nobody. Not one person. So we didn't even play. We bought a 12 pack of beer, sat underneath the Viaduct, and drank it. I think I drank most of it. And then just kind of said: oh well. Shrugged our shoulders. Maybe next time."

Jonathan Poneman and Bruce Pavitt agree on the location, but told Everett True the band did play, albeit to a small audience. "None of their original material was outstanding in the least," Pavitt said. "And to see this band and think: this is going to be the biggest band in the world in three years – no way. I'd put that at about a billion to one." Dawn Anderson recalls the cancelled Central show, but says it happened later in the year.

Michael Azerrad's *Come As You Are* has Nirvana's first Seattle show taking place at the Vogue, a club that was largely a disco but which featured live music on Tuesdays, Wednesdays, and Sundays; a *Rocket* ad gives the date as April 24, a 'Sub Pop Sunday.' The band arrived early for the show but then had to spend hours driving around town as they didn't want to pay for parking. While Dave Foster waited outside – still being underage, he wasn't allowed in the club except when performing on stage – Bruce Pavitt warmed up the crowd by playing Creedence Clearwater records. Kurt became so nervous he threw up in the parking lot.

He didn't appear any more at ease when the band finally took the stage. "I could tell they were all nervous," says Dawn Anderson, who estimates the number of attendees to be about 20 people, most of whom were underwhelmed by the band. "Blood Circus put on quite a grungy show, lots of hair going everywhere, and guitars flying," says Charles Peterson. "Then afterward Nirvana came on, and for whatever reason they had the lighting guy dim the lights really low, and Kurt just sort of stood there and stared at his feet. And the music came off as heavy and really difficult to play. I just didn't get it, I guess. It just didn't excite me for some reason.

"I took pictures of Blood Circus, but not Nirvana," he continues. "That was kind of unusual, and a very stupid move on my part. Part of it was that back then you're shooting film, and I wasn't getting paid for any of this. And I had to develop it all in my bathroom or kitchen, or wherever I was working out of at the time, so it's like, well, you know: I'm just gonna go easy tonight, and have a beer." He did take the time to approach Jonathan Poneman during Nirvana's set to ask him: "Jon, are you *sure* about these guys?"

"He'd just been ranting and raving about them and I'm like: sorry, I just don't see it," Charles explains. "I think it was probably partly due to the drummer, and partly due to Kurt's nervousness about playing this Sub Pop Sunday showcase. I don't know, because they were just so night-and-day the next time I saw them."

"All in all, folks came away impressed," Jonathan later said, although he also admitted that, while the band "rocked heavily," they did so "with less confidence than they later came to display on a regular basis." The band-members themselves shared this assessment. "We didn't play too bad but we were not really rocking," Foster told Charles Cross. And while his journals later described the audience as being insufferably judgmental, Kurt was equally demanding about his own performance. Dawn remembers him "grumbling, because he thought they sucked." Her own view on the group wasn't as harsh. "They weren't great, but they were good," she says. "I mean, if I saw them without knowing anything about them, I would have gone back and seen them again. I would have thought they were a promising band." She asked the group to do an interview with *Backlash*, and later, in the club's bathroom, made a point of telling Tracy Marander: "Man, I think Kurt has a great voice. You should tell him that, 'cause he thought he sucked." "Oh yeah – that's Kurt!" Tracy replied, rolling her eyes.

The band was far more relaxed at their next show, a house party in Olympia on May 14 – on Kurt's home turf, so to speak. With the closure of GESCCO, house parties and shows on the Evergreen campus were the primary outlets for all-ages gigs, and Nirvana were fast becoming a favorite act among the students. The May house party was for the birthday of Gilly Ann Hammer, then a member of local band Sister Skelter and later Calamity Jane, who lived in a group home dubbed the Glass House because of the large windows in the porch. Evergreen student Alex Kostelnik watched what he assumed was a roadie setting up the band's gear – "He was hunched over, the hair was always in his face, he moved slowly and methodically, like an 80-year-old man" – only to be completely floored when the 'roadie' turned out to be the band's passionate lead singer. "I came running downstairs, like: what the fuck?" he recalls of the moment the band started. "And I ran into the living room, and I thought that the whole living room was expanding and contracting. I had some kind of acid trip from the music! The minute I saw them I flipped out. The best sound I'd ever heard. It was fantastic. It was incredible! And you're just like: oh my God, oh my God, oh my God, oh my God, oh my God … he turned you on your head."

A May 21 show on Evergreen's soccer field provoked a similar reaction in another Evergreen student who would go on to work with

Nirvana, Jon Snyder. "I grew up a heavy metal kid in Spokane and that music was just really Guns N' Roses, crap like that," he says. "I was really into punk rock, but I'd grown up on heavy metal. And the first time I ever heard Nirvana it clicked with me so instantly because they were like this missing link that bridged those two worlds. I always was thinking: why the fuck is everybody listening to this grind metal crap when here's somebody doing something with some kind of heart and meaning and sounds just as cool? I was very aware of them. I was among a group there that was into them very, very early. They were a big part of my world before they became a bigger part of the world at large." For the next few years, Nirvana would become a fixture at Olympia's many house parties and dorm shows.

Up in Seattle, Jonathan Poneman remained keen for Sub Pop to work with Nirvana, and soon after the Vogue show he telephoned Kurt and arranged for a meeting at Seattle's Café Roma coffeehouse. Kurt arrived with Tracy and largely kept quiet; Krist made more of an impression by showing up in an inebriated state and drinking from a bottle of alcohol he'd smuggled in. They were disappointed that Sub Pop was only interested in putting out a single, but since there were no other offers pending they agreed to go ahead with it.

Tellingly, Dave Foster was not at the meeting, nor was he apparently told about Sub Pop's offer. Kurt in particular had become increasingly unhappy with Dave, not so much musically as personally. Kurt was now immersed in Olympia's alternative, bohemian counterculture, and Dave's more conventional appearance reflected a past he was desperate to get away from. Dave also had the dreaded moustache that was *verboten* in punk-rock circles (Bruce Pavitt told True that on first seeing Nirvana he found the drummer's moustache to be "problematic"). Kurt's worst fears about the impression his drummer created were confirmed at Nirvana's very first show with Dave at an Olympia house party, when an attendee grabbed the microphone to announce: "Gosh, drummers from Aberdeen sure are weird looking!"

Dave played what would be his final shows with Nirvana in May. Unbeknownst to him, there was an ad in *The Rocket* that same month looking for his replacement ("DRUMMER WANTED. Hard, heavy, to hell with your 'looks and hair a must.' Soundgarden, Zep, Scratch Acid"). It was a clear sign that Kurt's unhappiness with Dave had been immediate; the deadline for *The Rocket*'s May issue was April 17, so the ad had actually been submitted before Nirvana's show at the Vogue had even taken place.

Now Dave had the misfortune to be arrested for assaulting the son of the mayor of Cosmopolis, and as a result lost his driver's license and was unable to attend practices. Kurt and Krist saw this as an opportunity to ease Dave out of the band, simply telling him Nirvana was on hiatus. They briefly rehearsed with Aaron Burckhard again, but Burckhard soon engineered his own exit from the band.

"We left practice one night and Kurt drove me home," he recalls. "We got to my dad's place. My dad was on shift, so it was just me and Kurt there, and I told him: let me use your car to run up to the store to get a six-pack. But instead of going up to the store and coming back, I went down to the bar. And one thing led to another, and on the way back I got pulled over. And they took me to jail and the car got impounded. I called Krist up to come get me. Kurt was still at my dad's place and he was pissed. I did give him money that night to get his car back. But the next day he called me up and told me I was out of the band and, you know, what was I supposed to do? If I had known that they were going to become what they did, I would have worked things out. I still kick myself in the ass for it. I fucked up."

Aaron may not have been considered a serious replacement in the first place, since Kurt and Krist had already spoken to another drummer they'd had their eye on: Chad Channing. Chad was born in 1967 in Santa Rosa, California, and due to his father's job as a DJ, had been constantly on the move throughout his childhood. "I probably moved at least 80 times before I was even 18," he says. It also meant he was constantly exposed to new music, when his father brought home records from work. "I'd basically hear most every hit that was popular all through the 70s."

Chad was initially more interested in sports than music. "I just wanted to be a soccer player," he says. "My big hero was Pelé; I wanted to be just like that guy. I was pretty good too, until I mangled myself." That mangling was an accident in his early teens that shattered his thighbone, after which he taught himself guitar, bass, and drums. He got his first kit in 1983. "Drums were way more natural for me," he says. "It took me a little more effort for me to learn guitar, whereas it took little to no effort to figure out drums. The first time I sat behind a kit putting out a rhythm wasn't a struggle at all. It made totally perfect sense." He was particularly impressed with Led Zeppelin's John Bonham ("I was like: man, this guy's just it! Just the master of rhythm") and refined his drumming skills by playing along to Zeppelin's records. "I had this setup in my room and I'd put on the headphones and just play along with it until I learned it," he explains. "And I'd do that to every Zeppelin song, one at a time. It should be pointed out that I learned his drum *beats* but not necessarily all his drum *fills!*"

Chad discovered punk through his friendship with future Soundgarden bassist Ben Shepherd, whom he had met when both were in the fourth grade. "He was getting into punk rock at the time, so I was being introduced to bands like Dead Kennedys, The Clash, Sex Pistols, The Circle Jerks, and stuff like that," says Chad. His first group was a punk rock band he'd formed with friends in Anacortes, Washington, followed by stints in a band that played "messed up, dark New Age stuff," a "very Melvins-ish" band called Mind Circus (which featured Shepherd, playing a guitar he claimed Buzz Osborne had made), and a speed metal outfit called Stone Crow. By the mid 80s, Chad was living on Bainbridge Island, a few miles west of Seattle, and had dropped out of high school to pursue music more seriously.

Chad first encountered Kurt and Krist at the August 9 1987 show at the Community World Theater, when Chad was drumming with

The Magnet Men (later named Tic-Dolly-Row and also featuring Shepherd) and Nirvana was still called Bliss. Chad was taken by Kurt's stage apparel: "sparkly purple 70s flared velvet crush pants. They were pretty outlandish. It was pretty loud. It was a pretty good show actually." For their part, Kurt and Krist couldn't help but notice Chad's unique North drum kit, which had drums with unusual flared shells. Chad had seen the kit at a store called Lee's Music in Yakima, Washington, where he was living at the time. "I was like: that's weird – I want to get that kit!" he says. "It was about $2,000, and I didn't have any money, so I asked: is it OK if I make a down payment, and make payments when I can? It was like maybe two years or so before I finally paid it off, and the guy held it for me the entire time. I almost never did get that drum kit!" The kit's strange design made Kurt want to get Chad in the band on that basis alone.

A mutual friend introduced the three musicians at Malfunkshun's farewell show at the Community World Theater on May 6 1988. Kurt and Krist told Chad they were looking for a new drummer and invited him to check them out at their May 21 show. After their set, Chad was startled to be asked to join the band. "They were like: ah man, we really want you to be our drummer, will you do it?" he recalls. "And although I'd liked what I'd heard, I'd never even jammed with them before! I was like: what do they want, what are they looking for? Do they want somebody that sounds remotely close to their previous drummers? I had no idea. And so I was very tentative about it."

But Kurt and Krist were persistent, and suggested that the three get together for a practice session. "I'm like: OK, let's do that," Chad says. "And after practice, they were like: so, what did you think? In the early days, they were always asking me what do I think, what do I feel about things, because I never really said: OK, this is it – the word 'join' just never came out of my mouth. I was like: OK, I'll go ahead and practice with you next time. Then they said: well, we're getting a show together – you want to play that with us? And I was like: yeah, sure, it sounds fun. And after that show, there was never really another word about it. That was it. I was drumming for them. It just kind of happened that way. It was weird."

It was indeed a strange courtship, but one perfectly in keeping with the passive-aggressive nature of the band. (In another typical move, once Chad had joined, Kurt drafted a letter to Dave Foster informing him he'd been replaced, but couldn't bring himself to send it; Foster finally realized he was out of the group when he saw an ad in *The Rocket* for an upcoming Nirvana show he hadn't been asked to play.) But Kurt and Krist had found the perfect person to take Nirvana to the next level, for Chad, while an easy-going and amiable personality, was just as dedicated to getting ahead in music as they were.

"I think Kurt's attitude was: we are going to do something," he says. "Do or die, so to speak. That was my attitude, too, 'cause I dropped out of high school, for Pete's sake. I didn't have anything else to do. It was either that or be a dishwasher for the rest of my life. And there was nothing else I wanted to do. Right when I joined, that's when I decided: I think this is going to go somewhere. I don't know how long it's going to be before it does. But I'm pretty sure it's going to.

"Some of that was about the way I felt about Kurt and his songwriting. A lot of the ideas that he was coming up with – this whole sort of big guitar but not quite metal sort of thing, more pop-oriented sort of deal – was stuff that I was totally into at the time. I knew that he had something unique that was going to get him pretty far. I didn't imagine quite how far. But far enough."

CHAPTER 5

Happening Olympia Combo

Q: *"How long have you been around as Nirvana?"*
A: *"One long, hard, drawn out, excruciating, excruciating year."*

KURT TO *MATT LUKIN'S LEGS*, 1989

Now that Nirvana had a stable line-up, the three musicians threw themselves into rehearsal. "We built this rehearsal space in the basement of my house," says Krist. "I had enough money where I got a van. We'd cruise around job sites and lift plywood and two-by-fours, stuff like that, and we built this cool rehearsal space and padded it with rug remnants and stuff. We would have our rehearsals, and we'd get upset when a rehearsal went shitty. We should've recorded every rehearsal. 'Cause sometimes we would rehearse and just go through the songs and be really working, work ethic, and we're going to play all the songs, play them twice, or work on new songs. And sometimes we'd just go in there and play free form. And only a few examples of that ever made it on tape."

As they worked through the songs on the Dale Demo, Chad became increasingly impressed with Kurt's songwriting. "Most of the people I played with were very experimental," he says. "Whereas Kurt and Krist seem to have a specific idea in mind. Much more structured then most stuff I had done before, with very little time changes within the songs; a lot more straightforward compared to what I was doing in Tic-Dolly-Row. Honestly, I found it rather refreshing. It took a little getting used to, though; I wasn't really sure how much I could/should do for a while when I first started playing with them. But that was the cool thing about it – although it was a lot more basic, it was a lot more of a challenge. Kurt could take simple chord ideas and with these vocal lines that he'd come up with, really tie it all together. When you listen to most Nirvana songs, they're pretty simplistic stuff. But it's the way that he'd sing and the way the parts were put together just made a world of difference."

One reason for the extensive rehearsing was that Sub Pop had finally arranged a recording session for the band. The one Nirvana song Bruce Pavitt had liked was 'Love Buzz'; on first seeing the group, he'd leaned over to Jonathan Poneman as the band was performing it and said: "That's the single." Kurt wasn't happy the band was asked to do a cover. "He thought it was too poppy or something," says Krist. "He was worried that our credibility would be smashed." Krist was more confident of the song's appeal: "I thought it rocked." And Kurt himself later put a positive spin on the song choice. "It was one of the only palatable songs that we had," he said. "It was such a catchy song and it was so repetitive that we thought that people would listen to it right away and remember it."

The band also worked on new material for the upcoming session. 'Big Cheese' had already made its live debut at the March 19 show at the Community World Theater. "'Big Cheese' came together in one night," Krist recalls. "I remember Kurt played the riff, and I went: whoa, cool! So I started playing my bass, and somebody threw a chord change in there, probably Kurt, and I was playing off the drums. That song was a well-crafted song. Just the dynamics between the bass and drums and the guitar keeps it steady, but the bass and drums change and bring it all up into this kind of crescendo."

On its first outing, the song had different lyrics; now, as Nirvana prepared for their recording session, Kurt altered the lyrics to reflect his feelings about Jonathan Poneman, telling Michael Azerrad: "I was expressing all the pressures that I felt from him at the time because he was so judgmental about what we were recording." The most direct nod in Poneman's direction is a reference to going to the office; the character's dominance is suggested more by the music than it is lyrically. "That's actually still one of my favorite songs," says Chad. "I always liked that one a lot just 'cause of the intensity of it. The heaviness of it. I think it's the feel of the song, the way it flowed. I always pictured it as like being on a rowboat in the middle of a storm; sometimes it's mellow, and then it'd kick back up again. It was fun, too, because when I was playing with Nirvana I was just getting into playing with double-kick pedals again, and that song has a lot of that in it. So it was really fun. It was a really fun song to play for me."

'Blew' had also made its live debut at the March 19 show, in what would be its usual place toward the end of a set, although the lyrics, and the melodic line, which would ultimately give the song much of its power, had yet to be finalized. There were also some new numbers that had yet to be performed live. 'Blandest' is a droning, sinister number with disturbing references to razors and failure. Chad, who recalls the song first being worked on at soundchecks, felt that it never quite gelled. "I don't know what Kurt was thinking that he wanted to do with that song," he says. "He was never really too expressive about that, you know. He'd be like: well, I've got this idea – but if he wasn't hearing something that was right in his head it was like: let's not bother with this song. Like not giving the song enough time or space to figure it out."

'Mr Moustache' was at this stage a pile-driving number built around a seesawing guitar riff. 'Sifting' was slow and brooding, with a decided industrial quality that Chad recognized: "I always thought of factories playing that song. Just seeing some old factory with the robots working. Heavy song." And while Chad generally had the freedom to create his own parts, 'Sifting' was one song where Kurt had a very definite idea of how he wanted the drums to sound when the song went into the chorus. "If there was ever an opportunity where Kurt had some idea for a song, I was like: great, what is it?" says Chad. "Sometimes I'd say: get behind the set and show me what you mean."

The first session was scheduled for June 11, again at Reciprocal with Jack Endino. It was Jack's third session of the day. He'd spent roughly an hour copying a tape for a local musician, "then I did four hours in the afternoon with some band called Rising Evil, who pretty much disappeared from the face of the earth." After a dinner break came the Nirvana session, which lasted five hours.

The session began with 'Blandest,' then in the running as the 'Love Buzz' B-side. The song gets off to a good start but never quite takes off, due in part to Kurt's somewhat laid-back vocal, almost more of a scratch vocal than a final take, especially in the two screams, which warble rather than roar. "It wasn't very tight," says Endino. "It was kind of sloppy. It was the first song of the day. Nobody was warmed up, and it just doesn't sound that good."

"That was one that just never got anywhere," Chad agrees. "By the time we recorded it, we'd played it three or four times, so we never really had much time to work it out. A lot of times, the songwriting – you just play out the riff, and then after that you work out the details, the little things you want to do to it and stuff, and that song never had any details worked out on it. But it had potential, so we thought: well, we'll try it in the studio and see. So we took a stab in the dark with it, and we all listened to it, and it was just like the song title. It was. It was bland. But you've gotta have time with a song, and we never had the opportunity to spend that much time on it, really. But some songs are just doomed to go nowhere. And that was one of them."

The band then moved on to 'Love Buzz.' Kurt had brought along a cassette featuring a 30-second sound collage he wanted to precede the song, drawn from his record collection; he created various such collages in his spare time. "He said: here, just transfer it onto the tape," Endino recalls. "We actually put it on the half-inch tape on the eight-track before they did the song, because I'd take the cassette, transfer it on there, and then I'd send it out to their headphones, because they had to start the song right when the collage ended. So I had the collage on the eight-track before each take. Every time they did another take, I had to take that cassette and just copy it onto the eight-track again and again."

'Love Buzz' has a brightness unlike anything else the band had thus far committed to tape; it's catchy, as Kurt himself noted. It's also noticeably less sardonic than Nirvana's other songs, with Kurt's vocal performance giving it a decided edge, although on this first outing he sounds a bit self-conscious. Kurt and Krist had been performing 'Love Buzz' for over a year now, and the song's performance had become tighter, the taut bass line making the rush of the guitar's spiraling, descending notes that much more exciting. Next came 'Big Cheese,' with Kurt's sarcasm in full flower, scornful and taunting, and especially tortured in this first version; he comes out of one instrumental section with a mighty scream that lasts an impressive ten seconds.

The band then laid down early versions of some of the other songs they'd been working on recently. 'Mr Moustache' is taken at a noticeably slower pace than its final version, while the lyrics have not yet been finalized, with Kurt mostly singing nonsense syllables instead of words. In a nice change of tempo, the song slowly grinds to a halt at the end, coupled with Kurt's strangled cry: "That's the biggest tractor collection I've ever seen in my whole life!" Next came 'Sifting,' chugging and ponderous, Kurt again singing nonsense words and indulging freely in his use of the wah-wah pedal during an extended instrumental break (the main reason this take goes on for five-and-a-half minutes) – a rarity in any Nirvana song. The session ended with 'Blew,' again lacking final lyrics, but fairly close to its final version, and having some of the droning, Middle Eastern flavor of 'Love Buzz.'

Rough mixes of the songs were made for the band on cassette, and they returned to the studio for another five-hour session on June 30. They first cut a re-recording of 'Floyd The Barber,' which lacks the force of Dale Crover's hard-hitting version. "They immediately hated it," says Jack. Next came a second take of 'Love Buzz,' which everyone decided was better than the previously recorded version.

With that, the reel the band was recording on was full, and they opted to record over previously recorded takes they didn't like instead of spending another $50 on a second reel of tape. "I was carefully fitting new tracks over unwanted old takes, right in the middle of the reels if necessary, to save tape," says Jack. "Very, very typical of those days." Thus some of the songs recorded only survive as rough mixes on cassette, having been erased from the master reels.

'Blandest' was the first to be sacrificed. "They decided they hated it," Jack explains. "They told me to erase it and said they'd do a better version of it later. So we erased it, but they never got around to recording it again." "It was recorded very flat and very dry with no added ideas to it," says Chad. "So that's why it never really was a completed song. We all agreed that the song obviously wasn't ready yet." The band also recorded over the song because they'd decided to go with 'Big Cheese' as the single's B-side, at Jack's suggestion. "I thought 'Big Cheese' would be a little more exciting than 'Blandest,' as the release of their first original song," Jack explains. "And ultimately, they went with that."

A new recording of 'Spank Thru' was recorded over 'Blandest.' Although the re-recording of 'Floyd' hadn't proved to be satisfactory, the band perhaps thought that Chad's lighter touch would work better on their poppier material. The song is in a higher key than the Dale Demo version, with a more restrained vocal from Kurt (who nonetheless spirals off into a great scream before the first chorus). A second take of 'Big Cheese' was then recorded over the first version of 'Love Buzz,' in a lower key, which made the song heavier, with a harmony vocal on the chorus giving it an additional dreaminess. A third take of 'Love Buzz' was recorded over the early version of 'Blew' and the just-recorded 'Floyd,' but it was determined that take two of 'Love Buzz' had been the best, so no vocal was recorded (about a minute and a half of the re-recorded 'Floyd' survives on the master reels).

The second takes of 'Love Buzz' and 'Big Cheese' were then mixed for the proposed single. But after listening to the tracks, Poneman felt that Kurt's vocal for 'Love Buzz' needed to be re-recorded. He wanted a more straightforward performance, with fewer affectations. Kurt duly returned to Reciprocal on July 16 for a three-hour session to record a new vocal, which Jack then mixed. Kurt was also disappointed at Sub Pop's insistence that the opening sound collage be cut from 30 to 10 seconds and only two sound clips, one of which was of Natasha Fatale, the *Rocky & Bullwinkle* cartoon character, urging the listener to "do a twist, the surf, a wild watusi, a frug, or a swinging hully-gully!" "They were just constantly having control right away," he later griped. "Doing exactly what a major label would do and claiming to be such an independent label."

Kurt had also brought with him another sound collage that he wanted mixed in during the instrumental break on 'Love Buzz.' "We had to do it live when we mixed because we had used up all eight tracks," Jack explains. "So when we were mixing, we had to have this cassette going through the mixing board along with the eight tracks from the eight-track machine. And when we got to the middle part of the song, he had to reach over and press 'play' on the cassette deck right at the right time, every time I went through the mix. So we had a sort of virtual ninth track! It was a one-off thing." Thus the 'Love Buzz' record would have a unique single mix.

While the goal of recording a single had been accomplished, Jack was less than satisfied with how the sessions had gone. "I couldn't get the drum sound that I liked," he says. "The only way to get a really good drum sound is by beating the shit out of the drums, and Chad was a very light player at the time – he was barely touching the drums. And he'd only been with the band a couple of weeks. He barely knew the songs and they rushed into the studio to record. When Chad first joined the band, he had to sweat it a little bit, because he had to play some of the songs that Dale had played. Dale is brilliant, and Chad's a good drummer, but, I mean, Dale is Dale, and it took Chad a while to sort of get into the groove of it."

Chad had his own dissatisfactions, already feeling somewhat out of the loop in the decisions over what songs were going to be recorded. "I didn't really have a whole lot of say in that," he says. "I never really did. It didn't seem like I did anyway. I never really felt like what my opinion, or what I had to say, meant anything, you know? I'm not sure why I felt like that. Maybe it's just a you-had-to-be-there sort of deal. I mean, every other band I had ever been in I was always one of the main writers, and I was used to having an equal contribution to everything. This was the first time where that wasn't the case. It was just like being in the background, like I was hired on to play the drums, and that's that. It's like: well, I've played the drums. I've done my job. You guys decide whatever you wanna do. That's kind of how it felt to me." It was an early sign of a discontent that would continue to grow.

Aside from 'Love Buzz' and 'Big Cheese,' the re-recording of 'Spank Thru' would also see release in 1988 on the *Sub Pop 200* compilation released at the end of the year. "They were going to use the one from the Dale Demo," says Jack, "then they decided that they liked the one with Chad better." (The song was mixed on September 27, with Jack adding a backing vocal at Kurt's request.) 'Blandest' would finally see official release on *With The Lights Out*, drawn from the rough mix preserved on cassette, as the master had been recorded over. "I never forgot the damn song," Jack says. "It always was stuck in my head. It's not a particularly rocking tune, but it's got a weird little hook in it. When they were working on *Incesticide*, Krist asked me: you remember 'Blandest'? Do you have a tape of it anywhere? I said: no, I don't have a tape of it. You guys told me to erase it! And then years later I'm talking to some collector who informed me that he had a bootleg with a song called 'Blandest' on it. I said: oh my God, it can't be the one I'm thinking of – send me a copy. And he sent me a copy and it was the song. It's been widely bootlegged. It was a terrible rough mix with the drums way too loud."

Armed with a batch of new songs, Kurt began making new tapes to pass out to friends and prospective labels. One tape, called *Kurdt's Kassette* (with Kurt credited as "Kurdt Kobane"), drew on material from the Dale Demo, the 'Love Buzz' session, and Kurt's own home demos, with a running order of 'Floyd The Barber,' 'Spank Thru,' 'Hairspray Queen,' 'Mexican Seafood,' 'Beeswax,' 'Beans,' 'Paper Cuts,' 'She's Selling The Escalator To Hell,' 'Big Cheese,' 'Love Buzz,' 'Aero Zeppelin,' 'Pen Cap Chew,' and 'Montage Of Heck.' 'Montage' was an extended sound collage, one sequence featuring Krist repeating the phrase: "The landlord is a piece of shit from hell!" 'Escalator' is a short piece of vocal manipulation. 'Beans' was a jokey number, with Kurt singing a nonsense lyric while accompanying himself on a plunking guitar, the vocal sped up to enhance the song's 'nursery rhyme' quality. The cassette's J-card featured a picture of Kurt's visual art: a diorama crafted out of thrift store detritus (a Visible Man figure, a small Virgin Mary, a Batman doll) in front of a collage depicting pop-culture personalities like Andy Gibb, paper money, and pictures of diseased vaginas taken from medical journals. Another copy was entitled *Safer Than Heaven*, featuring a brilliant sun – or maybe a star – rising behind the band's name. Yet another copy, hopefully entitled *Touch And Go Demo*, was sent off to the record label, Kurt stressing in an accompanying note that the song selection emphasized the "Scratch Acid side of Nirvana."

There were a handful of shows over the summer, although the band lost a regular venue when the Community World Theater closed in late June. But a July 23 show at the Central marked the first time Nirvana opened for an out-of-town act, The Leaving Trains. The show had been booked by medical student Nikolas Hartshorne and his friend Dan Merrick, whose brother Sam played guitar in the LA-based band. "They said: let's bring Sam's band up from California!" says Courtney Miller, who was then dating Nikolas, and was also *The Rocket*'s ad manager; her involvement in the show extended to arranging a *Rocket* ad and getting posters made. "We were trying to make a little bit of money and have some fun by promoting a couple of shows," Nikolas explained. "We did three shows or something. So we did the Trains a couple times, I think we did The Hangmen, and Blood Circus."

They had originally hoped to get Mudhoney to be one of the opening acts. "It was just all of us thinking: who are our favorite local bands right now?" says Courtney. "Mudhoney was our number one choice. And it was a no brainer that there'd be Blood Circus, because they were really one of our favorite bands. We had wanted those bands to pull a crowd."

When Mudhoney were unavailable, Jonathan suggested Nirvana in their place. But as the band had only played Seattle a handful of times, they weren't much of a draw. "I have a specific memory of Nirvana playing to largely an empty room," says Courtney. "But they were very nice and polite. They played their show, and we felt bad that there weren't that many people there. But as it turned out, the way that the night ended up, we made enough money that in the end we could pay them $100 more than we had anticipated. And then they had to hurry and get home to Aberdeen, and there was a ferry involved that somebody had to catch. And it was like: wow, what nice guys. Too bad there's not more people here. I thought they were great." "Yeah, it was a phenomenal set," Nikolas agreed. He remembered the band's fee being increased only by $25, thus rounded up to $100 from the originally agreed-upon $75, and – more unusually – that the band turned down the extra money.

The turnout might have been light, but the fact that Nirvana was now opening for touring acts made its way into the band biographies that Kurt was busy drafting. "Looking for: EP or LP," he wrote in part. "Willing to compromise on material (some of this shit is pretty old). Tour any time forever. Hopefully the music will speak for itself." He soon had more clippings to add to the band's burgeoning press kit when the first published story on the band appeared, Dawn Anderson's piece 'It May Be The Devil And It May Be The Lord But It Sure As Hell Ain't Human,' which ran in the August/September '88 edition of *Backlash*. Kurt and Krist drove up to Seattle to do the interview, but the picture they gave Dawn for the story had their former drummer, Dave Foster; he was cropped out of the shot when the story finally ran. The article was notable for a daring prediction: "At the risk of sounding blasphemous, I honest believe that with enough practice, Nirvana could become – *better than the Melvins!*" "At the time, people were like: better than the Melvins? Those guys? No way!" says Dawn today. "You know: they're like five minutes old! They're just babies!" The article pointed out the difficulties of the band's first Vogue show, although Dawn also noted that she had "seen them twice since and they've gotten tighter each time."

K Records founder Calvin Johnson also wrote approvingly about Nirvana's upcoming single in his fanzine *Sand*, which came out around the same time. "Nirvana are the happening Olympia combo at present: transplanted Aberdeen natives raised on a diet of sawdust and pure Melvins. They've got a 45 coming out real quick on Sub/Pop Records … 'Big Cheese' starts out sounding like any other Sub/Pop axe-grinder till Kurdt Kobane starts in with his crooning, then you're hooked. The flip is a cover of Shocking Blue's 'Love Buzz.' Buy a half-dozen and keep them like you do your silverware. This guy's gonna make a million bucks."

Despite Johnson's prediction, the release of the 'Love Buzz' single was delayed, due to Sub Pop's ever-present cash-flow problems. It was a source of frustration for the band; although Kurt had offered to pay the band's production costs if Touch And Go signed them, when Bruce Pavitt called and asked for a loan of $200, Kurt hung up on him. But work on the single proceeded, albeit slowly, and in late summer a photo session was held to shoot the single's cover.

The photographer was Alice Wheeler, an Evergreen student who had met Bruce Pavitt when he worked at Bomb Shelter, and had arranged for him to DJ shows at GESCCO. The shoot, with Bruce and Tracy Marander tagging along, was held at a park near the Tacoma Narrows Bridge called Never Never Land. "It was like this little fantasy storybook land," says Alice. "There were all these weird characters, little elves under the trees, Humpty Dumpty, some other stuff. We went all over. We went in the woods, and I shot infrared, and then we went by the bridge. It took a few hours. It was a very lengthy photo shoot, and they were very cooperative. Chad had a Germs T-shirt on, and I just thought it was so weird that they were wearing other people's shirts. I couldn't understand why he would be wearing somebody else's shirt for a photo shoot of their band.''

Kurt and Krist were dressed equally casually, Kurt in a Harley-Davidson T-shirt (perhaps for its rock'n'roll connotations; Kurt was never known to ride a motorcycle), and Krist in a button-down short-sleeved shirt. The group is relaxed, smiling gently, obligingly lying on the grass. "Oh yeah, I was pushing them around – look at how many little poses I made them do," Alice jokes. "We were just having fun. I was nervous, of course. It was my first photo shoot, so I threw in every trick I had in the book, and I shot as much film as I possibly could. It was my first paying gig. I got paid 25 bucks." The photos chosen for the record were shot with infrared film, giving them a certain fuzziness. The front cover has Kurt looming in the foreground with Krist and Chad behind; the rear cover has Kurt standing alone under the Tacoma Narrows Bridge. Given Kurt's long hair, the fuzzy look of the photos, and the title 'Love Buzz,' there's a decidedly psychedelic flavor to the sleeve. "What was really interesting was when I first shot them, for the first probably 10 to 15 years, everyone told me what horrible photos they were!" says Alice. "And now, ironically enough, 23 years after the fact, they've become 'genius level.'"

Alice also spent time getting to know her subjects; being an Evergreen student, they had friends in common. "Kurt and I, we always just liked each other," she says. "We connected. So even if we hadn't seen each other for a while, we could just sit down and have a really long, heavy conversation. He knew a lot about music, but he was like a hungry sieve, trying to find out everything. And I was a little bit older, like five years older than he was or something, so I was just enough older that he would ask me all kinds of questions. Plus I'd lived in LA already, and I'd been in the punk scene when it was really happening, from 1979 to '80, and he was really curious about that.

We're also really interested in popular culture, politics – he was really against Reagan, so we talked a lot about that. We were like little devils together. Well, we were kind of innocent too, but we had the same kind of sarcastic, kind of bitchy, wry attitude toward the world."

Nirvana's next big show was their most prestigious gig to date, opening for the Butthole Surfers at Union Station in Seattle on October 28. The venue was a former railroad terminal, a large, bare room, lined with tile, that didn't lend itself to good acoustics. ("It just seemed like a giant box," says Chad.) But its size was seen as an advantage for the promoters. "Obviously it was going to be a big event," says Erik 4-A, a DJ with KCMU, the show's sponsor. "Butthole Surfers were kind of a draw band back then. You could fill a venue like Union Station, which is a pretty big room." Erik was also involved in doing some promotional work for KCMU, and had run into some problems in producing radio spots for the show. "You couldn't say 'Butthole Surfers' on the air!" he says. "You could not. It was *verboten*. And so what happened is, I called them 'Ballard Surfers.' And there was 'Surfers From Texas,' that was another good one."

Erik was not especially interested in Nirvana. "I was more into stuff that was more harmonic and harmonious and melodious," he says. "I was one of the first people to play [Bellingham pop group] The Posies on the air. And I was shafted for it. I got a big 'don't play this pop crap on the air!' There was a period between '87 and '89 where there was this real pop thing going, and nobody wanted to be part of it." But he thought 'Love Buzz' sounded "kind of cool" – like a lot of people, he didn't initially realize it was a cover – and was on hand at the Union Station show to represent KCMU. "They set the stage in sideways, instead of at the end of the hall," he recalls. "They put it on the side, because there was some dressing rooms or some sort of backstage area that they wanted. And they set up the sound system and they had a big screen and that's the Butthole Surfers thing, to show all these really bizarre films behind them, medical films, and you know, just disgusting stuff.

"Nirvana got their soundcheck and it sounded awful," he continues. "There wasn't much of a soundcheck. It was the typical pre-show stuff, you know, they tested out the sound system with the main band, Butthole Surfers, and then the second band never gets much of a soundcheck, 'cause the opening band is the band that is cannon fodder. I remember I looked at the drums and I said: that's weird, they look like pieces of macaroni!" Sound problems continued during the show. "They sounded like crap," says Erik. "They were out of time, and there were some problems with the PA going on; it was all just noise."

At least Nirvana escaped unscathed. During the next set, by Blood Circus, the stage came close to collapsing. "The audience did a big mosh pit and they were pushing up against the stage, and it started to move backward," Erik recalls. "And then finally it started to bend in the center. And it was like we were looking at like, this thing could collapse. And they had guys behind the stage, between the stage and the wall, with their legs against the wall, pushing the stage backward as it was sliding, so that it wouldn't slide anymore. Somebody had to go up on the stage and tell everybody: you gotta calm down. Somebody's going to get hurt. The stage is gonna collapse. And the audience getting really uptight about it: we want music! We want to mosh!"

If Seattle shows still tended to be problematic, back on their home ground of the Evergreen campus, Nirvana again received an ecstatic welcome, when they were invited to play a party at Evergreen's K-Dorm, which, being located at the edge of the soccer field, was unofficially designated the campus' 'insane party dorm.' Its reputation had drawn student Phil Buffington to move in during his second year at Evergreen. "I basically wanted to live in K-Dorm because they had parties, and I saw the potential for fun there," he says. "So I made the effort to live on campus that year, and worked really hard at having all these parties, kind of keeping the thing going, and not getting too out of hand. For the most part, everything went off without a hitch. I don't know how. One time, at one party, there was quite a bit of moshing and somebody was moshed out the window! Fortunately, because these dorms were still new, the landscaping was undone and there was basically just a lot of soft muddy dirt there, and the guy came back up, very pale looking, a little dirty, but he was not harmed in the least. I remember giving him another beer, and everything being OK. We were miraculously lucky that for all the craziness we had there, it just basically turned out to be a bunch of kids listening to rock music, drinking beer, and nobody got hurt, the building didn't fall down, or burn down or anything like that."

Kurt and Krist had attended a few parties in Phil's room, K208. "They were six-person units," says Phil. "Each person had their own room, and there was a shared bathroom/shower, and then there was a common area, that was sort of a living room/dining room/kitchen area. And if you cleared all the furniture out, it was a fairly sizable space. And so, between the kitchen and this outside wall – I guess it would be where they expected a dining table to go – is where the bands would set up, and then the rest of the space would be open for cramming people into it. Essentially, it's a rectangle with one corner given over to a kitchen, and then a kitchen bar and cabinets there, and that is where we set up our beer, trying to make our money back on the beer we bought. I held a unit lease on the K208, so everyone paid me rent, and then I paid the Evergreen Housing rent. And on these particular cases I would take all the rent money and buy kegs of beer, and then cross my fingers that I would make all the money back so I could pay rent!"

When Kurt and Krist asked if they could play a party sometime, Phil said "sure" before noting that he could only pay the band in free beer. A pre-Halloween gig was duly set up for October 30 with Nirvana and two other local bands, Landsat Blister, and Slim Moon's band Lush. Phil hadn't seen Nirvana before, but he soon found out how popular they were from his friends. "Some of the 'cognoscenti' that I knew were like: whoa! Those guys are playing? Those guys are awesome!" he recalls. As a result, he decided to record the show, and went to Evergreen's Media Loan department and checked out two microphones that he plugged into a boom box. "It was a General Electric boom box," he says. "And I just recorded it on a cassette tape. I had a two-channel in, so I could record stereo, when I had a sound level, so I could keep it from maxing out. And then I just taped the mics to the ceiling, mostly to keep them from getting damaged, because that was the only place I could put a microphone without fear of it getting damaged or stolen or something like that. And it just happened to capture the sound pretty good, even though the drum kit was there, and there was no real attempt at deadening the space or anything like that." Now expecting a good turnout, he purchased four kegs, charging two dollars a cup, with free refills until the kegs ran dry.

It didn't take long for K208 to fill up. "It was pretty crazy, as you might imagine," says Phil. "Halloween was always a pretty big holiday at Evergreen, sort of anticipating the retail expansion of that holiday by a number of years. It was chock-a-block with people. I would say as many as 80, throughout the living room/dining area, the hallways, the bathrooms, and some of the bedrooms. It was really, really packed." At one point, Phil went downstairs and noticed that the ceiling was moving from everyone jumping up and down.

The evening had already seen a fight during Lush's set, when Slim kicked over the drummer's kit and ended up with a punch in the face. The police arrived but let the show continue once Phil "convinced them of the tremendous effort of the bands and the event in general." Nirvana's set began with a raw version of 'School,' a new number that would quickly become a live favorite. "The minute they went on, the place went nuts," says Phil, who was just as impressed by the band himself. "I'd seen plenty of local bands and major rock acts, but when those guys plugged in and started warming up, you could tell that they were a cut above most of the other bands. It wasn't just that they were louder, they had this control, this presence, and it was obvious that they were kind of – well, by no means could I say that I

125

predicted their success or anything like that, but they were just a cut above the other bands we'd seen. Like that first time you have a decent glass of wine or something like that: oh, I've been missing out for all these years! No one else even came close to them as far as rocking the house." In the spirit of the evening, Kurt and Krist had each doused themselves with fake blood; Chad wore the same Germs T-shirt he'd worn during the 'Love Buzz' shoot.

The rest of the hour-long set was a mix of numbers from the Dale Demo and the songs they'd recorded during the 'Love Buzz' sessions; at this stage, there was also still a tendency for the momentum to stall during the set while Kurt retuned his guitar. Toward the end of the set, the band unexpectedly broke into 'Run, Rabbit, Run' by Finnish band Smack, followed by a cover of Led Zeppelin's 'Immigrant Song.' But the most significant moment came during the closing number, 'Blew.' The song's ending dissolved into a morass of noise and feedback which continued for nearly two minutes until Kurt provided the ultimate climax by smashing his guitar (which had been given to him by Jesse Reed's father). It was the first time he was known to have done this, and it took everyone by surprise. "He didn't have another guitar, so it was: holy shit, what are we going to do?" said Krist. It was the beginning of what would become a regular feature of Nirvana's shows, the end-of-set instrument destruction, which would also often see Kurt or Krist flying into Chad's drum kit. As well as providing a dramatic conclusion to a show, it also relieved the pressure of having to do an encore.

As the audience cheered, and some attendees rushed to pick up pieces of the shattered guitar, one wag in the audience called out "hey, you guys know 'Stayin' Alive' by The Bee Gees?" to laughter and more cheers. If the Friday night show opening for the Butthole Surfers had been a disappointment, the K-Dorm show fully restored the band's confidence. As Ben Lattin (who played with Ryan Aigner in a band called The Psychclodds) wrote in a letter to his sister about the show: "If you think they played good on Friday [October 28] you should have seen them last night!!! Ryan and I played security guards to a bunch of drunk, slammin' punks. It was great!" If it hadn't been for the four kegs, the show might have even been better documented. "It's unfortunate, because someone had a video camera," says Phil. "But they were a little too inebriated and forgot to put a tape in. Even though they filmed the whole time as if there was a tape in there."

'Love Buzz'/'Big Cheese' was finally released in November. Despite some of the band's shaky live performances, the single generated immediate interest. "I thought that was the most amazing song," Dawn Anderson recalls. "It was a cover song, but nobody remembered it, so it was like it was their own song. That bass line – God, it's so catchy." "What I felt when I first heard it was: that's beautiful, because listen to the bass!" says TAD's Kurt Danielson, a bassist himself. "It's a wonderful bass part, and it's played without error, and it's just perfect!" Charles Peterson changed his initial assessment of Nirvana on hearing the record. "I thought: this is a totally different band from the one I saw. This is brilliant," he says. "Just the sound, just everything about it was different. Despite the fact that it was a cover, they really made it their own song, I think. They could just as easily have written it. They were just a different band from the first time I saw them."

The single received good reviews in the local press. Veronika Kalmar, in *Backlash*, noted that 'Big Cheese' "sounds like the theme song to a slasher flick" even as she cited 'Love Buzz' as the stronger song. "Guys from weird, small towns in Washington State just naturally seem to rock harder," she continued, "and Nirvana's debut single proves it." In *The Rocket*, Grant Alden summed up the band's first effort succinctly: "Nirvana sit sort of at the edge of the current Northwest sound – too clean for thrash, too pure for metal, too good to ignore."

The band-members were excited about the increased exposure. "I remember reading the reviews and thinking: wow, the first single, the first piece of vinyl I was ever on. This is cool. It even got a review!"

says Chad. "And it was a real trip hearing the single on the radio for the first time. I knew it was getting airplay, so I always kept an ear out listening for it. And it wasn't until I was driving home at night with a friend of mine and we were listening to that station out of Texas that you used to be able to get way on the right end of the AM dial, Z-Rock or whatever. That's when 'Love Buzz' came on: 'This is from a band up in Seattle called Nirvana, it's called "Love Buzz."' And it came on, and we just kind of looked at each other and I go: whoa, this is a trip! And my friend's laughing like: right on, man, you finally fucking got something on the radio! It was a cool feeling. It was all just totally gleeful to me."

Kurt assured the band's Seattle airplay by dropping off a single at KCMU himself, then phoned in a request to the station, waiting patiently in Tracy's car until it came on. "He sat there hearing himself coming out of the radio with a big smile on his face," she later recalled. This accomplishment also filled Kurt with a new determination. "It was instant success and fame beyond my wildest dreams," he later told Azerrad. "I thought I would definitely like to hear my future recordings on the radio ... It made us step up mentally to another level where it was a reality that we could actually live off of this."

CHAPTER 6

The Distant Roar

"Hypnotic and righteous heaviness from these Olympia pop stars. They're young, they own their own van, and they're going to make us rich!"

SUB POP CATALOGUE DESCRIPTION OF *BLEACH*, 1989

Soon after the 'Love Buzz' single was issued, 'Spank Thru' was released on the compilation *Sub Pop 200*. The label opted to release the 20 tracks, which would have fitted on two albums, on three EPs, thus making the set appear more lavish. While the set featured Sub Pop stalwarts like Green River, Soundgarden, and Mudhoney, there were also contributions from The Fastbacks, folk-rockers The Walkabouts and Terry Lee Hale, and poet Jesse Bernstein. The only place outside the Northwest where 'Love Buzz' had generated much interest was Britain, and *Sub Pop 200* also received accolades overseas, most notably an article in the *Observer* by BBC Radio 1 DJ John Peel. After writing that the *Seattle Syndrome* compilations "dropped no hint that anything even remotely interesting would ever happen in Washington's largest city," he raved that Sub Pop's records had "the most identifiable house – as opposed to House – sound since early Tamla, a thick, angry, pressure-cooker guitar/bass/drums/vocals turbulence." "It is going to take something special to stop *Sub Pop 200* being the set of recordings by which others are judged for some time to come," he concluded. "Mudhoney and Soundgarden tour this year. The distant roar is the sound of queues forming. The God thing is coming."

Sub Pop 200's records were packed in a black box and accompanied by an illustrated booklet; Charles Burns, who'd drawn the covers of Bruce Pavitt's *Sub Pop* cassettes, contributed a pointed illustration of a sweaty guitarist, clad only in his underwear, wading through a garbage heap of broken records and cassette decks, with a monkey firmly lashed to his back. Sub Pop's penchant for embellishment was on full display inside the booklet, with Bruce and Jonathan Poneman pictured in suits and ties and credited as 'Supervisory Chairman of Executive Management' and 'Executive Chairman of Supervisory Management,' respectively. An impressive shot of the Terminal Sales Building was billed as 'Sub Pop World Headquarters,' when in fact the label only occupied a single office in the penthouse.

While most of the bands were pictured performing in dark clubs, Nirvana's shot placed the group in a rural environment, casually lolling on the ground, Kurt with a beatific expression on his face. It was a picture from their first session with Charles Peterson, whose photos would appear on nearly every subsequent Nirvana release. "I went over to Bainbridge Island, where Chad lived," says Charles. "It was a sunny day and I thought: why don't we do it here? It'll be easy. We drove all over the countryside with Shocking Blue playing on the cassette tape in their old white van that was falling apart. It was really fun."

The band's good spirits are evident in all of Charles's pictures. In one shot, the band is in a field, Krist on his knees, arms outstretched, Kurt, in a Scratch Acid T-shirt, smothering a laugh, and Chad, wearing tie-die, smiling benignly. "That's what there is on Bainbridge," says Charles of the pastoral setting. "There's no alleys. I think it kind of fit more who they were at the time, 'cause they really weren't much of an urban band at all. They were hicks from the sticks. They were shy, but sweet; Kurt, the shy kind of hesher dude, Krist the gangly, boisterous one, and Chad the hippie. A little bit of a motley crew in a way, but they all seemed to get along really well.

"Kurt liked having his picture taken," Charles adds. "He enjoyed the process, which you wouldn't think he would, of all people. You'd think he'd hate it, you know? Like [Screaming Trees lead singer] Mark

Lanegan, he just hated it. He's like: can I just hide behind something? It's like: no, Mark, you can't hide behind something, that's not having your picture taken. But Kurt, he was fine with the process. He's just: oh, what do you want me to do? Do you want me to stand here? Do you want me to do this? Never any complaints."

The band quickly capitalized on this flush of publicity. Tam Ohrmund, an occasional manager for the band (Kurt once wrote her a note to say the band was "completely pleased with your managing skills and enthusiasm. We love your very guts"), assembled a press kit/fanzine that included the *Backlash* profile, *The Rocket*'s review of 'Love Buzz,' snapshots of the Halloween show at Evergreen, and an ad for *Sub Pop 200*. One layout featured a picture of the band with the lyrics of 'Paper Cuts' running in a wave-like pattern across the page; a similar design would appear in the artwork for *Nevermind*, with lyrics from different songs running in the same wavelike pattern across the CD's inlay card.

Nirvana played only one show in November, and began December opening for another out-of-town act, Canadian punk band D.O.A., at Seattle club The Underground. Most of the month was spent in rehearsal for an upcoming recording session. Sub Pop was interested in having Nirvana record an EP, but the band – or more likely Kurt – had a more ambitious goal. "Sub Pop wanted to just do an EP, much like the Soundgarden and Green River EPs," Jack Endino explains. "That was their game plan at the time, release EPs with a lower sticker price. Nirvana wanted a full album instead. Nirvana however were not 100 per cent sure they wanted to do it with Sub Pop at all; that's what they told me at the time. So they wanted to pay for it themselves and then shop it. I doubt they shopped it much, though, 'cause Sub Pop went ahead and said OK after they heard it."

A friend of Chad's, guitarist Jason Everman, agreed to loan the band the money to pay for the sessions. "I had some money from working as a commercial fisherman in Alaska," he explains. "Kurt simply asked me at some point, and I had the money and am generous to a fault, so I agreed. I was simply helping out people that I considered my friends in a worthy endeavor." Reciprocal wasn't working with many clients during the holiday season, so sessions were booked for late December and early January for the album that would ultimately be called *Bleach*.

Krist was no longer living in Tacoma, having temporarily split up with his girlfriend, and had moved back to his mother's home in Aberdeen. His mother's beauty parlor, Maria's Hair Design, was used as an afterhours practice space. "It was the only place we had at the time," says Chad. "The shop closed at 6pm, and we would arrive there about 8 or so. We'd practice all night, and then we'd have to be out of there by 6, when the shop opened. It was a lot of driving! I'd get off work, drive out there, practice, come back home and work. And we did that for two weeks straight, just before we jumped into the studio. I can't tell you how much sleep I lost. Because the only time I slept was when I got back from practice; I wouldn't have to be at work until about 7:30am, so I'd get about an hour of sleep." On other occasions, Krist would serve as driver for the evening, picking up Kurt and Chad, and later driving everyone home. The hours spent together in Krist's van helped them bond, as they constantly listened to music, especially Celtic Frost and The Smithereens, reflecting a metal/pop mix that would emerge on the recordings.

"Most of the lyrics on the *Bleach* album are about life in Aberdeen," Kurt told journalist/musician John Robb shortly after the album's release. The twisted wordplay of the Dale Demo songs was abandoned in favor of short, sharp depictions of characters mired in rage and frustration, although an underlying self-deprecation keeps the outlook from becoming too depressing. And while the songs can readily be seen as the somewhat barbed observations of an outsider, they also reflected Kurt's struggles to find his own place in his environment. "Maybe Kurt was exasperated by humanity itself, [by] that weight of: oh, how do I fit in this world?" Krist observed. "[But] he would always turn it around. He'd say something and then he'd contradict himself moments later. And then he'd catch it a lot of times and just look at me and laugh."

The lyrics of 'Mr Moustache' illustrate this apparent contradiction of disdain and sympathy for one's subject. The title is generally assumed to have been inspired by the moustaches worn by Nirvana's previous drummers, which marked them as fans of heavy metal over punk. A moustache also had macho/redneck connotations, as seen in a cartoon of a 'Mr Moustache' Kurt drew at the time (reproduced in *Come As You Are*), which has the title character drinking beer as he presses his ear to his pregnant wife's stomach, dreaming of his hoped-for son becoming a football player.

But where the cartoon Mr Moustache gets his comeuppance, his face kicked in by his child's leg smashing through the mother's stomach and into his jaw, the portrait in the song is more nuanced: it's Mr Moustache that sneers at those who would patronize him, sarcastically asking to be graced with their "mighty wisdom." Chad calls it the funniest song Kurt ever wrote: "I mean, that song's a riot! It's totally hilarious." Similarly, the protagonist of 'Negative Creep' exalts in his outsider status, as the lyrics seemingly poke fun at the band's performance (the song deemed not only "out of our range" but also "a drone") over another fast-paced beat with unexpected starts and stops. According to producer Steve Fisk, the song's inspiration was a neighbor of Kurt's in Olympia, who would come over and pester his girlfriend Tracy.

"I enjoyed playing that one a lot," says Chad of 'Negative Creep.' "I really liked that main riff, that sliding back and forth thing. That was really cool, 'cause there wasn't really that many songs that had any kind of breaks, or dynamic type of areas, where things got quieter or things like that. Most of them were pretty much straightforward, a similar tempo, with that same kind of energy through the whole thing. And this was one of the songs where it was pretty much energy the whole way, but those little breaks in there just added something to it. I always liked that tune."

'School,' which the band had debuted at the October Evergreen show, was equally energetic, a 15-word rant against Kurt's perceived insularity of the Seattle music scene, with an opening guitar whine leading into the song's main riff. "It was Kurt's riff," Krist explains. "When I first heard it, I just stopped and said: oh my God, that is the most Seattle rock riff I've ever heard in my life! I said we should call the song 'School' because the whole Seattle scene is just like a fucking high school. And that's how it stuck!"

"That was actually a really fun song," says Chad. "Just because of what I was doing with the drums and stuff. Definitely one of the more fun songs I liked to play all the time." Jack Endino adds: "I think it's a very good example of economical songwriting. It's an entire song with three lines of lyrics, and frankly it reminded me of a Budgie song." What keeps the song from being a throwaway (even Kurt initially called the song "a joke") is the strength of Kurt's vocal performance, particularly when he howls "No recess!" during the chorus in righteous indignation, imbuing the song with a greater depth of emotion.

Both 'Big Long Now' and 'Sifting' had the doom-laden heaviness of the Melvins. Both also have a similar construction, with slow, simmering verses gradually coming to the boil in the choruses before sinking back down like a lumbering beast coming to rest. Kurt feared that 'Big Long Now' sounded too similar to the Psychedelic Furs. When the song later appeared on *Incesticide* he wrote in the press release: "I hope the Psychedelic Furs don't sue us." The song's title came from Chad. "It was nothing more than a silly phrase I thought of once," he says. "So I suggested it for the song title and Kurt liked it."

'Sifting' also alludes to the fallibility of teachers and preachers – authority figures (and at over five minutes, it's one of Nirvana's longest songs). A similar theme emerges in 'Scoff,' which reads like nothing so much as a teenager's gripe against a dominating parent who derides their child for being worthless. "It's almost an industrial song, the way some of those riffs went, you know?" says Krist. "Real primal. It was just simple, basic music. Few notes. That was always my take on it, just being a bass player. Just playing, being in rhythm and putting a lot of excitement and feeling behind it so you could really project it, just feel it or get lost in it. Then it kind of kicks in and rock'n'roll magic takes over. It's not real cerebral – it's more physical. Some dissonant bass work because it's just an abrasive song. It's almost an industrial song, the way some of the riffs went."

More interesting are Kurt's critiques of relationships. 'Blew' had been tightened up with a shorter running time, giving it more punch. Krist's thudding bass line kicks things off before the full band comes in, while the lyrics, rooted in passive-aggression, have the narrator alternately accepting and sneering at his perceived domination by a partner. 'Swap Meet' expands on the flea market setting Kurt first explored in the spoken word section of 'Mrs Butterworth,' which had the protagonist planning to sell such homemade crafts as seaside 'still life' sculptures – driftwood and seashells glued to a piece of burlap (references to the driftwood/burlap creations not only turned up in 'Mrs Butterworth' and 'Swap Meet,' but also in interviews and the band biography that accompanied the release of *Nevermind*). Over a jerky, stop-start rhythm, Kurt relates a story of a couple who make their living peddling arts and crafts, while their own personal relationship is fractured; while she loves her partner more "than he will ever know," he's unable to reveal the depth of his own feelings for her. "'Swap Meet"'s just another one with this kind of funky time signature," says Krist. "And it's rhythmic, just really rhythmic." Chad cites Kurt's lyrics as being among his favorites: "It was tongue-in-cheek, but at the same time it was an interesting story."

It's been speculated that the couple in the song reflected Kurt's feelings about his own girlfriend, Tracy. He never addressed that question, but readily acknowledged that 'About A Girl' was inspired by his relationship with her. Tracy had asked why he'd never written a song about her, and he responded by writing a song based on an argument the two had about his lack of interest in getting a stable job.

The resulting song is couched in bitterness, the verses pleading for attention from an inattentive partner, while in the chorus the narrator admits to his own manipulations. A home demo of the song was even more pointed, with references to the notes Tracy left for him listing chores she wanted done around the house (another home demo, belatedly named 'Clean Up Before She Comes' when included on *With The Lights Out*, also touches on this theme). And while the final version of the chorus has the partner being the one to "hang me out to dry," the early version not only says "you hang me" but also "I'll hang you."

The vitriol was tempered by an unabashed pop melody; Kurt later said he'd spent hours listening to *Meet The Beatles* before writing the song. "That's one of the reasons I liked the song so much," says Chad. "In a lot of ways, it was definitely a lot more toward the things that I was hearing as well, aside from the heavier side of stuff we were doing. I thought it was great. When he first was showing me the song, I thought man, what a totally cool song! It's so rhythmic and the vocal melody just flows. Flows so nice." The song's sweetness was somewhat disrupted when Kurt hit the distortion pedal during the instrumental break, but as Krist points out: "It's kind of the bridge between grunge and pop right there." On learning the song didn't have a title, Chad asked Kurt what it was about. "It's about a girl," Kurt replied. "And I said: well, why don't you call it 'About A Girl'?" Chad recalls. "And he just looked at me and smiled and said: sounds good to me. And that was the end of that!"

Another darker, acoustically based song written and demoed around this time but not recorded during the upcoming sessions was 'Polly.' The song was inspired by a newspaper account of a teenage girl's kidnap and rape. The narrative was made even more disquieting by Kurt's singing from the perspective of the attacker, relating the horrifying events with a cool detachment. "It's actually one of the earliest songs that I can remember playing with the band," says Chad. "There were times where we'd be hanging out and Kurt would just be playing the song on guitar, like at his apartment or something. Kurt had a lot of songs that he would write on acoustic and sing; I recall hearing him just kind of messing through songs, sitting down and playing the acoustic. He probably had a lot of songs that were like that, that nobody ever knew about. When you listen to a lot of the really early four-track things that he did, a lot of that stuff is just kind of weird, slow, just mellow trippy stuff that's very much in the vein of 'Polly' or 'Sappy' or stuff like that. Who knows how much stuff like that he had that he just never showed anybody." For the moment, 'Polly' was put on the backburner. "Nothing came of it for a while," says Chad.

One trait shared by most of the new songs was their simplicity. 'School' was an extreme example, but songs like 'Negative Creep' and 'Scoff' – both of which consisted of a single verse and chorus – weren't much longer. The stripped-down songs were also easier to perform live. "In the old days, Kurt had a hard time singing," says Jack. "You couldn't even hear the lyrics on stage. He'd be sort of mumbling into the mic and wailing on his guitar. That was one reason why he started writing simpler songs; the chord patterns became simpler because he realized he could sing better that way. So he basically put his effort into coming up with good melodies and being able to sing them, rather than coming up with trippy guitar riffs, like when he did the first demo, when he was more into a Melvins kind of thing."

A home video that captured one of the band's rehearsals before the *Bleach* sessions appears on the DVD included in *With The Lights Out*. Chad's North drums take up a good portion of the small room, a strobe light flashes, and friends mill around drinking Rainier beer, flicking the room's lights on and off, as the band earnestly runs through their set, Kurt trying to shield himself from any distractions by singing while facing the wall. "You know, in Aberdeen there's not much else going on," says Chad. "So if someone's got a band practicing or something, that's something to do." Kurt can't resist dropping to his knees during 'Love Buzz,' but mostly concentrates on his singing. The lyrics to 'About A Girl' have yet to be finalized. The video features the only known performance of 'Big Long Now,' after which Kurt segues into a raging version of 'Immigrant Song,' the band quickly falling in behind him. It's the best footage of early Nirvana in circulation, as the camera is never more than a few feet away; during 'Hairspray Queen' and 'Mr Moustache,' Kurt walks up to the camera, showing off his fancy finger work. Krist's brother Robert recalls the noise attracted the attention of teenagers walking by the house, "stopping and standing there listening with an amazed look on their faces, like it was music they had never heard before; they really didn't know what to make of it, other than it was good. That was the night I thought there maybe was something really special happening with the band."

Right before the sessions began, Nirvana played something of a hometown show at Eagles Lodge in Hoquiam on December 21, sharing the bill with Ryan Aigner's band the Psychlodds, and Aaron Burckhard's band Attica. "After I left the band, I was still friends with them and stuff," says Aaron. "I remember waiting outside of the Hoquiam Eagles, and Kurt showed up and he had his neck all painted red with lipstick, right – 'cause he was a redneck! But, yeah, that was a cool show." Nirvana opened with 'School,' now in place as the usual set opener – a position it would hold well into 1991. Aside from the inclusion of 'Paper Cuts,' the setlist was identical to the October Evergreen show, right down to the covers of 'Run, Rabbit, Run' and 'Immigrant Song.' The show was marred by sound problems with Kurt's guitar, people leaping onto the stage, and the usual extensive pauses between songs. The lyrics to 'Mr Moustache' had also not yet been finalized. But the cluster of fans in attendance nonetheless jostles excitedly at the front of the stage (it's not quite fully fledged moshing). And in sharp contrast to the band's stock-still performance at the Community World Theater nearly a year before, they're now quite animated: Krist jumping up and down as he lurches back and forth over his bass, stripping to his underwear after 'Spank Thru';

Kurt roaming the stage when he's not at his mic, swaying back and forth or dropping to his knees; Chad's flailing hair visible even above his large North kit. (Legend has it that Kurt and Krist dropped into the Pourhouse, a bar in Aberdeen, after this show, and played a short set; Krist has denied this, while Aaron says Kurt and Krist showed up on another date when Attica was playing the bar, and while Krist got up to jam, Kurt was unable to, as there wasn't a left-handed guitar available for him to play.)

Three days later, on December 24, Nirvana returned to Reciprocal. "We approached the recording of *Bleach* like it was a radio session," Kurt later explained. "The key to a successful album is to get the fuck out of the studio before you're sick of the songs." The band was able to work quickly because they were so well prepared. "We rehearsed a lot and made sure our chops were up," says Krist. "It was a pretty straight-ahead process: just replicate the live sound, just get it sounding good. Little bit of overdubbing here and there. Kurt would do his vocals, but he'd never do a comp track or anything. He always nailed it. He didn't ever have to do any trickery; he just did it straight-ahead. He just had that insane passion and drive or something. He tapped into something that was really compelling."

Jack Endino adds that on this outing the band had a clear idea of the kind of sound they wanted: "a dry, crunchy, 70s-rock sound." They used Jack's copy of AC/DC's *For Those About To Rock* as a point of reference. The band also experimented with drum sounds, stacking two snares on top of each other in one session. "The idea was to get heavy drum sounds," says Chad. "So the drum heads were tuned real low. Lower tuned drums, depending on how extreme you go, can result in a lessened response time. Kind of like the difference between hitting a drumstick off a pillow as opposed to a piece of wood. I think we went pretty extreme."

There were a total of six recording sessions for *Bleach*: December

24 (five hours), December 29 (five hours), December 30 (five hours), December 31 (four-and-a-half hours; the date mixing began), and, in 1989, January 14 (five hours), and January 24 (five-and-a-half hours). While there is no way of confirming which songs were recorded on which days, documentation left behind establishes the order the songs were recorded in.

The sessions began with 'Mr Moustache,' 'Scoff,' and 'Sifting.' Perhaps because it was the first session, the band indulged in a little bit of experimentation. "The band came in and actually said: we're gonna tune our guitars really low, and we're gonna try recording all these songs this way," says Jack. "All the strings were just slack. And of course they were way out of tune, and didn't sound too good. I think Kurt was having trouble singing and wanted to make it a little easier for himself, so they tried recording several of the *Bleach* tunes in this low tuning, and ended up hating it. They came back another day and re-recorded all of it." (Krist agrees with Jack's assessment of these early experiments. "It all sounded like shit," he says.)

It's possible that the entire first session was spent on those three songs, because when Nirvana played the *Sub Pop 200* release party on December 28, at the Underground, 'Mr Moustache' still didn't have final lyrics. New recordings of 'Scoff,' 'Mr Moustache,' and 'Sifting' (in that order) were ultimately recorded over the earlier takes, thus losing them forever. 'Scoff' is punchy if somewhat one-dimensional, but 'Mr Moustache' races along with great vigor (it's a half-minute shorter than the version recorded during the 'Love Buzz' sessions) and is given an unusual fade-in beginning to match the song's equally unique ending, which has the music slowing down and gradually coming to a halt, like a car running out of gas. Conversely, 'Sifting' was taken slightly slower than in the version recorded at the 'Love Buzz' sessions, giving it a greater sense of menace, especially when coupled with Kurt's double-tracked vocal, which veers between a low crooning and a more agonized wail. The song also features a longer guitar solo, which, unusually for a Nirvana song (aside from 'Love

Buzz'), doesn't simply follow the melody but is more improvisational.

The band then made the unexpected decision to record 'Hairspray Queen' again, but Chad's lighter playing – in contrast to Dale Crover's more forceful work on the Dale Demo version – diluted the song's impact. "Frankly, I didn't think 'Hairspray Queen' was that good," says Jack. "Basically, whenever they tried to do something that used to be a Dale song, it just didn't sound that good. That's the way it is with drummers; Chad was good on the stuff that they had written with him." Kurt had noted in his journals that he wanted to re-do a number of the Dale Demo songs, but most of the time, as with the re-recording of 'Floyd The Barber' during the 'Love Buzz' session, the results were unsatisfactory. Another probable reason why the new version of 'Hairspray Queen' was not released was that the band was losing interest in the song itself; it would be dropped from the setlist by the end of the year. As of this writing, Chad's version of 'Hairspray Queen' remains unreleased.

'About A Girl' was the next song to be recorded. While his bandmates had said they liked the song, Kurt still felt some hesitation about recording it. "I think he felt nervous about putting 'About A Girl' on there," Jack confirms, "but he was very insistent on it. He said: OK, I've got a song that's totally different from the others, Jack. You gotta just humor me here, because we're gonna do this real pop tune. I was like: great. Fine. You know: whatever. I think the question was raised at some point: gee, I wonder if Sub Pop is going to like this? And we decided, who cared, you know? Whatever. It's your album; put it on! And Sub Pop said nothing. In fact, I think they liked it. I think they liked it a lot. Jonathan is a total pop head."

The recording has a bittersweet plaintiveness that's irresistible, its pop quotient underscored by a tambourine that comes in during the instrumental break, and Kurt's overdubbing of the phrase "I do" providing a haunting echo throughout the song. 'About A Girl' also had an unexpected impact on the song that was recorded next, 'Blew.' Kurt and Krist tuned their instruments down to what they thought was the key of D, but as they were already tuned down to E-flat for 'About A Girl' (which starts out in E minor) they ended up tuning down to C-sharp. "It was so heavy!" says Chad. "I'm always just amazed that it even came out. Because it was such a low tuning, and there wasn't much bass or strings slapping. It was a trip. It just worked out. It was cool."

The newly recorded 'Blew' is tighter than the previously recorded version, being not only shorter but also faster (the earlier version was so slow, it tended to drag). Kurt also heightens the excitement vocally; whereas in the early version he kept his voice in a lower register throughout most of the song, only going up an octave on the final lines, in the new version he goes up an octave on the first chorus (the choruses also have a nice overdubbed harmony line). Chad also recalls this as a song where the two snares were stacked on top of each other.

It was a confident performance that illustrated how the band's musical skills continued to improve. "Frankly, I still think that the Dale Demo was really special and I was really sort of hoping that they would release some of those songs," says Jack. "I wasn't that impressed with the way they played at the 'Love Buzz' sessions. I didn't think the material was all that amazing. Chad didn't really have his thing down yet; he wasn't as good of a drummer as he became later. They didn't seem as impressive to me as a band. But six months later, at the *Bleach* sessions, they were a much tighter band. And I thought their stuff was much better."

Next up was 'Swap Meet,' originally titled 'White Trash' and then 'Swap Meat.' ("Why it became 'meet' on the record, I don't know, because it would have been much funnier if it was 'meat,'" says Jack.) Kurt finalized the lyrics during the drive to the studio. "He was always cramming at the last minute," says Krist. Chad concurs. "He'd be in the van in the front seat and he had his knee up with a pad there," he says. "And he'd always ask us: what rhymes with this? What rhymes with that? He used to always do that, even when we did the Madison sessions, before we went to record those, or in the hotel room and stuff, he's like: OK, what's a good word that rhymes with monkey? He had this whole booklet of lyrics, and for sure 'Swap Meet' and a few others were not quite finished yet." The song's jumpy rhythms underscore the uneven relationship of the couple depicted in the song, with a further note of desperation given by Kurt's shouted emphasis of the word "heart" (stretched out to *ha-art!*).

There were no underlying complexities in 'Negative Creep.' It's an out-and-out thrasher from start to finish – Kurt sounds like he's racing against the music to see who can get to the end of the song first – with an especially impressive throat-shredding scream from him after the second repetition of the song's sole verse; it's also the only Nirvana song to have a fade-out ending.

By this time, another reel of tape had been filled, so the tape from the 'Love Buzz' sessions was pulled out; the album's remaining songs would be recorded over more unreleased material from the previous session. 'School' (recorded over the first take of 'Big Cheese'), begins like 'Negative Creep' with a squall of guitar before the main riff comes tumbling in, and again it's a race to the finish (with the occasional shriek dropped in for good measure).

The last song of the sessions, 'Big Long Now,' was recorded over the first take of 'Mr Moustache.' It occupies a curious place in the band's catalogue: not only was it left unreleased at the time, it's not known to have been played in concert. Despite being somewhat ponderous, Kurt's vocal on the chorus is powerful, and the rehearsal video shows the band having fun pounding it out in performance. But it was never a serious contender for the album.

"I argued with them about it," says Jack. "I said: how come you're not using it? And Kurt said there were already enough slow, heavy songs on the record. He didn't want to weigh it down. And that is the slowest – other than 'Sifting' – it's the slowest, heaviest song. 'Sifting' is a better song. 'Big Long Now' is big and long and it's very slow; I just think it has an amazing vocal take on it. I pretty much just nagged them about it for a long time. When *Incesticide* came up I said: you guys have got to use this song, I've still got this out-take from *Bleach*. So it ended up on *Incesticide*. I kept reminding them about it: you guys, what about 'Big Long Now'? It's a brilliant song. It's got a great vocal."

On the final day of the sessions, a few earlier songs were remixed for inclusion on the album. "'Paper Cuts' was from the Dale Demo, but we added a vocal harmony part to it," says Jack. "You can hear it on the chorus. 'Floyd' is pretty much exactly the same, except we just mixed it to sound better. And 'Love Buzz' we remixed without the cartoon intro, because Kurt didn't have the cassette with him. But it was mixed so well that it didn't make a big difference. And really, the single mix isn't all that good. When I go back and listen to it, it's a terrible mix. It's got a really stupid reverb on it."

Kurt had also wanted to include 'Beans' but said Jonathan had dismissed the song as "retarded." The band then devised the running order: 'Floyd The Barber,' 'Mr Moustache,' 'School,' 'Scoff,' and 'Sifting' on side one, 'Love Buzz,' 'Swap Meet,' 'Paper Cuts,' 'Negative Creep,' 'About A Girl,' and 'Blew' on side two.

Jack duly spliced the tapes together in that order. "And then Pavitt listened to it, and he didn't like it," says Jack. "And he said: no, no, this is wrong – 'Blew''s got to be first. And I don't think Kurt was that confident to have 'About A Girl' be the third song but Pavitt was like: no, get that up there!" After Pavitt's rejigging, the final running became: 'Blew,' 'Floyd The Barber,' 'About A Girl,' 'School,' 'Love Buzz,' and 'Paper Cuts' on side one and 'Negative Creep,' 'Scoff,' 'Swap Meet,' 'Mr Moustache,' and 'Sifting' on side two. On the original UK release, 'Big Cheese' was substituted for 'Love Buzz.' The later CD release had both 'Love Buzz' and 'Big Cheese' as well as another Dale Demo track, 'Downer.'

"I frankly think side two – besides 'Negative Creep' – goes downhill," says Jack. "'Scoff' and 'Swap Meet' are the two least memorable tunes. Those just went nowhere. Basically, Pavitt put the sequence in descending order of the songs he liked the best; you can tell those first songs were his five favorite Nirvana tunes. So then the band called me up and said: Bruce wants us to re-sequence it, here's the new order. So then I had to go back and re-splice the whole thing again, and put it in a totally different order."

Chad still expresses amazement that *Bleach* came out as well as it did, with recording time coming to 30 hours and a total cost of $606.17. "That only happens once in a band's lifetime," he says. The songs were more straightforward than the Dale Demo material, but Kurt's sarcastic sense of humor remained, and the band's pop sensibility was increasingly developed. And if the preponderance of 'rawk' material on side two does bog things down, as Jack notes, three songs nonetheless remained in the band's setlist through their very last show: 'Blew,' 'About A Girl,' and 'School.'

Bleach can be considered an even greater success considering the time limitations. "It's nice doing a record quickly, but then it's nice to not be in a hurry," says Jack. "To be able to step back and go: wait a minute. Let's get a different drum sound on this song. Why don't we play with a different guitar amplifier? Let's see if we can get a different sound for this that would maybe work better with this song. That's the sort of thing you can't do when you've got a day to do an album. You just have to set up the mics and go. Which is why *Bleach* pretty much has the same guitar sound from beginning to end. You basically just roll tape. OK: start the first song. Here's the second song. Here's the third song. And that's what's fun about indie rock, but that's also what limits it sometimes. If you're literally just trying to make a recording of the band live, live recordings usually aren't very good. Bands don't usually sound that good live. So sometimes it's fun to spend some time in the studio."

Kurt himself was dissatisfied with the album. "We purposely made that record one-dimensional, more 'rock' than it should have been," he later claimed. This is at odds with Pavitt's – and even Poneman's – preference for Nirvana's less 'rock' material. It was after all the label heads who decided 'Love Buzz,' the band's poppiest effort at that time, would be the band's first single. But it was also typical of Kurt's assessment of his work, for throughout his career he invariably cast a critical eye on his recordings, beginning with 'Love Buzz,' which he dismissed as "the wimpiest recording we've ever done." The band's subsequent albums, *Nevermind* and *In Utero*, came in for similar critiques. "Things never came out the way he thought they would, or the way he heard them," says Chad. "I think that's common with most songwriters. That's just the way it is, you know. Most anybody that's got a real passion for what they're doing are probably never going to be 100 per cent satisfied with any song they ever write."

Others were more enthusiastic in their appreciation of the record. Nearly 20 years after recording *Bleach*, Jack met Iggy Pop at a show in Seattle, having been introduced to him as the man who'd produced Nirvana's first album. "Did you record the *good* Nirvana album?" Iggy asked, and when Jack replied that he'd produced *Bleach*, the Godfather of Punk shrieked with delight, talked excitedly about how much he loved the record, praised Krist's work ("That great bass player those guys had, he doesn't get enough credit!"), then gave Jack a bear hug before departing, leaving Jack in something of a daze: "The rest of the week I walked around going: did that really happen?"

CHAPTER 7
Instinct And Reaction

"When Melody Maker flies in for the first time in ten years, that's good for everybody."
BRUCE PAVITT TO THE AUTHOR, 1989

In early 1989, Nirvana played their first out-of-state shows at Satyricon in Portland, Oregon, on January 6 and 21. According to *Come As You Are*, Kurt may have met his future wife, Courtney Love, at the venue on one of these occasions, although other times and places have been speculated about elsewhere. (*Heavier Than Heaven* says the meeting took place at the same venue in February 1990; medical student Nikolas Hartshorne and future Hole guitarist Eric Erlandson say Love first saw the band at Raji's in Los Angeles later that same month; and *Nirvana: The True Story* says the two first met at the Hollywood Palladium in May 1991.)

Around the same time, Jonathan Poneman had suggested Nirvana get another guitar player, and Kurt agreed. Word that the band was looking for a new member reached John Goodmanson, who came by Kurt's Olympia home to ask about the position, using the pretext of soliciting some Nirvana songs for a cassette label he'd started with Donna Dresch as an excuse to visit. John was startled to be greeted at door by Kurt wearing nothing but his underwear.

"Whoa – I'll come back," John blurted.

"No, come on in," Kurt replied. "You want some toast?"

"He was painting, so it freaked me out to the point where I didn't feel like I could ask him if he needed anybody in his band," John recalls. "I chickened out and asked him if I could put the KAOS thing out on the cassette label instead. I remember him being totally fine with it, but we never did get around to it. And a week later, Jason Everman was in the band. So I was really bummed with myself that I completely missed out. Though it's not like I could have toured, 'cause I was going to college."

Jason was the friend of Chad's who'd put up the money for the *Bleach* sessions. Jason and Chad had also gone to school together and played in the band Stone Crow; since then, Jason had split his time between working as a fisherman in Alaska during the spring and summer and traveling abroad during the winter. "I played in some shortlived bands with friends in Germany, but nothing noteworthy," he says. "Before Nirvana and Stone Crow were a couple of high-school punk bands; just the standard garage or basement scenarios that every aspiring musician experiences during adolescence."

Jason had first seen Nirvana at the Community World Theater, possibly on January 23 1988, as he recalls a friend suggesting he check out "Dale Crover's new band." "The two features that struck me the first times I saw them live were Kurt's voice, and the craftsmanship of the songs," he says. "It was something special." It's been said the band even stayed at Jason's home in Seattle the night before the *Bleach* sessions began, which Jason doesn't recall, although he does say it "makes sense logistically, considering none of them lived in Seattle."

Kurt solicited Jason's interest in a typically roundabout fashion. "Not long after *Bleach* was in the can, Kurt mentioned to me that he and Krist were flirting with the idea of a second guitar player," says Jason. "I didn't infer that I was under consideration. But not long after that, Kurt asked me if I would be interested. I liked the band so I said yes. Kurt gave me a demo in order to learn the songs, and I played my first show with them some time after that at K-Dorm at Evergreen. At one point, Kurt even mentioned returning to the studio to add my guitar to the *Bleach* master, but it never went beyond that brief mention." Jason was nonetheless credited as a guitarist on the record, even though he didn't play on it. "We just wanted to make him feel more at home in the band," Krist said.

"We met [Jason] maybe a couple of months before we recorded [*Bleach*] and really liked him and started hanging out with him," Kurt later explained. "I started thinking that maybe I'd like to do a bit more singing and didn't want to worry about guitar playing that much." "It took a lot of the burden off of Kurt to sing and play guitar simultaneously – which is a challenging task live," Jason adds. "And a second guitar made the live sound of the band bigger and denser."

The K-Dorm show was again at Phil Buffington's room. "I don't remember how it all transpired," Phil says, "if I asked them to play again, or they asked. But obviously the first show exceeded everyone's expectations so I was like: sure! I guess the one thing that kind of surprised me about them playing the second time was that, I don't know, to me, as someone who never really played in a band, it seemed almost more trouble than it was worth. Because obviously no money was going to happen and you weren't really expanding your audience or anything like that. It was really cool that they played two shows there. It was sort of a phenomenal event, in hindsight.

"The second show was kind of crazy too," he recalls. "Because there was snow on the ground, and this was one where I really over-invested in beer, because it was the second Nirvana show. And the pipes broke in the unit below, so they cut the power to the whole place because they were worried. I had like six kegs of beer there, and all my rent was sitting there, and then the power goes out! It was horrible! After some pleading, they re-introduced power to the building, and fixed the broken pipe, or isolated it, and the show went on."

The band then began preparing for their first tour. "Nirvana, at least during my time with the band, rarely rehearsed," says Jason. "I played with them the first time live without ever rehearsing with them. Prior to the first West Coast tour, we rehearsed for a couple of days in an empty space next to a parking garage in downtown Seattle."

The tour's first date was February 10 in San Francisco, with one other confirmed show in San Jose; some sources say these were the only dates the band played. There was a smattering of press attention:

Calendar magazine, on the verge of changing its name to *SF Weekly*, ran an article I wrote at the time about the number of Northwest bands playing in the Bay Area that month, which I jokingly entitled 'Screaming North: Seattle Bands Take Over The World.' (The listings editor added the prophetic sentence "It's our big chance to see what may be the future of loud American music" to the end of the piece.)

The tour generated little in the way of payment. In San Francisco, everyone was forced to eat at a free soup kitchen, although Chad chose to emphasize the positive in a letter to his mother, bragging that the band had "played some smoken shows." Signs posted around San Francisco advising intravenous drug users to 'Bleach Your Works' as a way of curtailing the spread of the AIDS virus are said to have inspired the band to call their album *Bleach*. (Another title under consideration had been the more misanthropic *Too Many Humans*.)

The night after the San Francisco show, Nirvana shared a bill with Mudhoney in San Jose. "I remember looking in their van, and Kurt was in the back curled up into a ball, and they were all: yeah, he's really sick," says Mudhoney drummer Dan Peters. "But at the gig, he definitely came to and had a good show; I remember Steve [Turner, Mudhoney's guitarist] commenting on the fact that he was twirling around and ended up almost on his head, with his legs shooting straight up." It was similar to a shot of Kurt that Charles Peterson would later capture.

Back in Seattle, Nirvana played a high-profile show on February 25 at the HUB (Husky Union Building) East Ballroom, on the UW campus. On the day of show, Alice Wheeler had a photo session with the band on Seattle's waterfront. The group is pictured wearing jeans (Kurt's are especially tattered) and T-shirts, standing in a vacant lot, the city skyline behind them. Alice also shot individual portraits, one featuring Kurt with an especially winsome smile on his face. "When everybody tells me what a devil he is, that's when I whip out that picture and go: fuck you, he's a nice sweet little boy," she says.

In the audience was *Melody Maker* journalist Everett True, who'd been flown in specifically to talk up Sub Pop in the British music press. Everett had long been following the Northwest's music scene, beginning in 1985, when the drummer for Australian band The Cannanes turned up on his doorstep in London, bearing a copy of Beat Happening's self-titled debut album. "He was in London for 24 hours on his way back from Olympia to Australia," says Everett. "He'd been given two addresses to look up, and he decided on mine, because I used to do a fanzine called *The Legend*. It's lucky I was in! And I absolutely loved the album." Everett brought Beat Happening to the attention of Rough Trade, who ended up releasing the group's records in Britain.

He next discovered Green River after friends visiting the USA brought home their records and passed them on to him. "This was pretty much my first exposure to rock music," he says. "I was an indie kid. I never liked rock music. I started listening to music in '77, '78, just after punk, so I was taught to despise everything that'd come before. I liked Thin Lizzy, which I wouldn't admit to, but I liked Motörhead, which I *would* admit to, and AC/DC, which was just about allowable, but that was it. You weren't allowed to like anything else. And the whole of Britain was pretty much still like that, at that time, at least in terms of the music press. It was still completely unheard of to praise anything from the 70s – anything rock, anyway. It was a bit looked down upon to like anything in the 60s as well. Anything post-punk was fine, but before that? No.

"So I think that was partly the reason it was so exciting to hear a bunch of bands who had grown up on punk and hardcore, who'd clearly come from that kind of ethos, but had found it a bit too restrictive, and felt that they should rock out. They weren't ashamed of liking those bands in the 70s no one else admitted to liking, and so I think what was really thrilling was the fact that this was rock! You know, this was the first time rock was allowed into the British music press for a long time. Proper rock."

Bruce and Jonathan knew that quickest way to generate interest in their label was to attract the attention of the UK rock weeklies (which at the time included not only *Melody Maker* but also *NME*, *Sounds*, and *Record Mirror*), which were constantly on the lookout for "the thrill of the new," as Everett put it. They contacted London-based Southern Records Distribution, who handled Sub Pop's records overseas, and explained they wanted to bring a reporter to Seattle to cover their bands. "It was classic Sub Pop brinksmanship," says Everett. "They were almost all out of funds, they thought they'd have one last great hurrah before they went down, and they'd fly an English journalist out to do the story."

Anton Brookes, who was then working at Southern (he would later form his own company, Bad Moon Publicity, and retain Sub Pop as a client), had originally wanted to send the *Melody Maker* writing team The Stud Brothers. "But there were two of them," says Everett. "Simple finances dictated they couldn't go. And I'd just become reviews editor so I was just like: I want to go to America!" Everett was duly sent the latest batch of Sub Pop records. He spent the night in the magazine's review room, playing both 'Love Buzz' and The U-Men's 'Solid Action' over and over. "I was literally dancing on the table to these records," he says. "This isn't a lie! I have witnesses. I was dancing and head banging to these records. I was going absolutely berserk. They were the best rock records I'd heard since Hüsker Dü covered 'Eight Miles High.'" In a joint review which included both records as well as Olympia act Some Velvet Sidewalk's 'I Know,' he wrote: "Nirvana are beauty incarnate. A relentless, two-chord grunge beat lays down some grievous foundations for a sheer monster of a guitar force to howl over. The volume control ain't been built yet which can do justice to this three-piece! WHAT IS GOING DOWN OVER THERE?"

Despite loving Nirvana's debut single, Everett was initially underwhelmed by the band in concert. "They were dreadful," he says of the HUB Ballroom show. "They were really bad. I was just like: no, I don't understand this. They were heavy metal, basically, and at that point in time I didn't like heavy metal. I liked garage punk, like Mudhoney played. That was garage punk. And so is the first Nirvana single, and so is the U-Men single. Nirvana were dreadful. I mean, everybody would say that about that show, 'cause they were. Jonathan, even at that point, was really like: somebody's finally going to take on the world. And I was like: yeah, right. I don't think so!"

(Everett distinguished himself during the show by asking if he could perform as well. "Bruce and Jon were like: oh, shit!" he says. He ended up borrowing a guitar from Girl Trouble, a Tacoma band also on the bill, who begged him not to break it. He performed a short, four-song set. "The crowd fucking loved it," he later wrote. "I liked this city.")

Earnie Bailey, who would later become Nirvana's guitar tech, was also at the show. Earnie had previously run a guitar-repair shop in Spokane; then, after taking over management of an espresso bar at the Nordstrom department store, he was asked to run the bar at one of Nordstrom's Seattle stores. While in Spokane he'd caught a riotous U-Men gig that had been shut down by the Fire Marshall, and he regularly attended rock shows in Seattle. One of his employees was Rob Kader, a huge Nirvana fan who had known Jason Everman in high school.

"Rob was one of their first real diehard fans," Earnie recalls. "I think I had already seen Nirvana at that point, opening up for other bands. When Rob came to work for me, he would be ranting and raving about Nirvana all day, and in the back of my mind I was like: God, are we talking about the same Nirvana? Because the shows I had seen weren't really that great. Rob was a couple of years younger than I was, so I thought, well, maybe I just don't get it. Rob badgered me into going out and seeing them, so I agreed to go catch the show at the HUB, hoping to get him to stop hassling me about seeing this band."

The two arrived to find that the show was sold out – an indication of the scene's growing popularity – and snuck in through a side door. "Rob headed straight for the front," Earnie recalls. "I stood by the soundboard, watching Rob do swan dives off the stage. The thing that was very memorable right off the bat was Kurt's voice, because you just didn't hear anyone sing like that. I remember them having really crappy amplifiers, at a time when most people prided themselves on having a good nice tube amp; they had all these really cheap solid-state things up there. And to make it worse, what was even stranger was that Kurt was getting all this solid-state feedback, really kind of abrasive sounding. I was trying to figure out if he was doing it because he enjoyed it, or if it was really because he had really bad amplifiers. I didn't really understand the sloppiness, for the most part."

But to Charles Peterson, down at the front, the band were clearly in their element. "Kurt was doing these Pete Townshend jumps, and he'd be on the ground playing, and really, really animated," he says. "And Jason Everman was always moving his head. All over! They just seemed excited, excited about what they were playing, and that gets me excited, gets the audience excited. They ended up throwing their instruments up, trying to hit the overhead hanging florescent lights, so I got pictures of Krist's bass and Kurt's guitar hitting up there, and they were being all wacky." The band's antics were fueled by the red wine they'd brought to the show, and the damage they caused resulted in a ban on rock shows being booked at the venue for a short time. In some of Charles' shots, an example of Nirvana's 'set dressing' can be seen: a tapestry of Elvis Presley that Kurt had altered by painting Alice Cooper-styled eye make-up around Presley's eyes. They called it 'Elvis Cooper.'

Soon after the HUB show, Everett was taken by Jonathan to a park near Sub Pop's offices, next to Pike Place Market and overlooking Puget Sound, to meet Nirvana, who were excited, as he recalls, to meet a music writer from England. (It was an attitude shared by others, as Jonathan later told Everett he was "in awe" at having "a real live British music journalist in our midst, particularly one from *Melody Maker*.") The meeting was friendly enough, although Nirvana made little impression at the time. "I never thought they'd be big," Everett says. "I just remember their Northwest sense of humor – my kind of humor. I loved it. Dry, light, they just made me laugh. But they were always a bit separate from the rest of the Seattle bands. They were always a little bit on the outside. And they're a little bit stranger, probably, than Mark [Arm], Tad [Doyle], and some of those people. They didn't quite fit in." There was certainly no sense then that Everett would become exceptionally close to the band, interviewing them more than any other writer.

The first fruits of Sub Pop's bid for publicity came in *Melody Maker*'s March 11 issue, which had a cover story on Mudhoney: 'Mudhoney: Sub Pop, Sub Normal, Subversion.' The two-page story's subhead stated 'Suddenly Seattle Is The Centre Of All Things Grunge' – a word Everett had previously used before to describe the music of Manchester's Happy Mondays – while the article began: "Britain is currently held in thrall by a *rock* explosion emanating from one small, insignificant, West Coast American city." Another two-page spread followed the next week titled 'Sub Pop: Rock City' and including brief descriptions of the label's other bands. "Basically, this is the real thing," the article stated about Nirvana. "No rock star contrivance, no intellectual perspective, no plan for world domination. You're talking about four guys in their early twenties from rural Washington who want to rock." It was a description that nicely, if a tad condescendingly, summarized the band, and has been quoted in numerous Nirvana biographies since – ironically, since it was actually a quote by Jonathan, although Everett had no hesitation about passing it off as his own. "It was taken word-for-word from Jonathan," Everett admits. "I was running really late on my deadline, and I can actually remember being in the office, calling him up and going: Jonathan, can you tell me something to say about Nirvana? It's been quoted in loads of places; I've seen it quoted so many places, and it's Jonathan's quote, not mine. I loved the single, sure, but, no, no, that quote wasn't me." Still, given Sub Pop's penchant for exaggeration, it was a perfectly fitting gesture.

Throughout the spring, preparations were made for *Bleach*'s release. At the HUB show, Alice Wheeler had taken stark headshots of the band backstage, which were considered for the album's cover (the pictures can be seen in *Come As You Are*). "They were pretty standard stuff," she says. "But the band didn't like them. And that's cool; I don't want someone to have pictures they don't like of themselves for their record. If I had to do it over now, of course I would have done a much different job. But Bruce liked them. He probably liked that idea of the scary hick from Aberdeen. And I think that kind of hurt Kurt's feelings."

Indeed, Bruce had told Michael Azerrad that he liked the pictures because of what he saw as their authenticity: "These guys were *ugly* – this was the most un-LA look you could come up with. I really wanted to use these photos to dramatize the fact that these people are *real*." But for Kurt, the condescension stung as much as it had when his band was made fun of for having a drummer with a moustache. "It was just obvious that [Bruce] thought of himself as an educated white upper-middle-class punk rocker who knows everything and I'm just this idiot from Aberdeen," Kurt told Azerrad. "That was always something we sensed and we totally resented him for it."

"Because Kurt and Krist came from Aberdeen, they could be publicized and promoted and exploited as backcountry hicks," says Kurt Danielson, whose band TAD was often portrayed as a motley crew of backwoods freaks by Sub Pop, with lead singer Tad Doyle shown holding a chainsaw in press photos, and the accompanying band bio invariably making reference to his former job as a butcher. "We all resented Sub Pop to an extent for that," he says. "But on the other hand, we understood it as a necessary promotional gimmick, a gimmick that seemed to work. What you want is to have people at your shows and buying your records; if these things accomplish that, then so much the better. But shortly thereafter we discovered that we were painted into a corner, that nobody cared so much about the music – they wanted to see the fat butcher on stage, clowning around, and that got old fast. But we can't turn around and say: well, it's Sub Pop's fault, they painted us with this brush. We let them do it. We were enthusiastic about it as a matter of fact. Nirvana, too. But in fact, Kurt was a very sensitive, artistic individual, who, if anything, wanted to get as far away from that image as possible."

Ultimately, a live shot from an April show at Olympia's Reko/Muse Gallery, taken by Tracy Marander, was used for the cover. It was Kurt's idea to print it as a reverse negative. "I think he liked the way everyone looked like they were rocking out," Tracy explained. "They weren't just standing around playing." The picture caught Kurt in mid-head bang, creating a look, as Dave Grohl later recalled, of "big burly unshaven logger drinking guys" – ironically, not much different from the aesthetic Pavitt had seen in Alice Wheeler's pictures. A poster included in early copies of the record featured Charles Peterson's pictures from the HUB Ballroom show.

The record also featured the first appearance of the Nirvana logo. The cover was designed by Lisa Orth, who also worked as a production assistant at *The Rocket*; the artwork was laid out in the magazine's production room. When she asked Grant Alden, then the magazine's managing editor and typesetter (and later the co-founder of *No Depression* magazine) to set type for the cover, she told him to use whatever typeface was on his Compugraphic typesetting machine; it happened to be Bodoni Extra Bold Condensed. (Although it's sometimes said the typeface was Onyx, Alden says he didn't have that typeface on his machine.) Alden produced the type, and the logo that would adorn countless albums, T-shirts, and baseball caps was created for the sum of $15.

Over the next three months, there were only six Nirvana shows, and it was during this relatively slow period that Kurt made one of his few guest appearances, on a record by Olympia band The Go Team. The band had formed in 1985, and had a constantly changing line-up revolving around Calvin Johnson and Tobi Vail (later of Bikini Kill). "The Go Team was about process," Vail explained. "I liked to go make stuff, partially as an excuse to hang out with people – that is where the collaboration came from – but then the tapes would be rolling; and the result would turn into a K release ... Some people, most people probably, thought we sucked because we'd often improvise or play stuff that was unfinished sounding. That this was deliberate – an aesthetic/conceptual choice – really confused a lot of people."

It was quite different from the more precise music Kurt was making with Nirvana, but he nonetheless joined Tobi and Calvin at Tobi's parents home on April 21, for a session in the garage, playing a third guitar alongside Calvin and Donna Dresch, with Louise Olsen on bass, Tobi on drums, and Tam Ohrmund (who'd also played with Tobi in the Olympia band Doris) on vocals. Two of the songs recorded at the session were released on a one-sided single, 'Scratch It Out'/'Bikini Twilight.' The droning 'Scratch It Out' is held together primarily by Ohrmund's forceful vocal, the musical backing a bit too listless in comparison with the song's angry lyrics, which are directed at a former acquaintance. 'Bikini Twilight' is decidedly livelier, an instrumental with a surf-rock feel. According to Calvin, Kurt only played on 'Bikini Twilight'; the stronger guitar line suggests this could be the case. Tobi recalled five or six songs being recorded at the session, including a cover of The Stooges' 'Loose,' on which Calvin played bass. (Krist believes that 'tourette's,' which later appeared on *In Utero*, was written around this period.)

The single was released in July 1989 on K Records, part of a series of singles The Go Team was releasing each month that year (Everett True, credited as 'The Legend,' had sung on the March single). "We had this grand plan that we were going to package each single in a bag, with a label on top," says Candice Pederson, who worked at K and later became the label's co-owner. "But after the first month, my God, we were hand-stapling them, stuffing them, pressing the bags, hand-cutting the labels – it was a very laborious project and I was like: this is really a nice concept but it's not going to work for 12 months!" As it turned out, the series ended with the September '89 single, when The Go Team broke up.

Sometime that spring – the exact date is unknown – Nirvana entered the studio to record a track for a compilation on C/Z Records. The label's owner, Daniel House, had been working at Sub Pop since 1988, handling sales, while running C/Z at the same time. "Sub Pop let me keep my records down in their basement," he says. "I had developed such a strong direct-to-retail account base at Sub Pop, and I was the salesman, so I would, representing Sub Pop, buy records from C/Z to sell direct. C/Z Records were selling great! The misconception that Bruce and Jon had was that I was going overboard trying to sell C/Z at the expense of Sub Pop, because at the time there were a couple records I put out that actually did better than records that they put out simultaneously, and that kind of pissed them off!"

Daniel freely indulged in the same kinds of playful hijinks as did Sub Pop, at one point putting out a C/Z T-shirt that read 'Bruce Pavitt Gave Me Head' as a way of getting back at his boss for perceived jabs at Skin Yard in his 'Sub Pop' column and what he felt was a lack of promotion on the label's part when they finally released a Skin Yard record. "Bruce had it coming for years!" he jokes. "At the time Bruce thought it was kind of a cute idea and said it was OK, because he looked at any attention, be it positive or negative, as being, simply, more attention. But it also brought a lot of attention to us. And I think had Bruce known how popular those shirts were going to become he would have thought twice! But that shirt helped put us on the map."

Daniel had first heard Nirvana when Jack Endino passed him a copy of the Dale Demo, on which Jack had written 'Nirvana Is God.' ("Daniel is the only one I would've written 'Nirvana Is God' on the tape for, 'cause he would've gotten the joke," says Jack.) "So within a week of them recording that first demo, I'd heard of them, had received a tape of theirs, and had fallen in love with their music," says

Daniel. Skin Yard also shared the bill with Nirvana at two shows in 1988 and two in 1989, including the HUB Ballroom show in February. Daniel remembered the group as being initially "very, very timid. Very gawky, awkward looking; this big, tall, lanky bass player, who didn't look comfortable in his own body, and this timid frail guy who seemed to be afraid of getting too close to the mic. But their music was still really powerful. Early on, they were not a real dynamic band. I mean, Kurt was timid and scared, you know? He didn't let loose until they'd been playing a year, a year and a half out. And then it just started, you know. I don't know what happened; I don't know what epiphany Kurt had that somehow allowed him to just explode and emote."

Daniel had wanted to put out a Nirvana single himself, but says: "Jon jumped on them so fast it was just blinding. Back then I never really did that. I was pretty casual about everything. I lost Helmet the same way. I knew Helmet before Amphetamine Reptile ever heard of them, and we had agreed to put out a single, but it was just very casual, and kind of like, whenever we get around to it, you know? And Amphetamine Reptile just jumped on it. Same kinda deal." Even so, Daniel was able to get Nirvana to contribute a track to a Kiss tribute compilation being put together by Steven Stavrakis at Australian label Waterfront, who'd already lined up a number of Australian acts for the record. "He wanted to get some US bands, and so we struck a deal where I would help him to get a number of US bands and make his product more of an international thing," Daniel explains. When Sub Pop passed on licensing the record for US distribution ("They thought it was too gimmicky"), Daniel snapped it up for C/Z.

Krist thinks it was his idea for the band to record 'Do You Love Me,' originally released in 1976 on Kiss's *Destroyer* ("I thought it was kind of rockin'," he says). A quick session was arranged at Evergreen with Greg Babior producing. Greg, who'd been in Slim Moon's band Lush, needed to do a recording for a class project and jumped at the chance to work with a band he'd long admired. "Nirvana was one of my favorite bands that I would always, always go to see wherever they were playing," he says. "I would go to Kurt's place occasionally and he would play me some of the stuff he was working on and we would talk about it. I just thought he was a terrific songwriter. I had a sense that they had a pretty good shot at going somewhere. I certainly never got the impression that they knew that they were going to be as big as they were. But when it happened it didn't surprise me at all. This session felt like a mutual favor kind of thing. I really liked them and I really wanted to record them. And it was convenient for them and they didn't have to pay for the session. So it worked out for everybody."

It was also the only session the band would do with Jason Everman on guitar ("It was my first time in a real recording studio," he says). There was no rehearsal, indicating the lack of seriousness about the project. "Krist just called me up and said: hey, we're gonna be doing these recordings in Olympia," Chad recalls. "I was familiar with the song, but not that well. So when we were on the way to the studio we spent the time listening to the song on tape. It was definitely a very non-serious type of thing." The band-members also shared a gallon jug of red wine between them. "Ernest & Julio Gallo rosé," says Krist. "And then we just went in there and just had fun. Free studio time at Evergreen! That was pretty much it. We just made a spoof on it."

"Quite frankly, I'm a little shocked that we even did it," says Chad. "Because I don't remember Kurt or Krist ever being very much of a huge Kiss fan. I wasn't! So it was kind of a head scratcher, like: why are we doing this song again? What's the point? Ah, who cares. Give me that wine!"

The studio was in Evergreen's Music Building (where KAOS was also located). "There was a smaller room with a piano in it and a larger sort of performance room, and I had them set up in the larger performance room," says Greg. "And one thing that I did, which I think is a really stupid idea now – it was something that I wanted to try out because we'd been talking about it in class – I had them playing in the big room, but I had the amplifiers isolated in the small room. So they were actually hearing themselves on headphones when they were playing. And I wouldn't do that now. I think it'd be really important for them to just be playing like they would normally."

Despite the fact that it was Nirvana's first time in a 24-track studio ("Apparently the board was the exact kind of board that Led Zeppelin used," says Chad), they didn't take full advantage of the new setup. "It was all very straightforward," says Greg. "There really wasn't any special overdubbing. Essentially, it was just the band and then Kurt would go and sing the vocals afterward. Or Kurt and Krist, for the Kiss song. I can't even imagine that we used all 24 tracks."

'Do You Love Me?' would be Nirvana's most shambolic recording, bashed out with gusto if not precision. Unusually, it's also the only song to feature a 'harmony' vocal from Krist, who joins Kurt in bawling out the song's title during the chorus, as well as singing the bridge, which concludes with a nice scream from Kurt at the end (at one point the two drag out the word "money" so it sounds like "Mudhoney"). They really go to town during the fadeout, each adlibbing manically on rival channels until the song collapses into a welter of noise and Kurt finally shouts: "Fuckin' turn it off!"

Of greater interest is the early version of 'Dive' that was also recorded at the session, apparently spontaneously. "I think because of the fact that we were just having fun with that session, that could have been one of those times Kurt decided: well, let's just go ahead and jam this thing out," says Chad. "I don't think we played it that many times before we went in there. I don't think it was something we were planning to record." Kurt later dismissed the song as "yet another re-write of the heavy string-bend grunge formula," but it has a livelier, lighter, feel than *Bleach* material like 'Sifting.' "Kurt and I sat in his garage in Olympia and we put that song together," says Krist. "He had the first part, and then I had the second part, that bridge part, and so we worked on it. We were just sitting around working on it without drums. We started playing off each other, and in not too long a while we had a song. And the next time we had a rehearsal we busted it out. It's just working with dissonance again."

After some menacing opening bass notes, the song explodes into a churning riff that rises in intensity while leading into the chorus. It was one of the few songs where Chad remembers Kurt specifying how he wanted the drums to be played; usually, Chad was free to create his own parts. "When we were going into the chorus, he told me what he heard and showed it to me, like: this is what I want," he explains. "He came up with the drum thing before the chorus. And so I followed that and just went through the song."

The song's lyrics had yet to be completed ("Kurt was busy writing the lyrics as we were listening to the playback," says Greg), but the underlying theme was already fixed: the verses express a desire to be chosen, while in the chorus, it's the singer who's doing the choosing. "I remember him saying something about remembering when he was a little kid and being picked last for a team," says Greg, of an idea alluded to in the phrase "pick me."

At this stage, 'Dive' ran for nearly five minutes. And unlike on 'Do You Love Me?' Kurt was determined to turn in a good vocal performance, startling Greg by screaming repeatedly before recording. "He really sort of worked himself up into a frenzy right before he sang the song!" says Greg. "You'd try to talk to him, but it would just be like he was out on the edge of instinct and reaction. He was concentrating, he was into the song, and wasn't being distracted; like accessing some immediate part of himself." Chad recalls this being a common warm-up technique of Kurt's. "A lot of times before he'd sing a song, even during the *Bleach* sessions, he'd just scream and yell," he says. "That was his way of warming up his voice. There's some live recordings of shows where it starts out with him screaming and he'd do the exact same thing in the studio before he'd sing. It was kind of the backward way of warming up your voice; instead of starting out mellow and getting the vocal chords warmed up, he'd just go balls-out at 'em, right off the bat. Then he figured his voice was ready after that."

Both Greg and Chad feel there was a second session for mixing – and possibly even recording the vocals – attended by Kurt and Krist but not Chad and Jason. "I remember that I actually had some disagreements with them about various things," says Greg. "I pretty much went with what they wanted, except I might've made some changes that I wanted after they left. I remember one of the things I really, really liked was the sound of Kurt's voice, and so I really wanted it as dry as possible and I think they wanted more reverb on it. You'll notice, on 'Dive,' it's just bare; it is just dry as a bone. But the Kiss thing there's a lot more reverb. I think Krist wanted the bass to be louder, but the bass was already pretty loud. I don't remember the details exactly. I know that they were really into the hard pan in the Kiss thing when both Kurt and Krist are doing their little improv rants toward the end of it. They were really into the hard pan; essentially they're both in different channels there, left and right, so you can actually turn your balance on your stereo and hear them individually if you so desire!"

Greg also wanted to capture the sound of the tape stopping after Kurt's demand to "Fuckin' turn it off!" "It was totally exposing the recording process," he explains. "You knew that it was a tape stopping: wow, this isn't a CD, this is something that was recorded on a tape, and the tape is stopping. And I actually always kind of liked that. Because these are big-ass tapes – they're like two-inch huge reel-to-reel things. So when you hit 'stop' on the machine, it doesn't just stop immediately, it kind of slows down, almost like somebody scratching a record." But the concept didn't survive the mastering process. "The thing I picture is, I see the people doing the mastering sitting in there going: What the hell is this at the end! This is so unprofessional, my God, they've got the tape stopping!" says Greg. "So they just faded it out. But that's fine."

When Greg was finished with the final mix of 'Do You Love Me?' he gave it to Kurt, who said: "Oh yeah, thanks. The deadline for this is today." "He hadn't even communicated that it needed to get done or anything like that," says Greg. Greg also recalls that a second song was needed for a split single with Northwest band Alphabet Swill, but the version of 'Dive' is so rough, it's hard to believe it would've been considered for release. Then again, its very roughness may have killed the project. In any event, the song remained unreleased until its appearance on *With The Lights Out*.

Nirvana are known to have performed 'Do You Love Me?' only once, on June 10 1989 at a show in Portland. The Kiss compilation, eventually titled *Hard To Believe*, was finally released in August 1990, shortly after which Chad, by then no longer a member of Nirvana, heard it on the radio. "That song had just disappeared off the face of the earth as far as I was concerned," he says. "I never heard it again until right when the compilation actually came out. And I just laughed – right on, that's funny! I thought it was cool. I remember reading reviews about it, one was talking about it like: 'So and so did this cover, it's pretty cool, and then there's Nirvana. Egads! What the hell were they thinking? Good grief, they could've at least tried.' But I thought that was great. It's a Kiss song! Why try? You have to joke about it. You just have to. You can't get too serious about a song like that. I don't think Kiss did either!"

There were four different versions of the album, with double and single album sets in Australia, and single album editions in Europe and the USA, each with slightly different track listings. There was a final amusing postscript, when Gene Simmons threatened to sue the label for unauthorized use of the Kiss logo and the band's likenesses on the cover. "So I did a whole new package," says Daniel. "It's primarily black, and it says K-I-S-S, but instead of the 'I,' it's a pair of lips. Like a kiss. It's actually Anna Woolverton's lips – the receptionist at *The Rocket*. C/Z was down the hall from *The Rocket*, and I was like: OK, we need a kiss. Who's got the perfect pucker? Who's got the ideal lips for a kind of Marilyn smooch? So I ran down to *The Rocket* and I asked her if she would mind giving me some impressions of her lips to use. And she's like: no, I'd be more than happy! She got her lips all painted and did a number of impressions on some paper, and we scanned it in and used it! It's perfect. And on the inside it says: 'Love ya, Gene, baby! Please don't sue us!'" (To the consternation of completist collectors, this edition featured yet another track that wasn't on any other edition of the album.)

Around the same time, Nirvana opened for Skin Yard at a gig at Green River Community College in Auburn, Washington, on May 26. The band was no longer the shy, timid act Daniel had first seen; now they roamed the stage in front of the 'Elvis Cooper' tapestry, Jason occasionally playing on his back, and the excited crowd shouting out requests.

"It was when it was all exploding, it was all happening," Daniel recalls. "The last time I played with them was also the last time they ever opened for us. They were second on the bill of three, and it was really, really depressing, because it was really, really obvious that everybody was there for them. They played this blistering, amazing, unreal set; it didn't matter how good we could play, there was no way we could play after them. And yet there we were. We were scrambling to get everything on stage, get set up, because people were just filtering out. By the time we went on, there was probably two-thirds of the audience that there had been for Nirvana. And by the time we were done, it was probably down to about half.

"What I felt like was that we were going down the toilet, but what was really happening is that they were just in their ascendency. And we were being just kind of left where we had been. It was very obvious. We were like: well, they're not here for you, dear. You know, that show, they should have headlined. That was it. From there, it was just – it was just over."

CHAPTER 8

Lost In America

"In 1989, it was inconceivable for a band like ours to be on mainstream radio – and forget about television! But there was an alternative universe, and we found it alive and well in most corners of the US."

KRIST NOVOSELIC, *OF GRUNGE AND GOVERNMENT*

Bleach was finally released on June 15, the same month another important event took place: Nirvana signed their first recording contract on June 3. The band, and Kurt in particular, were not entirely comfortable with or trusting of Sub Pop, which is one reason why they paid for the *Bleach* sessions themselves. To add insult to injury, Bruce Pavitt was again forced to call Kurt to ask if he could borrow money in order to release the album. "Which sounds absolutely insane, but that's where we were at financially," said Bruce. "You have to be really shameless." (He eventually borrowed the $5,000 he needed from a friend.)

Kurt had also been reading the industry guide *All You Need To Know About The Music Business* and discussing what he read with Krist (Chad was once again left out of the loop). Some time after the *Bleach* sessions, Bruce Pavitt returned to his home from a party next door to find an angry Krist on his doorstep, demanding that Nirvana be given a contract. Although he was intimidated by Krist's demeanor ("he's a big guy"), Bruce managed to calm him down and promptly contacted his partner, Jonathan Poneman, who cobbled together a one-year contract (backdated to January 1 1989) with two one-year options, offering $600 for the first album, $12,000 for the second, and $24,000 for the third; given the state of Sub Pop's finances, the latter two figures were decidedly fanciful. For Bruce, who championed the indie ethic and didn't believe in contracts, the event had an emotional, as well as a practical, significance. "I remember thinking: this could be important," he recalled.

Bleach's release coincided with another event the label was planning: a June 9 showcase entitled Lame Fest – a name well in keeping with Sub Pop's 'loser' aesthetic. The show, which featured Nirvana, TAD, and Mudhoney was advertised as 'Seattle's lamest bands in a one-night orgy of sweat and insanity!' The venue was the Moore Theatre, which had around 1,500 seats, and usually featured out of town acts. "Three local bands playing at the Moore Theatre was fairly unheard of at the time," says Mudhoney's Dan Peters. "Especially for a ragtag bunch like we all were. When that was being talked about, doing a show there with us as the headliner, and we were all like: are they crazy?"

It was not completely unknown for local bands to play the Moore; Dan's previous band, Bundle Of Hiss, had played an early-80s event called the Northwest Musicians Festival at the venue. ("We played two o'clock on Saturday afternoon to about four or five people," he says.) Craig Montgomery, who did sound at local clubs and worked extensively with Sub Pop acts, was not at all surprised at the scale of Bruce and Jonathan's ambitions. "Maybe they didn't know if they would sell it out, but I think they had a pretty good idea that people would show up," he says. "By then, things were buzzing pretty good about the whole Sub Pop scene, and everybody was wearing all kinds of Sub Pop shirts, and 'lame' this and 'loser' that, Nirvana shirts were popular and stuff. So I think it was pretty well established that there was a fan base out there of whatever size – even if it's only several hundred people, that'll be fine in the Moore Theatre. I don't think it was that big of a stretch. Bruce and Jon were about pushing the envelope, seeing what they could get away with, trying to make things bigger."

Nonetheless, it was still something of a surprise that the show sold out. "It was a definite turning point, that show," Bruce remembered. When Chad arrived at the theater, he looked up at the marquee, thinking it was "kind of cool" to see Nirvana's name there; his parents snapped a picture of the marquee and hung the photo on their wall. Copies of *Bleach* (the initial run on white vinyl) were on sale in the lobby, and selling "like hotcakes," according to Aaron Burckhard. Fan Rob Kader scooped up four, giving a copy to Earnie Bailey, who was attending the show with him. Kurt gave Craig Montgomery a copy. "I was excited about the show," says Craig. "We had a big sound system. It was a chance to do a bigger place and see how it would go."

Nirvana opened, suddenly finding themselves spread out on the biggest stage they'd ever played, Krist stage left, Jason stage right, and Kurt in the center, with Chad on a riser behind him. "We were so used to playing small clubs and stuff, three feet away from each other, pretty much," says Chad. "And here everybody seemed like they were miles away. It was the first time I played a show that was on a really big stage and seeing how much different the sound plays. Because the sound was so much different – it's like you hear some reverberation from the drums, you hear an echo after everything that you play. It struggles with the timing in your head when you're playing – it's almost like there's somebody else playing this right next to you."

The only Nirvana footage from the gig to have surfaced shows the band's final numbers, 'Negative Creep' and 'Blew.' Jason is the liveliest, off to the side, headbanging, "in his own little world," in Chad's words. TAD's Kurt Danielson, who first played with Nirvana at the *Sub Pop 200* release party the previous December, felt the band had much improved in six months, even as he felt Jason's abilities weren't a perfect match for the group. "Oh, they were much better," he says. "Much better. It wasn't the band we would end up touring with in Europe. Yet. And this was partially because of Jason's role in the band. Because he was kind of a hard-rock player, and he had the sort of stage mannerisms, and presence, of more of a guy you'd expect to be playing in Alice In Chains – not to disparage anybody, but just to be honest about pretensions. I mean, some bands have a lot of guitar solos and things like that, whereas Nirvana was the antithesis of that kind of hard rock image. Looking back, it seems very obvious; you could see that in retrospect it was bound to fail, that he wasn't going to last, because he just didn't fit. But he filled some kind of void. Kurt wasn't sure they could pull it off as a three-piece."

For Earnie Bailey, the performance of 'Blew' in particular began changing his mind about Nirvana. Having seen bands like the Pixies at the Moore, he'd already found it "bizarre to see local bands filling the place up. And I remember when they played 'Blew' thinking: wow, there it is again, that really bizarre song. It was the first song that really kind of set a hook for me in terms of having a pop element to it. But it wasn't a pop song, so that was the confusing thing about it; they had such a dirty, sloppy sound, and yet there was a complexity to the pop end of it too. Which I think you figured out the next day, when you couldn't get the songs out of your head when you're at work. Kurt's got a really strange timing thing that he's doing with his guitar; it's like somewhere between a blues riff and something else altogether. I remember marveling: how does he sing and play that at the same time? It just seemed so difficult to do. Listening to what he was playing as a guitar player, and singing on top of it, there's a realization that he's really, really good."

He was more taken aback by the set's ending. As the band ground out the final chords of 'Blew,' Krist began tossing his bass in the air, followed by Kurt swinging his guitar over his head by the guitar strap while running back and forth across the stage, finally throwing himself into Chad's drum kit. "I remember being really caught off guard by that," Earnie says, "Like: wow, what in the world just happened? And Kurt got himself up, and there was just a mess of drums back there, and he comes walking back out to wave goodbye, and he's got his Univox guitar, I believe it was, tangled up in his hair!

It's just hanging from his hair, like dangling off the side, and he's waving goodbye. And I remember thinking it was the most brilliant ending to a set that I had ever seen. That moment right there, that's when everything changed for me. It was really cool. It was hilarious!"

Backlash rated Nirvana's set as "totally intense" and "quite riveting," and chided the bouncers for being so heavy-handed during Mudhoney's set. The *Seattle Times* critic also noted that "the war between the slam-dancers and bouncers upstaged the music." But while acknowledging that this new strata of Seattle bands was gaining in popularity, he was clearly mystified by the performance itself, describing the musicians as "grungy, foul-mouthed, self-despising meatheads who grind out undifferentiated noise." After grudgingly admitting TAD had "more character," he added: "I'm glad after reading Tad's imbecilic lyrics, however, that I could not understand one word of them. ... If this is the future of rock'n'roll, I hope I die before I get much older."

Bleach found a more positive reception in the rock press. Robert Allen, in *Backlash*, noted that the album "occasionally suffers from a sense of detachment" but praised Kurt's vocals and guitar as "the core of Nirvana's sound. His guitar can implode as well as explode – little snatches of tension make 'About A Girl' and 'Paper Cuts' work." The *NME* found the album "slightly top-heavy with too much filler" (citing 'Sifting' as an example), but went on to say: "Nirvana are undoubtedly at their best when they're playing short and punchy songs ... This is the biggest, baddest sound that Sub Pop have so far managed to unearth." In an article for *Melody Maker*, Everett True emphasized the songwriting, which he said was "crafted around a firm base of tune, chorus, harmony. OK, so they might smother them a little with licks that'd do prime-time Sabbath proud, but what the heck?" (In a review I wrote for *The Rocket*, I noted the variation of the band's musical styles "giving a nod toward garage grunge, alternative noise, and hell-raising metal without swearing allegiance to any of them.")

Less than two weeks after the Lame Fest show, Nirvana headed out on their first US tour. It got off to a grueling start when, after a gig at the Vogue on June 21, they drove straight to San Francisco for a show at the Covered Wagon Saloon the following night. They had no road crew, but did have a stash of merchandise – their first band T-shirts, designed by Kurt, and paid for by Jason. The front had an illustration Kurt had seen of the Circles of Hell as depicted in Dante's *Inferno*; the back had a phrase coined by Krist: 'Nirvana: Fudge Packin, Crack Smokin, Satan Worshippin Mother Fucker.' The police would occasionally ask people seen wearing the shirts to turn them inside out because they were deemed 'offensive,' a risk the band-members themselves acknowledged. When Krist gave a shirt to his sister's boyfriend, he warned him: "Don't wear that to my mom's house, 'cause if she saw that she'd throw me out!"

After San Francisco, the band's next stop was Los Angeles, where they did their first interview with a national magazine, *Flipside*, during which 'Kirk' (as he was credited in the story) and Krist unexpectedly plugged the Gyuto Monks. "They are one of the only things that I've ever been affected by off of a record to where it really made me feel spiritual or it made me feel human, like someone was really directing their energies," said Kurt, with Krist adding: "It has a very eerie effect on you." Co-writer/editor Al Kowalewski concluded: "If you like to totally lose yourself on occasion, giving in to loud thundering rock and then fucking diving into brick walls 'cause it feels good, then Nirvana can be just the band to take you there."

The band also did their first in-store performance while in California at Rhino Records in the LA suburb of Westwood. "That whole stage was just slightly shaking," says Chad. "It was bouncing." The 11-song set featured most of the *Bleach* songs (with the exception of 'Paper Cuts,' 'Mr. Moustache,' and 'Swap Meet'), as well as 'Spank Thru,' 'Dive,' and the debut live performance of 'Polly.' 'Blew' was now in place as the standard set closer, which gave the shows a powerful conclusion. "And right before that would be 'Negative Creep,'" says Chad. "So we'd kind of blast ourselves out. In 'Blew,' there's no real intense vocal screaming until toward the end; it's kind of a midrange thing, and he's not really having to stretch his voice out through most of the song. So it gave Kurt plenty of time to give his voice a little bit of a rest from the intensity of doing 'Negative Creep.' And then his vocals were pretty much good and ready to give it out for that final chorus for that song." The tour also marked the last time 'Blandest' was performed live. "I think it's probably because when we recorded it, it didn't come out exactly the way we wanted the song to come out," says Chad. "And maybe Kurt decided: well, it wasn't that good a song."

After California, the tour headed through the Southwest, then up through the Midwest to Michigan and Wisconsin, finally arriving on the East Coast on July 9, when they played Wilkinsburg, Pennsylvania. Attendance at the shows varied greatly. "It was sort of hanging by the seat of our pants," says Chad. "We had some shows that weren't that well attended, then we'd play another show and there'd be a whole bunch of people there. It was just a grab bag." Generally, audiences were bigger on the coasts than the middle of the country. In footage of a show at Rockin' T.P. in Santa Fe, New Mexico – a venue that looks more like a large rec room in someone's house than a club – a small group is shown milling around in front of the band, a few kids bopping away at the edge of the stage, adults shooting pool in the back, and others lounging on hard chairs, seemingly unmoved.

Payment was also erratic. "One show we'd be lucky to get 50 bucks, and we'd have to put it in the gas tank to make it to the next show," says Chad. "And then some places were better. It was just kind of up in the air." There was never money for a hotel, he adds, although there were often people at shows willing to put the band up for the night. "Staying the night at people's houses and stuff was pretty regular for us," he says. If they couldn't find anyone to put them up, they'd end up sleeping by the side of the road. "We were a hardy bunch," Krist recalled from a more comfortable vantage point in 1992. "It was Kerou-wacky." Footage of the tour can be seen on the

DVD in the *With The Lights Out* boxed set; in one scene, the band-members are seen hauling mattresses out of the van to bed down for the night.

"The tour was interesting for me," says Jason. "Although I had traveled quite a bit through Western and Eastern Europe by that point, it was the first time I had really seen and experienced America other than the Pacific Northwest – it was an eye-opener. The only other tour I had done was the Nirvana West Coast tour earlier that year. I really don't remember the bad times, but I'm sure they existed. It was in many ways the same experiences that most bands have on low-budget van tours: buying a single plate for the salad bar at a Wendy's in Texas somewhere, and rotating the entire band through that one plate. Sleeping in the van, or outside, because you don't have a place to stay and no money for a motel. Trying to get enough money from the promoter in order to purchase gas to get to the next town, when in fact he lost money because you played in front of eight people. Getting shaken down by the cops because you're a bunch of unwashed, longhaired guys in a van who mistakenly drove into an upscale neighborhood. Every band has these stories. Kurt never confided in me whether he had a bad time, good time, anything."

"In some ways those early American tours were more brutal than the European ones," says Kurt Danielson, who traveled with Nirvana on a later US tour. "Because in Europe, the touring circuit has been set up for years, and it's a well-worn routine; the hotels are set up, the restaurants, the venues, the promoters, and the distances aren't nearly so great. Whereas in the States you have these immense distances and at that stage you have no crew, you just have yourself, and their van was not in the best condition. We were lucky enough to have the Sub Pop van for some reason – I don't know how we managed that – and it was brand new, so it didn't break down. But luckily Krist is mechanically inclined and knows engines, and before they hit the road he made sure that van was in good shape."

The others adapted to the rough living better than Kurt, who was prone to getting colds. He also suffered from a chronic and painful stomach condition, never properly diagnosed, that he described as "burning, nauseous, like the worst stomach flu you can imagine." The condition would inevitably flare up on tour. "Once he got sick, it would make everyone miserable," said Jason.

On July 13, the band arrived at Maxwell's, a legendary rock club across the river from New York City in Hoboken, New Jersey, where they were to share the bill with TAD. Mudhoney was playing a show with Sonic Youth in New York the next night, so there was a sizeable Northwest contingent in the audience. "The Maxwell's show was fun," says Craig Montgomery, who did sound for the gig. "It was just a typical tornado of a TAD and Nirvana show, stuff getting broken, crowd flying around everywhere. Good time had by all." In footage of the show, Nirvana are clearly having a good time; during 'Love Buzz,' Kurt and Jason seem to be trying to out-do each other in seeing who can headbang the hardest. "They actually played really well," says Dan Peters. "They were really focused. The Sonic Youth guys were in the crowd, and so they wanted to put on their best. I remember thinking they were really great."

It was the first time Sonic Youth's Thurston Moore and Kim Gordon had seen the band perform, although the connection between the two groups dated back to the 'Love Buzz' single, for which Sonic Youth's lighting designer, Susanne Sasic, had devised the label art. "As soon as I walked into the room, I knew there was this total rock-godhead thing going on," Moore later told *Rolling Stone*. "These guys were like the *Children Of The Corn*. They wore ripped flannel, had greasy long hair. Total backwoods freaks." Moore was already interested in the band – he later played *Bleach* to co-producer Ron Saint Germain during mixing sessions for *Goo*, saying he wanted Sonic Youth's record to have the same sound – but was taken aback after the set when the band-members asked him if he would wear a Nirvana T-shirt at Sonic Youth's upcoming show. Nonetheless, it was the start of an important relationship between the two bands. Sonic

Youth had recently signed with DGC, an imprint of Geffen Records, and Gordon had already advised Mark Kates, head of the label's promotions department: "The next band you sign should be Nirvana." ("There's a phrase about A&R people," says Mark. "Some of them have a good nose, some of them have a good ear. Kim and Thurston always had both.")

Sounds writer John Robb was also at the show, accompanied by photographer Ian Tilton. John had been following Nirvana since 'Love Buzz' caught his attention. "I got the single before it was released," he says. "Someone in a shop gave it to me; I'm not sure how they got it so early. No one seemed to like it; people said it was the first bad record on Sub Pop. But I loved it – I thought it was amazing. I loved the singing; it made me think of John Lennon at his raspiest and most soulful. I made it 'Single Of The Week' in *Sounds*." Just prior to the show, after soundcheck, the band went outside with Ian for a quick photo session. Many of his shots have the members posed close together: sitting on steps; playfully leaning against each other while posed in front of what looks like a power station; sitting by the Hudson River, with the Manhattan skyline looming behind them.

"I liked the steps, so arranged the band on there," says Ian. "I also have a photographic thing for industrial structures so placed them in front of that. Krist: very funny and Kurt's good mate. Kurt: quite shy and quiet, humorous, not the obvious leader. Jason: cool, friendly to me, his heavy rock image didn't quite fit. Chad: really funny, positive, happy in a good childlike way, the butt of many jokes – aren't most drummers?" Ian also shot individual portraits of the group, with Kurt, Krist, and Chad relaxed and smiling; only Jason has a solemn expression. He also took shots of TAD and Nirvana in their dressing room, everyone clowning around and grinning.

Nirvana's set had what John Robb recalled as a "cataclysmic" ending, with Krist spinning like a top before diving into Chad's drums, while Kurt determinedly smashes his guitar. "I had seen plenty of footage of The Who smashing their instruments live on stage, but this was different," Ian says. "The Who could afford to do that, but Nirvana were piss-poor. It was so exciting, but I was torn, wondering if they were doing it just for the camera. Someone later told me they did it on a pretty regular basis so it couldn't have been for my lens. I really admired them after that."

"Kurt was just amazing," says publicist Anton Brookes, who was seeing Nirvana for the first time. "I was like: wow, this is just brilliant! Fantastic!'" He considered taking a chunk of Kurt's guitar with him, but wondered: "How am I going to explain a broken guitar at customs?" "It's an awesome demolition job," Robb later wrote. "Nirvana are quite possibly the best rock'n'roll band in the world right now."

There was no time to get a replacement guitar for Kurt for the next show, July 15 at Green Street Station in Boston's historic Jamaica Plain neighborhood, so he was forced to play without one. They spent the night at the home of photographer J.J. Gonson. "They literally, from the stage, said: can anybody put us up?" she recalls. "And we took them home. Because of touring with Hullabaloo [Gonson's boyfriend, 'Sluggo,' was Hullabaloo's guitarist, while Gonson managed the group], and because of shooting bands when they came to Boston, we always put bands up. I'd had endless people come through and sleep on my floor. And because of that I had this relationship with all these people in the Northwest, even though it's so isolated. I was surrounded by the Throwing Muses/Pixies sort of thing in Boston, but the stuff that was coming out of Seattle I knew was really important. I remember Skin Yard coming through, and just knowing that this was not like anything that was happening in Boston – I was like: this is really visceral! I was the only person that knew what was going on in Seattle at that point, in my world. Nobody was paying attention to Seattle. It was not even on the radar. It was all Boston rock."

Gonson was immediately won over by Nirvana. "There were 15 people at that show," she says. "The room was empty. There was nobody there. But it was phenomenal. That show changed my life. There's been maybe two or three times that I can remember watching a band and thinking: this is important. This is not just a band playing music. This is significant and life-changing, and nothing will ever be the same after this moment. I remember walking around for weeks afterward, being like: oh my God, you have to hear this band – they're the best band ever! You should go buy their record right now, because this is important and this band is going to be important. And, really, that's all I could think."

Although she took no pictures at the show, Gonson did shoot pictures of the band at her apartment, capturing Kurt and Krist as they slept on their bedrolls next to her stereo. Kurt also acquired a new guitar by swapping his broken Fender Mustang for a guitar that Sluggo owned. "Sluggo had also just smashed a guitar, but it wasn't as badly smashed as Kurt's, so they traded," says J.J. "And Kurt smashed that guitar a couple nights later. This was what these guys did. They smashed guitars. They were into it. It's like: what the hell, you guys, you don't have enough money to pay rent, and you're smashing guitars!" Kurt autographed his guitar before the trade, writing: "Yo, Sluggo, thanks for the trade. If it's illegal to rock'n'roll, throw my ass in jail." He signed it 'Nirvana.' In 2008, the guitar sold at auction for $100,000.

The guitar smashing had become something of a sore point for Jason, who'd made the biggest financial contribution to the tour. "I was trying to deal with the logistical side of things, and being pragmatic doesn't make for an interesting rock'n'roll narrative," he says. "If you do not have the necessary equipment, it creates a challenging situation in regard to the next performance. In Soundgarden [Jason's subsequent band], I learned that this function is an actual profession with the title of 'Tour Manager.'" It was a sign of a growing unhappiness, for relations between Jason and the other band-members had progressively cooled over the course of the tour. "Yes, I remember by the time we got to the Northeast, things were strained," he agrees. "I'm generally quiet by nature, but was probably talking less by that point."

A schism in musical tastes had been revealed as well. On July 14, the night Sonic Youth played with Mudhoney at The Ritz in New York, speed-metal band Prong was playing at CBGB's. "The show you chose to go to showed your allegiance," says Kurt Danielson. "It was Sonic Youth on the one hand, and Prong on the other. And your choice revealed where your sympathies lay. So you can imagine what Jason chose: Prong! And he was the only one, I think. The rest of us ended up at Sonic Youth. And it was a great show, too. They're a band I've always considered one of the major icons of the age, and still do. Always will. And it was clear that Kurt thought of them that way, even more so, he sort of put them on an even higher pedestal. I think it showed him the rift that existed between himself and Jason, and just Nirvana as a whole."

Amid the increasing tensions, the band returned to New York, where they were set to make their Big Apple debut on July 18 at East Village club the Pyramid. They spent the days before the show at the apartment of Janet Billig, then working at Caroline Records, who distributed Sub Pop's records in the USA, and who routinely let bands sleep on her floor. (She went on to work for Gold Mountain, who would become Nirvana's management company.) Her floor was more crowded than usual that week, with members of TAD and *Sounds'* John Robb and Ian Tilton also seeking out space in the 300-square foot room.

"It was really hot, really humid," says Kurt Danielson – as could be expected of New York City in July. "The Nirvana guys were just exhausted. Kurt didn't even come upstairs at first. It was just Jason, I believe, and maybe Krist followed later, because somebody had to stay in the van to keep an eye on it. That was always the case in New York, if you left a van unattended, it would either get broken into or graffitied very quickly." John Robb, in between tending to Ian, who had been hit by a city bus and was forced to recuperate at the apartment as no bed was available at the hospital, recalled the band having "the burned-out look of a young band at the end of their first toilet tour: suffering from weeks on the road without food, an audience or any acclaim." Craig Montgomery concurs. "The Nirvana guys all seemed really down and quiet," he recalls. "In general, they were tired and road-weary. And also their relationships within the band didn't seem to be going well."

The July 18 show turned out to be the final date of the tour. The show has been described as an off night, but the live video suggests otherwise. While the band plays with less energy than at Maxwell's (even though Jason, wearing a Prong T-shirt, headbangs as usual), they're sharp enough to make it nearly all the way through 'Floyd The Barber' before Jason and Kurt, with a little help from Krist, unceremoniously shove a drunk off the stage. Chad, at the rear of the stage, missed the altercation with the drunk. "When you sit in back there, behind Jason and Kurt and Krist, it's just in the shadows most of the time," he says. "The lights were on them; they blocked me out."

Chad was having more trouble trying to keep his kit together. "This club did not have a rug to play on," he says. "They had a wood floor and a rubber mat. And my drums kept on sliding away. Every other song I'd have to pull the kick-drum up. Drove me nuts!" There was to be no instrument smashing this night: Kurt and Jason simply work to coax more feedback from their guitars while Krist swings his bass back and forth by its strap and talks gibberish into the microphone, after which Jason and Kurt climb on top of him.

The show was not only the last of the tour but also Jason's last performance with Nirvana. There are contradictory versions of his departure from the group. In one account, while in New York, Kurt decided Jason was out of the band, although he only explicitly told Krist. Jason himself told authors Michael Azerrad and Mark Yarm that he had quit, although Krist insisted to Azerrad that Jason didn't quit: "We were just too maladjusted to tell him [he was fired] to his face. We just didn't want to hurt anyone's feelings and that compounded the problem."

"The fact that there was a dearth of communication during these last days of that tour is probably the salient feature of that event," says Jason. "I was definitely done, and I told Chad in most likely those same words. I'm sure Kurt and Krist were 'done' as well. The 'he said'/'she said' quality of these accounts are obvious and tired. I think that the most objective way to sum it up is that it was implicitly mutual.

"I didn't think that the Pyramid show would be my last show with Nirvana," he adds. "I assumed that we would suck it up and finish the tour." But the tour's remaining seven dates were summarily cancelled, and the band drove straight back to Seattle in two-and-a-half days. Legend has it no one spoke during the entire trip; for Jason, things were "not quite that dramatic, but there was some tension for sure. What stands out the most for me, in retrospect, was when they dropped me off in the alley behind my house in the U-District [Seattle's University District], I didn't believe I would see any of those guys again, even Chad, and I was at peace with that. I went into my room, dropped my pack and guitar on the floor, and felt just completely relieved. In a sense, I was free."

The band-members were more open with interviewers about Jason's departure than they were with each other. A few months later, Kurt explained to writer Nils Bernstein: "[Jason] just wasn't into exactly the right type of music, especially for the direction that we're going now." The 'musical differences' theme surfaced again in an interview Kurt did the following year: "We kicked him out 'cause he didn't like to do the songs that we like. He wants to play slow, heavy grunge and we want to write pop songs."

But for Jason, any musical differences were secondary to Kurt's creative domination of the band. He shared Chad's frustration in not being able to contribute more, as Kurt had assured them both would happen. At one of the band's rehearsals, Jason recalls: "Chad, who is a great songwriter in his own right, had a song idea that was summarily dismissed. After that I didn't really consider throwing any of my ideas into the ring." (He offered a more blunt assessment of the situation to Azerrad. "I always felt kind of peripheral ... Basically, anybody besides Kurt or Krist is kind of disposable. At the end of the day, Kurt could get in front of any bass player and any drummer and play his songs and it's not going to sound that much different.")

But Jason has no bad feelings about leaving Nirvana. "I think that musical/artistic differences was a friction point, and probably something that would have most likely led to me leaving the band at a later time anyway," he says. "That, and the fact that I would have been shut out creatively. I think that the popular narrative is that I was this knuckle-dragging heavy-metal guy who just didn't 'get it,' but that's not an accurate assessment. At the end of the day, I just wasn't a good fit for Nirvana, and that is borne out in the way events took place. I have never looked back on that split with regret, and conversely, I appreciate the experiences that I had with Nirvana, both the good and the bad. I have always owned the decisions that I've made, regardless of the outcome, and I have made decisions which entail far more intrinsic gravity than playing with a certain rock'n'roll band or not."

Even those who were unaware of the inter-band dynamics had sensed that Jason was peripheral to Nirvana. "I never felt that Jason was quite 'there,'" says Greg Babior, who produced the one session the band did with Jason. "I always felt that it was sort of like: there's Nirvana, and then Jason." According to Dan Peters, "Jason didn't add anything to the band, as far as I could tell. Not to take anything away from him, but it just wasn't really necessary. I mean, I can see why Kurt might want to be freed up to do some more stuff, but it really didn't add much." Chad also agrees having a second guitarist "didn't make that much of a difference. Because the songs weren't written for two guitar players, you know? And Kurt always played his solos, so, you know, the other guy was just there playing rhythm all the time."

Nonetheless, Kurt would toy with the idea of adding a second guitarist for some time. "There were a lot of guys who wanted to be in the band," says Kurt Danielson. "I know a lot of guys tried out on guitar. And I've heard stories – it's something that Krist never talks about and Kurt never talked about either – but I would hear rumors that said they wanted Tad to play drums. But Tad wouldn't do it because he insisted on doing his own thing. I even heard that Gary [Thorstensen, TAD's guitarist] tried out." Ben Shepherd, Chad's friend and former bandmate in Magnet Men/Tic-Dolly-Row, was also considered, as was local musician Robert Roth. In a game of Seattle musical chairs, Jason would next join Soundgarden on bass after bassist Hiro Yamamoto's departure; Ben Shepherd would then replace Jason in the band; and Robert Roth would team up Yamamoto and Screaming Trees drummer Mark Pickerel to form the band Truly.

Earnie Bailey, for one, felt that staying a trio had other benefits for Nirvana. "Their personality became really apparent then," he says, "because I think that when Jason was out, it just seemed to strip away one identity and reveal another, and that was that you had these kind of goofy small-town guys. And I think that Jason was anything but goofy. I think he was extremely serious. He was just really, really intense, and I think that while Nirvana were intense during the songs, in between songs the tension would go away, and there'd be these really funny moments. Krist would do these funny impersonations of 70s TV show characters, and I remember thinking that I just kind of had an instant friend right there!"

CHAPTER 9
A Matter Of Will

"We're moving towards simplicity and better songwriting all the time."

KURT TO *MELODY MAKER*, 1989

Having returned so abruptly from their East Coast tour, Nirvana had no other shows scheduled. They played only one more date that summer, on August 26, at Seattle art gallery Center on Contemporary Art (CoCA), as part of a two-day showcase of Sub Pop bands. By then, Kurt and Krist had teamed up with Screaming Trees singer Mark Lanegan and drummer Mark Pickerel to form a side project. Pickerel had first seen Nirvana when they played Ellensburg, a city just over 100 miles east of Seattle, the previous April; the show had ended in a fight when Krist leaped off the stage to tackle a bouncer he saw harassing his girlfriend. Pickerel envisioned this new venture as a modern-day blues group, along the lines of Cream or Led Zeppelin.

"We were all becoming big blues fans during a similar point in time," he explains. "I think Lanegan approached me with it 'cause he knew that I was already a big Leadbelly fan and just a blues fan in general. And since Kurt and Krist were both becoming fans of the same genre, we thought it'd be cool to be the first band out of the Northwest that already had some notoriety to try and forge ahead with a different sound or a different vision." Kurt in particular was interested in the work of folk/blues musician Huddie 'Leadbelly' Ledbetter, having discovered his music through an article written by beat author William Burroughs; Slim Moon then loaned Kurt a copy of Leadbelly's *Last Sessions*, after which he became "totally obsessed" with the singer/songwriter.

Initially, the four musicians gathered at Nirvana's Seattle practice space and pored over the blues tapes they had brought with them to pick out songs to cover. "I believe we learned a version of 'Where Did You Sleep Last Night?' from a cassette that I had," says Pickerel. "I think Kurt brought a cassette version of 'Ain't It A Shame'; 'Grey Goose' might've been Lanegan. I think we started exclusively with Leadbelly and then we were going to branch out from there. The idea originally was to just do a session devoted to Leadbelly and then go back in later on and do some other blues artists as well.

"Mark's vocals with Kurt's vocals could've led to something really powerful, I think," Pickerel continues. "But the irony is, it was that combination of those two personalities that slowed things down." Both men had very strong ideas about their own work, and never hesitated to provide direction when working with their own bands, but they seemed to tread lightly with each other. It reminded Pickerel of "junior high kids at a dance, a couple of wallflowers … I felt like I was the cheerleader of the entire session, always making suggestions, and trying to get us to move in a certain direction or to try a certain song or even sometimes suggesting who might sing the song. Neither Mark or Kurt really wanted to take the initiative to make a lot of decisions." It was an attitude that most likely played a role in the project's failure to fully take off.

There was a second rehearsal, and a session at Reciprocal was then scheduled for August 20, with Kurt and Krist staying with Pickerel the night before. The session, produced by Jack Endino, lasted six hours. A total of four songs were recorded, beginning with 'Where Did You Sleep Last Night,' which had Lanegan on lead vocals. "'Where Did You Sleep' was probably the most interesting song," says Jack, "because that was the only really powerful tune that we finished that showed where things could've gone." The stark opening has Krist playing the opening lines solo; the drums come in next, followed by the whine of Kurt's guitar, before Lanegan begins singing in a deep bass growl, his voice rising both in pitch and intensity throughout the number.

Then came 'Grey Goose,' a rather draggy instrumental consisting of a single eight-note melody played through the entire song. "It's fairly forgettable because it's only two chords," says Jack. "It maybe could've turned into something really cool if there had been a really powerful vocal on it." Perhaps the reluctance of anyone to really take charge prevented somebody suggesting that Kurt or Mark provide a vocal. "Everybody was being very polite with each other, but nobody was really running the show," Jack observes.

The energy level increased dramatically with a rollicking 'Ain't It A Shame,' with Pickerel laying down a locomotive beat as the band barrels through the song, Kurt starting his vocal in a low register, then going up an octave after two verses. "That's the selling point," says Pickerel. "And it's really powerful. And then the music gets louder and more aggressive."

"It's almost a joke song," says Jack. "It's like a novelty tune. It was funny, because the bass track is all screwed up. Krist's bass was actually crapping out, there was some bad connection inside it; the signal was going in but it had all this noise on it. So I had to roll all of the high end off it, take all the high end off the bass and sort of compress it and tuck it in the mix. And it works just fine."

The final number recorded was 'They Hung Him On A Cross,' which Kurt performs by himself, revealing the plaintive, expressive voice heard on his home demos but not as yet fully unveiled to the public, either in performance or on record. The session now over, Jack asked if the group had a name, and Pickerel suggested The Jury; hence, the recordings became known as 'The Jury Sessions.' "It's funny now that everybody's calling it The Jury because no one else seemed to be all that excited about the idea at the time," says Pickerel. "Kurt really wanted to call it Lithium. It seemed as though Mark was satisfied with that name but not necessarily excited about it, and I don't remember if Krist had an opinion one way or the other about it, but Kurt definitely did not want to call it The Jury. And the funny thing is, I don't really care for that name anymore. But it's a little late for that."

A session was scheduled for August 21, but no one showed up at the studio, and a three-and-a-half hour session on August 28 was probably just spent mixing 'Ain't It A Shame' and 'Where Did You Sleep Last Night,' according to Jack. "I think at that point they had figured well, all we have is two songs that are finished, so maybe we'll have Sub Pop put out a seven-inch, and Mark sings one and Kurt sings the other," he says. "And that's kind of where they left it. I mixed the two songs and spliced them onto a reel and I called it 'The Jury seven-inch' and put it on the shelf. And then plans changed or something; Sub Pop never ended up putting it out and we ended up taking 'Where Did You Sleep Last Night' and putting it on Mark's first solo record [1990's *The Winding Sheet*] instead. We ended up remixing it."

'Ain't It A Shame' became particularly legendary over the years, especially after Jonathan Poneman said it featured "one of Kurt's greatest vocal performances." It was finally released, along with 'Grey Goose' and 'They Hung Him On A Cross' on *With The Lights Out*. But The Jury never reconvened again, leaving Mark Pickerel to wonder if things could have turned out differently. "Who knows what we might have done if we'd been able to get together once a year for a couple weeks?" he says. "Lanegan and I have massive record collections, so there would've been a wealth of music for us to listen to, to learn from, research, and recreate. I really regret that it didn't happen."

Soon after the Jury sessions, a Nirvana session was arranged; European dates were being scheduled for the fall, and Sub Pop wanted to have an EP ready for the tour. The band had five new numbers to record, with only 'Polly' and 'Stain' having been performed live ('Stain' had made its debut at the August 26 CoCA show). Lyrically, the songs were as brief as those on *Bleach* – 'Even In His Youth' and 'Stain' each have a single verse – but the musical feel was much lighter, with a decided move toward pop.

"A lot of the time it was kind of hard to say what direction Kurt wanted to go," says Chad. "But I definitely remember talking about how he wanted to get things a little bit more pop oriented. He didn't want to lose the heaviness, he wanted to keep that, but just get things a little more pop-wise than just, I dread to say this, grunge-wise. That started showing up a lot more on this session; there wasn't anything like a 'Sifting' or a 'Scoff.' There wasn't anything up-tempo like a 'Mr Moustache,' nothing brutal like 'School.' But I didn't see them as being that much different. They were just a little more pop, a little more along the lines of 'About A Girl,' so they felt really comfortable. The progression that we made felt pretty natural. Kurt was pretty much a pop songwriter in the first place, just putting a harder edge on the whole thing."

Playing shows more consistently – the US tour was the first time Nirvana had played so many consecutive shows within a month – undoubtedly pushed Kurt into thinking about where he wanted to take the band artistically. "Grunge rock was just some mutant form of heavy metal, and you can only mutate it so much," says Krist. "Kurt as a songwriter was developing. We'd listen to other bands' records, bands that were getting touted for something or other, and Kurt would get all pissed off and say: where's the song? I don't hear the song. He honed his skills, developing, in a song, where hooks are, just kind of going for hooks. If you're going to go for hooks, you might as well get into pop music. What's more hooky than a good pop song?" Kurt himself pointed up the band's growing pop tendencies to *The Rocket* later that year. "We're writing a lot more pop songs, like 'About A Girl' – some people might think of that as 'changing' into something, but it's something we've always been aware of and are just now starting to express," he said.

But as was typical of Nirvana's songs, the pop mood was matched with a darker lyric. The upbeat 'Stain' has an interesting lyrical twist in that the sole verse (which is repeated three times), describing a lonely, luckless outsider, is in third person, while the chorus (a single line) reveals the outsider to be the narrator himself. The more mournful-sounding 'Even In His Youth' is a variation on the same theme of inadequacy, and even has a similar construction, with a single verse (repeated twice) sung in third person, and a chorus sung in first person. It's tempting to read an autobiographical element into the lyric about a man who's been a disappointment to everyone in his life from childhood on, especially his father; the "yeah, yeah" at the end sounds especially downcast. (A lyric from one of the Fecal Matter songs, about keeping one's body clean, also resurfaces.) For whatever reason, the song was only briefly performed live, during the fall European tour.

'Been A Son' is an especially catchy number addressing society's preference for boys over girls. (It is also said to refer to Don Cobain's feelings about Kurt's sister, although Kurt never specifically addressed this.) 'Token Eastern Song,' built around a droning bass riff, was the only number without an underlying message. "Oh, that's all my fault," Krist says. "I came up with that stupid bass line and named the song 'Token Eastern Song' to get myself off the hook. The bass line ruined it. See how important a bass line is to a song? Everybody thinks the bass player doesn't do anything. They don't know anything about rock'n'roll. It can make or break a song, and I broke it." Despite Krist's reservations, the song's main riff is actually quite appealing, with the same hypnotic groove of 'Love Buzz' (a song that also has a touch of Middle Eastern flavor). But the band would quickly find it unsatisfying, and after four months of performing it live would drop it from the setlist.

The session was set up at a new studio for the band, the Music Source, located in Seattle's Capitol Hill neighborhood. The studio, which opened in 1969 as the Music Farm, primarily catered to commercial clients, but recorded rock bands during the week after 6pm and on weekends. "We had three 'celebrity consoles,'" says Steve Fisk, one of the studio's producers. "One console, the original *Ghostbusters* soundtrack was tracked on it, but that was done some place back in New York. One was from [radio program] *Prairie Home Companion*, and one was from Steve Miller's old home studio." Although it was still a small studio, the Music Source was substantially larger than Reciprocal, and would mark the second time the band recorded in a studio with a 24-track set up.

Jonathan Poneman set up the sessions, asking Steve to produce. "He called me when I was working with some other bands and asked me if I wanted to work with Nirvana," says Steve. "And I said: yes." Steve was another Evergreen student, who had worked at KAOS and been in Tiny Holes and War With Elevators with Bruce Pavitt. He had been in numerous other bands, and also worked as a producer; while working at Velvetone Studio in Ellensburg, he produced Screaming Trees, Soundgarden, and Beat Happening, among others. He'd been at the same Nirvana show in April 1989 that Mark Pickerel had attended, and ended up walking out. "Basically, it wasn't as if Nirvana was so bad, it just was that it was so loud and unlistenable," he says. "It was hurting my ears. And the PA guy had a sleeveless black T-shirt and was folding his arms like everything was cool."

The exact dates for the sessions aren't known, but it's believed to have been in September. "They came in for one night, like a Wednesday or Thursday, and then they came in the next week to do the overdubs and the mixing," Steve says. "I forget why it got separated like that. I think back then there was this whole thing about giving bands a lot of control over the process. With Screaming Trees, for example, they would track something and mix it the same evening, but that was just taking it too fast. So with Nirvana, we recorded all the basics and rolled roughs the first night, and then we got back the next week and did the vocals and the guitar parts. And then the mix-downs was all about working on sounds on all of that."

The first step was trying to get the band's gear into workable shape. "Novoselic had been running around all day trying to get things fixed up, because they'd been knocking things around a lot," says Steve. "There was two 15-inch speakers in this cabinet; one of them didn't work, even though it was supposed to be fixed, and it made a real low distorted tone. And the other one that did work didn't work that well. And I think the amplifier was messed up too, so we spent a long time working on the bass and trying to get something useable out of it. There was no bassiness for the bass; it was just 'rrrrr,' and not in a good way. It was kind of low volume, and very uninteresting.

"And the kick drum was cracked like the Liberty Bell," he continues. "It had reams and reams of duct tape wrapped around it to hold it back together. And you understand about those drums? How they fit in music history and how weird and interesting it was that Nirvana used them? Well, they were made for jazz-fusion drummers that needed to make a lot of noise. So the kind of elegance or subtlety that you might have in wooden drums was just completely out the door. These were for live use and they were for maximum volume. And they always had a double kick drum and way too many tom-toms. And because [the shells] were made out of molds, they all sounded exactly the same; the tom-toms just sounded like samples of each other. There was no difference in them at all. And that was one of the things that I thought was an egregious thing on the *Bleach* record is all the insane tom-tom stuff. Jack told me how he did the tom-toms, so I sort of mimicked his miking of them, and then Chad hit the tom-toms I think six times in the whole session! There were no tom-tom songs, there were no tom-tom fills or anything."

As before, the band had to operate on a small budget. "Sub Pop was broke," says Steve. "They wanted to do everything as cheap as possible, so any corner we could cut, we would cut; we recorded on used tape." On the upside, there was less pressure. "We weren't pressed for time," says Chad. "We weren't sitting there trying to crank out an entire album in a week like we did with *Bleach*. Steve spent more time on certain things, like when we were working on the snare sound we spent an hour and a half just listening to the snare drum and trying to get that right."

"The songs were together," Steve says. "They didn't record 'em quick; they did a lot of trying it again. There was a little tension, some talking to each other in between takes. I just tried to help; I didn't really have any great ideas." No out-takes were saved. As at Reciprocal, if the band didn't like a take, they'd simply record over it. "They'd just say: hey, let us do it again," says Steve.

For recording, Kurt and Krist's amplifiers were put in isolation booths off the main room with the doors left open. "The idea was that they weren't aiming into each other's mics," Steve explains. "So the drums could be open in the room, and then no one had to wear headphones. I didn't invent that, that's just a good way to record rock bands, because if you don't have to have headphones, everything just comes out a lot better. In fact, if I recall, I think Kurt also sang without headphones – and was really businesslike about it."

'Stain' was the first song to be recorded. "These were relatively fresh songs," says Chad. "We didn't really spend a whole lot of time working on them. So although I liked 'Stain,' it was one of those where I wished I would've had the opportunity to spend more time on it." In addition to doubling his vocal, Kurt also doubled his guitar solo. "Just like Screaming Trees!" says Steve. "And they lock together a couple places and a couple places they go out and do different things. You get a little bit of Thin Lizzy in there. If you listen to the version on *Incesticide*, they're on the left and right channels, both equal volume, like squabbling hens. And that's exactly how you do Screaming Trees records. And if I would've explained about not saying 'fuck' so much in the lyrics, that song could've been a hit! That could've been a really big song. But I just didn't have the forethought then as a record producer to say: Kurt, you can't say 'fuck' that many times. It just won't fly on the radio."

'Been A Son' was next. The previous December, Kurt had hesitated to suggest recording 'About A Girl' for *Bleach*, fearing it was too poppy; now he readily doubled his vocal to provide, in Steve's words, "*Rubber Soul*, John Lennon kind of harmonies. Just a lot of descending parallel thirds and fourths and all of that." A sticking point for Krist was the song's bass solo, which he never liked. "It probably would've been better having a guitar solo than a bass solo," Steve admits, "but I was into the idea of trying to do something weird with it. The thing about the bass solo is, it peters out. It starts really strong, and then it kind of dribbles off. It's this bass solo that's twice as loud as the song, so when it stops the band sounds kind of wimpy. The bass is one of those instruments that you can't turn it up and down. It's sort of like raising and lowering the floor; you notice when it goes back down."

'Stain' and 'Been A Son' were the only tracks to be finished; the remaining songs had no overdubs and only scratch vocals. "The overdubs all happened in the second session," Steve explains. "We were going to work on all of the songs, but we just worked on these two first and then the other three we never got to. But we were supposed to finish the other three. That was always the plan."

'Even In His Youth' is the most noticeably unfinished of the songs. The lyrics had yet to be finalized, nor had a solo been worked out for the instrumental break that follows the second chorus. "You can tell there's nothing going on there – a solo's supposed to happen here or something," Steve says. "Or some kind of flashy guitar business. We would have never called that done. You can also hear Kurt doesn't do his big screams live. He holds back. The folk myth is that his chest hurt, he had that stomach weird thing, in the solar plexus, so when he hit a big note it hurt. Or maybe he couldn't hit the note and keep playing the guitar, and he wanted to get the guitar right and was going to re-do the vocals." This version of the song also opens with 15 seconds of guitar squalling (similar to the improvisations on 'Endless Nameless,' the 'hidden' track at the end of *Nevermind*) that wouldn't appear on the later version of the song, recorded in January 1991 at the same studio and released as a bonus track on the 'Smells Like Teen Spirit' single.

The session marked the first time the band would record 'Polly,' this time as a full band, electric version. "We'd done different versions," says Chad. "Sometimes it was strictly acoustic, and sometimes there was drums in it; we were always trying out different things. It had a lot of transformations in a way, but always still structurally kept the same, with the lyrics and the basic song idea and stuff like that." In this version, there's a rather awkward shift from the relatively quiet beginning into a louder, more 'rock' performance. "They were having a hard time getting that to gel," Steve says. "And you can hear it in the take; it starts fast and then it slows down. I think that's the reason they didn't want to use it." It would take two more attempts in a studio before the song would be fully worked out.

'Token Eastern Song' was the last to be recorded, and seems like something of an afterthought. "I don't think I played that song more than a handful of times before we went in the studio with it," says Chad. "It's was one of those things where Kurt goes: I've got an idea for a song I've been working on a little bit. Here's what it's like. Let's jam on it. And it's like: OK, let's try it. And we pop in the studio the next week and it's like: hey, let's try that one song. So we try it, and it sounds like we haven't spent all that much time on it, like it was something we just kind of quickly whipped out." It was the only time the song would be recorded with vocals, and Chad, for one, feels it was a song with some potential. "Who knows how that song would've turned out if we'd had a chance to actually put in the time?" he asks.

However, only 'Stain' and 'Been A Son' were worked on at the next session, with a lot of time spent working on the drum sound. "We were talking about making the snare bigger," Steve explains. "I was playing with early-80s ideas, with mid-80s toys. We had a very expensive digital reverb that we were fooling with, and I told them it was the kind of thing you would use in a different situation if you were trying to make something sound like silly radio shit. We had three tracks with exactly the same guitar part, and exactly the same EQ – one in the middle, one on the left, one on the right – and we were turning those down and turning the snare up. And Kurt got all excited about it, 'cause then it was a good Top 40 drum sound."

Kurt and Krist were equally excited to hear 'Been A Son' booming out over the studio's large monitors. "I don't think they had played a lot with giant monitors," says Steve. "And they really liked these because they were so big and silly and huge sounding. And when 'Been A Son' was done, Kurt and Krist asked: can we jump on the tables? Can we dance on them? I said OK, so they jumped on one table and I jumped on another, and it's like me and Krist were almost up to the ceiling – Chad was in the other room watching TV or something like that. And we listened to the song, and we rocked. And it was like: Ah! That's cool! That's fucking cool. Not a lot of people ever got to do that. I got to do that. I got to nail the mix and jump up on the furniture and rock with Nirvana. That's fucking cool."

'Been A Son' and 'Stain' would appear on the upcoming *Blew* EP; 'Even In His Youth,' 'Polly,' and 'Token Eastern Song' would remain in the vaults until the release of *With The Lights Out*. "They were talking to me about working on their next album, which would've been *Nevermind*," Steve recalls. "They were talking about they had a lot of money to spend, because Jonathan was going to let them spend $10-12,000 on their next record, and that they really liked working at the Music Source, and they liked working with me, and they wanted to talk about working some more. Kurt's one of the best singers I've ever worked with. And they were really nice, really cool, really polite, really demonstrative, and really appreciated everything we did." Nirvana did later return to the Music Source, but they would not work with Steve Fisk again.

One reason the *Blew* sessions are assumed to have been in September is because Steve recalls that the band was about to head out on another US tour, possibly even leaving on the night of the second session. A brief tour had been arranged, beginning September 28 in Minneapolis and ending October 13 in Boulder, Colorado, to make up for the dates they'd cancelled at the end of the previous tour. Ben Shepherd, who was then in consideration as the band's second guitarist, came along for the ride. He had rehearsed with the band before they hit the road, but says that in the end he "really didn't do anything except be a friend on tour. I was always like: you guys should just stay a three piece."

"We went back to being a three piece and stayed that way for a while," says Krist. "Try to make it interesting. I thought Kurt and I had a pretty good interplay between guitar and bass. Kurt was a very unconventional guitar player: very original and just dissonant, and melodic too. Some guitar solos would just be wack – kind of Greg Ginn-crazy. And the song: if it wasn't some pounding kind of riff-song, vocal melodies were the clincher. So it just seemed to work, the three piece. There was a good dynamic."

During the tour Ben was able to see how devoted the band's fans had become. After an October 8 show at the Lifticket Lounge in Omaha, Nebraska, the audience refused to let the band leave. "You guys didn't play all your songs, man," they protested. "You skipped out on us last time, come on! Play the rest of 'em." After that, Ben recalls, "they came back on rather sheepishly and blew the fucking doors off the place."

Without Jason, the trip was free of the underlying tensions of the previous US tour, and the band passed the time listening to music during the long drives. Everyone picked up on each other's tastes. "They introduced me to The Vaselines," says Chad. "I introduced them to Shonen Knife." Shonen Knife were a Japanese pop-punk trio whose songs tended to focus on 'cute' subjects like food and animals. (Sample song titles include 'I Like To Eat Chocobars,' 'Fruit Loop Dreams,' and 'I Am A Cat.') K Records was the first label to release Shonen Knife's work in the USA, beginning with the 1983 tape *Burning Farm*, while 'One Day At The Factory' had appeared on *Sub Pop 100*, making it curious Kurt hadn't heard of the band before, although he quickly became a fan.

The Vaselines were a Scottish group, based around the core duo of Eugene Kelly and Frances McKee, whose light music and lilting voices made their tales of sexual obsession sound even more twisted.

As Krist later noted, theirs was "simple songcraft, and at the same time there was a lot of sexual innuendo." Nirvana would soon add 'Molly's Lips' – said to have been about Scottish actress Molly Weir, star of the TV series *Teatime Tales* and *Rentaghost* – to their setlist. Kurt referred to them as "my favorite group ever."

Chad also piqued Kurt's interest in another performer who would have an influence on Nirvana's act. "When we were in Boston I went to a record shop, and I found David Bowie's *The Man Who Sold The World* album," he says. "It had a poster inside, which I thought was great. And whenever it was that we next stayed at some people's house, I bought some blank tapes and recorded some of the records that I'd bought on tape. I'd never heard them listening to David Bowie before, and when I played the tape Kurt looks back and says: what are we listening to? I said: David Bowie. And he goes: really? I go: yeah, you guys listen to much David Bowie? He says: no, not really – this is cool! I said: hell yeah, it's David Bowie! I think they were more familiar with stuff like 'China Girl' and 'Let's Dance' and things like that. But I grew up with records like *The Man Who Sold The World* and *Hunky Dory* and especially *Ziggy Stardust & The Spiders From Mars*; those were pretty staple records that I listened to a lot." (When Nirvana later performed a cover of 'The Man Who Sold The World' on MTV's *Unplugged* in 1993, it would provide the show with one of its most poignant moments.)

The tour was not without its drama, however. After the Minneapolis gig, Kurt collapsed from stomach pain and missed a few shows. "Krist said he took Kurt to the emergency room, that his stomach was giving him a great deal of trouble, and that he hadn't been able to eat," says Kurt Danielson. "Like when Krist would stop and eat a hot dog somewhere, Kurt wouldn't eat, or if he did, he threw it up. I remember after that Krist became a vegetarian, because of those very hot dogs." Krist had wondered if the "crap food" Kurt tended to eat was in part responsible for his stomach problems.

According to Kurt Danielson, Kurt himself felt there might have been a relationship between his stomach ailments and his singing. "He and I talked about this," he says. "I told him I thought his singing was good, I liked what he did. There was something sinister about it, yet very melodic, and I wondered how he could do it. And he said that it was a matter of will, but that he had these stomach problems at the same time and he wondered if they were connected. And I don't know if he continued to think that; maybe that was just a passing fancy. And it seemed that his stomach would bother him most when he was on the road; this may have been because of the bad food, it may have been because of the singing. I don't know. It's a mystery. What I could never understand is why it was never properly diagnosed, considering all the medical attention he got later."

More crucially, while in Colorado on October 12, Kurt purchased a used 12-string Stella acoustic guitar for $32.21. "He put nylon strings on it, six of them," Krist recalls. "And it would never stay in tune. So he would tighten down the screws on it as tight as he could, so when he wanted to tune it he had to use pliers." Defective as it was, Kurt found a way to make the guitar work for him, and he would use it on two of Nirvana's most evocative recordings.

"He always had some new tool to explore with, and he'd come up with cool stuff," says Krist. "He'd smash a guitar and we'd go find him a guitar. And I had this habit for years, I don't do it anymore, but I used to walk by pawnshops and I'd out of habit just look for a left-handed guitar: there was the cool guitar I saw in Tacoma, you gotta get it, it's a great deal, or whatever. Or it's a guitar you could string up left-handed and it would work. We were at this party at Evergreen or somewhere, and somebody had this Mustang: a left-handed Mustang, all stripped down. And I'm like: hey, you want to sell that guitar? He goes: yeah. I go: how much do you want for it? He goes: oh, I don't know, I'll take 50 bucks. And Kurt and I looked at each other and we go: whoa! We were just running to go get 50 dollars. And Kurt was so into it: it's a Mustang! He was totally into it. It was a left-handed Mustang. He strung it up. Then he painted it. And he ended up smashing it, but he was into it, so he would play it all the time 'cause he just got a guitar. So we would write all these songs on it. Whenever he got a new guitar he'd be totally into it. So it was always good to get Kurt a new guitar. He'd bust something out on it." Kurt later designed his own custom guitar, the Jag-Stang, which melded together elements of two Fender guitars, the Mustang and the Jaguar.

The fall of 1989 was shaping up to be a busy time for the band. A week after the make-up tour ended, Nirvana, along with TAD, headed to Europe, for their first overseas tour.

CHAPTER 10
Innocents Abroad

"The good God grunge is getting ready for a new kinda kick."
JOHN ROBB IN *SOUNDS*, 1989

Mudhoney were understandably the first Sub Pop band to venture overseas, as the band's 1988 EP, *Superfuzz Bigmuff*, had been on the UK indie charts for a year. They first toured the UK and Europe in the spring of 1989, opening for Sonic Youth for half of the dates. "When we went out with Sonic Youth, we were playing in front of packed houses every night and it was incredibly insane for us," Dan Peters remembers. "We never expected anything like what was going on – to be able to just go out and play shows and tour and stuff – and it was just crazy to us. I remember at one point someone saying: oh, yeah, you'll be able to headline those venues next time you come to Europe or England."

A May 12 date at London's School of Oriental and African Studies (SOAS) became particularly chaotic, after singer Mark Arm jokingly announced: "I'd like to take this opportunity to invite everybody to join us on stage" after a few songs, provoking a stampede that nearly toppled the stage. It was a performance later hailed as the first big grunge experience in the UK. "I remember seeing Mudhoney when they came over, and it was just phenomenal," says publicist Anton Brookes. "Every time they played there was a stage invasion, and the venues would just go mad, especially at things like 'Touch Me I'm Sick.' It became an anthem. It was just like: wow!" Such a response not only raised Mudhoney's profile but also Sub Pop's. "That tour had a tremendous impact," says Kurt Danielson, "and it had a lot to do with the fact that our tour was even possible. Because there wouldn't have been enough of a potential audience to invest in such a tour without the interest created and generated by Mudhoney."

As a result, there was much anticipation about the Nirvana/TAD tour, which was scheduled to begin October 23. The tour would encompass 36 shows in nine countries, with the bands swapping headlining duties at each show. *NME*'s Edwin Pouncey had already written favorably about *Bleach*, and in an article that previewed the upcoming tour, he was just as enthusiastic: "By the time they tour Europe this coming October, Nirvana's future as the next BIG thing will be in the bag." For the first time, Nirvana would be touring with both a tour manager, Edwin Heath, and a live sound mixer, Craig Montgomery. Craig, from Seattle, had started out as a musician, playing in local bands The Happy Campers ("We played punk rock at frat parties, which was cool, because nobody else was doing that – it was all Bob Seger covers or whatever") and power-pop act Pure Joy. But he gradually moved into sound engineering, first working for Room Nine then mixing sound at the Squid Row club. While working at Yesco/Muzak, he met Jonathan Poneman and Bruce Pavitt, and soon began doing sound for Sub Pop bands on a regular basis.

Craig had already done sound for Nirvana on a few Seattle dates, but didn't really get to know the band-members until the European tour. "Chad was the sweetheart, one of those people who's the nicest person you could ever meet," he recalls. "You wish you could be as nice as Chad. Always had a positive attitude about things; he's the kind of person who just sees the good in everybody, doesn't have anything bad to say about anyone. Krist is like … I hate to say the 'hippie stoner,' 'cause I don't think he was a hippie or a stoner, but that kind of an intellectual, you know? But also super-hilarious. The best analogy I could ever think of for him was he was like Andy Kaufman – that kind of humor. Kurt was a little more impenetrable. He loved to laugh, super-funny, very dry sometimes, and his humor could be pretty cutting. Also, with Kurt I kind of had the vibe that he had had a hard life; that he'd been through a lot as a kid – sort of similar to my childhood in some ways, although his was much more drastic. He and I got along pretty well. But he was the kind of guy that … the social lubricants that we all use just to make things easier on each other, he wasn't great at that. If you were going to talk to him, you had to have your homework done or he would call you on it. He wasn't always very tolerant of people's shortcomings."

Everyone was excited about the tour, the first trip to Europe for both bands. "I couldn't believe that we'd actually made it out of America," Krist said. "People seemed to know who we were. And it seemed to us that we were more popular there than we were at home." On arrival in London on October 21, Nirvana found they'd made the cover of *Sounds*, albeit a split cover, with Tad Doyle, billed as 'Seattle's biggest bulk export' taking up most of the space, along with the pungent headline 'Tad & Nirvana: Grabbing America By The Balls.' A flyer with tour dates issued by Glitterhouse, Sub Pop's UK distributor, added further hype: "Worth going! Worth kissing! Worth f***ing!" A poster for a November 25 date in Switzerland billed the show as 'Heavier Than Heaven R 'n' R From Seattle,' leading it to be belatedly dubbed the Heavier Than Heaven tour. The tour's own itinerary billed it as the Bleach God's Balls tour, *God's Balls* being the title of TAD's 1989 debut album.

There was a day off before the first show at the Riverside in Newcastle, England. Mudhoney had previously played a "brilliant" gig at the club, local fan Chris Knight later recalled, "so Newcastle was really ready for Nirvana." Newcastle wasn't disappointed. Having had time to recover from jet lag, Nirvana turned in a strong performance. "It was a crazy gig," Craig remembers. "It was stuffed full of people." Knight was especially taken with Kurt's voice ("I couldn't understand how a fella with such a little frame could produce a gravelly voice that had so much pain in it"), while Jim Maudsley, another attendee, was overwhelmed by Krist's performance. "I was stunned by the height of the man and the lunatic way he jumped around," he said. "You just knew that this band was going to happen." After the show, Nirvana were surprised to meet fans who'd come all the way from Aberdeen, Scotland, to meet them. "It was pretty awesome," Chad recalls, "because they all came up to us, a group of maybe 11 or 12, and they were like: you should come to Aberdeen! in these thick Scottish accents that I really had to bend my ear to understand. We had a great time; they came to our green room and we bullshitted with them for a while. I was like: hell yeah, I'd tour in Scotland, that'd be fun!"

Edwin Heath was a bit more dismayed by the antics of his charges, especially when Krist smashed his bass through his amp during the very first show. It's been said he did it in response to being hit in the head with a beer bottle, but Craig suggests the quality of the band's rental equipment may also have played a role. "The gear that's been rented for both bands to share, it's not really a great fit for the way they play," he explains. "For bass, these guys need a big, powerful tube bass amp, and what they got was this smaller, more high-tech Trace Elliot amp, and it just wasn't happening, sound-wise. It was frustrating; the amp was clipping out before it got loud enough, and not making enough low end. I don't really know what motivated them to smash gear, but on Krist's part probably some frustration and probably a lot of alcohol. And he was just the kind of drunk that gets out of control. I don't think that's news. So he started smashing his bass into the bass speakers, and I guess he perforated one or more of them.

"So before our next show, in Manchester, we had to go back down to London to the place where we had rented all the backline gear, and swap out the damaged stuff," he continues. "And this time we got the right kind of bass amp. I think we got another bass cabinet, but we had to power the bass amp with a Fender Twin guitar amp the rest of the tour; we had to do this hodgepodge of stuff, but we managed to make that hodgepodge last the rest of the tour. I didn't really take the gear smashing personally, myself. Maybe a little bit, 'cause I don't run my life with that kind of abandon – I would be thinking, geez, we got another show to do tomorrow, guys. And it would affect me in that it would make our next day a lot more difficult; instead of having whatever time to relax, we'd have to be solving all these problems. I can't help but think of the consequences of my actions. And I guess that's why I am who I am and other people are famous rock stars."

After shows in Manchester and Leeds, Nirvana returned to London on October 26, where they taped a radio session for the *John Peel* show at the BBC's Maida Vale Studios in Studio 5. Although the band had been impressing British audiences with their aggressiveness, they chose to stress their pop side on the program. As with their last radio appearance on KAOS, Kurt called the shots. "I think Kurt already had in his head the idea of what songs he wanted to do," says Chad of their radio appearances. "He was the one who was picking the songs; he was like: I'd like to do this song; you guys want to do this song? I was like: sure, I'll do whatever song you want to do. It was a more relaxed atmosphere, doing radio shows; it wasn't like we were in the studio and OK, this really matters, we have to do this totally perfect sort of a deal. There wasn't that kind of pressure. And there were certain songs that we did, like we played 'Love Buzz' because it was a pretty big hit and it was expected of us to play it. There was always a couple songs with doing the radio stuff that we played mainly because those would be the songs that people would want to hear."

Unsurprisingly, the Peel session opens with the band's first single, 'Love Buzz.' The pace is brisk, and while Kurt's vocal is somewhat subdued, he stretches out a bit on the guitar solo, conveying some of the playful energy of the band's live shows. Next up is 'About A Girl,' the rasp in Kurt's voice clearly revealing the exertions of having just sung three nights in a row. Then came 'Polly,' a somewhat surprising choice considering that the song had yet to be released. The instrumental backing was more restrained than on the version the band had recently recorded with Steve Fisk, coupled with a new element: a harmony vocal from Kurt, taking it a step closer to how the final version of the song would sound. The session closes with a confident, full-bodied performance of 'Spank Thru.' The session's producer, Dale Griffin, found the band to be well rehearsed ("All too often not the case with many bands, especially on the John Peel sessions"), and like other Peel shows, the session was recorded onto two-inch tape, then mixed onto quarter-inch tape; the two-inch tapes were then recorded over for the next session, meaning the multi-tracks were lost forever. The show was broadcast the following month, on November 22, but has yet to be released officially despite being bootlegged extensively.

The next day, Nirvana played SOAS, the same venue where Mudhoney had created such a stir the previous spring. After months of reading about the band in the music press, a London audience was finally going to see Nirvana, and anticipation was high, drawing another large crowd. "When you play at a college, the college kids will show up," says Craig. "It almost doesn't matter what it is. It was in a college cafeteria room, with a temporary stage, and speakers up on tables. The stage couldn't take the bouncing, so it was really bouncing up and down. There was little or no security; they weren't prepared for the ferocity of the crowd reaction. There are famous pictures out there of that show, people getting up on top of the speakers and jumping off into the crowd. We were used to this by now. The main thing I felt was dread – these things are so out of control, and if they're going be in these environments, where there really isn't much thought for safety or security, somebody's going get hurt. Fortunately, nobody did, seriously. You might see a bloody nose or a tooth get knocked out or something, but nothing serious. Nobody breaking their neck or anything. Nobody carried out on a stretcher."

Anton Brookes felt the venue "wasn't as full as when Mudhoney played," but nonetheless thought the show was "just amazing. You could tell they were a special band. I suppose because of their attitude, everything – I remember seeing Soundgarden at a soundcheck, and thinking: wow, these guys are going to be big. You could tell. It was an air about them. And it was the same with Nirvana. They had an air about them, but they were quite unassuming. They just had something special, they just had this real poppiness, the most catchy little songs ever. From one extreme to the other, you'd have something like 'Negative Creep,' which is just riff central – it's just a belligerent sound – and then you've got 'Love Buzz,' which is just beautiful. Even now, you can listen to *Bleach* and a few tracks will be dated, but other tracks still sound good today."

Also among those in attendance was *Sounds* journalist Keith Cameron, who would go on to be one of the band's biggest supporters. "I was really into Mudhoney, and Nirvana were being mentioned as the next great band on Sub Pop," he says. "I remember hearing *Bleach* in the *Sounds* office, early summer '89, and I thought it was amazing: great rhythm section, and the singer definitely had an unusual quality to his voice, very different from anything else at the time. But at the SOAS show, I actually thought TAD were better that night. Nirvana were great – it was one of their more consistent performances – but if I'm honest I thought it lacked a certain something. What with Mark Arm and Tad Doyle, we'd come to expect a bit more charisma from Sub Pop front men, and Kurt didn't have it. Of course, as I soon realized, he had a different sort of charisma."

Kurt himself felt the band's set needed something more after the final song. "I need to do something and I don't know what," he told Anton as he came off stage. "Why don't you let off a fire extinguisher?" Anton suggested, and Kurt duly complied, thus giving the set a suitably dramatic ending. He later cited the show as his favorite of the tour, adding that the audience was "more energetic than a Seattle crowd." Critics were just as impressed. "Nirvana were superb, cranked-up, desperate, and fucking loud," Neil Perry wrote in *Melody Maker*. A decade later, journalist Jenny Bulley described it as the moment when "all the loyalties starting shifting from Mudhoney to Nirvana."

Even in the UK, however, these bands were still something of an underground success. As Anton recalls, most of the mainstream rock press was too busy promoting homegrown acts to pay too much attention to Sub Pop. "Everybody put their money on Manchester [bands], because they were British, and it was exciting!" he says. "You've got Happy Mondays, and The Stone Roses, two diverse bands, but both of them very important, so it was kind of that 'proud to be British' thing. And a lot of people were just skeptical about Nirvana. *Bleach* got a couple of good reviews; we had our core followers, but editorial-wise, when it came to getting big features and things, it was harder. The Seattle thing was kind of like: what's all this noise?"

After three more UK dates, the tour headed to the continent on October 31, beginning with a journey by ferry to Amsterdam. Things got off to a rocky start immediately on arrival, Krist having shared a considerable amount of whiskey with Kurt Danielson on the ferry ride over. "We made it to the hotel, which turned out to be run by a couple of really nice guys," Danielson recalls. "It's a hotel that's used by a lot of bands." As Krist hauled his bass up the long stairs to the front entrance, he got into an altercation with the owners. "They took offense," says Danielson. "They took his bass, and threw it all the way down the stairs – it fell out of its case and clattered on the stone steps – and then they took him and threw him down the stairs! And he was sprawled all over the sidewalk. We had to find a different hotel. Edwin was furious! Oh, my God! Kurt was laughing the whole time." Kurt invariably forgave his bass player's excesses. "It never seemed like a big deal to me at all," he told biographer Michael Azerrad about Krist's drinking. "Everyone gets drunk, and he didn't get drunk every single night, it was just every *other* night."

They had all pulled themselves together by the following day, when Nirvana played their second (and final) live radio show for VPRO Radio's *Nozems-A-GoGo* program, broadcast from Villa 65 studio in Hilversum, the Netherlands. 'Love Buzz' was again the opening song – a natural choice, given that the Dutch audience would likely recognize it as a Shocking Blue cover – and Kurt clearly has fun with the guitar solo. A booming, fuzzy version of 'Dive' comes next; although Kurt's voice nearly breaks on the high notes, he manages to hang on, turning in a strong performance. 'About A Girl' was the final number, the roughness of Kurt's vocal giving it additional poignancy. Although each song was greeted with a smattering of applause by the crew, the show's host Fons Dellen was not overly impressed: "We had loads of bands playing our show in those days and Nirvana was just one of 'em."

Now the real grind of touring began. During the month of November, there would be only four days off. "It was really grueling," says Craig. "I was excited, because I was excited to see Europe. The other guys didn't seem to be into it all that much – 'the food's different, it's cold, nobody speaks English' – they weren't really grooving on the fact that they were in Europe. It *was* cold. Our van was crowded. You couldn't really sleep well in it, because there were nine of us sitting shoulder to shoulder. It was tough. There was always somebody getting sick. There were blowups. There was tension within the TAD band for just normal inter-band stuff, when two bands are crammed together in a van for eight weeks."

"It was a baptism by fire," says Kurt Danielson. "It was the kind of thing that made you a much better musician, and I think all of us appreciated that aspect of it. It was like basic training, being in the army. Once you get through that, then you're a stronger fighter, the theory goes. But I think it's true, and in this case it made us better musicians, certainly much tighter players. But at the same time there were various privations which are typical of tours, especially when you're just starting out and you don't have any resources. Nobody has a credit card, for example, so whatever you get to eat at the venue, that's it. And oftentimes it was not really healthy food."

Kurt's recurring stomach problems meant that he had a harder time, faced with a diet Chad describes as largely consisting of "stupid baloney spread and rock hard biscuits." "Eating was a real problem, especially for Kurt," says Craig. "I don't know what he used to eat, but he was just really not open to trying new food. He was like: just get me a piece of meat with nothing on it, that's all I want." But even Kurt didn't suffer the gastrointestinal difficulties Tad Doyle experienced. "Tad was having unfortunate and terrible diarrhea as a result of drinking too much and eating really bad English food," says Kurt Danielson. "Like, tuna and corn pizza – I don't know what else was on it, but it was stuff that shouldn't be on a pizza. And another thing that was really bad: I like lamb, and kebabs can be really good, but if you get one from a bad, cheap shop in the middle of the night, chances are you're going to get sick. And, indeed, that's what happened. And so Tad had this terrible case of diarrhea that lasted days and would hit him at most inopportune moments, especially on stage. I remember there was a particular song, I think it was 'Pork Chop,' where Tad had to scream at the end of the chorus, and when he screamed his scream, he sort of lost control of his sphincter, and that episode became – it was the basis for a lot of jokes, let's put it that way." (It was perhaps an appropriate affliction, since Tad had once told Everett True: "There's a certain frequency, 27 Hertz or something, that's been proven to make people shit their pants. We're searching for that frequency.")

Audiences also varied more widely on the continent. "Some of the shows, hardly anybody was there, and some of them were big," says Craig. "It was a comedown in one sense, 'cause in England the shows were big, and the sound systems were pretty nice. Then we go to this little dump in Germany and it's almost like being back in the States." The "dump" in question was B-52, in Mönchengladbach, where the bands also drew the ire of club's in-house sound engineer for being too loud. "It was a tiny place, low ceilings, even smaller than the Vogue," Craig remembers. "And I'm trying to do sound, and the sound guy is telling me: this is too loud! Well, that's what they're playing, I can't do anything about that. So all I could do in that situation really is just try to get the vocals working. So you could hear 'em above what the band is doing." On occasion, even the band-members felt the music was too loud. Chad recalls a show in Melkweg that ended with an impromptu version of 'Vendetagainst' after Kurt smashed his guitar, "and all Kurt was doing was screaming as loud as he possibly could in the microphone. And the monitor was a couple feet from me and it just completely blew my ear out. It was deafening. And it's actually permanently damaged from that."

Despite the varied audiences, the bands found that touring under the Sub Pop banner prompted a lot of interest from those who had been following the label. "The way Sub Pop marketed their bands made it seem like we were bearing the scepter of a new movement," says Kurt Danielson. "Which in fact, in some ways, we were. And so it didn't really matter what your music was like. As long as you were associated with Sub Pop, people would come; if Sub Pop was mentioned on a poster, or in the press, chances are there would be some people at the show – maybe not a big crowd, because it was still a new phenomenon, but more than there would be otherwise. We were told quite often by our tour manager, Edwin, that Sub Pop bands got treated differently by Paper Clip, the booking agents, than any other bands at that time. We had better guarantees, we got perks on our riders that other bands wouldn't get – nothing big, but you notice it when you have no resources. Just getting a hotel room instead of having to spend the night on somebody's floor is a big difference."

On November 11 the tour crossed paths with history, arriving in Berlin just two days after the government of East Berlin announced its citizens could travel freely to the West – the first step in the country's eventual reunification. "It was amazing," Krist recalled. "It's just one of those moments when history is in the air, and you can just feel it." The tour van ended up stuck in traffic for hours observing the commotion. "We're in line waiting to go through the border, and in line with us are all the East Germans who have been to West Germany to visit long-lost relatives and buy all kinds of consumer goods," says Craig. "All these little Trabants full of toilet paper. And on the overpasses, over the road, all the Germans have come out, and they're all waving, 'cause they're all so exuberant. And waiting on the other side of the border, to get out of East Germany, was a line about 60 miles long, parked on the freeway, and still more people on the overpasses. It was incredible. Then we get to Berlin and it's just like a holiday. Everybody's out being all festive and partying." "It was like witnessing a reunion," says Kurt Danielson, who found the sight of West Germans pouring into the roads, bearing gifts of fruit and champagne for the East Germans, "a bit strange, a bit surreal."

The show that night drew a full house, although as Craig points out: "We didn't know if it was full because people wanted to see these bands, or people just wanted to go out." Nirvana's set ended early when Kurt became fed up with equipment problems and threw his guitar to the floor – the band's usual response to malfunctioning gear. The bands had been told they'd be sleeping above the club, and later trooped upstairs to find that their 'rooms' were actually the club's offices. "There weren't any beds or anything, hardly even any furniture," says Craig. "We just had to lay on the floor with our coats, and then get up and drive all the way back up to Oldenburg, and that's a long day of driving."

The song Nirvana had been playing when Kurt threw his guitar down in disgust was a new one the band had first played on the fall US tour, and which was now titled 'Immodium,' after the anti-diarrhea medicine Tad was using on the tour. (The medication is actually spelled 'Imodium,' with one 'm.') Lyrically, the song was unfinished, with Kurt singing nonsense words during the verses, but musically its brisk pace was similar to the more pop-driven songs the band had recently recorded at the Music Source. Chad recalls the musical arrangement coming together quickly. "It was just: bam!" he says. "That's the idea of what we want and it stayed that way. Very few changes were ever made to that song. It has the same exact arrangement that it does on *Nevermind*." 'Sappy' was another new song, which the band first played live in Oldenburg on November 12, and another indicator of Nirvana's continual moving away from the heavier material on *Bleach*.

"Kurt was conflicted at this time," Kurt Danielson notes. "His natural aesthetic was to write pop songs. But the ethos at that time was very aggressive and heavy. You might be convinced that Kurt had a total hard-rock esthetic, after seeing a performance or having a conversation with him. And then you'd turn around and read something in the press, or see him at a party, and he'd say something completely the opposite. So you never knew where he stood about certain things, and I would step back and watch him, fascinated to see what he'd say or do next. I felt like I knew him, and fairly well, too, as time went on. Yet in the end, I would say that that's not really true. I knew certain facets of him – those he chose to present, or those he was able to present at a given moment. And it's like anybody else: you never really truly know a person completely. Even if you're closely allied with them, or close friends, or married, or whatever, it's a mystery. Human beings are a mystery. And Kurt was certainly an example of that."

Danielson had first met Nirvana when TAD shared a bill with the band at the *Sub Pop 200* release party in December 1988. "Krist had these enormous mutton-chop sideburns," he recalls. "I guess it was because we could all grow them for the first time in our lives, and they were ridiculous. I hadn't seen any as nice as the ones Krist had, and I complimented him right away, and he just beamed. He was very pleased that I'd even noticed. And it's absurd, but that became the basis for a long friendship. Krist played a very important role in Nirvana, when it came to practical duties especially – for example, driving and/or repairing the van, as well as acting as liaison between the band and various outside agencies, which was critical in the early years, before there was a road crew. He was loquacious, a very capable individual, and especially in the early days, a guy who, when he had a few drinks, just loved to sort of take things to the extreme."

Like most people, Danielson found Chad to be pleasant and easygoing: "Warm, talkative, a very conscientious guy. There was sort of a childlike charm to him, owing partially to his diminutive size, but also to his personality. I don't say childlike in a disparaging way, I mean it in the best way possible – the sort of enthusiasm that you find in children. Yet at the same time an accomplished musician. Chad isn't the kind of guy that carouses around and parties; he's totally devoted to the music. Also, he likes living out in the countryside. Not an urban person. Just likes to commune with nature, in sort of a hippie kind of way – and I mean that in the best sense also. He just has a connection with nature, with natural things."

Danielson was especially interested in taking the opportunity to get to know Kurt better, often sharing a room with him and talking late into the night. "We'd just stay awake and talk in the dark, like I used to do with my brother," he says. "You could have a nice conversation with Kurt if the two of you were alone. He was, on the one hand, darkly comic, a very funny person, with an ingenious sense of humor, very cutting, very acerbic, black humor – the blackest. But on the other hand, he was a gentle, empathetic, sympathetic, kind, very nice person. He was homesick, and he said more than once that he wished he could go home. He would talk a lot about Dylan Carlson – he really looked up to Dylan a lot. We talked about the freaks from our respective hometowns, and Kurt definitely used that. One thing he was really good at was absorbing whatever was in his environment and then kind of regurgitating it in his own image.

"This is what artists do in general, and I noticed that ideas I would mention would show up in his lyrics. For example, 'Lithium.' We were talking about anti-depressants and mental illness, depression in particular, and the various pharmaceutical agents available to treat such a problem. And I was talking about lithium, a salt that is naturally found in certain lakes, like in Northern Germany, I believe. Anyway, he was fascinated by that – and besides, the word itself is beautiful, it sounds good, and it's a great title. And there was another anecdote I told him, about a woman I heard of who had an aneurysm, and the story is interesting because it burst when she was having sex. It was a horrible episode in her life. I told Kurt this story, and then there comes 'Aneurysm,' the Nirvana song."

It was apparent to Danielson that despite appearances to the contrary, Kurt took his career very seriously, constantly critiquing and revising his work. "He was very self-aware. He may have presented a front that denied that, but in fact it was a front. He pretended like he never practiced, but in fact he practiced incessantly. And he demanded a lot from the band, and he was a relentless taskmaster. After a show, or an interview, Kurt would sit there and parcel out comments to Krist and Chad, saying things like: oh, that was really good, you did a good job, Chad. Or: Krist, I like what you played there. Or maybe Krist would say: well, despite that fuck up, I think it worked. And Kurt would say: really? And then they'd make that a part of the song, whatever it was. And sometimes, he'd sing a song over and over again at various shows, and later he'd admit he was just singing something he'd made up off the top of his head, and he'd write the real lyrics at the last minute and then record them." Such would be the case with 'Immodium,' which Nirvana would first record the following year, under a new title and with substantially different lyrics.

The tour continued with a date in Hungary, a country, like Germany, whose political situation was changing as the nation gradually loosened its Communist ties. When the bands arrived for their November 21 show at the Petőfi Csarnok in Budapest, they faced an audience that had rarely seen rock bands from the West. "It was damn near like playing in the Key Arena or something," says Chad, referring to a large concert venue in Seattle. "It was like they just picked the biggest possible place they could find, 'cause they were having a rock show in Hungary. And so many kids showed up because I don't know if any other rock bands ever played there. The way they reacted, it was all new to them. That particular night, TAD opened up, and when they stopped, some of the lights got flipped on and everybody started leaving, because they thought the show was over. So someone got on the mic and explained to them: hey, it's not over yet! We had to really fly to get my drums up." The bands were paid in forints, which they had to spend before leaving the country. Krist bought a bottle of brandy, and Chad bought a snowman candle and two rolls of film, while Kurt Danielson recalls a purchase of "very cheap blue tin space-ray-type guns that shot sparks through a red plastic barrel. We also bought many packs of very stale Marlboros that were nigh on unsmokeable."

By now, after a month on the road, everyone was starting to feel worn-out, aside from Chad, who had little difficulty adjusting to the constant change. "I probably enjoyed myself more than anybody," he says. "I had a great time. I'm totally into traveling. I made it a point to get up really early, an hour or so before we'd have to move out, just to check stuff out before we had to leave. Because I wanted to take in as much of the atmosphere as I could before we had to move on. That was kind of a bummer thing – there wasn't much time for sightseeing or anything. Our days off were usually put there specifically because we needed that much time to get to our next show. So our days off were spent driving."

The musicians could always blow off steam on stage – another reason for the instrument smashing – but when stuck in the van they had to find other ways of relieving the boredom. A porno magazine purchased in Hamburg was passed around, but the thrill undoubtedly wore off after a few viewings. "For some reason, we started making fun of junkies," says Danielson. "Kurt thought it would be funny to get vampire blood, and put it on his arms, and pretend like he had track marks, and then go on stage and play with a short-sleeve shirt on, but we didn't have any of those props while we were on tour. Kurt always loved to provoke people if possible. He was bored silly, as the rest of us were too, and one thing he would do was try to be an *agent provocateur*."

Even their illnesses could become a source of amusement. "Tad had bronchitis," says Danielson. "And he was a smoker at that time, so every morning he would cough up a lot of phlegm, and he would choke on it and vomit. It happened every day. It usually happened in the van, so he had a bucket for him to puke in. And Kurt liked to hold that tub – he liked to watch it happen. It was just one of the twisted pieces of entertainment – we were so starved for entertainment, so bored, that that served as entertainment. I was fascinated by it too – I think everybody was. Part of it was just because we were so bored, but part of it was because it *was* fascinating. And part of it was the clownish way in which Tad did it."

Toward the tour's end, however, sickness began having more of an impact on the shows. Kurt was too ill to perform on November 25, when the tour reached Fribourg, Switzerland, according to Danielson, with Tad performing in his place, although Chad says Kurt did perform most of Nirvana's set. "Kurt did miss that show in Switzerland, with all due respect for Chad's memory," says Danielson. "Kurt's voice was shot because of a serious cold, so Tad did stand in for him to appease the promoter. Kurt didn't want to miss that gig, he felt bad about it, but in the end he was too sick to be so stubborn; he realized that if he didn't take a night off he might lose his voice for the rest of the tour. Someone got him some medication and took him back to the hotel." Kurt repaid the favor the next night in Mezzago, Italy, by singing 'High On The Hog' and 'Ritual Device' when Tad was too ill to finish his set; Craig Montgomery also filled in on guitar.

By November 27, when the tour moved on to Rome, Kurt was feeling especially run down. "That was a hard tour," says Krist. "Kurt was straight the whole time. He never did any drugs, he never drank; you never saw him drunk. He had a freak out in the middle of it. It was the stress. But he wasn't drinking or smoking, so he didn't have any crutches, like I did. A few of us other people would just drink and smoke and get our ya-yas out. So I could see how he snapped." Kurt put it more bluntly a few years later in an interview with Jon Savage: "I was ready to die."

There was also a surprise waiting for the musicians at the venue:

Bruce Pavitt and Jonathan Poneman had flown in for the show. "There they were, out of the blue," says Danielson. "It was like we came from a different planet all of a sudden, and here were these earthlings that came to see us." While Danielson gave them both a hug, the other musicians were more resentful. "Everybody was mad at the Sub Pop guys for putting them through this grueling tour, and then they show up in Rome," says Craig. "There was a little bit of: oh, here's these guys, living high on the hog, and they haven't even paid us the money they owe us yet." Jonathan belatedly recognized the impression they gave, telling Azerrad: "I can see them thinking: these arrogant sons of bitches … here come the moguls."

TAD played first that evening, and while their set went well, Craig remembers the show as "a mess, chaotic. It was one of those shows where the crowd may really have just been there for the disco that was gonna come afterward. TAD's set was relatively fine. But Kurt – it wouldn't take much to set him off. He was having problems. He wasn't getting along with the local monitor guy; he couldn't hear his monitor or something. It was always a problem for him. And Kurt wasn't the kind of guy who hit it off with people he didn't know, so there would always be attitude between him and local monitor guys. I would try to smooth things over, but at this point I couldn't. I was out in the middle of the crowd."

Kurt's frustration with the equipment led to his "working the audience into a frenzy, even though it wasn't really a positive frenzy," as Danielson recalls. "It was kind of a riot-like atmosphere." Ten songs in, during 'Spank Thru,' Kurt surprised everyone by suddenly smashing his guitar, then climbing the speaker cabinets on the side of the stage. "They were probably 30 feet, if not taller," Danielson says. "And then there was a significant drop from the stage itself, maybe five or six more feet, so if Kurt would have fallen or jumped he could have been seriously injured, if not killed. I think there was a kind of desperation that drove him up there. It was real, and it wasn't just for show. He was going to jump and kill himself. That's what he said."

Having reached this physical – and emotional – precipice, Kurt hesitated. "I didn't know how he was going to back down out of there," says Danielson. "It was kind of like he challenged himself to go through with it, and if he backed down he would look like a chicken." Footage of the incident shows that it didn't take long; after a few moments, Kurt decided not to push things further and he jumped back down to the stage. "He saw what he was doing was crazy," Danielson says. "And I think everybody else agreed, and just let him off the hook."

The show was over, but Kurt's crisis was not. When the club's owner began arguing with Edwin Heath over whether Kurt had broken a microphone or not, Kurt grabbed the mic, smashed it on the ground and announced: "There, now it's broken!" He then burst into tears and announced he was quitting. Edwin, thoroughly fed up with both the tour and the musicians' behavior, said he was quitting in response, prompting Krist and Chad to say they were quitting as well. But theirs were the reactions of immediate frustration; for Kurt, the despair ran deeper and cut harder. "I see all these people in the crowd and they're fucking idiots," he sobbed to Jonathan. "I don't know what I'm doing this for. I miss my home. I just want to go back to Olympia. I can't stand riding in the van with those guys; they're making me crazy. My guitar is fucking up. I don't have any money." "That was the first time I heard him say anything along the lines of: I'm playing for a bunch of bumpkins," Jonathan observed.

By the next morning, Kurt had calmed down, joining the others on a visit to the Coliseum. Thinking it would help to give Kurt a break from riding in the van, Jonathan arranged to travel with him by train to Switzerland. But what should have been a quiet, uneventful journey became more complicated when Kurt's wallet and passport were stolen while he was asleep. "That meant we had to spend a day getting his passport restored, instead of resting," says Craig. "So yeah, that was a nightmare. But somehow we did manage to get the tour carrying on. And the Switzerland shows were better than the shows that had come before, because we were better taken care of. They had nice food for us, and comfortable dressing rooms, so it was a little bit of relief after Italy."

There were two shows in Switzerland, followed by one apiece in France and Belgium. The tour's final show was December 3 at the Astoria Theatre in London, another Lame Fest, which also featured Mudhoney. "We had to take a ferryboat from Belgium and we barely made it there," says Craig. "It was another long, grueling day and by the time we got there we were all just frazzled. The sound system was kind of a mess, just the way all the equipment was patched together at the mixing board, so I remember having to spend time re-patching things in a way that made sense and improved the sound – at least for what I wanted to do with my bands."

With Mudhoney headlining, Nirvana and TAD flipped a coin to determine who would go on first. "Kurt definitely felt that Nirvana should play second," says Danielson. "But in fact we won the coin toss, and Tad chose to play second. Kurt was pissed, I could tell. And when he made it a condition that Nirvana would headline when we played with them later, it was definitely in response to this coin toss outcome. Even though it wasn't our choice, it was chance, he made sure that that didn't happen again."

As the bands had arrived at the venue late, there was no time for a proper soundcheck. Nirvana simply warmed up right before they played, then went into their set. For the band, the show was something of a let down: "It stunk," was Krist's frank assessment, perhaps recalling the show's more shambolic moments, such as a jam that drifted into a ramshackle version of 'I Wanna Be Your Dog.'

Mudhoney's Dan Peters was also unimpressed. "They all looked like shit," he says. "Especially the TAD guys. Nirvana's set was horrible, in the sense that they had several major technical difficulties. Kurt's guitar kept going out and they could barely finish a song without something fucking up. And I think out of frustration they started just destroying everything, before it was the 'Allotted

Destroy Time.' At one point Krist's swinging his bass around by the strap and I was standing by the side of the stage, and I'm like: ah, man, I wonder if that fucking bass is gonna fly off – and it did, and it came flying right at me, and I was able to put my hand up and grab it.

"It's funny because people talk about how if you missed that show, you missed one of the greatest shows of all time: Nirvana just blew everybody away, and they were the greatest things, they were fucking amazing. And it's like: sorry. They weren't. It wasn't what it's been built up to be in Nirvana's post-superstardom. It was just not a good show for them. Which was unfortunate. I remember feeling bad for them, because it was a big show in London. And I was psyched for all the bands to be there, and have a killer show, but they had a hard go of it, and a bunch of technical difficulties and frustrations and string breaking. That's what I remember from the show."

Others recall the show quite differently. Bruce and Jonathan were loyally supportive, with both men later citing it as one of Nirvana's best shows. "I remember them being pretty good," says Everett True. "I remember I was sitting at the side of the stage, and there was Anton, Keith Cameron, Tad, Matt Lukin, and Nirvana were playing, and all of us went off the stage, one right after the other – boom boom boom boom boom! Tad went straight after Lukin, and landed on him. The crowd saw Tad coming and parted – it was like the parting of the Red Sea – and Tad landed straight on Matt. And that took a while to sort out."

"It was the most amazing band I'd ever seen," Keith later told Azerrad. He'd been particularly impressed by that night's instrument destruction, during which Kurt heaved his guitar at Krist, who, wielding his bass like a baseball bat, took a swing and smashed it to pieces (uncharacteristically, Tad also smashed his guitar during his set, in the hopes that Jonathan would buy him a new one, and was much chagrined when Jonathan refused). Keith also spoke briefly to Kurt after the show. "He was very sweet," he says, "clearly mischievous, and seemed totally convinced that his band were very special. As I later discovered, I obviously caught him on a good day."

Anton was also overwhelmed by the show. "Kurt was throwing himself around and jumping up in the air and landing on his knees," he recalls. "His knees were all cut up and bruised after the show, and his jeans were even more split than what they normally were. After the show, I was just kind of: wow, that's the future of rock'n'roll! And the reviews from that show, from the people in the know, were just like: forget Tad. Forget Mudhoney. This is the band! It's amazing. They're gonna be huge." Anton wasn't the only one to think so. In an interview with Phil Alexander (then writing for *Raw*, later editor of *Mojo*), Kurt calmly revealed that his goal was for Nirvana to be "the biggest band in the world." "It wasn't a boast, but neither did he mumble," Alexander later recalled. "He just said it as if this was the most normal thing in the world."

Indeed, even Nirvana's soundcheck was favorably critiqued. "A mini-LP of Nirvana's soundcheck would not be a totally unlistenable artifact," the *NME* declared, before concluding: "Nirvana are Sub Pop's answer to The Beatles." Two songs from this performance, 'Polly' and 'Breed' (as 'Immodium' later became known) would later appear on the live album *From The Muddy Banks Of The Wishkah*, thanks to Craig's foresight in taping a number of shows on the tour. "It's always fun to listen to the show afterward in your headphones," he explains. "Just in case something good happened. Nobody else cared if I taped or not. They didn't want to hear it. But the tape from that show came out fairly decent, 'cause it was in a big room. The stuff that got used on the *Wishkah* helped pay for my house. So I guess it was prescient to put a cassette in the machine and hit 'record.'"

Nirvana returned home on December 6. They would not tour so extensively overseas for another two years. For Kurt, it had been an especially draining experience. "The last tour we did in Europe was so bad," he told a journalist in 1990. "We're not going over there again unless we get some guarantees. We worked every night for seven weeks and haven't seen a dime. Plus, we starved; we were only given a budget for one meal a day." Much as he enjoyed the thrill of performing live, Kurt was never overly enamored of touring, or travel.

As the rental van was cleaned out after the tour, Kurt Danielson found an unexpected artifact. "The van was a total mess, and it was littered with beer cans, half-full bottles of vodka, and just trash everywhere," he says. One piece of paper turned out to be the lyrics for 'Polly,' which Kurt had written out before Nirvana's John Peel session. "I saw Kurt was writing out the lyrics to 'Polly' in pencil on a piece of notebook paper," says Danielson. "And once they were done with the session, he brought the lyrics back into the van, crumpled them up and threw them on the floor, and they joined the rest of the stuff. When I found the paper later, it was stomped on with footprints, soaked with beer. Nevertheless, legible, in Kurt's hand, were the lyrics to 'Polly.' I held it in my hand – even then, it was obvious Nirvana was going somewhere – but my malaise and exhaustion were such that I wasn't really thinking too clearly, and I just threw it away! Many's the time I've thought I could have used the proceeds from such a sale. However, if I had it, I would never sell it."

When Nirvana returned to Seattle, they were on the front cover of *The Rocket*'s December issue, a live shot by Charles Peterson from the August CoCA show with Krist in the foreground and Kurt behind him, wearing a *Sub Pop 200* T-shirt. "I just remember having this kind of feeling of: they've got to be on the cover! Everybody felt like we were on the verge of something big," Courtney Miller, *The Rocket*'s ad manager, recalls. The article, 'Berlin Is Just A State Of Mind' by Nils Bernstein (who would later run the Nirvana Fan Club), was the biggest article on the band yet to appear in a local publication. Along with covering the band's recent European tour, the article noted the newfound collectability of their records, with the 'Love Buzz' single selling for $30 and white vinyl copies of *Bleach* going for $25. 'Kurdt Kobain' again complained about provincial misperceptions about the band: "I feel like we've been tagged as illiterate redneck cousin-fucking kids that have no idea what's going on at all. That's completely untrue."

There were also two new record releases toward the year's end. Daniel House began a series of compilation EPs on C/Z, inspired by Amphetamine Reptile's *Dope Guns 'N Fucking In The Streets* series. "I liked the concept, but I wanted to represent a much broader spectrum of music," he explains. He chose the name *Teriyaki Asthma*, with the first EP, released in November in a limited edition of 1,000 copies, featuring 'Mexican Seafood' from the Dale Demo (the other acts were Coffin Break, Helios Creed, and Yeast, a band Daniel played drums for). The song next appeared on *Teriyaki Asthma Vol. I–V*, an album that gathered together the first five EPs in the series.

Around the same time, the *Blew* EP was released in the UK on Tupelo. Although it's been said the record wasn't available until December, the first review appeared in *Melody Maker* in October. Along with 'Blew' and 'Love Buzz' (the latter tune having not appeared on the UK edition of *Bleach*) the EP also included 'Been A Son' and 'Stain' from the Music Source session with Steve Fisk. The cover featured a shot of Kurt lying on the stage, hugging his guitar, taken by Tracy Marander during a show the previous May at Green River Community College in Auburn, Washington. The back cover shot, also by Tracy, was an austere photo of a doctor's examination room.

The EP received mixed reviews. "Nirvana have clearly been holed up somewhere for the past 20 years in a home studio held together with paper clips on a Blue Cheer album for comfort," *NME*'s Ian McCann wrote, adding that he was "none too sure about the VD clinic sleeve," referring to the back cover shot. *Melody Maker*'s Simon Reynolds dismissed the record with the withering comment: "These warhorse riffs are only fit for the knacker's yard." But Dan Peters liked Nirvana's new material. "That's the stuff that I really thought was great – 'Been A Son' and stuff," he says. "Before that EP came out, Matt [Lukin] had a copy of that tape. We were doing a tour and ended up down in Eugene [Oregon], and after the gig we ended up at a house party, and I was just kind of over it, and me and Matt said: fuck it, let's go out to the van. So me and Matt went out to the van and sat around and drank beer and smoked cigarettes and listened to that tape over and over, and just thought it was great. I remember sitting there and playing that, and when the bass solo comes up, and cranking it."

Blew also inadvertently ended up creating a rarity when the two *Bleach* songs were not re-edited back into the master tape when cassettes of *Bleach* were first manufactured; thus, the first run of tapes were missing both 'Blew' and 'Love Buzz.' Daniel, then still working at Sub Pop, recalls that there were no returns. "People actually went out to the store and began buying them up, because it was a mistake and a collector's item!" he says. "All it did was serve to sell the entire rest of the pressing out in record time." Jack Endino recalls being given a bunch of defective cassettes by Bruce. "I think they threw most of them away," he says. "But Bruce gave me a little shoebox of them and said: here, you can use them at the studio, record over them or whatever because we can't sell these. I used to use them as telephone answering machine cassettes. A few people bought them on my website and then posted them on eBay, so I quit selling them."

Unlike the hectic activity of the previous year, when Nirvana had been busy rehearsing for the *Bleach* sessions, this December was quiet for the band. Krist and Shelli got married at the end of the month, and the only musical activity came when Kurt attended one of the sessions for Mark Lanegan's solo album, *The Winding Sheet*, contributing backing vocals to 'Down In The Dark.' "And possibly a little guitar," says Jack Endino, who produced the sessions. "But it was totally inaudible. There's no way to hear it." 'Where Did You Sleep Last Night,' from the Jury sessions earlier in the year, would also appear on the album; Nirvana's own version of the song would provide a searing conclusion to their *Unplugged* appearance in 1993.

Kurt's aunt Mari had picked up the December *Rocket*, thrilled at her nephew's success. "I was so excited for Kurt," she said. "It looked like: wow, they're really doing something." She was surprised to arrive at Kurt's mother's home in Aberdeen for a Christmas party and hear the *Bleach* album playing loudly. "After all those years when Kurt was upstairs practicing his guitar and she was telling him to turn it down, I walk into the house and the *Bleach* album is blaring so loud, nobody could hear each other," she recalled. "And I'm like: what happened? It's really kind of funny when people begin to 'make it' or whatever; it seemed like there was a turn in everybody's perspective or something. And I often wonder how Kurt perceived that, you know. I don't know, it just seemed – it seems kind of sad in a way."

CHAPTER 11
A Full Phenomenon

Q: "Tell me about your new material."
A: "There's a lot more melody. There's driving
songs. There's gonna be melodic songs. There's
not gonna be anything real slow or grungy on it."

KRIST TO *PEACE* MAGAZINE, 1990

Nirvana had a habit of holding recording sessions at the beginning of the year. Their first professional demo was recorded on January 23 1988, and the concluding *Bleach* sessions were held in January 1989. Later, the band would return to Seattle's Music Source studio on January 1 1991 and record demos for *In Utero* in Brazil on January 19–21 1993, while the band's final recording session took place at the end of January 1994 at Robert Lang Recording Studios in Shoreline, a suburb of Seattle. So it wasn't surprising that Nirvana were on their way back to Reciprocal Recording as 1990 began. What was unusual was that the two-day session, held on January 2 and 3, focused on a single song: 'Sappy.'

The song was relatively new, having made its debut on the European tour. Kurt had previously recorded a demo version, accompanying himself on guitar, and singing in a slow, lethargic fashion, as if he'd just woken up. Lyrically, the song makes reference to finding comfort in the illusion of happiness, a theme that would resurface in later songs, most notably 'Dumb.' The demo version had an instrumental introduction and was relatively brief: two verses and a chorus.

The reasons for Nirvana going into the studio to record the song are uncertain; no releases were scheduled, so perhaps Kurt simply wanted to hear how the song sounded in the studio. The first studio recording is substantially different from the demo. It kicks off immediately into the verse, without the instrumental intro; the tempo is faster; the song is longer, with a brief instrumental break and an additional verse; and Kurt sings in an upper register throughout.

For his part, Jack Endino was unimpressed. "That was the first time I knew that Kurt was fallible," he says, "because everything he'd done had been brilliant to me up to then." More puzzling was the amount of time spent on the song: seven hours on the first day, and three hours on the second. "A tremendous amount of time," says Jack. "By Nirvana's standards, from what I was used to, that was a long time. They were pretty particular. They wanted to get this song down and Sub Pop didn't have any plans on releasing it or doing anything with it. I couldn't really see exactly why they were doing it. It was a strange session."

Of more interest is that the session demonstrated Kurt's increasing interest in the workings of the recording studio. Just as he had been during the Music Source sessions with Steve Fisk, Kurt was in search of a new sound. He was most interested in getting "an Albini kind of sound," according to Endino, referring to Steve Albini, who in addition to playing in Big Black had produced a number of bands Kurt admired, chiefly the Pixies. But Kurt had difficulty explaining what he wanted to his producer. "He wasn't sure how to express it or describe it to me," Endino recalls. "Basically, he just had me try a bunch of different stuff, with a lot of different miking techniques. And that version of 'Sappy' really sounds very Albini-esque. It's not something I would have done normally; it was very much him telling me exactly what to do. What you hear was me trying to get exactly the ideas he was expressing. If I had just mixed it, it would have sounded more like *Bleach*."

"I think it was one of those songs that could not come out that well in the studio, because of its real basic simplicity," says Chad. "I mean, when you listen to it, it's pretty much the same thing over and over and over again, with those soft little breaks in the middle.

Basically, the song's only built on two changes; it's got the main melody riff going on, that stops for about a quick four measures into something different, then goes right back into the main melody again. And when it comes to the solo that he did, that's just playing it right over the melody line again. There were only two parts to that song. And it was up to what we did, especially with the vocal – the way he'd sing that song – and putting in a guitar solo, that was going to be able to make that song fly. And I think it did."

Over the course of the ten hours spent in the studio, just two takes of 'Sappy' were recorded. "Only one was finished," says Jack. "They're almost identical. I'm not aware that any other take has surfaced." Nirvana would tinker with the song repeatedly over the years, recording a second version three months later, with subsequent versions recorded during the sessions for *Nevermind* and *In Utero*. The *In Utero* version was the only one released during Kurt's lifetime, appearing as a 'secret' track on the *No Alternative* compilation album (for which the song was retitled 'Verse Chorus Verse'). The Endino version remained unreleased until 2005, when it appeared on *Sliver: The Best Of The Box*. "I didn't really get the song," Jack admits. "When Poneman heard it later, he didn't really get it either. I remember he said: what's up with that? The people at Sub Pop were very puzzled by it. It was this song that just didn't seem that interesting, and Kurt was determined to get it, you know? And I was like: no, it's just nothing. Write some more songs, Kurt!"

Nirvana returned to live performance on January 6 for another show at the HUB Ballroom, with local acts Crunchbird, The Gits, and TAD sharing the bill. The rigors of the European tour resulted in a considerably more polished sound, and they turned in a commanding performance. "It was a real crazy show," DJ and promoter Erik 4-A recalls. "They trashed stuff again and got a lifetime ban; I think the powers that be at the UW said: this is getting out of control!"

"It was an amazing show," says Charles Peterson. "And they were definitely more mature at that point, you could just tell, like music-wise and set-wise, less pausing and fiddling around between songs, and it just seemed to flow better." During Nirvana's set, Charles got a dramatic picture of a stage diver in mid-flight, soaring over the audience, some of whom have raised their hands in anticipation of the diver's descent; the photo appears on the title page of Charles' first book, *Screaming Life*, and the back cover of Nirvana's live album *From The Muddy Banks Of The Wishkah*.

It was the first time Rob Nyberg, then an Evergreen student who would later intern at Sub Pop, had seen the band, having become a fan after hearing *Bleach*. "It was a pretty big show considering they were a local band," he says. "It was definitely the era of the super mosh pit. It got pretty chaotic at the end, and Kurt was on Krist's shoulders and things were breaking, and drums were blown apart that night. Mudhoney and Nirvana both would end their shows in chaos, where the pit would bleed onto the stage, and the band and crowd would be indistinguishable. But this was more of a love pit, I felt. The first shows I went to in the mid 80s, the pits were violent, and then it got more thick because of the influence of ecstasy and MDA. People just kind of rolled around on the floor, and fell down, and people would help you up – more of a pleasant pit. It wasn't necessarily dangerous. But it was crazy."

Evergreen student Phil Buffington had also come to Seattle for the show and hung out briefly with the band backstage. Having first seen Nirvana in his dorm room, he now felt their performance pointed the way to bigger things. "Even at that time you kind of knew that they were well on their way to something," he says. "I don't think anyone anticipated *Nevermind* or anything, but even at that time, watching them just thrill a packed house of that size, it was like: wow!"

After a January 12 show in Portland, Oregon, the band returned to Olympia on January 19 for a show at Rignall Hall – a performance many attendees recall as being particularly galvanizing. "It was so amazing," says Courtney Miller, *The Rocket*'s ad manager. "It was one of those transcending shows where you're like: oh my God, this is really something! I saw them in a completely different light. It was just something that clicked like: this is so infectious, this has really got this pop sensibility, this is just really fun! And I remember it was a really low ceiling and Kurt was jumping up and down, and he was just getting closer and closer to hitting his head on that ceiling. My brother remembers that after the show Kurt had steam coming off of him." Footage of the gig shows the band crammed into a small room, on a low stage, the seething audience literally inches away. There were no spectacular leaps from Kurt during this performance; there simply wasn't any room.

Rob Nyberg was also at the show. An inveterate music fan, he was used to traveling to see his favorite bands, but he was surprised to see a number of people he knew from Seattle at this Olympia show. He also recalled how Kurt used fake blood to draw track marks on his arms, making good on an idea he'd thought up during the European tour. "It seemed stupidly shocking," says Rob. "It didn't faze me at all. I'd heard rumors of the heroin scene here, and that there were a lot of people involved with it, but people were mocking it at the same time. So I just thought it was stupid heroin humor."

The following night, the band drew an equally enthusiastic crowd at the Tacoma club Legends. The stage was flanked by bouncers, who struggled to keep audience members from stagediving. Matt Lukin had no difficulties there: he simply walked on from the backstage area, leaped off, then went around backstage to do it again, much to the consternation of the bouncers, who eventually attempted to kick him out. There was a momentary disruption, as Kurt pleaded: "That's our friend!" (Krist, trying to mollify the situation, sang a bit of 'All You Need Is Love.') After a few minutes of confusion, and Krist's impromptu rendition of another Beatles song, 'If I Fell,' the show was allowed to continue. Chad was pleased to see Nirvana's peers enjoying the show. "I remember looking down off to my left, just over my hi-hat, and I saw Mark Arm there," he says. "And he turned and looked right at me, and he was bobbing his head. I remember thinking: how cool!" The show marked the last time 'Token Eastern Song' was played in concert.

In February the band headed out on a nine-date West Coast tour with TAD, beginning on the 9th with a show at Portland's Pine Street Theatre. The show was later released as a bonus disc in the 2009 anniversary edition of *Bleach*; the recording bristles with self-assurance, the sound of a band coming into their own. "By this time, it's a full phenomenon," says Craig Montgomery. "They were really hitting their stride." That Kurt was feeling a growing surge of confidence could be seen in his demand that Nirvana headline over TAD during the tour. "He never did that before," says Kurt Danielson. "The European tour was characterized by flip-flopping back and forth; one night Nirvana headlined, the next night TAD. But the condition for this next tour was that Nirvana would headline. We accepted. Tad was not happy, but I could see the writing on the wall; I didn't protest. Kurt had a very shrewd sense of publicity; I mean, he knew what he was about. He and I had conversations about this quite often, actually, when nobody else was around. He wouldn't say anything about this kind of thing if anybody else could hear it; he'd only tell it to you in the strictest of confidence."

Danielson also observed the other side of Kurt's personality on the road. "There were times when Kurt's shy, meek side would come to the forefront," he says. "Like after a gig, when they would be selling T-shirts, Kurt would stand up there with a Nirvana T-shirt and be holding it up, and no one would be paying any attention to him at all. He couldn't sell a shirt to save his life! I remember Jonathan saying: what's he doing? That's not how you sell a T-shirt! You know: that's not how you promote yourself! And Jonathan would always be giving him object lessons in how to be doing things correctly. Not that he knew himself, but he did have a natural sense of how to promote a band, and a lot of us didn't know how to do that – or, if we did know, we didn't want to do that; that was somebody else's job. We considered ourselves artists, above that kind of thing. And I think Kurt felt like: fuck this, I'm not supposed to sell T-shirts. Usually, what Kurt would do is he would slink outside and avoid the whole situation, and he learned to do that very well. But at this time, I think he gave it a try, or he felt like just making a lampoon of it, possibly."

In contrast to the European tour, each band had their own van, and as a result the mood was laid back, and the band antics more playful. "We bought all these redneck-type hats," Chad recalled. "'I'd Rather Be Hunting.' I think mine said 'CBS Sports' or something about fishing." Krist later told Everett True of an occasion when they stopped to ask for directions and Kurt leaned out the window to shout "Hail Satan!" before driving off. He was also in the habit of brandishing a large crucifix out of the van's window at people walking by, then taking a picture of their startled reactions.

Kurt Danielson sometimes rode in Nirvana's van for the change of pace. "Kurt, when he drives, he loses interest after about a half hour," he recalls. "Krist wouldn't let him drive for longer than that, and eventually he wouldn't let him drive at all. And that was fine with Kurt: he would just sit in the back and listen to music, strum his guitar, whatever. And Chad, he liked to drive, but he would do some crazy shit. One time Krist and Kurt and I were sitting in the back, not really paying attention. Chad was driving, and he has a really playful side to his character, and it would come out under stress, or conditions like that on the road. I think he was driving with his chin – or maybe he was driving with his feet – and anyway, finally the van swerved and Krist turned around and he noticed what Chad was doing. It was something crazy, on the freeway, going like 70, and Chad is driving with his feet, and talking to himself in puppet voices."

Everett True accompanied the bands down the coast and described Nirvana's show at San Francisco's Kennel Club as "stunning: the Washington trio blow every other fucking band in existence off-center with the potency and ferocious intent of their music." There were more than just music fans in the audience. In San Francisco, DGC's Mark Kates, who'd been advised by Sonic Youth to sign Nirvana, finally saw the band perform live. "It got me to go back to listen to *Bleach*," he says. "I bought it when it came out, based on Kim's suggestion, and I remember listening to it and thinking: you know, I've just never been into Black Sabbath, and I think that's kind of a prerequisite for really appreciating what's going on here. But seeing the show, I certainly noticed 'About A Girl.' As a listener and as a fan of music, I've always been about melody and they definitely reached me in a bigger way than they had on the record."

On February 15 the tour arrived in Los Angeles for a show at Raji's. For Charles Peterson, who saw the shows in San Francisco, LA, and Long Beach, Raji's was "definitely the highlight. It was such a perfect kind of sleazy little club, and the band was just totally on. It was one of those nights where the bands were on, and I was in the perfect spot to photograph them." Charles took a series of shots showing Kurt throwing himself backward into Chad's drums during the closing number, 'Blew.' The pictures subsequently appeared on the cover of the 'Sliver' single and on the inner sleeve of the *Bleach* CD. "The only thing that I worried about when they jumped on my drum kit was the possibility of bending or breaking something," says Chad. "Because we didn't have a lot of money. Repair jobs were done with duct tape! And it would usually guarantee that we wouldn't be coming back on stage for any encores."

Members of LA-based band L7, who had just released their first single for Sub Pop ('Shove'/'Packin' A Rod'), were also at the show. "Nirvana's energy and style of music and everything was what I'd dreamed about my whole life," says Jennifer Finch, the band's bassist, who also lived in Seattle occasionally. "I grew up in LA hardcore, and there became such a mechanical feel to LA hardcore at a certain point in the early 80s that you just abandoned it. It felt like not having any kind of community at all from '85 to '87, '88. And then, going to Seattle it was really like – as I've heard Donita [Sparks, the band's guitarist] say in interviews – we've found our tribe. And it wasn't in our own city." The tour also took in Nirvana's first visit to Mexico, where they played Tijuana club Iguana's on February 17.

A proposed UK trip that would've taken place at the end of February was cancelled. March saw only one date, a show in Vancouver, British Columbia, on March 12. During the momentary lull, Kurt tried to get a more ambitious venture off the ground: putting together a video that the band could sell on tour. "I heard about it like a couple weeks in advance," Chad recalls. "Kurt was like: OK, we're gonna go in and make these videos. And I was like: cool! I wasn't exactly sure what the plans were for them, but it sounded fun."

Kurt made the arrangements for the session himself, contacting Evergreen student Jon Snyder, whom he knew had access to the television studio on campus. "We talked on the phone," Jon recalls. "And the way Kurt explained it to me was that they wanted to have a lot of stuff to sell on the road, and one of the things they wanted to do was a home video. The idea, the original concept, was to do stuff in the studio and then go to Aberdeen and shoot a bunch of other stuff, and then turn it all into some hour-long thing that they would sell to fans."

Because it wasn't a college project, the Evergreen session was done surreptitiously; the March 20 date for the session was chosen because it was during spring break. Jon got together with Kurt and Krist the day before the shoot to discuss details. Kurt wanted to make use of the hours of footage he'd taped from television – maybe it could be projected behind them? "I said: oh, yeah, we can do that in the TV studio, 'cause we've got a Chroma Key curtain," Jon recalls. "A Chroma Key curtain is a big blue curtain, like they used in movies, where they'd shoot actors against a blue screen and put special effects in later. I brought Kurt and Krist out to the college, into the VHS editing suite, and showed them how to edit videotape." Afterward, Kurt took Jon out to dinner. "I was just thinking: this is sweet!" he says. "I was on food stamps, I was on financial aid. I didn't have any money then, so getting a free meal was great. And they paid me $75. I was psyched! That was great money for me."

Greg Babior was brought in to do the sound, and Jon also contacted Maria Braganza and Alex Kostelnik to operate the cameras, knowing they were Nirvana fans. They in turn invited another Evergreen student (and Nirvana fan) named Jeff. "He was a huge Sub Pop record collector," remembers Alex. "So we called him and said: you want to film Nirvana? He's like: I'll be there in 15 minutes. He got in his car and drove there as fast as he could. That was a huge treat for him."

Shooting began in the afternoon. After the band set up in front of the Chroma Key curtain, a few adjustments had to be made: a cement block was dragged in and propped against Chad's bass drum to keep it from sliding around, and Krist put white tape on his pants, because his legs couldn't be seen against the blue screen. "The thing about these videos that most people don't realize is that it's all live," Jon explains. "We did no editing and we did no after effects. We were switching between cameras in the studio control booth, which makes it look like it's been edited, and then all the effects were running off the tapes in another room so they could be combined in as we were shooting. [It was] the same with the sound. The sound was live engineered sound and nothing was done to it later." As the band performed, they faced the control room, which had a TV monitor, so they could watch themselves as they played.

There was little in the way of preparation. "We were winging it," says Maria. "We'd agree before the song approximately what we'd do, and Jon could see both of our camera movements on the monitors, and decide which camera to mix in at what time." The first song shot was 'School,' one version breaking down, the other complete. The backing footage was a montage of clips featuring Leif Garrett (who would later record a cover of 'Smells Like Teen Spirit' with the Melvins) and Kristy McNicol dancing together, Shaun Cassidy, the Christian bodybuilders dubbed The Power Team, a boy-girl dancing team on *Star Search* (often incorrectly identified as Donny and Marie Osmond), and commercials for Lee Press-On Nails. "[Kurt would] sit and watch television for hours!" Krist said about Kurt's video montages. "He had the remote control on the VCR and he would watch the most ridiculous things and he would compile them ... just the most kitsch stuff." Much of Kurt's footage couldn't be used during the shoot, as he'd recorded in SLP (Super Long Play) mode, which couldn't be played back properly on Evergreen's equipment. "It really annoyed him," says Alex.

Nirvana hadn't dressed up for the shoot. Kurt wears a gray sweatshirt, while Krist and Chad wear T-shirts, although Chad adds some rock'n'roll cool by wearing sunglasses. Their appearance makes a striking contrast when set against the clean, pre-packaged smoothness of the characters in the footage projected behind them. For Alex, the video's point was obvious: "Making fun of stupid people, gross plastic people, conservatism, mainstream America. 'School''s got the best lyrics, and what could be cornier than 'no recess'? It's funny. People always overlook Nirvana's humor. Nirvana was funny!"

After 'School' there was a break to boost the sound of Krist's bass. When they were asked to play something to test the bass level, the band surprised everyone by playing a new song, 'Lithium,' which they had yet to perform live. "The song was so new that we were still working out the ideas ourselves," says Chad. "It was kind of like when we were working out 'Blandest,' just warming up with it for soundcheck at a show. It was just an excuse to play it a little bit." It was Kurt's most tuneful song since 'About A Girl': even in this rough, early stage, in a halting performance and without its final lyrics, the song drew an immediate positive response. "We thought it was so awesome," says Alex. "I'm like: Krist, man, this song is so cool! But we couldn't really understand exactly what he was saying. I thought he was begging some girl: 'I love you. I'm not stoner trash. I miss you. I'm not stoner trash.' But this is that pivotal moment. It's like they did a whole change – like they already impressed everyone, and then they did this song, and you thought: they're doing it again. They're upping the ante." As Maria puts it: "We were like: oh my God, they're gonna make it! Because they'd gone over into pop land."

The cameras then caught an instrumental jam, built around a jerky, repetitive guitar riff. "That must have been just a warm-up thing," says Chad. "Or we were just having fun. I remember it being a pretty relaxed atmosphere situation. Not too much unlike the Kiss recordings session, because we were having a lot of fun with it. We were just goofing off and having a lot of fun; we probably just felt like jamming for a bit." If it was a song idea, it was abandoned, as the melody never surfaced in any other song. Two versions of 'Big Cheese' were shot next, the backing footage drawn from Benjamin Christensen's 1922 silent film *Häxan* (later released as *Witchcraft Of The Ages*). "It's a creepy, cool silent film that's in the public domain, that some Seattle video artist had prepared for them to do a video," says Jon. "But they didn't like working with that person so they just took the footage and kept it." It's the most atmospheric of the videos, with witches flying on broomsticks and a hapless nun being tormented by demons.

The final number was 'Floyd The Barber,' which made too much use of a 'feedback loop' effect that multiplies the image, making a person look like they have multiple arms. Of greater interest is the backing footage, drawn from Super-8 films Kurt shot of his art projects. "I don't know if anyone will ever see that footage any other way," says Jon. "It shows these stop-motion doll parts, and melted wax, and burning pieces of toys – really, really interesting stuff that he had been fooling around with. It totally foreshadows this aesthetic that emerged on the *Incesticide* and *In Utero* album covers, this fascination with thrift store toys and the Visible Man bodies and all that kind of stuff. It shows how he was visually creative as well as musically creative." As with his video collages, Kurt trawled through the detritus of popular culture for objects he'd then alter to express his own sardonic views about humanity. The dolls were particularly striking: in addition to painting their faces and gluing hair to their heads, he'd sometimes cover them in clay and bake them in the oven. "I didn't mean to make the dolls look evil," he told Everett True. "But somehow they always ended up that way."

At the end of 'Floyd,' Kurt clambers on top of Chad and his drum kit – "as per usual," says Chad. "I think at that point he was just kind of tired from being in the studio all day," says Jon, who was nonetheless pleased with the band's work. "What's cool about it is just the guitar solos and stuff," he says. "The only bad thing about Dave Grohl being added to Nirvana was that Kurt's guitar playing changed a little bit. You see a different kind of – a bigger guitar solo on 'School' that seems really different to me than what they did on later stuff. And it's also cool because Kurt's hair was so long. People aren't really used to seeing even photos of him when he was in his long hair stage. And when we were shooting, he was just whipping it all over the place and it was hanging all over his face a lot too. And that was pretty cool."

But the project fizzled out soon after it was completed. "I tried hard to get in touch with them, and I called Kurt a bunch of times," says Jon. "But they went out on the road. And when I finally got ahold of Kurt he was like: well, we really wanted to do that but I don't think it's going to happen now and blah blah blah." Fearing he'd lose the master tape, Jon only gave Kurt a dubbed copy of the footage; although widely bootlegged, the videos have yet to be officially released. What's most interesting about them is the glimpse they provide of Kurt's visual perspective of the world – and, in retrospect, the way the performance captures the band about to go through another change.

Prior to the band's next tour, Nirvana held a photo session with Charles Peterson at his studio. Charles had hung up a large piece of white paper for the backdrop. "I didn't know what to do with them," he says. "I was never much of a portrait photographer. A lot of

Nirvana's more portrait stuff was done by Michael Lavine in New York City, and he had a big studio, and all these lights, and he had this style of processing, and that just wasn't really my thing. I tried to get fancy at one point, but really the photos of mine that are the best are where I just took them into an alley, or put them in a field, and shot black-and-white.

"So with this session I was like: well, OK, I'll get some studio lights, and my Hasselblad medium-format camera, and I'll just try and keep it really simple." The setting proved to be too simple for Kurt, who, on walking in, looked at the backdrop and said: "White paper in the back? This is boring, let's do something else." When Charles had no ideas of his own, Kurt suggested: "Well, maybe we can draw something there, or write something there." "OK, knock yourself out," Charles replied.

On looking around the studio, Charles found a can of black spray-paint and handed it to Kurt. "Here," he said. "Do something with that." Kurt shook the can, considered the backdrop for a few moments, then walked up and spray-painted a large plus sign on the left, and a minus sign on the right. "And that was that," says Charles. "I don't think I ever asked him what it meant, or I may have, and he probably just was like: I don't know."

It wasn't until later that Charles noticed something about most of the shots taken that day; Kurt was sitting under the plus sign and Chad was sitting under the minus sign. "It's not like we purposely put Chad under the minus sign or anything," he says, although the events of the next few months made him wonder about the underlying significance of the pose. "I mean, hindsight is always 20/20," he says, "but it seemed like Kurt and Krist were always the most comfortable with each other."

CHAPTER 12
On The Road Again

"Let's just say that Nirvana will influence world culture in a massive way."

BRUCE PAVITT, TO EVERGREEN STUDENT NEWSPAPER *COOPER POINT JOURNAL*, 1990

At the end of March 1990, Nirvana headed out on another US tour, with a stop scheduled in Madison, Wisconsin, so they could record their second album, tentatively entitled *Sheep*. Jonathan Poneman had decided Nirvana should record with Bryan David 'Butch' Vig at Smart Studios, having admired his work as the producer of Killdozer's 1989 album *12 Point Buck*. In addition to producing, Butch had also played drums in various Madison bands; one act, Fire Town, had recorded an album for Atlantic Records, and post-Nirvana he would form the band Garbage.

Butch began his career as a producer in the late 70s, when he and his friend Steve Marker started recording bands in Marker's basement. By 1987, Smart Studios had moved to a two-story brick building on E. Washington Avenue, on Madison's east side, not far from the Wisconsin State Capitol. Jonathan had called Butch "out of the blue" as Butch recalls, telling him how much he'd enjoyed *12 Point Buck*. "I remember he specifically said: I love this record – it sounds amazing but it's kind of crazy. It has a loose energy that we want you to bring to some of our artists at Sub Pop. I hadn't really bought that many Sub Pop albums. But a friend of mine, Dave Benton at Mad City Music, the indie record store in Madison, subscribed to the Singles Club and got all the Sub Pop stuff. So I would go into the store and he would play me whatever. So I definitely knew who they were, and that's how it sort of gelled from there."

Butch was surprised at how enthusiastically Jonathan spoke about Nirvana. "They can be as big as The Beatles," he told Butch. "There's this amazing buzz, this amazing underground hysteria around the band. I think once you get them in the studio, you'll realize that they've got something special."

"I'm thinking to myself: yeah, right," Butch continues. When Jonathan later sent him a copy of *Bleach*, he was equally unimpressed. "I put it on and I was really tired," he recalls. "I'd done a session the night before. I put it on in the morning and I listened to it and I thought: it's all right. And then 'About A Girl' came on and I stopped and went: this is fucking brilliant. That was the song that jumped out because it had this melodic thing going. The rest of the record I thought was OK. It was cool punk, had a great energy, I thought Kurt had a great voice. But I didn't think any of the songs were that remarkable except for 'About A Girl.'"

The band played a show in Chicago on April 1, then drove directly to Madison, checking into their hotel to get a few hours sleep before the sessions were due to begin. Kurt still had Steve Albini's production techniques in mind. "We were listening to the Pixies," Krist recalls. "By that time we had a trailer. We were pulling all our gear in a trailer so the van was nice and open. And there was this like ottoman, a little couch, against the back door. Chad was driving, and I was sitting, I was kind of looking around. I'm looking at Kurt and Kurt put up his finger and goes: and our snare sound shall sound like this! He lifted up his finger, like he proclaimed it. He was sitting on that couch like he was a ruler on a throne. He decreed. And then the tire blew out! The back tire. So we had to pull over and I changed the tire."

When the band arrived at Smart, they unpacked their own gear. "Kurt was sort of sitting around while we're setting up the drums," Butch recalls. "And Krist was very charming and pretty energetic and talkative. Basically all they said [was that] they just wanted the record to sound heavy. I brought some plywood in because there were parts of the main room that were carpeted, and parts that were hard drywall. The room itself was pretty live sounding, but we wanted to make it even 'live-r' so I put plywood under the drums." Engineer Doug Olson suggested using a Marshall tube amp instead of Kurt's transistorized Sunn guitar amp; Kurt scowled: "No, I don't want to do that." But Chad did agree to make use of Butch's Yamaha snare drum, later used on Smashing Pumpkins' *Gish*. Afterward, Butch took the band across the street to the Friendly Tavern Bar for grilled cheese sandwiches.

Most accounts indicate that the sessions started on April 2, yet the tracking sheets are dated April 3 and list all eight songs from the sessions as being recorded on the same day (on three reels). The drive from Chicago to Madison is no more than three hours, meaning the band could easily have arrived on April 2 in time to start work. So were the sheets misdated? Chad, for one, thinks it unlikely that basic tracks were all laid down in a single day. Regardless of the exact starting day, they still didn't have much time; Nirvana had to leave Madison on April 7 for their next gig in Milwaukee on April 8.

"We did everything relatively quick," says Butch. "So you've pretty much got to get everything set up pretty quick and get rolling. I didn't really dissect the songs. Most of the songs seemed like, once they played them, the arrangements were pretty tight. We pretty much tracked the songs live. I got Kurt to double-track some of the rhythm guitars even though he wasn't into it. In some cases there was just one guitar, so I would do an automatic double, which is where you pan it left, then you run it through a delay and pan it to the right to make it sound more of a stereo image. Kurt would record a scratch vocal, then go back and do the final vocals and the harmonies. There were very few overdubs. Kurt might add a second guitar, and he dropped in a couple of lead guitar things here and there, but the band was pretty much tracked live." As usual, unsatisfactory takes were recorded over. "I was always very economical," Butch says. "I was always like: well if it wasn't a good take, there's no point in keeping it.

In hindsight, I wish I could have kept everything, but it was just a budget thing. The bands were like: just tape over the stuff we're not using."

Chad found Butch's style as a producer closer to Jack Endino than Steve Fisk, who he describes as "a little bit more of a *finesse* sort of guy. Jack had a really good sense of getting thickness out of recording, getting a good solid-sounding kick drum and snare sound. And when you'd say you wanted the guitar to be really big sounding, Vig could do that – like Jack, he could bring that out. But Vig played with a little more stuff. When we sat there finding different sounds for the snare, he had a machine that had like 150 different effects to put on the snare – there was something called 'Elvis Beat' and 'Monster' – whatever, and the list goes on. And we just sat there and pretty much listened to just about every one of them. But like Jack, he was able to get some really thick, thick sounds."

The songs were a mix of old and new material. 'Immodium,' 'Dive,' 'Sappy,' and 'Polly' had been in the band's setlist for some months; 'Lithium' and 'In Bloom' were newer; and 'Pay To Play' and 'Here She Comes Now' had yet to be performed live. The band began with the older material, getting off to a good start with 'Immodium.' While live performances of the song were occasionally ragged and sluggish (partially due to Kurt's not having the lyric finished), in the studio it was a streamlined assault, as frantic in its way as the *Bleach* version of 'Downer,' but with a simpler lyric – a single verse repeated twice. It was the same lyrical brevity found in 'Stain,' with a similar theme of insecurity, as Kurt sang "I don't care," "I don't mind," and finally, "I'm afraid," while his agitated guitar nags beneath, similar to the 'squabbling hen' sound of 'Been A Son.'

When it came time to record the vocal, they ran into a problem that would recur through the sessions. "Kurt would sing so hard he literally blew his voice out," says Butch. "I was lucky if I could get him to do another take. On 'Immodium,' he did one take and I got him to double-track some of the other sections of the song and then his voice was so shot I think that was the last he sang for that night. He was hoarse the whole time he was there."

The band also played around a bit with sound effects; during the instrumental break, the guitar solo pans from the left to the right channel, at Krist's suggestion. "I think it was on a Jimi Hendrix record, where they were panning the thing," says Butch. "And Krist said: why don't you trying doing something like that in the mix? We did the same thing [with the song] on *Nevermind*. It's just: let's make the guitar move back and forth during the break sections."

As the next song, 'Dive,' had been in the band's setlist for nearly a year, it too was quickly recorded. "That one sounded great," says Butch. "The first time they ran through it, it just sounded amazing. It was super powerful sounding. That was one of the songs I was really keyed into." The song had been tightened up since it was first recorded the previous year at Evergreen, and now ran one minute shorter. Kurt's vocal taunts sarcastically through the verses, building to the climactic roar of the chorus, consisting of a three-word command: "Dive in me."

The 'whispery' hissing heard at the song's beginning came from Kurt "fucking with the mic on the overdub; he was making those sound effects with his voice," says Butch. "He actually did that quite a bit on songs. There were things on *Nevermind*, like on 'Drain You' and 'Come As You Are,' just little things that appear on the tracks where he just sort of fucks around with the sound effects from his voice, basically." It was the same thing Kurt's aunt Mari had noticed him doing the first time he recorded at her home, when he liked to add "weird sounds" to his songs. Butch also doubled Kurt's guitar and double-tracked his vocal.

Nirvana had just debuted 'In Bloom' at their April 1 show in Chicago. The band had been working on the song in rehearsal, Kurt refining it further at home, getting so excited he called up Krist to play him the song over the phone. "I'm like: wow, that's really cool, that's cool, man. Let's rehearse, let's practice, let's play it," Krist recalls. "So we got in rehearsal and then it came together pretty fast." "That song was almost good to go right off the bat," Chad confirms. "When I first started playing drums to it, I played the drums exactly the way they always have been and are today."

The song's anthemic strut is obvious from the opening bars, guitar, bass, and drums booming with authority, creating a welcoming, celebratory mood that encourages the listener to join in. This makes the bite of the lyrics that much sharper, for the chorus takes a broad swipe at the band's audience, pointing a disdainful finger at a man who likes the songs but is blissfully ignorant of their meaning; that this figure is also a described as a gun owner links him with the backward-thinking 'Mr Moustache.' In a press bio for *Nevermind*, Kurt would explain the song's meaning in one word: "Reproduction." In other interviews he was more straightforward; asked about the song in January 1992, he replied: "I don't like rednecks, I don't like macho men. I don't like abusive people, and I guess that's what that song is about, it's an attack on them." Which makes it all the more curious that the song is also said to refer to Kurt's best friend, Dylan Carlson, although Kurt himself never addressed this subject in interviews.

Butch immediately recognized the song's strength. "That was the track I focused on the most, I think, out of all of the songs," he says. "It sounded to me like a single. That's probably the song that we did the most takes of – probably not more than four or five – but I think it took a bunch of takes to get a good master. That was a little bit harder for Kurt to get the vocals on. We went back and overdubbed just guitar on that because I was like: we can make this sound better. I wanted it to sound better than the scratch guitar." When the song was deemed to be a bit too long, Butch simply sliced an instrumental section out of the tape with a razor blade.

Butch recalls Kurt being especially unhappy with Chad's work on this song, something that became increasingly obvious as the sessions continued. "We'd do a take and Kurt would say: no, I don't like that fill you're doing there, you've got to hit it harder in that section," Butch recalls. "I remember several times Kurt actually got over on the drums and tried to show him, but Kurt was not a good drummer. He was trying to show Chad more as a feel – trying to figure out what he wanted for that section. 'In Bloom' was one of the songs where he got behind the kit and was trying to show Chad a drum fill. The arrangement on that section of the song is different from what Dave played. I think that Kurt felt like they were struggling to get it to sound super-tight and powerful."

The abrasive 'Pay To Play' was akin to 'Immodium' in being another pummeling number that went all out from start to finish. "That one has a bitchin' bass line in it," says Krist. "Just pumping it, driving it – keep it going with the drums, keep the melody but not the same riff, playing off the guitar. It was a raw song. We just went in there and busted that song out." Whereas the title refers to the practice of some clubs who made bands sell tickets to their own shows in order to get paid, the lyrics are another seemingly random litany of words. More notable is Kurt's unhinged vocal – you can practically hear his throat tearing itself apart as he repeatedly screams out the title at the song's end, the instruments then falling over themselves in an audio approximation of the end of the band's stage show. The song was neatly transformed on *Nevermind* by a simple change of title to 'Stay Away'; now, instead of a rant, the lyric became a warning.

The band then tackled 'Sappy' again. "We just kept playing it," says Krist. "Maybe we thought we'd hit it. But I never changed my bass line because I really liked what I was playing on bass, so I was pretty content with it. I think what happened was we thought we'd finally use it this time." Several other changes had been made from the previously recorded version with Jack Endino; there was now an intro instead of a cold opening, and the full band didn't come in until after Kurt sang the first line. It was also a less heavy version; even the guitar solo during the break is more restrained.

"Kurt really liked 'Sappy' a lot," says Chad. "He just wanted to get a version where he could finally put it out on record. It was just one of those things, where, OK, this could be a really cool song and somehow it's not coming out sounding the way we want it to for some reason or another. He just wasn't going to let it die. Get this song down, damn it, no matter what it takes!"

Next was 'Lithium,' which was much improved from the rougher performance captured during the Evergreen shoot. It was the first song to exhibit the trademark formula of Nirvana's later hits: the soft verse and raging chorus. "I pumped up the chorus," says Krist of his bass line. "I went to make it the big chorus – I'm doing the verse, I play higher, then I do this thing where I don't follow the guitar, I just play off it, notes that are melodically appropriate. And then when the chorus comes in, you go down to the E, fatten it up. You kind of put it on a silver platter, like: there it is – there's a big huge chorus."

"That fell into place pretty easily," says Chad. "When we started playing it, I had these ideas, like the whole intro idea, with the rim shots – that was something that I was doing with that song from the beginning, from the very first time we played it. From the time we first started playing it to when we eventually recorded it, there's very little difference in the song at all."

Kurt's lyric weds another disturbing story to an upbeat melody, in this case an atypically bright and even optimistic one. As the title suggests, the song's theme is madness, lithium being an antidepressant. "People who are secluded for too long go insane and as a last resort they often use religion to keep alive," Kurt explained. "In the song, a guy's lost his girl and his friends and he's brooding. He's decided to find God before he kills himself." Yet in the first line comes the pronouncement "I'm so happy," and a later verse insists "I'm not sad"; the underlying disquiet is only revealed in the bridge, in the accelerating litany of "like it"/"miss you"/"love you"/"kill you."

"It was a great song," says Butch. "It had a gorgeous melody over the chord progression. Krist and Kurt seemed to have an intuitive feel, back and forth. The great thing that I noticed right off the bat was that Kurt wrote these amazing songs, but Krist wrote these super-hooky bass lines. The bass lines are really melodic. A lot of times the chords are pretty much cowboy chords, with the back-and-forth kind of rhythm, and the hook of the song was actually in the bass. That worked so well with Kurt's vocal melody. They had a really cool, interweaving quality. I don't know that Krist ever really got much credit for how hooky the bass parts are, but they are damn hooky. A lot of Krist's bass parts sort of remind me of Black Sabbath, in that a lot of the punk bands I'd been recording up to that point pretty much followed whatever the guitar player did – it was very unimaginative – so it was refreshing to have this counter-play between the bass hook and the vocal melody and the rhythm guitar."

'Lithium' would also be the most difficult song to record. "That one took a bunch of takes to get," says Butch. "Even to me today it still sounds a little shaky – it sort of pushes and pulls, and not in a good way. Probably a lot of people think it sounds fine, but I can hear it. I could tell when they were tracking it that it was not going down very well. Kurt stopped after a couple of takes, just sort of got pissed off and went and sat down and didn't want to play. We went back to it later that night and tracked it again. I think he was just so frustrated that it wasn't sounding like the way it did in his head that he didn't even want to record at that point. So I was like: why don't we just work on something else?" (This is perhaps one reason why Nirvana aren't known to have played the song live until August 1990, even though it was finished in April.)

Butch found it tricky to deal with Kurt's suddenly changing moods. "He could be very charming, very articulate, very focused for an hour, then he would shut down for an hour," he says. "He had these extreme bipolar mood swings. That was the most frustrating thing. So I would address Krist about stuff: I think we should work on this, or this should be tighter here, or the guitar sound could be better in the song, let's try maybe a different amp. Kurt would sit in the corner and not really respond – about half the time he did, and half the time he didn't. I couldn't get a handle on what made him turn on and turn off."

Even so, Butch was intrigued by Kurt's constant creativity. "Kurt was always playing songs," he recalls. "We'd be setting stuff up or I'd be changing a mic or Krist would break a string, and Kurt would sit around and play stuff on that little acoustic guitar or he'd be strumming the electric – not plugged in, he'd just be playing quietly in the corner. He was always playing Velvet Underground covers or a lot of Beatles things. He was always playing these little things that sounded amazing to me. I was like: what's that? That sounds really cool. And he goes: oh, it's nothing; I'm just fooling around. It was the same on *Nevermind*. I'd catch him playing stuff and I was like: you should record that. And he'd say no and stop playing. But there were all these little riffs of things that sounded amazing to me. He'd be singing some sort of scratch lyric, some melody over a chord progression, and they were all pretty cool. But I think a lot of it for him was … part of that was a nervous energy and because he loved doing that. As soon as I'd try to draw it out of him, a lot of times he would shut down."

Kurt's guitar-doodling on Velvet Underground songs had a point to it, for it was during this session that Nirvana recorded a version of 'Here She Comes Now' (from the Velvets' second album, *White Light/White Heat*) for the compilation album *Heaven And Hell Vol. 1: A Tribute To The Velvet Underground*. This came as a surprise to Chad, who, yet again, hadn't been told about an upcoming project. "I had no idea we were supposed to be doing a Velvet Underground song," he says. "I'd never heard the song before! I had no idea how it went. And they just started playing this riff and I was like: what's this? OK, whatever, I'll just start playing." Unlike Nirvana's reworking of 'Love Buzz,' the arrangement and sound of 'Here She Comes Now' are initially similar to the Velvets' original. But where the original fades out after two minutes, Nirvana spin the song out to five minutes, rising in intensity as it goes, especially when Kurt's vocal goes up an octave.

After running through the song once, the band recorded it in one take. "They didn't spend very much time on it," says Butch. "And it was pretty long. I think I did a little editing on that. From the original version I just cut it down; I maybe cut like 30 seconds out of it." Ultimately, it became something of a throwaway for the band. "We had never played that song before and we hardly ever played it after," Krist said. Nor did the band get a good response when they first played the song live a month later, at a May 2 show in Charlotte, North Carolina. "Kurt, you just completely ruined my favorite Velvet Underground song. I hope you're happy," one attendee jokingly told Kurt after Nirvana's set. "If you thought that was bad," Kurt replied, "wait till you hear the version we recorded!"

With the last song, 'Polly,' Kurt opted for something new. Even his original demo had been recorded with an electric guitar; now, he said, he wanted to do an acoustic arrangement. "Kurt just wanted to make it really, really simple," says Chad. "When we played it live, it was always backed with drums. But for whatever reason I guess he just decided that he wanted to have a more mellower version of it." "Obviously, the song is very dark, and I think that sometimes the band gets in the way," says Butch. "Trying to make the band work with the track, he thought, sounded intrusive. He just felt like it was getting in the way of the song, which makes perfect sense."

Kurt pulled out the Stella he'd bought the previous year, despite Butch's suggestion he use a better guitar to get a "pristine sound." "No, no," Kurt replied, "*this* is the sound, this dark sound." "It had almost a plucky, ukulele sound, which I thought was kind of cool," says Butch. Using the Stella was a key decision – the final touch that makes the song especially evocative, all the more so for being paired with Kurt's haunting, dispassionate vocal.

After a quick run through, the song was recorded in one take. "Kurt sang a scratch vocal, and just sort of mumbled it just to get through the song. He wanted to concentrate on playing the guitar. When he recorded, he played it really quiet. It was like he sort of would almost want to get into a corner and play it for himself. It wasn't like he was trying to project with it. I remember I had to really bring the mics up. There's actually a fair amount of tape hiss on everything. Once he started, I should have brought the levels up, but he was already into the take so I didn't want to adjust the levels. I realized doing those sessions that once I was hitting 'record' it wasn't like I could stop and say I needed to adjust the sound – I had to be able to capture on the fly."

After recording the vocal, Krist then overdubbed his bass part, and Chad, sitting in a separate booth, added a few cymbal splashes. "It was just the cymbal stand and me," he says. "They moved me into a booth with one of my cymbals, and there I was. And I listened to the song on headphones, and put the cymbals where they were." "It took literally 30, maybe slightly over 30 minutes, but not much more than that," says Butch. Butch has mistakenly said that the line "Polly said," sung right before the final verse, was a "mistake" that they decided to leave in. In fact, Kurt had frequently (although not always) sung the line in live performance, and in the 1989 BBC rendition of the song, not to mention the original demo.

Toward the end of the sessions, a show had been scheduled on April 6 at Madison's Club Underground. Jonathan Poneman flew out to check on the band's progress and attend the show. "Club Underground was a long, narrow room," says Butch. "It didn't have much of a PA. I'd never seen Nirvana live, so it was great; I thought they were amazing. A lot of the local music scene was there, everybody who knew who they were; Killdozer was there. That was the first inkling that there was some super buzz on the band because the place was packed. And it was all people in the know in the underground in Madison – people who ran clubs and a lot of musicians and people from record stores. You could tell there was a buzz about them."

Nirvana was again sharing the bill with TAD, and Kurt Danielson was stunned on first hearing 'In Bloom.' "That was a quantum leap, that song, from what they did before," he says. "It just took my breath away, in a similar way that 'Teen Spirit' did later. And I'm certain that Kurt knew what it was." Danielson also noted Kurt's increasing improvement as a live performer. "In the beginning, he seemed a little lost on stage," he says. "Then at some point the confidence built in him, and he became a commanding performer – he began to own the stage. The development was imperceptible; it happened over time, and there were little evolutionary leaps along the way. And 'In Bloom' was probably the biggest one that I saw."

By the end of the show, however, Kurt had blown his voice out again, while Krist had swung his bass around with such vigor that he managed to poke a hole in the club's low ceiling. "Kurt's voice was just shot the next day," says Butch. "He was like: I don't want to attempt the last couple of songs. And I was like: well, we could record the basics on them, but he said: no, my voice is shot. And he wasn't feeling very well. That's also when I noticed he had problems with his stomach; all of these ailments that would grow worse on *Nevermind* and later were definitely bothering him when we were in that recording session. So we just did some rough mixes."

Since Nirvana had a show scheduled for April 8 in Milwaukee, the sessions were effectively over. Although Nirvana hadn't quite managed to record an album's worth of songs, they did come close; with 'Here She Comes Now' already headed for the Velvets tribute album, there were still seven completed tracks. "Generally, you could fill an album with eight to ten songs," says Chad. "And we recorded eight songs, so we were only a few songs shy from actually having a full album." Butch was also under the impression the album was nearly done. "I told Jonathan: I'll go through these tracks, I'll mix these down and send them to you, and we'll schedule a time for me to finish later," he says. "We'd been talking loosely about me going to Seattle to finish them, or having them come back after the tour." But the songs would never appear on a Sub Pop album, and would instead trickle out over the years. 'Here She Comes Now' was the first to appear, released that fall on the *Heaven And Hell* compilation on

Imaginary Records in the UK (and on Communion in the USA the following year). 'In Bloom' was used for the band's first professional video. 'Dive' would appear on the B-side of the 'Sliver' single, also released in 1990. 'Polly' would appear, remixed, on *Nevermind*, and 'Pay To Play' would be the first posthumous Nirvana release when it appeared on the 1994 compilation *DGC Rarities Vol. 1*.

In 2011, all of the songs, including some previously unreleased mixes, appeared on the deluxe 20th anniversary edition of *Nevermind*. By then, the songs had been bootlegged extensively, in part because the band-members passed out so many copies themselves. "Oh God, yeah," says Butch. "So many people later would say they'd got an original copy of the Smart Sessions. I'd hear it and it was just overdubbed from cassette like ten times over. It was kind of funny."

With the Smart session completed, the tour continued, heading east, with a brief swing up into Canada for two dates. On April 18 Nirvana arrived in Cambridge, Massachusetts, where they met WFNX DJ Kurt St Thomas, who would later produce the *Nevermind: It's An Interview* promo CD. Krist gave him the newest Nirvana T-shirt, which had Jonathan Poneman and Bruce Pavitt's heads superimposed on the nude bodies of John Lennon and Yoko Ono (taken from the cover *Unfinished Music No. 1: Two Virgins*). They also reconnected with photographer J.J. Gonson, who saw the band perform on the 18th, as well as a subsequent show at a fraternity party at the Massachusetts Institute of Technology in Cambridge on April 21, and an Amnesty International Benefit show at Hampshire College in Amherst, Massachusetts, on April 27. Gonson recalls the MIT show in particular being "a free for all. I don't remember there being a grown-up in the entire place. It was just pure, crazy, kid joy – just a zany frat party with tons of beer. There were these spear-like things in the room and Krist started throwing them at the audience, for fun." (Krist pushed the limit when he took apart a sign made out of bones that spelled the fraternity's name and passed them out to the audience, but the bones were retrieved without incident and the show continued.)

J.J. recalls Kurt throwing a mild tantrum before the show, lying on a table and kicking his legs, a result of his being tired and homesick. "Kurt was in a really crabby mood," she says. "I think at that point they were exhausted. I remember he was talking about his animals a lot, and his girlfriend." In an interview that same day, Kurt spoke about the rigors of the road: "I like playing just for the hell of it, but not for seven weeks. Playing the same set every night is as boring as a construction job. You get tired of it." And although he may have been thinking about his girlfriend, he wasn't necessarily missing her. On Tracy's birthday – the same day as the Amherst show – he called her up and said he didn't think they should live together any more.

Kurt also gave J.J. a copy of the Smart sessions songs on cassette, jokingly writing 'Blow Job' on the tape as a play on the name of their previous record, *Blew*. "They were amazing," she says. "I felt like they were just waiting for the world to figure that out. They wanted the world to hurry up, because *they* knew. Kurt certainly knew. There was never any question in my mind that he knew that he was going be a superstar. From the day I met him, I knew that: that he knew. And I knew, because before I met him, I saw him play. So I knew it too."

In between the Massachusetts shows, the band hit New York, where they shot a video for 'In Bloom,' directed by Steve Brown. Chad has few memories of the shoot. "It was just in some guy's photo studio in NY," he says. "We had a boom box set up, playing 'In Bloom' while we acted like we were playing the song. No real direction was given except to act like we were playing the song right there." The video is something of a *cinema verité* primer of life on the road, with black-and-white footage showing the band unloading their gear and carrying it up to the room where they're later seen playing, intercut with color footage of the band walking around town, eating hot dogs, and playing live (at the Pyramid and at Maxwell's). The video first appeared on the *Sub Pop Video Network Vol. 1* collection and later on the DVD included in the *With The Lights Out* boxed set.

On April 26, Bruce Pavitt arranged a photo shoot with photographer Michael Lavine, another former Evergreen student. Lavine was given a copy of the Smart sessions and played it at his next shoot, with Iggy Pop, who liked it so much that Lavine brought him to the band's show that night at the Pyramid. According to *Sounds* writer Sam King, the show suffered from a poor sound mix, culminating in a bout of instrument smashing described as "an orgy of frustrated violence." The band was unhappy with the show as well, Krist shaving his head that night in "penance" (which is why the 'In Bloom' video shows him both with and without his hair). "I just felt we were playing really badly and I wanted to kill the other members of the band and myself," Kurt told King. "Afterward I went into the van, lit a cigarette, and said for the 30th time: I'm quitting."

Once again, however, there were others who enjoyed the show. Iggy Pop liked the way Kurt "hopped around like a Muppet or an elf or something," and while Kurt may have felt embarrassed that he happened to be wearing a Stooges T-shirt that night, Iggy was pleased to see it. More importantly, Sonic Youth's Thurston Moore and Kim Gordon were in attendance, and brought along DGC's Gary Gersh as part of their ongoing promotion of Nirvana to the label. And Sam King was full of praise for Nirvana's April 28 show at Maxwell's. "Nirvana are astonishing," he raved. "In little more than 45 minutes they remind you that when they're on form they're one of the most visceral, intense, and beautiful bands on the face of the planet. When they're on form you can understand why Jonathan [Poneman] is spending such a long time on the phone on their behalf."

Craig Montgomery joined the band halfway through the tour. "They were having a lot of fun together," he says. "There was a lot of drinking going on, but it was fun. I mean, there started being tension between Kurt and Krist and Chad, when they started getting tired of Chad. But there wasn't any of this angst or tension that you hear about. Everybody seemed to have their head on pretty straight to me. Other than, you know, Krist and Kurt liked to get drunk and fuck shit up and get out of control and do crazy stuff. They were like the typical buddies from childhood who'd egg each other on, to see what the other guy would do, see how far they could take it. And sometimes they lost me. I'd be like: I'm not getting involved in this!"

One such incident came after a show in Tampa. "A lot of times we'd stay at people's houses, and this guy at the show offered to let us stay at his house," Craig explains. "So we drive, and we're going along Tampa Bay, and we end up by this really fancy, nice, big house – the guy's obviously got rich parents, there's big TVs, stereos. We slept in this rec room/den kind of thing where the 'entertainment center' was. And I guess the guy had to go to work in the morning or something, and I don't know what Krist and Kurt were on, but Krist didn't handle his liquor very well. Somehow, in the middle of the night, he decides he should get naked and go running around the cul-de-sac that we're on. Then in the morning they decide they're going to make breakfast, but nothing edible ever comes of it. They're just pulling all this food out of the cupboards, and making a big mess, and I'm like: guys, this isn't cool. This kid offered to let us stay at his house, he's doing us a favor, and now you're messing up his kitchen. Their way of making amends was to leave a hundred-dollar bill on the counter before we left."

After leaving the East Coast, the tour headed west, through the South, the Midwest, and up to Boise, Idaho, where the band played a final date on May 17 at the Zoo. It had been a tour largely free of incident, and, with the recording of new songs, had the band looking to the future. During the tour, Kurt had commented on their changing audience, a reflection of the band's growing popularity; along with "a mixture of white trash and punks who at least appreciate the arts," he also noted that there had been "some jocks at a few of our recent shows, and they liked it a lot. That's scary." But when asked about his objectives for the band, he stressed the main goal was to "write the best music we possibly can. That comes before anything else; it comes before philosophy, image or playing live. It's always been the main point. Just songs. As a unit we've come a whole lot closer to getting where we wanna be as collaborators."

But the 'unit' of Nirvana was about to undergo a major change due to Kurt and Krist's increasing unhappiness with Chad. Butch Vig had noticed it during the Smart sessions; now others were aware of the growing discontent as well. "I knew once in a while there would be some dissatisfaction with Chad's drumming," says Craig Montgomery. "Sometimes he wasn't the most solid player, and he would drop a beat. Drums were not his first instrument of choice. Krist and Kurt would talk to me about it when Chad wasn't around; Kurt may have even called me and said: we're thinking about getting rid of Chad, what do you think? I was against it at first, just 'cause I was resistant to change. I didn't want it to happen, 'cause the three of them had such a great chemistry. So I didn't think it was a good idea."

The discontent was not entirely one-sided. Chad had also become increasingly dissatisfied with his role in Nirvana. "I never really felt like I was quite part of the band," he says. A songwriter himself, Chad had hoped to have more creative input in the band besides just writing his own drum parts. "Kurt was saying: yeah, after *Bleach* comes out, it'd be cool if you wanted to come up with some ideas and stuff," he says. "And I was looking totally forward to that, 'cause that's one of the things that I really, really wanted to do. Just to contribute more. But it never transpired and it was never going to transpire. It was never going to happen. And then I just started losing interest. Slowly but surely."

Kurt later admitted to Michael Azerrad that he didn't like Chad's music: "It just wasn't good and there was nothing else to be said about it." But with neither Kurt, Krist, nor Chad predisposed to dealing with conflict, the situation was allowed to linger without being addressed. Chad readily admits his playing was beginning to suffer. "Whatever you do, whether it's music or anything else, if you're not satisfied with what you're doing, you're not really gonna do that good of a job anymore, 'cause you're not gonna be that interested," he says. "I was just not performing as well as I used to back in the old days. So I started the whole slow downfall; I just started not caring all that much. I was burning out on it, and when you're burned out on it, it totally shows. And I just never got around to saying: boy, I'm really burned out on this, I can't take this anymore. I just let it go. I just let everything go until eventually it was pretty blatantly obvious to those guys, and they were like: man, he just doesn't seem into it anymore, let's get another drummer. It was just a matter of who was going to come to who first."

In the end it was Kurt and Krist who went out to Bainbridge Island to see Chad and finalize a breakup everyone knew was pending. It was the only time Kurt and Krist met in person with another band-member to tell them they were out. "It was really kind of a big relief," says Chad. "It was like a big weight off my shoulders. Because we'd done so much together, and in the early days we had so much fun. Aside from the band stuff, we got along; we got along really well. So that was what made it so difficult."

Nirvana had grown a lot in the two years Chad Channing was in the band. But with his departure, all future plans were now on hold.

The Turning Point

"Nirvana is recording this summer for their next record due to be released this fall."
SUB POP NEWSLETTER, SUMMER 1990

Once again without a drummer, Nirvana were in a state of limbo. They would not play live again for two months – their longest break between shows since 1987. But events were pushing them to make some crucial decisions about the direction of their career.

By 1990, more alternative bands, including acts from Seattle, were signing with major labels. Mother Love Bone, the band formed by members of Green River and Malfunkshun, signed to PolyGram in 1989, and were on the verge of releasing their major-label debut, *Apple*, in March 1990, when lead singer Andrew Wood died of a heroin overdose; Soundgarden had signed with A&M and released their major-label debut in 1989; and Alice In Chains would follow with theirs on Columbia in 1990.

Seeing some of their former charges moving on prompted Sub Pop to consider an alliance with a major label themselves. "Everybody that we came in contact with who were already part of the major-label system – of which there were quite a few because the major-label system was so much bigger at that time – would keep on advocating: you guys have got to do a deal, you're going to lose all your bands and blah blah blah," says Jonathan Poneman. "Bruce and I never really saw it that way because Bruce in particular, to his credit, saw our enterprise as being more of a local familial endeavor as opposed to being a national or multinational music company. But we also saw in the wake of a lot of local bands' success that we needed to have additional resources if we wanted to keep playing on the same turf that we were playing on."

As Sub Pop began negotiating with the majors for a distribution deal, they presented their bands with new contracts. Both Kurt and Krist were hesitant to sign, being well aware that more bands were signing directly with a major label themselves. "Everybody was getting a major deal, like Sonic Youth and Dinosaur Jr.," says Krist. "It seemed like the labels were signing all kinds of bands. And if Sub Pop was going to sign to a major, it was like: why do we need to have a middle man?"

The two set up a meeting with Soundgarden's manager, Susan Silver, to ask her advice. "We met up with Susan to say we wanted to sign with a major label ourselves," Krist explains. "And she's like: well, I'm going to be down in LA in a couple days – why don't you meet me there? So the next day we just got in the van and started driving. And we pulled into LA and we found a motel, the Saharan Motor Hotel, on Sunset Boulevard. We hung out there: no visitors, no this, no that, just a flea bag motel. Saw some friends. And Susan, she introduced us to a few people. God bless her. And she set us up with this attorney, so we had a Hollywood attorney."

The attorney was Alan Mintz, who at the time was working for the law firm Ziffren Brittenham & Branca, and had worked with up and coming alternative acts like Faith No More and Jane's Addiction, two acts Krist felt "broke ground for us." Mintz told Charles Cross he found the two musicians "naïve but ambitious," with Kurt especially outspoken in his determination to leave Sub Pop. Kurt and Krist gave Mintz a copy of the Smart sessions tape; the songs they'd recorded for a second Sub Pop album now became a demo to help the band secure a major-label deal.

Since returning from their last tour, Kurt and Krist had been busily dubbing copies of the Smart sessions – sometimes on cassette copies of *Bleach* – and passing them out to everyone they could think of. As a result, the songs were bootlegged extensively; Smart's engineer, Doug Olson, was surprised to find that bands arriving for sessions at the studio had a copy of the tape. Anton Brookes was amused to find that his copy of the demo abruptly cut off in the middle of 'Lithium'; you had to flip the tape over to hear the song's ending. "Krist gave me one and said: don't tell Jonathan that I gave you this," Jack Endino recalls. "I thought 'Dive' was brilliant. 'In Bloom' was great. And 'Pay To Play' was pretty cool." Craig Montgomery was also impressed by the band's musical progression. "They were figuring out what their voice was," he says. "It was more focused. Some of the more riffy kind of things from *Bleach* weren't there anymore; there's some stuff on *Bleach* that they never did anything like that again. They got more straight ahead, I think. Kurt made no bones about the fact that he wanted to go in more of a pop direction, even back then."

Nonetheless, Kurt and Krist decided to record one more record for Sub Pop. But they still needed a drummer. One night at the Vogue, Shelli and Tracy (who had finally broken up with Kurt but remained friendly with him) ran into Dan Peters, who was himself at a loose end, as Mudhoney's guitarist Steve Turner was contemplating a return to college, leaving the band's future in question. "Shit, as far as I was concerned, we'd just started," says Dan. "I was loving going out on tour, and playing live and stuff, and the last thing I wanted to do was fucking stop! And so when I ran into those guys at the Vogue, and they said, Chad's out of the band, they're looking for a drummer. I was like: wow, I'd like to play drums for them. And they passed the word on, and I got a call from Kurt, and we hooked it up."

From the beginning, Dan made it clear he wasn't interested in being a fill-in. "I point-blank asked those guys: am I going to be in the band?" he recalls. "I don't want to audition. If you're going to keep rehearsing drummers after me, I'll bow out. I don't want to try out for the part. If you want me, you want me, and if you don't, you don't. And they're like: oh, no, no, no, no, it's cool."

At the time, Nirvana was rehearsing at a warehouse space just south of downtown Seattle called the Dutchman. Although he'd known Kurt and Krist for some time, Dan found his new bandmates to be surprisingly reserved. "With Mudhoney, at practice we'd sit around and drink, hang out, smoke cigarettes, party – you know, just have a good time," he says. "And that wasn't really what was going on with those guys. I didn't really click with them like I did with Mudhoney. The ease factor wasn't there. Kurt didn't really talk much, he'd just plug his guitar in and crank it up super loud – and then they'd tell me that they couldn't hear my drums. And I'm like: yeah, no shit, neither can I! I could tell that they wanted me to play a big ol' drum set, and I was really not willing to make that concession. It was probably somewhat of a strange ego thing that I had at the time – I don't need a big ol' drum set! And now of course I have one. But my time spent with those guys practicing wasn't, to me, very fun."

Nonetheless, Dan was impressed with Nirvana's new material. "Kurt came over to my place and we went into my bedroom where my stereo was, and he said he had some stuff to play," he says. "And the songs were great. One of the first songs I ever heard from that new stuff was 'In Bloom.' I just thought that was one of the greatest songs I ever heard from any of my contemporaries, my friends. I thought that was a crazy good song, and was completely psyched about it."

Dan's tenure in the band also coincided with the writing of a new song, 'Sliver.' There had been autobiographical elements in Kurt's songs before – 'About A Girl' and 'Even In His Youth' come to mind – but none had been as direct as 'Sliver.' The song is a simple reminiscence of childhood, with Kurt recounting an evening he spent at his grandparents when he would rather have been at home. A demo, which appears on *With The Lights Out*, is largely similar to the final version, the only major difference coming in the final verse; on the demo, the verse is about being burned by a cigarette, while in the released version the narrator is simply reunited with his parents. "I decided I wanted to write the most ridiculous pop song that I had ever written," Kurt told Michael Azerrad. "It was like a statement in a way. I had to write a real pop song and release it on a single to prepare people for the next record." The song had the childlike pull of songs by Kurt's beloved Half Japanese and The Vaselines, with a hint of something more disturbing going on beneath the surface.

The song's arrangement came together during rehearsals. "Kurt started up the riff," Dan recalls, "and it's obviously a really straight ahead song, and it just came very easily. Everybody was like: yeah, that sounds good. How about doing this? It definitely wasn't: this is my song, this is how it goes, start to finish, because it was just a riff. It seemed really kind of off the cuff; there was no set way to do it or anything. I love that song. I think it's a great song." Considering that the liner notes to *With The Lights Out* say the 'Sliver' demo was recorded in 1989, the song was evidently more finished than Danny realized. But at Krist's suggestion, some of the chorus repetitions of "Grandma, take me home" were cut back.

With Nirvana scheduled to go out on tour in August, Sub Pop was anxious to get the song recorded quickly. "On July 11, I had TAD in the studio," says Jack. "And Jon called up and was begging for Nirvana to cut this one song, really fast, and is there any way they could just use Tad's equipment? I said well, let me see. Tad was kind of testy about it; he was like: this is our time, you know; we're trying to record something here. And I said: well, you guys take a dinner break, OK? You guys go and eat dinner. I'm sure we can do this in an hour."

And they did. With Dan using TAD drummer Steve Wied's kit, the basic tracks for 'Sliver' were laid down in one hour at Reciprocal. "We just went in and banged it out," says Dan. "There was a bit of finessing here and there on my part, drum-wise, but it was pretty straight ahead, and good to go." A second, ten-hour session was held on July 24, when Kurt recorded his vocal and the song was mixed. It was "an ungodly amount of time, for then," Jack notes. "I was a little worried, because it was another song that has no bridge," he adds, recalling that 'Sappy' also had no bridge. "It doesn't even have a solo. I thought: man, what is happening to their songwriting? Have they forgotten how to write songs? There were two in a row that seemed to me really rudimentary songs. But of course, as it turns out, we had nothing to worry about."

Kurt later described 'Sliver' as "an experiment in dynamics and simplicity," something apparent from the song's arrangement. The first verse has Kurt singing to the sole accompaniment of Krist's bass line and Dan's taps on the hi-hat cymbal, Kurt's guitar finally entering when it ushers in the chorus with a whine. The full band plays on the second verse, and Kurt heightens the tension by raising his vocal an octave on the third verse. In a neat twist, on the fourth verse the music is again scaled back, while Kurt continues to sing in an upper register, underscoring the narrator's frustration at his situation. "I loved the way he screamed out 'After dinner, I had ice cream!'" says Dawn Anderson. "That was one of the greatest, *greatest* phrasings I'd ever heard! Only Kurt could take that line and put so much angst into it." As a final joke, the band tagged on a conversation between Jonathan Poneman and a very hungover Krist that Krist's answering machine had inadvertently recorded. The song was paired with 'Dive' from the Smart sessions and released on Sub Pop in September; the answering machine conversation only appears on the single. The front cover shows a purplish Visible Man model, standing out in stark relief against a blue background; the back cover has one of Charles Peterson's shots from the Raji's show of February 15, printed as a reverse negative, à la *Bleach*. The initial run of US seven-inch singles was available on blue or pink vinyl.

One reason for Sub Pop's haste in getting the single out was their growing awareness than Nirvana was planning to leave the label. Typically, Bruce and Jonathan learned of Nirvana's unhappiness through rumor, rather than being told directly. "I just don't understand how you're expected to come right out and tell someone something like that," Kurt later admitted. Bruce took the band's decision especially hard. "It really fucked with my head for a while," he later said. Jonathan agrees. "I think Nirvana's leaving [Sub Pop] was very demoralizing for Bruce," he says. "I remember at the time that that really wounded him. Not so much from the business standpoint, but just the feeling that anybody and anything could be bought and sold in the marketplace; he thought that our relationship was grounded more on common values and not so much on dollars and cents."

Bruce went to Olympia to meet with Kurt, bringing copies of The Shaggs' *Philosophy Of The World* and Daniel Johnston's *Hi, How Are You* as gifts. "My intention was to essentially communicate to him that, at the end of the day, Sub Pop was going to support unusual points of view," he explained. They spoke for hours, but Kurt still couldn't come right out and confirm Nirvana were leaving the label. He was more open later with Azerrad in addressing the crux of the matter: "We felt we deserved a little bit more than what we were getting." Kurt knew his material was getting stronger, and he didn't feel an independent label like Sub Pop had the muscle to get the greater exposure he desired, pointing to the lack of ads Sub Pop had taken out for the band's records as one example of the label's ineffectiveness. "We weren't being promoted very well," he told *Backlash*. "I challenge anybody to find a *Bleach* ad." In his defense, Bruce told Mark Yarm that Sub Pop tended to do group ads that promoted more than one act on the label. "I felt that [Kurt] was truly missing the big picture, because we were so effective at garnering press," he said. "Literally a year and a half after he was sleeping under bridges, he was on the front cover of *Melody Maker* in England. I'd say that's pretty effective label promotion."

But Sub Pop also had another growing crisis on their hands. Their efforts to hype the label had resulted in Bruce and Jonathan spending money they didn't have. Negotiations with major labels had also resulted in hefty legal bills, creating more debt. Record sales weren't enough to cover the bills. "They hit rock bottom," Krist told Azerrad. "They tried really hard to pay us because they really appreciated us, and that's cool, but it was just too much of a burden."

Amid this growing estrangement, Nirvana headed out on an eight-date West Coast tour, opening for Sonic Youth. Kurt and Krist informed Dan they had previously arranged for Dale Crover to be their drummer on the tour. "I was like: yeah, whatever," says Dan (in fact Mudhoney was scheduled to be on tour at the same time, including their first appearance at the Reading Festival). Dale had agreed to the tour on the condition that his drum kit was off limits during any end-of-set instrument smashing; his forcefulness on the subject was such that neither Kurt nor Krist smashed any of their gear on the tour.

The tour saw the debut of a new song, 'Verse Chorus Verse.' The song has an appealing, somewhat lilting melody (more apparent in live versions of the song than in the studio version), with lyrics detailing Kurt's typical ambivalence about relationships. One could easily imagine it being recorded during the Smart sessions, but the song was never finalized, as the constantly changing lyrics in the different versions reveal, and the band only performed it a handful of times. "It was too straightforward," says Krist. "It had no personality." Nonetheless, Nirvana recorded a rough version of the song during the *Nevermind* sessions in 1991; this version was later released on *With The Lights Out*. Confusingly, the song's title was later given to 'Sappy' when Nirvana's version of that song, recorded during the *In Utero* sessions, was released under the name 'Verse Chorus Verse' on the 1993 *No Alternative* compilation.

More importantly, the tour gave Nirvana the chance to build on the interest they were getting from major labels. DGC's Mark Kates attended the tour's opening night, August 16 in Las Vegas, meeting the band-members for the first time. He also attended the show the next night, at the Hollywood Palladium, taking note of the audience's response. "I remember checking them out and liking them, and just thinking: yeah, these guys are cool!" he says. "There were clearly people that were aware of them, and knew the songs. I remember noticing that there was definitely something going on there, and I probably said something to Gary [Gersh, DGC's A&R rep], who was standing there with me." Also in attendance at the show was MCA's A&R rep Bret Hartman, who had long been interested in signing Nirvana.

Kurt and Krist made another key connection during the tour when they were introduced to Sonic Youth's manager, John Silva. Silva was then working at the management company Gold Mountain Entertainment, co-founded in 1983 by Danny Goldberg. Goldberg was a music industry veteran who had got his start in the business as a journalist at *Billboard*; he went on to do PR for Led Zeppelin in the 70s and co-direct and co-produce the film of the 1979 No Nukes concert at Madison Square Garden before moving into artist management in the 80s.

John Silva was a recent hiring at Gold Mountain. "I wanted to bring in somebody younger, who was really fluent in what was happening in the punk/alternative scene," Danny explains. "John's strengths were twofold. He was really into punk music and the indie scene, so he was culturally one of them. And he has a tremendous attention to detail; he's just a very disciplined guy, who makes lists of things, and checks everything off on the list. He certainly had a passion for the music, but he wasn't just a fan: he was also somebody who had a great work ethic. You need to have both to be valuable to an artist." Sonic Youth had been introduced to Silva by their friends in Redd Kross, another band Silva managed. Silva had brought both Redd Kross and House Of Freaks to Gold Mountain and secured major-label deals for them; with Sonic Youth, who'd already signed with DGC (their major-label debut, *Goo*, was released in June 1990), Silva helped ease the transition from the indie realm. Slowly but surely, Kurt and Krist were forming alliances with the individuals who would be crucial in the next stage of their career.

The tour reached Seattle on August 24 with a date at the Moore Theatre. Evergreen student Rob Nyberg was now interning at Sub Pop, and when Sonic Youth's Lee Renaldo came by the office and offered to put everyone who wanted to attend the show on the guest list, he happily signed up. "I was able to be in the orchestra pit," Rob says, "although I also watched it from further back. The Moore show was interesting. It was more of a 'rapt attention' type of show than it was crazy. You could feel the Nirvana train was definitely starting to chug a little harder and people were paying more attention to them." The performance was somewhat restrained; Kurt dropped to his knees while playing 'In Bloom''s squalling guitar solo and spent time coaxing feedback from his guitar during the closing number, 'Blew,' but there was no instrument destruction. (The tour ended the following night in Vancouver, British Columbia.)

The band's next Seattle show, at the Motor Sports International Garage on September 22, definitely fell into the 'crazy' category. As the name suggests, the venue wasn't a proper club, but a garage, with a makeshift stage set up for the bands – "a big, echoey-sounding garage," according to Buzz Osborne. "Not my favorite venue. It was big, noisy, bad-sounding." The show drew well over a thousand people, making it Nirvana's biggest show to date, and had them headlining over local band The Derelicts, Chicago's Dwarves, and the Melvins. "That show was total chaos," says Rob. "That was the only show in my life, during the Dwarves' set, that I ever rode the pit." The Dwarves also provided the gig's first moment of anarchy. "It got ugly because the Dwarves were just out of control," Craig Montgomery recalls. "The bass player threw a glass bottle off the stage into the crowd, and it hit somebody right in the head. Then somebody near that person picked up the bottle and threw it back, and hit the bass player right on the head! Knocked him out!" "He was in a world of hurt," says Krist, who took the time to find an ice pack to soothe the injured musician.

Craig was also unhappy about the audience's wild behavior. "That show was frustrating for me because it was really poorly organized and there was no security," he says. "People were jumping on stage and knocking all the mics over, and stepping on Kurt's cord and pedals and stuff – we couldn't get through a song. And for me the songs are God, you know? To me, it's about the songs, and these people were ruining every song! You couldn't even see the band for all the people on stage. I got on the talkback mic and asked if anybody was going to keep the audience off the stage. And finally they managed to rustle up somebody. But it was out of control. I don't know if we ever got through a song without any mishap."

Dan Peters concurs. "It seemed like every song was interrupted by somebody jumping on stage and unplugging something or knocking something over," he says. "But obviously that was the vibe of the show. Mudhoney had played a show there – I think we did the very first show at the Motor Sports – but that Nirvana show was definitely way more packed, and had a lot more fire behind it. It was pretty wild, and it was a pretty damn big show. It was chaotic and inspired – a crazy show, but fun." This was evident in Dan's expression; Rob remembers Dan "having this huge, beaming smile on his face. It was almost as if, even though he was playing, he was watching the show as well."

The audience was equally enthused about Nirvana. "Once again, the buzz was in the air," says Rob. "They tore it up. It was one of those cool, glorious rock'n'roll shows, where everyone's like: yeeeaaah!" "That one just changed absolutely everything," says Earnie Bailey. Earnie had loved the 'Sliver' single ("Right then and there was when I pulled up my anchors for any other band and just dedicated myself to Nirvana"), and was amazed at the size of the Motor Sports show. "It was pretty incredible," he says. "It was punk rock on a huge scale. There were tons of people in there, and a real PA, so they could get as loud as they wanted to. And I remember the sound just being phenomenal."

When the Dwarves bassist was hit with the bottle, Earnie worried it might lead to show being shut down. "There was an atmosphere of tension," he recalls. "And when Nirvana came on, Kurt had a completely different look about him. He didn't have all this long hair in front of his face so you couldn't see what he looked like; you could tell that he was actually a really good-looking guy. It was the first time I had heard a lot of the *Nevermind* songs. And I remember watching

Kurt at that show and thinking to myself that it was like seeing Springsteen in a club, just knowing that you're in the presence of something special. Just watching him and thinking that he was a really important songwriter." Krist, as was often his habit when playing live, was barefoot. ("It seemed to blur the line between hippie and punk," Charles Peterson later noted.)

The show attracted greater media interest as well. "That was the first time there was a bunch of people, not just me and Tracy and Charles," says Alice Wheeler. "There were all these other photographers – like all of a sudden there was a mass of people there. Kurt got Dylan to come find me, because that was the first show you needed a backstage pass for." Dylan gave Alice his pass so she could get backstage and speak to Kurt. "Save some film for the end," he told her. "I'm going to do something special. Just wait."

By the show's end, the photographers were all crowded stage left. "There was a kind of space at the front of the stage, and I started off in that," says Charles. "But it was a fairly high stage, and you're really looking up nostrils from there. And also, it just got so crowded with stage-divers and the security running people in and out, we all just had to get out of there at a certain point. We all ended up on the side of the stage. That side was the easiest access, but also that was the side Kurt was on – and you want pictures of Kurt, you know?" Kurt's 'surprise' came at the end of a searing performance of 'School,' which had him throwing himself around the stage as audience members climbed out of the churning mass packed down front, getting up on the stage and jumping off at will, much to Craig's frustration. With feedback wailing, Kurt began smashing his guitar, then climbed onto a speaker, swinging the guitar by its strap as Dan and Krist continued to play. He then leaped back to the stage, trying to break the guitar's neck, eventually smashing the instrument in two, causing a few fans to scramble up and grab the pieces before being hustled off by the bouncers. Alice noted that before 'School' had begun, Kurt actually changed guitars, swapping his Mosrite Gospel for an Aria Pro Two;

while he appreciated the dramatic touch smashing an instrument added to the shows, he took care not to smash his favorite guitars, and was by now acquiring spares to use during the end-of-set destruction.

Alice took a great shot capturing Kurt in mid-guitar twirl; another portrait she took was a haunting double-exposure that had Kurt looking somewhat the worse for wear. "He's got this kind of almost sad, numbed look on his face," she agrees. "He looks sad, but it didn't feel sad to me. It wasn't sad at all. It was completely overjoyous. Nirvana was great. It was exciting." *Sounds'* Ian Tilton shot the most well known picture from the show, of a seemingly distraught Kurt sitting on the ground afterward, face screwed up in a grimace. When Kurt first burst into tears, Tilton knew instantly that such an image would produce a strong photo, but he hesitated before taking up his camera. "Should I take it, because it is a vulnerable moment?" he wondered. "I am not a paparazzi, I am a documentary photographer." In the end, he decided to take the shot, and despite later writers finding it a "prophetic" image of Kurt "floored in anguish," Kurt's malaise was momentary. By Tilton's third shot, he was smiling. "He had just trashed his gear on stage, and it was simply a release of energy," Tilton explained. "He simply came off stage, sat down, and cried for about half a minute. Then he was fine."

The Motor Sports show marked a turning point for Nirvana. It was their biggest headlining show in Seattle to date, but it was also one of their last; over the next three-and-a-half years, they would play just eight more shows in the city. "I remember watching them and thinking that this was as perfect as a band could be," says Earnie Bailey. "And not really expecting anything to happen after that point. I just remember thinking that I had seen a band in its apex, and that that was it – it's really just a matter of time now before something happens and it's gone. And I really didn't expect any – I really didn't imagine what was going to happen in the next year."

Interest in Nirvana was quickly moving beyond fans of alternative music. Mark Kates, in Seattle for the record-release party for *Dear 23* by The Posies (another DGC act), also attended the September 22 show. "It wouldn't have been random that I was there," he says. "Because Kim [Gordon] had told us to sign them, and we had just seen them on tour with Sonic Youth, reaching people. That show was like: whoa! Something's going on here. OK, they're from here, but this is a lot of people to be going to see any band in any city and reacting this way. There were a few A&R people there. It's funny to think about gigs like that and who's there – everyone's checking each other out, and really funny things happen; people decide they want to sign a band, and then they leave the gig so that the other A&R people will think they *don't* want to sign them, et cetera."

Nirvana's now inevitable move to the majors was the focus of Keith Cameron's next article for *Sounds*, tellingly entitled 'Take The Money And Run.' Keith had also been at the Motor Sports show, which he calls "one of the greatest shows I've ever seen, not just one of the greatest Nirvana shows. I thought Dan did great." He and Ian were put up at Krist's home (they slept on a mattress on the floor, and awoke to the sound of Krist serenading them with Black Flag songs), so were on hand for a barbeque Krist and Shelli hosted the day after the Motor Sports gig. "They were all really nice, especially Krist, who was a great host," he recalls. "Interaction with Kurt could be a bit awkward, but I soon got used to the fact that he sometimes just sat there and didn't talk to anyone for considerable periods of time. I thought he was just shy. Fair enough." Keith also gave the Nirvana members long-sleeved *Sounds* T-shirts; Kurt ended up wearing his on stage at a number of shows over the next year, including a March 8 1991 show in Vancouver, British Columbia, that produced one of Charles Peterson's best known shots of Kurt, playing guitar while seemingly balanced on his head. ("Just that Vancouver show alone, there's probably been more images reproduced from that than all the others I photographed put together," he says.)

Despite his occasional reticence, Kurt was clear enough about his determination to move to a larger playing field, even as he tried to downplay his ambition. "It's really not hard to keep your dignity and sign to a major label," he told Keith, while hastening to add: "A year ago we wouldn't even have considered signing with a major, or even looking into it." He trod a similarly thin line when he said: "Maintaining the punk rock ethos is more important to me than anything," before offhandedly casting rock'n'roll as his only employment option and confessing a yearning for stardom. "I don't wanna have any other kind of job, I can't work among people. I may as well try and make a career out of this. All my life my dream has been to be a big rock star – just may as well abuse it while you can." Still, while Kurt was able to discuss the matter with Keith, he had yet to officially tell Sub Pop of Nirvana's intention to leave, merely assuring Keith the label was "aware of what we're doing right now, and hopefully we can all agree on something." ("Sooner or later they will have to sit down with us and make a deal," Jonathan Poneman replied in the same article. "I get bummed out about the lack of communication.")

"It's been pretty obvious for some time that if any of the emergent US underground bands are to break through into the mainstream, Nirvana will be the ones to do so," Keith noted. "Just about the only thing to throw a spanner in the works could be the self-destruct capability that lurks within the volatile personal chemistry of this highly strung three-piece," he concluded, presciently. Although he didn't know it at the time, there were further changes already underfoot. When Dan mentioned he'd have to borrow his wife's car to attend the barbeque, Krist and Kurt told him not to worry about it – even though a *Sounds* photo shoot was scheduled to take place at the event. Dan ended up making it to the party, and all appeared to be well; a playful shot of Kurt sticking a cigarette between Krist's bare toes was chosen for the magazine's cover, with the accompanying headline 'Get Yer Socks Off With Nirvana.'

The *Sounds* story was set to coincide with a UK tour scheduled for October. But as the days passed, and Dan finally asked Kurt for an update on the arrangements, he was in for a rude shock. "Kurt called me and so I'm like: yeah, so what's up with the tour of England? And he says: well, that's what I'm calling to tell you: we got another drummer. I'm like: oh, really? I wasn't pissed that they got another drummer. I mean, I was fine with it, actually; in fact, if anything, I might've been relieved. But just the way it was handled bummed me out. When I found out later on that everyone else knew except me, that's when I started getting pissed."

Indeed, Kurt had announced that Nirvana had a new drummer during an interview on Calvin Johnson's *Boy Meets Girl* show on KAOS on September 25, admitting he had yet to tell Dan he'd been replaced. Nor had anything been said as the three posed for pictures for *Sounds*. "I just like felt like a fool," says Dan. "Because when the thing for *Sounds* magazine came out, there's me on the cover, and you open it up and a headline or whatever saying: Dan, before being told to bugger off." (The actual quote from the article is: "Mudhoney's Dan Peters lasted just one gig and a *Sounds* photo shoot before being told: bugger this – you're off!")

"They weren't upfront with me," Dan continues. "They kind of knew I wasn't gonna be in the band anymore, but they didn't have the balls to tell me. Not to sound bitter, by any means – I'm not. The only thing I'm ever pissed about is just the way it went down."

A month later, music fan and critic Tom Kipp and his co-worker Jim Harrison were on their way to a show by satiric goth/metal band Gwar in the woods outside Fairfax City, Virginia. The outdoor event was being held on the extensive property owned by the Cedar Crest Country Club, renowned for having a skating 'half-pipe' on its grounds. Tom had previously lived in Montana, where he was the original vocalist in Deranged Diction, the band that featured Jeff

Ament and Bruce Fairweather, before the latter two departed for Seattle and the ranks of Green River, Mother Love Bone, and Pearl Jam. (Tom would move to Seattle as well in 1992.) He remembers having to navigate an unmarked, rutted road into an increasingly dense forest to get to the show. "We suddenly emerged into an impressive, unexpectedly large clearing, with the much-ballyhooed metal half-pipe at its center, and an array of largish bonfires surrounding it," he says. "Scores of kids from about 12 to 17 were scurrying here and there, and the fires were blazing away, as we observed what we soon learned was the second opening band, with the memorable moniker Coat Hanger Delivery, about to start their set."

After the band's set (described by Tom as "generic Pistols-styled punk, the set closer being 'Sonic Reducer' by my beloved Dead Boys"), Jim suddenly spotted a familiar face among the attendees. "Hey Tom," he said, "that's Dave Grohl over there! I met him a few times back when he used to drum for Scream – let's go say hello." The two walked over, and, after some pleasantries, asked Dave what he was up to these days.

"I just moved to Washington State," Dave replied. "I joined this band called Nirvana."

CHAPTER 14

True Hardcore Drummer

"All I really had was a suitcase and my drums, anyway, so I took them up to Seattle and hoped it would work. It did."

DAVE GROHL TO *MUSICIAN*, 1991

By the time Dave Grohl joined Nirvana, he was already a musician of considerable experience, having recorded with four different bands and toured more widely than Kurt and Krist. He had made his Washington State debut when he was the drummer in Washington DC hardcore act Scream, who played the Community World Theater on October 24 1987. (Nate Mendel, who played in another band on the bill, Diddly Squat, would later join Dave's post-Nirvana band, Foo Fighters.) Kurt attended the show with Slim Moon, who recalls him being unimpressed: "He kept saying it sucked when good bands turn into Van Halen."

Things had changed when Kurt and Krist next took note of Scream in 1990, when the band was on the verge of breaking up. Craig Montgomery recalls accompanying Kurt and Krist to a Scream show in San Francisco on August 13 1990, just prior to Nirvana's tour with Sonic Youth: "We just happened to go, I don't remember why exactly. But I remember Kurt and Krist going: I wish we could get a drummer like that!" But Krist remembers seeing Dave a few months earlier, after the trip when he and Kurt first went to Los Angeles at Susan Silver's suggestion. "And then we went back to San Francisco, and thought: let's go see Buzz and Dale," he says. "And so we stopped in and saw them. And Scream were playing and so we showed up there. And they were cool. And then we drove back to Seattle."

Both stories could be accurate. Scream were nearly always touring, so Kurt and Krist could possibly have seen the band in the early summer and then later in August. And the mutual acquaintance that finally brought Kurt, Krist, and Dave together was Buzz Osborne, whose own band had inspired Nirvana from the beginning, and who would now help to provide the final piece that would make the band complete, for despite growing up on the opposite side of the country, Dave Grohl was as much in thrall to the Melvins as Kurt and Krist had been.

David Eric Grohl was born January 14 1969, in Warren, Ohio (a street one mile from the hospital where he was born would later be named David Grohl Alley in his honor in 2008). In comparison to Kurt and Krist's upbringing, Dave's was decidedly middle class. His father, James, worked for the Scripps-Howard news agency; his mother, Virginia, was a teacher. In 1972, the family (which also included Dave's older sister, Lisa), moved to Springfield, Virginia, just outside of Washington DC, and James entered politics, working as a speechwriter and campaign manager for the Republican Party. James and Virginia divorced in 1974.

Dave's interest in music was encouraged by his parents, who themselves had artistic leanings. James was a classically trained flautist, and he and Virginia had met at a community theater group. Dave's first instrument was the trombone, which he played briefly in the school band, but he was always more interested in rock music, beginning with The Beatles. By age nine he'd picked up an acoustic guitar that his mother had originally bought for his father; although the instrument only had two strings, he managed to teach himself to play Deep Purple's 'Smoke On The Water.' He also took guitar lessons for a year.

By that time, like Kurt and Krist, his listening interests had progressed from 60s pop to 70s rock – Lynyrd Skynyrd, AC/DC, Alice Cooper, Black Sabbath. He also had a great fondness for Edgar Winter's prog-rock classic 'Frankenstein' ("It changed my fucking life, I swear to God"), and, like Kurt, discovered new wave when he saw

The B-52's on *Saturday Night Live*. "I remember that moment like some people remember the Kennedy assassination," he later observed.

And then came punk. During the summer of 1982, when Dave was 13, he arrived for his annual visit to a friend of his mother's who lived in Evanston, Illinois, a suburb of Chicago. Her teenaged daughter, Tracey (incorrectly identified in other accounts as Dave's cousin), met him at the door in full punk regalia. "It was the most fucking awesome thing I had ever seen," he said. Dave spent the rest of his visit going through Tracey's collection of punk singles; she also took him to a Naked Raygun show at Chicago club Cubby Bear's. Grohl was enthralled by what he heard. "I had learned my basic three chords, but after hearing punk rock I realized you don't have to be Eddie Van Halen to be in a band," he said. "You can pick up a guitar and with those three chords write a song." He also took note of the fact that a number of Tracey's singles were released by the Washington-based label Dischord.

By then, Dave had already played in a few local bands. He'd received his first guitar, a 1963 Sears Silvertone, with a built-in amp in its case, for Christmas in 1981. He'd also begun to play drums, after hearing Rush's futuristic concept album *2112* ("It was the first time I'd heard music where the drums were almost the most prominent instrument," he explained), teaching himself to play by setting up a makeshift drum kit in his room made out of pillows, chairs, and the bed, and playing along to his favorite records. But for the moment he stuck with guitar, playing in various shortlived bands at house parties; he also teamed up with a friend to play nursing homes, playing covers of songs by The Who and The Rolling Stones.

Discovering punk pushed Dave in a new musical direction. On July 3 1983, he attended a free Rock Against Reagan concert, an all-day festival staged next to the Lincoln Memorial and headlined by San Francisco's Dead Kennedys, which drew a heavy police presence in addition to thousands of punk fans. As helicopters roared overhead, and the Kennedys worked their way through a set that included 'When Ya Get Drafted' and 'Religious Vomit' as well as the band's signature songs 'California Über Alles,' 'Holiday In Cambodia,' and 'Nazi Punks Fuck Off,' Dave experienced his own personal epiphany: "That's when I said: fuck the world, I'm doing *this*."

By the early 80s, Washington DC was home to a lively hardcore scene – or "harDCore," as the scene's denizens liked to write it. "There was an extraordinarily vibrant, if sometimes troubled, punk underground, one that in many regards I think we can look back on now and say was perhaps the single most creative and influential punk underground of the 80s and 90s," says Mark Andersen, who moved to the DC area from Montana in 1984 and went on to co-found the DC chapter of Positive Force, an activist group that organized benefit concerts for various progressive causes and organizations. "I say that fully understanding that Seattle and the Bay Area have produced far more million-selling acts. But I think DC's significance comes from something deeper than popularity, something more profound than moneymaking. It's a sense of commitment that punk was not simply a form of rock music, but a call to a different and more profound kind of life."

The bands also had more of a political edge, by virtue of being based in the nation's capitol. "It's a very political city," says Jenny Toomey, who performed in numerous bands in the area, and co-founded the label Simple Machines. "It just seeps into everything; in Washington, you really do see yourself in relation to the rest of the world, because of the government being there. A lot of these folks were kids of people who worked at the World Bank, or, you know, lawyers that worked on political things. Even the people who say they're not political are responding to an idea of politics that doesn't exist in other places.

"On the Minor Threat records," she continues, referring to Ian MacKaye's pre-Fugazi band, whose song 'Straight Edge' popularized the alcohol/drug-free 'straight edge' lifestyle, "if you go back and look at them, there's a kind of anti-politics that's going on, but you also see a very, very 'personal is political' thing going on. Like they'll make fun of hippies, or they'll make fun of people who are being overtly political, but they're responding to a political context. They were trying to get some message across, even though they were pretending like there wasn't politics. It was very 'personal is political' in DC. It was less 'Fuck Reagan' and more 'change your life.'"

There was a good network of clubs supporting the scene. "Both DC Space and the 9:30 Club let people come in underage," says Jenny. "And Positive Force was starting to function and they did benefit concerts, so there were lots of bands who played benefit concerts through Positive Force. And Dante Ferraro, who runs the Black Cat in DC – his father owned the health food restaurant Food For Thought, and they would do matinees and shows there, so you'd see Rites Of Spring or Grey Matter playing on this teeny little stage in the back of the health-food restaurant. And there were halls that opened up for a time, like for a summer – I remember seeing Sonic Youth playing at some crazy warehouse somewhere. But a lot of the venues stayed for a long time, things like Fort Reno, a project the DC government had, like a 'keep kids busy' project, which was a stage out in the middle of a field, very close to the grounds of Wilson High School, which was where Ian [MacKaye] and a bunch of the punk rockers went. They had free shows every Thursday, two or three bands playing, and that still happens to this day."

Dave had picked up a number of flyers for local punk gigs at the Rock Against Reagan show; now he threw himself fully into the club scene, and in 1984 joined hardcore band Freak Baby on second guitar. The band was only together for a few months, but during that time Dave made a crucial connection when Freak Baby set up a recording session at Barrett Jones' Laundry Room studio; Barrett would go on to work with Dave's subsequent bands, including Nirvana (as both producer and drum tech) and Foo Fighters.

Barrett had grown up in Arlington, Virginia, playing in local bands, the best known of which was 11th Hour. He began moving into production when he found a sound mixer in his parents' attic. "From there I basically just kept buying more and more equipment until I had enough to actually record a band," he says. "I went to Boston University for a little bit in '84. I was there for a very short time, about three months, and withdrew, and with the refund of my tuition I convinced my parents to let me invest in studio equipment. And that's when I started recording other bands, in my parents' house in the laundry room, and that's where the name came from. I've gone back and forth with hating it and wanting to change it and keeping it. In the laundry room – that was where the control room was – I made this cabinet that could close up and be put out of the way that had all the gear in it, the mixing board and whatever; I could close it, and then when I opened it, I could pull the mixing board out. That room was probably 10x10 [feet]. And then everybody played in my bedroom, which was just up a short hallway, and it was probably 15x15 or something. Very small."

Freak Baby set up a session at the Laundry Room after hearing about Barrett from the brother of Freak Baby's singer, Chris Page. They recorded a tape, which they then sold at a local punk-friendly record store, Smash, but the band soon broke up. One day before rehearsal, Dave had sat behind the drummer's kit to play, and the other members were so impressed by what they heard they kicked out their bassist, moved their drummer to bass, put Dave on drums, and became a new band, Mission Impossible. "Freak Baby wasn't too different from Mission Impossible, but they weren't nearly as good, because their drummer was really bad," says Barrett. "The first time I saw Dave play drums, in Mission Impossible, I was blown away. He was better than most drummers are after years and years of practice. He just was really on top of it. He played fast, very, very fast. True hardcore drummer!"

The band's first release, a cassette recorded on January 20 1985 at the Laundry Room, helped generated immediate interest in both the band and Dave's skill as a drummer. "I got their first tape at

Smash, and it captured them very well," says Mark. "It was very friendly, very 'kids, let's do a cassette!' I was very impressed, thinking: wow, of all the stuff I've heard, this is one of the few things that actually makes me feel like there's something I'd wanna see! I saw Dave play for the first time at a practice in the basement of the singer, Chris Page. I loved that band! They carried some of that hardcore energy. You could definitely hear Minor Threat, you could hear Bad Brains in there, but there was also this broader emotional openness – it wasn't just a very narrow band that centered on rage. And part of their special chemistry was Dave's drumming. He was very, very fast, very energetic, and very … propulsive, I think, is the word. It wasn't just him. Dave Smith, the bass player was good, and Bryant Mason, the guitar player, he was also very good. But from the beginning, he just had one of the most wild and energizing styles of drumming that I had encountered, and it is too bad that Mission Impossible was not more well documented, because they were a very powerful band."

Mission Impossible released two tapes and a split single, and appeared on three compilations, but "none of this stuff was ever released in anything more than 500 or 1,000 copies total," says Barrett. "It never really got distributed." Dave paid close attention to how Barrett worked in the studio; as he watched the producer working on his own songs, playing and recording all the instruments himself, Dave became increasingly intrigued, thinking: "Man, I want to try that." The two friends also began spending more time together outside of the studio. "We were in the same circles," says Barrett. "There was a lot of partying going on back then, a lot of hanging out. We had fun. Somewhere around then I got my first CD player, and my first CD was [Led Zeppelin's] *Houses Of The Holy*. I'd never been into Zeppelin before that, really. We all bonded by listening to that really loud in the house." ("This coincided nicely with the start of my love affair with marijuana," Dave later joked.)

Led Zeppelin became an obsession for Dave. "They were the perfect combination of the most intense elements: passion and mystery and expertise," he told *Rolling Stone*, and he was especially taken with drummer John Bonham. "I think he will forever be the greatest drummer of all time," he said. "You have no idea how much he influenced me. I spent years in my bedroom – literally fucking years – listening to Bonham's drums and trying to emulate his swing or his behind-the-beat swagger or his speed or power." He soon got his first Zeppelin tattoo, the three interlocking circles that formed Bonham's personal insignia on *Led Zeppelin IV* and were later used on his kick drum. (Years later, Dave's dreams of being in Led Zeppelin would come true when Robert Plant and John Paul Jones guested at Foo Fighters' June 7 2008 show at Wembley Stadium; he would also co-found the side project band Them Crooked Vultures with Jones and Queens Of The Stone Age's Josh Homme.)

Becoming immersed once again in classic rock led to Dave moving away from hardcore in his next band. According to Mark, Mission Impossible were torn apart "by the bane of teenage punk bands, which is college." When the band's singer and guitarist departed for institutions of higher learning, Dave and Mission Impossible bassist Dave Smith decided to stick together, and, with guitarist Reuben Radding, formed the band Dain Bramage. "If you wanted to compare them to somebody, I think the general comparison people would make would be Hüsker Dü," says Mark. "It's upbeat guitar rock with lots of melody, and some pretty powerful driving energy." This is borne out by footage of the band's first show on December 20 1985; the songs are a good deal more melodic than the hardcore thrash of Dave's previous bands, with Dave attacking his kit like he's at an arena show instead of a community center in the suburbs. "It was like watching a young Keith Moon," said Radding of Dave's drumming, while Jenny Toomey, who first saw Dave playing drums at a Dain Bramage show at Fort Reno, recalls: "He always looked like Animal from *The Muppets* to me. He just had this incredible flop of hair, and he was so gangly, he just had those insane long arms and knees and he just played like a maniac!"

However, by the time Dain Bramage released their sole album, 1987's *I Scream Not Coming Down*, Dave had already moved on. In late 1986, he noticed an ad reading 'Scream looking for drummer' pinned to the bulletin board of a music store, where he'd gone to buy drumsticks. Scream were DC stalwarts, formed in 1979 by Pete and Franz Stahl (singer and guitarist, respectively), bassist Skeeter Thompson, and drummer Kent Stax. The band was a punk/garage-rock act until Bad Brains inspired them to go in a more hardcore direction. Scream recorded for Dischord and toured incessantly, and by the fall of 1986 Kent Stax, who'd recently become a father, felt it was time to leave the group.

Dave was a big fan of Scream, and decided to audition just to have the pleasure of playing with one of his favorite bands. To his surprise, he was offered the job. After first declining, he changed his mind and agreed to join, to the chagrin of his Dain Bramage bandmates. "The guys in the band were actually very upset," says Barrett, "because they were supposed to do a tour, things were just starting to go for them, their record had just come out, and Dave just kind of up and left to join Scream. They were kind of blindsided by it; those guys were heartbroken. I don't know if they ever got over it."

Dave's joining Scream was a sign of his growing ambitions. It also marked a turning point in his life; Scream toured extensively, and Dave was still in high school, so in order to join the band, he dropped out. (When he first auditioned for Scream, he'd lied and said he was 20 instead of 17.) "I didn't get the sense that Dain Bramage were planning to be road warriors," says Mark, "and so I think Dave could probably have slotted that in and still continued with high school. Scream was not gonna be that way. Scream, you're gonna go till you drop, basically. And then you were gonna get up and do it some more. And as it turns out, that was something that Dave loved."

Over the next three years, Scream toured the USA five times and Europe three times. Dave discovered it was a life he felt completely at home with. "I'd never been past Chicago, and it was a good two-month tour," he said of his first outing with Scream. "Everywhere from Fender's Ballroom in LA to the Botanical Center in Des Moines. It was seven dollars a day per diem. Whether it was learning how to perform live, how to live within the fucking confines of a Dodge Ram or learning how to fucking score chicks, I learned everything ... Cigarettes were cheap, and Taco Bell was everywhere."

"Scream was playing punk rock shows all over, and it was pretty crazy," says Barrett, who toured with the band as a soundman and roadie in 1988. "They usually weren't playing clubs, they were more like community centers, set up by kids. This one place in Texas, it was an old headstone factory or something like that, and they didn't have a PA system, and somebody had to go scrounge up something to use as a PA. And then, on the night, the promoter didn't want to pay them, and he had a gun and was threatening them. It was crazy. So yeah, there was always wild stories about the craziness of that, and Skeeter was always quitting."

In Amsterdam, while on his first tour of Europe, Dave stumbled upon another musical influence. Flipping through the record collection at the home where Scream was staying, Dave found a copy of the Melvins' *Gluey Porch Treatments*. "I thought: here's another hardcore record," he later recalled. "But when I put it on it *really fucking blew my mind*." He was especially overwhelmed by the force of Dale Crover's drumming: "He would do things with time signatures that no one else could have done, and still no one can do ... While Dale Crover is around and playing drums, I'm always going to be number two." He later claimed to have listened to the record every day for the next two years. He soon struck up a friendship with the band, with whom Scream occasionally shared the bill.

Scream released one studio and two live albums while Dave was in the band, and in December 1989 began work on their next studio album. Dave brought in a song he'd first demoed at the Laundry Room the previous year, 'Gods Look Down,' which became his first solo track. There's a touch of dirge in the grinding guitars, while

Dave's lead vocal is classic hard rock (which one could say about the song's title as well). Although it was the only song of his to appear on a Scream album, Dave had been working steadily on his own material for some time. "At that point, we were hanging out a lot more when he wasn't on tour," says Barrett. "He would help me record stuff, and he'd throw his songs on during those sessions when he was recording with me. He'd seen me do it and said: I can do that." There were also various side projects. Dave occasionally played in Barrett's band Churn; Dave, Barrett, and Skeeter were in a band called Them Cover Boys, playing Zeppelin and AC/DC covers; Dave, Barrett, and two other friends recorded five songs later released in 1996 under the name Harlingtox Angel Divine. "I always thought it was so great that it needed to get out somehow at some point," says Barrett of the latter venture. "Interesting little novelty item."

By 1990, however, it had become increasingly apparent that Scream's fortunes were on the downswing. They were no longer as strong a live draw; Mark Andersen recalls leaving a punk show, hearing music coming from the club next door, and looking in to find Scream playing "for maybe a dozen people. And they're playing their hearts out. It's like: why is Scream here?" Sales of their last studio album, 1988's *No More Censorship*, hadn't given the band's career the boost they'd hoped for. There were growing substance-abuse issues, and money was a continual problem. "They toured constantly, but they didn't make any money," says Barrett. "It was not an easy life."

"No band that I've ever seen deserved more to break through than Scream," says Mark. "They worked really hard, they were absolutely impeccable musicians – they were the real deal. Somehow, it didn't come together. Maybe if they had somebody helping them organize things, it could've worked, because they had it all. But when it looked like it was gonna take off for the skies, it fell apart. And they didn't seem to know what to do, except to keep pushing it as hard as they could."

It was around this time that the band met Glen Friedman, who managed Suicidal Tendencies, and who offered to help Scream find a new record deal. Scream headed back to Europe, only to return and find that Pete and Skeeter had been evicted from their home. "Every time Scream would go on tour, pretty much, their phones got turned off, and they would be in danger of being evicted," says Mark. With no other options, the band decided to get back on the road again. "Our plan was: let's just book a tour and get the fuck out of here," said Dave. "It was an escape, it was almost like we could survive on the road better than we could at home."

Not this time. The tour was plagued with cancellations, and Dave became increasingly despondent. "I was starting to question this as a life decision," he told his biographer, Paul Brannigan. "I was like: do I really want to be homeless for the rest of my life? I was tired of having absolutely nothing; I was tired of being hungry, tired of being lost, and tired of being tired – I just wanted to go home." The situation worsened when Scream arrived in Los Angeles and Dave and the Stahl brothers awoke one morning to find that Skeeter had again disappeared. The remaining shows were cancelled; the remains of Scream were now stuck in LA. Glen Friedman had not had any luck with finding a record deal, although some A&R reps had expressed interest in Dave's drumming. Friedman later recalled Dave being "totally exuberant and really excited about having me on board and trying to get them a label deal. Dave called me more than the other guys, and we became good friends. Everyone wanted it, but Dave *really* wanted it."

Too embarrassed to call home and ask for money for a return bus ticket, Dave took on a job tiling floors at a coffee shop while he tried to figure out his next move. On learning that the Melvins were coming to town, he decided to give Buzz Osborne a call, explaining his current circumstances and confessing he had no idea what to do next. Buzz's response was unexpected. "Dave," he said, "you should join Nirvana."

"I thought Dave was a great drummer," Buzz explained. "I thought Scream was really great. They were one of the best bands that I ever saw. And so, when I suggested that he join Nirvana, I thought it was really good, because I always thought that a great drummer is a great thing for a band. You should really concentrate on finding somebody that's a really good drummer that's capable and understands the Neanderthal quality that comes out of Keith Moon and Mitch Mitchell, and, to a lesser degree, Buddy Rich. It's nothing to do with being perfect timing or any of that kind of stuff ... I've always said that guys like Crover and Grohl have something that more accomplished drummers don't have. They have the ability to envision music in a way that is organic and human. It has nothing to do with perfect rhythmic time or any of those things." Buzz passed Krist's number on to Dave, and also gave Dave's number to Kurt.

Dave had actually crossed paths with Nirvana a few times in recent months. Scream had played a show at the Reko/Muse Gallery in Olympia on August 3, and had afterward dropped in at a party Slim Moon was hosting. Kurt was also in attendance, later describing the Scream band-members as "rocker dudes ... [Dave] brought up this Primus tape from their car and tried to play it and everyone got mad at him." Shortly afterward, when Nirvana were in San Francisco rehearsing for their West Coast tour with Sonic Youth, Kurt and Krist were pointed out to Dave when everyone was hanging out backstage after a Melvins show. Dave had heard *Bleach* and thought from the cover Nirvana looked "almost like a metal band." He was surprised to find the band quite different in person, Krist loud and raucous, Kurt sitting hunched in a corner, speaking to no one.

What Dave (and apparently Buzz Osborne) didn't know was that Nirvana already had a new drummer, Dan Peters, as Krist informed him when Dave first called. Dave took the news with a shrug, telling Krist to give him a call when Nirvana were next in LA. But after conferring, Kurt and Krist began to reconsider. Perhaps it wasn't too late to work with Dave after all. "It wasn't that we were unhappy with

Dan's drumming, it was just that Dave has qualities which match our needs a little closer," Kurt told *Melody Maker* in October. "We were blown away by him when we saw him playing with this band Scream a few months ago, and Krist and I agreed we'd ask him to join Nirvana if we ever had the chance. Ironically, that chance came just weeks after we got Danny in." In the end, the temptation to work with Dave was just too great. "You can't pass up an opportunity to play with the drummer of our dreams," Kurt told Michael Azerrad. Krist then called Dave back, suggesting he should come up and audition, while also sounding him out on his favorite bands. "I thought I should ask," Krist says. "I'm trying to ask him these questions, and Kurt's like: shut up! Why are you asking that shit? Tell him to get up here! So I'm like: OK, just come on up."

Now Dave was left to break the news to the Stahl brothers that he was leaving them behind. Although he wrestled with the decision, in the end there was really only one clear choice; just as when he'd left Dain Bramage and dropped out of high school to join Scream, he opted for the path he felt had the most potential. He tried to soften the blow by telling the Stahls he was only going up to audition. "I don't know if I have the gig," he stressed. But Franz suspected otherwise, and told his bandmate he wasn't coming back. "Deep down," Dave told Brannigan, "I knew it too." And so, on September 21, Dave flew up to Washington State with his drum kit packed inside a cardboard box. He would initially stay with Krist and Shelli in Tacoma.

The next night was the Motor Sports show. Jenny Toomey, who was living in Olympia for a few months, attended the gig and was pleased to see Dave, a friendly face from DC. "I was amazed how big, how huge that show was," she says. "In DC, nothing like that would have ever happened. The biggest Minor Threat shows were like 300 people." Dave was also impressed, and a little intimidated, by the size of the crowd, and the number of fans with Nirvana T-shirts. "They must have sold 200 T-shirts that night," he told Azerrad. "That's *insane* for a local punk show." Dave had been told to keep a low profile at the gig, as no one was to know he was auditioning for Nirvana. "Dave didn't know anyone," says Jenny. "He wasn't being told whether he was going to be in the band. And of course Kurt couldn't be hanging out with Dave at the show! I think there was almost like guilt, you know – I think they loved Dan Peters, but they didn't want him to be the drummer as much as they wanted Dave to be the drummer."

Dave also tried to be inconspicuous at the barbeque at Krist's the following day; he can be seen hovering in the background of one of Ian Tilton's shots, reading and seemingly uninterested in what's going on around him while Kurt poses in the foreground holding a can of Prairie Belt Smoked Sausage, a crazed grin on his face (the sausage can would later feature in the 1993 video for 'Sliver'). Yet something about his presence at the party stuck in Keith Cameron's mind. "This guy Dave, who told me he was a drummer and his band had just split up, was hanging around and helping out," he says. "And I'm not sure if I really processed it at the time but when Anton Brookes told me that Nirvana would have a new drummer for the UK tour, I said: don't tell me – his name is Dave. I was pleased in the end, because I loved Mudhoney and hadn't really wanted them to break up, which is what people thought would happen if Dan joined Nirvana."

Krist had found Nirvana a new rehearsal space in Tacoma. It quickly became apparent that Dave's style matched that of one their key influences: a band whose drummer had played on Nirvana's first demo. "He was like Dale," says Krist. "He locked right in, and he was a hard hitter. And it was dynamic. He played a big drum set, it was thundering. That was it. He gave a spark like a – I don't know. Something happened."

It was not an entirely smooth start, however. The band's second rehearsal with Dave didn't go nearly as well. "Kurt and I just messed around at practice for some reason," said Krist. "We all left together, and I could feel that Dave was a little distressed … Perhaps Dave was feeling a little remorse at that moment for betting it all on these two guys from Washington." If he was, the feeling had dissipated by the end of the next rehearsal. "We got into the groove again and played most nights," Krist said. Krist had been responsible for providing the Melvins with their final drummer, when he introduced Buzz to Dale; now Buzz had returned the favor, having introduced Nirvana to their own final drummer.

There was some residual bad feeling about Dave's departure from Scream. Over the next few months, whenever he called to talk to the Stahl brothers, Franz would refuse to speak to him (although he would later join Foo Fighters for a two year stint). Glen Friedman also later threatened legal action, saying he'd invested his own money while working for the group; the matter was settled out of court (and the demos he'd been shopping were released as the album *Fumble* on Dischord in 1993). There were no regrets on Dave's part. Although he knew his decision had upset the Stahls, he was pragmatic about it. "I had to do what I had to do," he said. And to others that knew him, the move was understandable. "When we found out he was going to be in Nirvana, it made total sense," says Jenny. "Like, why wouldn't you want him? I don't think there was anybody who ever saw him play who didn't think: wow, I'd like him in my band!"

Characteristically, Dave said Kurt and Krist never explicitly told him he was in the band. But Kurt had no hesitation about saying so when he appeared on Calvin Johnson's *Boy Meets Girl* show on KAOS in September. It was an impromptu appearance, Kurt having simply called up Calvin to ask if he could come on the show. It was also a musical appearance, with Kurt said to have performed eight songs. Only three have surfaced so far: performances of 'Lithium,' 'Been A Son,' and a new song, 'Opinion,' all of which appear on *With The Lights Out*. 'Opinion' was a short satirical number that touched in part on media manipulation; sadly, the song was not developed further, and was only performed on this one occasion. Kurt was also supposed to have debuted 'Dumb' on the show, as well as performing 'Polly,' and a cover of the Wipers track 'D-7,' which would soon be added to

Nirvana's set. Calvin Johnson duetted with Kurt on the latter song, in a performance he recalled as being "rather good."

Some of Kurt's banter with Calvin has appeared on bootlegs. "I just wrote most of the lyrics this evening," he says in reference to his new songs. "While I was driving with one foot … I wanted it to be as spontaneous as possible, you know?" But the moment when he revealed Nirvana had a new drummer hasn't surfaced. According to *Come As You Are*, Kurt made a Melvins reference when he said of their newest member: "His name is Dave and he's a baby Dale Crover. He plays almost as good as Dale. And within a few years' practice, he may even give him a run for his money" – an echo of Dawn Anderson's remark in the very first story about Nirvana, in which she'd speculated that, with enough practice, Nirvana might become "better than the Melvins."

"Dave's drumming is so crucial to Nirvana, and in realizing the vision that Cobain had as a songwriter," says Mark Andersen. "No offense to any other drummer that was in Nirvana – I haven't studied them, I don't know them – all I know is that Dave Grohl's drumming is the top of the mountain, at the motherfucking peak. And the kind of breakthrough that's present artistically – I'm not just saying commercially, but artistically – in *Nevermind*, you can't credit it all to Dave, but without Dave it would not have worked. That's my belief. And that Dave Grohl spark was there from the first time I saw him play in the basement of his friend's house."

CHAPTER 15

The Crest Of The Wave

"In our [record] contract we were dealing from a position of strength because there were other labels competing for us, so we get complete, 100 percent creative control. So we can do whatever we want."

KURT TO *BACKLASH*, 1991

Nirvana spent most of the three weeks after the Motor Sports gig rehearsing with their new drummer. When they weren't practicing, Dave was trying to learn their songs by listening repeatedly to *Bleach* – using headphones, as he was aware that Kurt and Krist were tired of hearing the album. He was more keen on the band's newer material, later noting that songs like 'Immodium' were "more up my alley, just because I came straight from playing with a hardcore band."

Dave made his live debut with Nirvana on October 11 at Olympia's North Shore Surf Club. When the band arrived at the club to find a line stretching around the block, Dave was so excited he called his mother. "I was amazed," he told Paul Brannigan. "With Scream the band usually outnumbered the audience." But the show got off to a rough start. After opening with a fierce cover of 'Son Of A Gun' (which Kurt described as "our second favorite Vaselines song"), the band segued into 'Molly's Lips,' only for their amps to suddenly cut out. Further frustration ensued when the amps cut out for a second time during 'D-7,' and then again during 'Blew.' "It's time to pay the electric bill!" Krist said when 'D-7' was interrupted. "You can get government aid and stuff if you can't afford it."

"That put a little bit of a damper on the show," says Rob Nyberg, who was in the audience. "It's Dave Grohl's first show and the gods were just like: no, this can't happen!" But once the problem was finally repaired, Nirvana played as if there had been no break at all; perhaps spurred on by the earlier interruptions, the band's energy never flagged.

"It was great," says Jon Snyder, who was also overseeing the filming of the show, as well as shooting still photographs. "We had a couple cameras, and I was mostly stressing about making sure they were still going. I was working with a small crew and trying to get this working. There are four camera angles of this show, but they're all crappy and there's all the technical problems with the audio and power going out. But there were snatches where I could get totally caught up in the music, and when I watch that footage today, I can go back to that place really quick. Especially on 'Love Buzz,' which is my absolute favorite recording of that song. I mean, you just sit there and watch Kurt bend that string during the chorus – that's it, that's what rock'n'roll is all about, right there. It's a pretty clear snapshot of their musical evolution." (The performance appears on the *With The Lights Out* DVD).

Dave played with such ferocity that at the end of the set Kurt held up the snare to show the audience how their new drummer had broken the drum head with the force of his playing; Dave then tossed a piece into the audience. "We thought Dave could hit real hard and he had a lot of energy, and that was impressive," says Alex Kostelnik. Jon Snyder agrees. "You were kind of seeing the music transform with what he could do on drums," he says. "I thought it was great. I mean, I could tell that the music had a different energy." The four-song encore ended with another new addition to the set, Devo's 'Turnaround,' a song the band would play on only one further occasion. Jon used some of the pictures he shot in a video he created for 'Lithium,' which also drew on the show's live footage, as well as footage from the March 1990 session; the video, along with a similarly styled video of 'School,' aired on *1200 Seconds*, a two-episode music video show created by Evergreen students that was broadcast on campus and public access cable. Jon was more pleased with his still pictures, especially one of Kurt leaving the stage, his face in shadow, the crowd packed behind him. "I like that shot a lot because it's kind of a precursor to what's coming up," he says. "Not that it's depressing or dark, but just more like, there was just going to be a lot of people around him and trying to get to him in a way that there hadn't been before, every day after that shot. I think that picture hints at that a little bit."

Jon also noted that the large size of the crowd was due to the fact that a lot of non-Olympia residents were in attendance, something that left him with mixed feelings. "People were actually coming from out of town to see them because they were so big at that point," he says. "There were a lot of people from Seattle there that were kind of, I don't know, like hard-rock jocks. The mosh pit was furious. And so in a way it was a little weird, because it was like the beginning of them blowing up a little bit. It was the biggest show that I'd ever seen to that point, the biggest venue I'd ever seen them play in. So that was a little bit bittersweet for me, because it was clear that it was only going to get bigger from here. But it was exciting." Jon wasn't the only one who could sense bigger things ahead. After 'Turnaround,' the club's MC called out: "Thanks a lot Nirvana, you guys were great! We'll see you on MTV!" Krist then reminded the audience they had T-shirts for sale.

Amid breaking in Nirvana's new drummer, Kurt also found time to become involved in another side project during October. Dylan Carlson had formed a new band, Earth, and had booked recording sessions at Smegma Studios in Portland. The studio was located in the house of producer Mike Lastra; it was "perched on a cliff," Dylan recalled, "full of cats and hamsters, and surrounded by raccoons." Earth had a droning heaviness reminiscent of the Melvins, and indeed bassist Joe Preston would later join that band. Dylan invited Kurt and Dickless lead singer Kelly Canary to come to the sessions and contribute vocals, offering them payment in "Pabst and Percodan."

Kurt ultimately appeared on two numbers. On 'A Bureaucratic Desire For Revenge' (a line taken from Ingmar Bergman's 1968 film

Hour Of The Wolf) he provides backing vocals; he can be heard more clearly on 'Divine And Bright' (described by Dylan as "a love song written to the H-bomb"), singing the song's title repeatedly in a low voice, accompanied by Kelly's wildcat screaming. 'A Bureaucratic Desire For Revenge' and another number, 'Ouroboros Is Broken' (for which Kurt assisted with the sequencer), were the first numbers to be released, on the EP *Extra-Capsular Extraction*, which was issued by Sub Pop in 1991 with 'Kurt Kobain' and Kelly Canary credited as 'specialists.' The release was accompanied by a unique promo item: a video cassette that used the music as a soundtrack to a collage of apparently found footage of aircraft carriers intercut with 50s-era soft-core 'porn' of couples spanking each other. The tape was packaged in a white case, in a limited edition of 100 copies; "I got the last one," says Jack Endino. 'Divine And Bright' was first released as a bonus track on the 2001 reissue of *Sunn Amps And Smashed Guitars*; the songs are more readily available on the 2010 CD *Bureaucratic Desire For Extra Capsular Extraction*.

On October 19, Nirvana flew to the UK for a short tour. On the 1994 home video *Live! Tonight! Sold Out!!*, the three band-members are shown goofing off on the plane ride over, and, once in London, trying to adjust to cars that drive on the opposite side of the street. "I can't get used to the traffic situation," Dave jokes to Krist, who's filming him. Krist responds with a mock bellow at the passing cars: "Well, *fuck it*, man! Start driving *normally!* What's your *problem?*" The band was ensconced in the Dalmacia Hotel in Shepherd's Bush; even though they were sharing a basement room, for Dave it was a taste of luxury he hadn't previously experienced on tour. "When I was in Scream, we were living off five dollars a day, sleeping in the van, on floors," he later explained. "So to be playing big places, having my own bed and being able to smoke two packs of cigarettes a day was a big fucking deal to me."

First up was another John Peel session, for which the band returned to the Beeb's Maida Vale studio on October 21, with Dale Griffin producing. The four songs recorded were all covers – unusually, given that the tour was meant to promote the 'Sliver' single, although as had been the case with the *Blew* EP, the single wasn't available overseas until after the tour was finished. (The CD single added live versions of 'About A Girl' and 'Spank Thru' from the February 9 1990 show in Portland as bonus tracks; the 12-inch vinyl single added only 'About A Girl.')

The session begins with straightforward renditions of 'Son Of A Gun' and 'Molly's Lips'; perhaps Kurt's love of The Vaselines kept him from adding any embellishments of his own. But the band put some of their own spin on 'D-7,' taking the song at a faster pace than the Wipers version, with a more frenzied vocal from Kurt and a squall of guitar at the end. Devo's 'Turnaround' also rocks harder than the original, although again it adheres closely to the original arrangement. "There was not a lot of time invested in those songs," Krist concedes. Nonetheless, on the whole the session was Nirvana's most energetic to date, due in no small part to Dave's spirited drumming. Dave was also a singer, which meant Nirvana now had live backing and harmony vocals for the first time. The show was first broadcast on Radio 1 on November 3. The songs were first released on the 1991 EP *Hormoaning* (released only in Australia and Japan); all but 'D-7' later appeared on *Incesticide*.

The band's first live date was at Goldwyn's Suite in Birmingham on October 23. L7 was also on the tour. Jennifer Finch was surprised to learn Chad Channing had been replaced by Dave Grohl, whom she knew from having previously booked Scream in LA. "My early memory of them bringing in Dave was kind of like: it's a professional choice," she says. "It seemed to me like they were getting this young hotshot in. I knew that Chad had inconsistencies, but I thought he was just such a livewire, that I had these thoughts of: oh, they're selling out, they're trading in a member, you know?" There weren't too many bad feelings, however. Jennifer and Dave began dating during the tour, while opening for Nirvana gave L7's career a boost as well. "That was amazing," says Jennifer. "The shows with Nirvana were our first shows in front of a larger audience, and it was just mind-blowing at how many people would even be interested! L7 always did well in smaller clubs, like Raji's – pack 120 people into a 70-person space. But then to really expand it out where there was a [stage] barrier in front of us – I think it was one of the first times we'd played with a barrier. It was crazy."

For his part, Craig Montgomery found Dave "really a breath of fresh air. Here's this young kid, and he's super funny, happy to be there, great attitude, and great player – tons of energy, a solid drummer, and he can sing, he's got an ear for pitch and melody, along with being a good musical drummer who also has the power to hit as hard as those guys wanted. It was like he was made to order for Nirvana. Kind of made you forget all the drummers they'd had before. It took it to the next level and made *Nevermind* possible. I've never said that before, in any of my dozens of interviews, but yeah, I did think getting Dave was the piece that made *Nevermind* possible."

After the Birmingham show, Nirvana returned to London, where interviews with *NME* and *Melody Maker* at the Dalmacia had been scheduled for the following day. *NME*'s Steve Lamacq arrived at the hotel to find the band watching *The Wizard Of Oz* on TV, with both Kurt and Krist nursing colds and Krist additionally burdened by a hangover. Nonetheless, Lamacq, who called 'Sliver' a "shockingly good boy-ish pop-guitar thrash-along," found Kurt affable enough. "We're finally coming out of the drains and saying: we like pop music," he told Lamacq. "I like R.E.M. and I like The Smithereens and I'm not afraid to say that anymore."

Photographer Martyn Goodacre then had the group go outside for photographs. "I was very familiar with Nirvana," he says. "I had bought a vinyl copy of *Bleach* a year or so before and couldn't understand why this band were not huge. For me, they were the missing link between Sabbath, Butthole Surfers, Hüsker Dü, and The Beatles. Not many journalists liked them in the UK; in the UK, most music was ecstasy-related, so they were viewed as a punk throwback. I turned up, and they were dressed similar to myself – the just-got-out-of-bed look wearing ripped old clothes. But it wasn't contrived – that's what we all looked like, mainly because of being skint. It became the grunge look about a year later."

Martyn didn't expect to make much money from the shoot ("about £40," he says), and had only brought two rolls of black-and-white film. He ended up with about 60 shots. "I do wish I had taken a little color, but thinking about it, it was a very gloomy, gray day," he says. "The band were cheerful and up for anything. They were quite playful, even though it was really cold and miserable. Kurt said very little. Dave was shy. Krist was the most animated, like a big gangly friendly spider. I felt I had known him for years – he was so personable. They were very easy to work with, but I wasn't too demanding." Krist and Kurt appear the most relaxed in Martyn's pictures; Dave, still very much the new guy, is more tentative in his expressions. The band is seen sitting on the front steps of their hotel, standing at a bus stop (for which Martyn positioned Krist directly behind Kurt to deal with problematic height issue), in a laundromat, and crossing the street in a crosswalk in an attempt to emulate The Beatles' *Abbey Road* cover.

Martyn also took individual shots of the band, with his portraits of Kurt being the most notable. "There was no direction – just a quick five or six shots of Kurt staring into the lens," he says. One pose in particular stood out to Martyn, even during the session. "I felt that something weird had happened when I took that shot," Martyn recalls. "There was a sort of connection; Kurt just opened up his soul for a second. It's blatant if you see the contact strip. When I started printing, I couldn't stop. It was so much fun. Everything was perfect, from the grain of the film to the look in his eyes. I remember showing a copy as I was printing to my girlfriend at the time and telling her that Cobain had the look of the last great rock star. Which I guess he was in the end." The shot has Kurt looking directly into the camera lens with a complete lack of self-consciousness, eyes heavily rimmed with eyeliner, hair casually falling in his face. His expression is open, but also ambiguous; Kurt could be tired, contemplative, bored, apprehensive, depressed, or none of the above. It's the kind of expression people are drawn to because so much can be read into it, and Martyn was disappointed it wasn't used for the story.

Then came the interview and photo shoot for *Melody Maker*. The reporter, Push (a pseudonym for writer Christopher Dawes), called 'Sliver' "one hell of a pop song," and, like *NME*'s Lamacq, found the band looking to the future. "I hate *Bleach* so much now," said Kurt, while Krist addressed the public misperceptions that came along with Nirvana's rising fame: "I hate the way that every single thing you do or say is seen as being of such great importance just because you're in a band. We've been portrayed as redneck illiterates just because of where we're from, and while we don't mind admitting that we're from a redneck town, we've always had trouble dealing with the attitudes which prevail out there. By the same token, we're not an underground band because we had records out on Sub Pop and we're not a teenage pop group because we now want to sign to a major label."

After the interview, the band went to a meeting with Island Records. That night Nirvana played the Astoria. Ten months previously, they'd played the same venue at the end of their first exhausting European tour, flipping a coin to determine the running order for the gig. Now, there was no question about who was going to close the show. As Keith Cameron later wrote: "In less than a year, Nirvana had evolved from an intense but hit-and-miss live outfit into an awesome rock'n'roll group, a paragon of the art of the power trio, where the possibility of havoc is part of the thrill."

"The 1990 UK tour with Dave was amazing, really the first time I was able to drag other journalists along and show them this band and they stood there with their mouths hanging open," Keith says.

"Until then, in terms of the press, it was just me and the usual people who wrote about US underground stuff. Dave added an extra power dimension, no question about that. Once he was in the band, you realized something serious could happen."

After the show, Kurt agreed to yet another interview, answering a few questions for Tina Caruso of *Submerge*. Caruso had found the show "wild" ("The Astoria was solid with sweaty bodies and long haired men – just what the doctor ordered!"), and wondered how the band would fare should Nirvana become bigger. "We'd still be doing spontaneous things like playing clubs that only hold 200 people and playing there five nights in a row so people can see us play in a small venue," Kurt assured her. "I don't think we'll get that big, our music isn't that commercial, there's no way we'll get as big as Guns N' Roses."

Kurt was franker with people he knew and trusted. "One day in London, we'd been to see a couple of record companies and publishers and things," says Anton Brookes. "And a few of the people were quite dismissive of Nirvana; they didn't really know what to make of them or Kurt's music. And afterward, we were having a conversation and he just had a look – I remember how he kept eye contact in the conversation. He was telling me: you know, I've got tracks which are going to be top ten singles, they're going to be huge, they're going to be number ones in America. And I was like: yeah, I believe ya! But I don't think he believed that it would happen so quickly. I think he believed it would be a process of time; you take your albums out on tour quite extensively, you get on MTV, and probably get one hit, and no more, that's it."

There were four further UK dates in Leeds, Edinburgh, Nottingham, and Norwich. The Edinburgh date was especially exciting for Kurt as The Vaselines, who had split up the previous year, had agreed to reform for the gig. Eugene Kelly had been surprised to learn Nirvana had been covering their songs ("we were incredibly obscure"), and even more surprised at how nervous Kurt was to meet him. "Kurt was quite introverted," he later recalled. "I just remember him wearing fingerless gloves, sitting on a chair saying: hi, so great to meet you." Kurt was equally thrilled that Shonen Knife were on the bill. "When I finally got to see them live," he later told *Melody Maker*, "I was transformed into a hysterical nine-year-old girl at a Beatles concert."

Playing with some of his favorite bands, and energized by his new drummer, Kurt was in good spirits throughout the tour. "Finally we found the perfect drummer," he enthused to a journalist. "If he leaves, we quit. It's as simple as that. The drummer dilemma is officially over, period." On another night, while drinking at a disco after the band's show, Kurt came up to Dave and told him: "I'm so glad you're in this band. I'm so glad you're down-to-earth." ("I was like: wow!" Dave later recalled.) The tour made it clear that Kurt wasn't the only person who was enthusiastic. "The buzz was definitely out there by then," says Craig. "You knew that Nirvana was on the way to something, because every kid on the street was wearing a Nirvana shirt! You could definitely tell things were bubbling under – that they were looking to make a step, label-wise, and they're realizing that there's an audience out there. You know something is going to happen and we're thinking: oh, we could do something like what Sonic Youth is up to, you know? – something like that kind of level, Sonic Youth or Henry Rollins – the mid-level indie rock of that time. You think: oh, maybe we could get up to that." Anton viewed Nirvana's potential for success along similar lines. "To me, being huge and big was only like doing two nights at the Brixton Academy, something like what Sonic Youth or the Pixies would do," he says. "If Nirvana could have sold a million records around the world, over two albums, three albums, that would have been massive, you know?"

When Nirvana returned to the USA, Dave moved in with Kurt in Olympia, sleeping on the couch, noting to his chagrin that the aquarium Kurt kept his turtles in was longer than the couch he was forced to fold his six-foot frame onto. The turtles also kept him awake at night, with one in particular prone to banging its head repeatedly on the glass. "All he wanted to do was escape," Dave observed, perhaps reflecting his own feelings. It was Dave's first winter in the Pacific Northwest, and he initially had a hard time adjusting to Olympia's gloom; the skies are overcast for three-quarters of the year, with far more rainfall than in Seattle. "The sun, if there's any at all, it'll come up at nine and go down about three in the afternoon," he said. "Those winter months are wet and dark and cold. There was a hole in [Kurt's] window, so it was fucking freezing all the time."

"He was pretty depressed," says Barrett Jones. "He was having a tough time at that point. Actually, he sent me a Pixelvision thing – I'd love to find it again – that's just him walking around Olympia, and he was depressed and bummed out, and missing people from home, and told me I should come out there. But I remember him saying the practices were great, and they were writing these really great songs. He was psyched about it." Dave also cited Mark Lanegan's moody solo album, *The Winding Sheet*, as "the soundtrack to my first six months in Olympia. I listened to it every day – when the sun wouldn't come up, when it went down too early and when it was cold and raining. I was lonely ... It was a huge influence on our *Unplugged* thing."

Major labels were now seriously courting the band. Soon after the UK tour, Kurt and Krist flew to Los Angeles to meet with MCA; while they were in town, they also stopped by Gold Mountain management. John Silva also flew up to Washington to take the band to dinner, and on another LA trip, the entire band finally met with Gold Mountain's Danny Goldberg. Danny had yet to see the band live but was familiar with *Bleach*. "I knew it was good, I knew it was critically acclaimed, but my real passion for Nirvana didn't take place until I saw them live," he says. "I was reticent to sign other acts. For example, John really wanted to sign Dinosaur Jr. but I was just nervous about it. In retrospect, I feel a little foolish – Dinosaur's such a great band – but I was just nervous about paying the bills, you know? It's so much work to run a small business, and this is a great business when you have superstars, but when you have mid-level acts, you've gotta pay the bills. But I felt a little remorse that I hadn't followed up on the Dinosaur thing, so when they were all talking about Nirvana, I didn't want to crush them again. And by that time, I had such confidence in Kim and Thurston's judgment of the scene, I'd got to know them a little better, that it was just blind faith. And of course I was very lucky that I chose that particular one time to trust them; later when I saw Nirvana live I realized how lucky I was. But at the time I was just doing it on blind faith and Kim and Thurston's judgment."

In Danny's first meeting with the band, Krist commanded the most attention. "Dave didn't say a word," says Danny. "So my impression of him was that he was really good-looking – he had movie-star good looks. Krist was the most gregarious and did most of the talking and just seemed like a great guy; we talked a little bit about politics. Krist Novoselic has been the same from the day I met him to the last time I talked to him – he's one of the most real people, and what you see is what you get. And Kurt was very quiet; it was only in subsequent meetings that I realized how powerful he was in the dynamic of the band."

Nonetheless, Danny quickly picked up on Kurt's underlying resolve. "Kurt was just intensely ambitious," he says. "I walked on eggs when I first met them, asking if they wanted to stay with Sub Pop, because for some artists that really is a big issue with them; they like to stay indie, and I didn't know if that was going to be an issue with Nirvana. But he said: definitely not! Oh, OK – got it! He was just emphatic about not wanting to stay with them. There's no question they wanted out."

Nirvana eventually decided to sign with Gold Mountain and the negotiations with labels continued, even though DGC already seemed the obvious choice. "I think even at that first meeting we talked about Geffen [DGC's parent company] as probably being the best place, as long as they were going to make a competitive offer," says Danny.

"Because they hired people from the indie world; they had Ray Farrell, who had been with SST, and Mark Kates, who knew the indie/alt radio scene really well. And the other labels didn't have guys like that, so in the major world, Geffen had an advantage at that time. I was pretty sure they'd pay well and make the right kind of deal, but John really wanted to meet with everybody that was interested. But to me it was kind of a foregone conclusion that it was going be Geffen."

The band-members were happy to make the rounds of other labels, not least for the free meals. Although Dave's subsequent comment to Michael Azerrad about feeling like "snotty little hot-shit kids … getting away with something" reveals a touch of insecurity, Kurt – despite his reserve and the fact that Krist usually did most of the talking in meetings – remained focused. "It was interesting to see how Kurt operated," says Jennifer Finch, who occasionally went along with the band when they were taken out for a meal by a record exec. "I think maybe a lot of people don't realize that he was very professional in that capacity. He wasn't like: I don't care, whatever. He had very specific questions that he wanted to know, he was interested in what the compromises would be, and he had an understanding of how everything worked, the sort of mechanical side of the record industry. I don't remember conversations about 'selling out,' because the major record labels at that point were really trying to present themselves as being artist-friendly. So the real question was: is it possible to be shelved? Are you exchanging money for losing your career? That was more of what was discussed. And the band that completely paved the way for it at that time was Sonic Youth: they were one of the first alt/indie bands that did sign with a major and they had a great experience with it. So there wasn't, at that point, any example of bands from our scene that had a bad experience."

The band spent most of their time in rehearsal or writing new songs. Dave quickly fell in with their usual songwriting routine. "It starts with Kurt might have a riff and he'll bring it into soundcheck or whatever, he'll start playing it," he later explained. "Krist and I will just start following along. We'll jam on it until verses and choruses pop up out of it. It's usually just jamming, there is no actual composing or writing." "We just started experimenting with these really extreme dynamics," he said to another journalist, citing the Pixies and Black Sabbath's *War Pigs* as influences. "We just sort of abused it with pop songs and got sick with it – silly with it. It was fun: feeling good in some mellow verse and then smashing your way into some big, huge, distorted chorus. I suppose it's a cheap way to make the chorus seem a lot bigger than it really is." Dave also noted Kurt's habit of moving his jaw around when he played guitar, "like he was playing the drums with his teeth."

'Radio Friendly Unit Shifter' was an example of a song that came together out of a jam, aptly described by Krist as "a rocker. When we wanted to, we could really rock." The song features a pile-driving main riff played throughout the song on the bass, with the guitar joining in after the intro – the kind of catchy, melodic riff that was key to Nirvana's best work. But while the band would soon debut the song live, the lyrics wouldn't be finalized for over two years, when it was resurrected for *In Utero*. Such was the case with a number of the songs that were worked on during this period; early versions of the songs that have surfaced reveal that while the musical arrangements are largely similar to the final versions (aside from the occasional change of key), the lyrics were left unfinished until the song was recorded. ("[Kurt] really downplayed his lyrical skills," Dave recalled. "He always said: melody first and lyrics second.") 'Oh, The Guilt' was another riff-driven song – "just another rocker," in Krist's words. The taut lyrics run down a series of observations – or maybe indictments – of an unnamed woman, building to a chorus of Kurt screaming out the word "Go!" It would later appear on a 1993 split single with The Jesus Lizard.

Both 'Radio Friendly Unit Shifter' and 'Oh, The Guilt' emphasized Dave's muscular drumming, as did 'Aneurysm,' which also showed the band reaching beyond straight-out rocking to create something more complex. "'Aneurysm' was like a classic collaboration song," says Krist. "Everybody just stepped up to bat on that one and threw their two cents in, and it came together." The song had an unusually long intro for a Nirvana song, opening with Kurt playing a descending guitar riff, the guitar line slowly ascending as the rest of the band comes in, then lashing back and forth for nearly a minute and a half before the guitar begins another ascent, then dropping out, leaving the bass and drums to maintain the beat. This soft/loud dynamic continues throughout the song, but it's not quite the familiar Nirvana 'formula' of a quiet verse bursting into a loud chorus; the soft/loud interplay occurs during the verses themselves, with Kurt singing a line backed by bass and drums, the guitar coming in as he sings *"Ah-haa"* then dropping out again as he sings the next line.

There are only six lines to the song: a four-line verse, a single-line chorus, and a single line sung at the song's end. The verse is sarcastic, with an exhortation to dance until you "have a fit," and Kurt's declaration of love tempered by the punch line "makes me sick." After two repetitions of verse and chorus, the song heads back into its melodic climb, Kurt launching into a scream that rises in intensity with his guitar line, finally climaxing into a mighty roar. Dave's drumming adds another dimension to the song. He plays with a forcefulness that gave all the new songs a greater power and energy.

'On A Plain' was in a much lighter vein, rightly described as "a total pop song" by Krist. The buoyant music readily conveys the song's optimistic mood – something that's also apparent in the lyrics of the chorus, in which Kurt makes the rare concession "I can't complain." 'On A Plain' would later appear on *Nevermind*. 'All Apologies' was also considerably lighter, musically, in its early version, as opposed to the more melancholy number it became as the elegiac closing track on *In Utero*. But the lyrics darkened the mood, even at this early stage; despite Kurt's assertion he wanted to create a feeling of "peaceful, happy, comfort – just happy happiness," the confessional tone of the lyrics undercuts that intention.

Several other more contemplative songs were written during this time: moody, atmospheric numbers along the lines of 'Dumb,' which Kurt had first performed on KAOS in September. 'Dumb' had emerged nearly fully formed, with only the lyrics of the bridge changing from the first time the song was performed to its eventual recording on *In Utero*. Although Krist described it as "kind of a sweet pop song," the lyrical sentiments are decidedly melancholy, with Kurt singing from the perspective of the perennial outsider looking in, alternately envying those who remain blissfully ignorant and gently chiding them at the same time. "The song's not about me, but it has been," Kurt said. "And just using the word 'happy' [in the song] – I thought it was a nice twist on all the negative stuff we've done before."

The haunting 'Pennyroyal Tea' takes its title from the herb said to induce abortions, used here as a metaphor for washing away one's "bad evil spirits," Kurt explained. But Kurt's mournful vocal suggests this is a battle that can't be won, as he made clear in another interview, right before the song was finally released on *In Utero*. "The song is about a person who's beyond depressed," he said. "They're in their death bed, pretty much." 'Something In The Way' was equally despondent, a bleak depiction of Kurt's immediate post-high school years, when he had no fixed home and slept where he could – friends' couches, apartment building hallways, and even, he claimed, under a bridge two blocks from the house where he'd lived as a child. Putting his feelings of abandonment into words apparently came easily to Kurt, for aside from some very minor lyric changes (and a change to a lower key), the song remains largely the same from its first live performance to its recording for *Nevermind*, which featured the same acoustic guitar Kurt played on 'Polly.'

There was a darker undercurrent to this productive time as well. Sometime during the fall, probably after the UK tour, Kurt began to use heroin. (The lyrics of 'Aneurysm' allude to drug use, while Kurt decided to feminize the name in his journals, referring to it as "heroine.") Although Kurt told Azerrad he first used the drug while living in Aberdeen, friends who knew him at the time have disputed this. Now, he telephoned Krist to casually announce: "Hey, Krist: I did heroin." Krist was shocked and warned his friend he was "playing with dynamite." Krist also relayed the news to Dave, who was in LA at the time. Kurt assured his bandmates he wouldn't use it again, but he soon did, even though for now he remained a casual user. He told his ex-girlfriend Tracy that the drug made him feel "more sociable," and that it helped alleviate his persistent stomach aches.

Kurt's heroin use came at a time when he began to experience more stress in his life, both personally and professionally. After breaking up with Tracy, Kurt had gone out with Tobi Vail, then on the verge of forming the band Bikini Kill. Since Kurt's appearance with The Go Team, Kurt and Tobi had occasionally played music together, recording their efforts on Tobi's father's four-track – songs Slim Moon described as "the minimal quiet pop songs that Olympia is known for."

"Kurt had a lot of cool ideas about how to approach songwriting," Tobi later told Everett True. "He told me the first thing you have to do is decide a singing style. This was a big revelation ... I didn't have any idea that you could shape the sound of your voice like it was a guitar." But the relationship ended after a few months, leaving Kurt a "wreck," in Dave's recollection. Charles Cross's *Heavier Than Heaven*, in quoting Kurt's journal entries at the time, reveals a personality mired in self-loathing.

And while Nirvana's career seemed firmly on an upward trajectory, there were still hiccups along the way. From May to September, the band had played with four different drummers. And while Kurt had worked hard to get Nirvana to the next level, he also had some ambivalence about the move. "The punk rock scene there was so claustrophobic," Dave recalled. "Everyone was so deathly afraid of doing something wrong." Despite Sonic Youth's example, Kurt continued to worry that signing with a major might compromise Nirvana's – or his own – integrity. Even after *Nevermind*'s success he told his biographer, in a continued attempt to promote his indie credentials, that Nirvana had come "really close" to signing with K Records. In fact, K was not even in the running; at the band's next show, November 25 at Seattle's Off Ramp Café, A&R reps from Columbia, RCA, and Capitol, among others, were the ones vying for Nirvana's signature. The show was one of the most wide-ranging that Nirvana ever played; half of the numbers in the 20-song main set had yet to be released, beginning with the opening song, 'Aneurysm'; they also debuted 'Oh, The Guilt,' 'Something In The Way,' and 'Radio Friendly Unit Shifter' at the show, as well as 'Dumb.'

"That's in my rock'n'roll top ten of shows," says Rob Nyberg. "It was the first show with Dave Grohl back in Seattle after they had just toured Europe, so you could see how he had settled into the band. It was an amazing show – just amazing, song after song after song. It's like they played their entire catalog." The band resurrected *Bleach* numbers like 'Mr Moustache,' 'Swap Meet,' and 'Sifting,' none of which they'd played in over a year; performed the Vaselines and Wipers covers they'd recently added to the set along with 'Here She Comes Now' and 'Where Did You Sleep Last Night'; and included a rare performance of 'Verse Chorus Verse.' Six of the songs that would ultimately appear on *Nevermind* were also performed.

Given the number of A&R reps in the audience, there was an excellent incentive for the band to showcase as much of their material as they could. But it was also clear they were playing just for the sheer joy of it, enjoying themselves so much that as 2am approached – the cutoff time for liquor sales in Washington state – a plan was worked out so that the show could continue: everyone left the club, the alcohol was locked up, the club re-opened, and anyone who wanted to stay was readmitted. Nirvana went on to play at least another 11 songs (the circulating recording cuts off at that point).

For Dan Peters, the experience of watching his replacement was bittersweet, but even he was won over by the band's performance. "I thought they were great!" he says. "I thought they had made the complete right decision. When I saw Dave, it made complete sense to me why he was the drummer and I wasn't." Dan also received an acknowledgment from the stage for his brief tenure in Nirvana. After performing 'Sliver,' Krist said: "Thanks Danny! Dan Peters helped us write that song."

The commercial appeal of the new material was obvious to those in attendance. On hearing 'Lithium,' Soundgarden's Ben Shepherd went up to his bandmate, Kim Thayil, and said: "That's the hit. That's a Top 40 hit right there." (Dave Grohl agreed with this assessment: "I always thought that 'Lithium' was going to be the big deal on the record," he said.) There was no shortage of offers from the majors, and Jeff Fenster, of Charisma, was seemingly the initial winner; two days after the Off Ramp show, Alan Mintz called Fenster and confirmed that Nirvana would sign with the label. Fenster, who had been following the band for several months, was pleased, but became increasingly concerned as the days passed with no other word. Then came the news: Nirvana were signing with DGC.

"I remember John [Silva] calling up and saying: we're managing these guys now. They want to talk to you, we know you want to talk to them," Mark Kates recalls. "The next thing that I remember is that Gary [Gersh, DGC's A&R] asked me to call Krist and just talk to him, and I was very used to doing that part of the job. It was very much a dialogue among a very small group of us at the company; the top of the company was probably focused on signing the bands that everyone knew about, that were either sure things or massive bidding wars. That's a very hard thing to convey in the wake of how big Nirvana got, obviously. But there's a theme here, if you look at the music business, that most of the biggest bands were not about bidding wars, or powerful lawyers, or powerful managers that were playing the record companies like a marionette; most of the biggest bands were not signed with the expectation of what would happen. And most of the ones that *were* signed with that expectation *didn't* happen. I'm telling you, you could do a graph, and it would be highly entertaining.

"If I had to give you one answer why Nirvana signed with us, it would be that Sonic Youth was on our label and they were happy," he continues. "We had taken them from selling 80,000 copies of *Daydream Nation* to 200,000 copies of *Goo* – which, to be honest with you, as time goes on, I understand less and less how we did that, 'cause all I can think about are the things that we *couldn't* make happen for that record, particularly getting the 'Kool Thing' video played. But anyway, I think that no one in their life, including their management, had more influence on Nirvana than Kim and Thurston. There's a very nice list of bands from that era who one could say were 'adopted' by Sonic Youth that went on to be really successful. Or at least more successful than they would have been if they weren't adopted by Sonic Youth." Jeff Fenster apparently agreed, later telling a panel at the South By Southwest music conference: "I had Nirvana. They agreed to sign with me. Then Gary Gersh came along. Danny Goldberg wheeled in Thurston Moore. He said: Gary's all right with me – and that was it."

DGC's contract gave Nirvana a $287,000 advance, part of which went to a $75,000 buyout fee for Sub Pop (Sub Pop would also get two percentage points from sales of the band's next two albums, generating an influx of cash that would rescue the label from its financial doldrums for good). The contract was finally signed on April 1 1991; in the meantime, Gold Mountain put each member of Nirvana on a retainer of $1,000 a month. Although this has been characterized in other accounts as "barely minimum wage," it was actually rather higher than that, for the minimum wage in Washington State in 1990 was $680 a month. Kurt had also received an additional $3,000 from a publishing deal he'd signed with Virgin Publishing (giving his song catalogue the name The End Of Music). It was the first time in Nirvana's career that money was not a pressing concern, leaving the band free to focus on rehearsing and songwriting. For the next five months, they would play just eight shows.

Dave took advantage of the downtime to return to Virginia. He had already made one trip to his former home when Nirvana was in New York City meeting with record labels. His joining Nirvana had pushed the group into greater productivity, and it had sparked his own interest in songwriting as well. When Kurt retired to his room after band rehearsals, Dave would stay up in the living room, recording songs on Kurt's four-track, singing quietly so as not to awaken his bandmate. Dave admitted he was "in awe" of Kurt's songwriting talent, and was hesitant about bringing his own material to Nirvana's rehearsals. But one night, Kurt walked in while Dave was listening to a playback of a song. "What *is* that?" he asked. "Oh, just something I just recorded," Dave replied nonchalantly. Kurt then asked Dave to show him how the guitar line went, and the two musicians ended up jamming together. "Wow," Dave thought. "Maybe I *can* write songs."

If he was too intimidated to suggest playing his songs at Nirvana rehearsals, he felt more comfortable in front of his old friend Barrett Jones. And so, on December 23, Dave returned to the Laundry Room – then operating under the name Upland Studios, as the house where the studio was located was on Upland Street – and cut his first solo tracks. "I just wanted to see how poppy or how noisy a song I could write," he later explained. "It was always just for fun." But the versatility of the material recorded showed that Dave underestimated his abilities; even as a young songwriter, the songs display economy, imagination, and wit. 'Pokey The Little Puppy' is an upbeat instrumental, reminiscent of faster Nirvana numbers like 'Pay To Play' and 'Immodium.' 'Petrol CB' (with backing vocals by Jones) and 'Throwing Needles' are harder rock numbers, but nonetheless tempered by a clear pop melodicism, such as when the distorted, gnarly lead vocals on 'Petrol CB' unexpectedly lead into a more laid-back, dreamy chorus. Just as deceptively, 'Throwing Needles' begins with a few quietly strummed notes before exploding into a breakneck pace, Dave's cool harmonizing suddenly erupting into harsh screams. 'Just Another Story About Skeeter Thompson' is a delight, a spoken-word piece about life on the road with his erstwhile bandmate, complete with a twist ending.

But the most striking songs, and the ones that best display the influence Kurt had on Dave's early songwriting, are 'Color Pictures Of A Marigold' and 'Friend Of A Friend.' "Those are definitely Kurt-influenced, I think," Barrett agrees. "Kurt taught him how to write quieter, more pretty songs. Before that he was just doing loud, screamy stuff, more Melvins-like." The delicate 'Color Pictures Of A Marigold' was the song Kurt had heard Dave working on; this version has an acoustic guitar providing the sole musical accompaniment, coupled with a surprisingly gentle vocal. 'Friend Of A Friend,' the first song Dave ever wrote on an acoustic guitar, was even more striking. The song is a pen portrait of his new bandmates: Kurt, locked in his "quiet room" with his guitar, and Krist, worrying about his drinking. An air of melancholy hangs over the song, reflecting Dave's uncertainty about his new circumstances, observing his new friends yet somewhat detached at the same time. "'Friend Of A Friend' is an amazing song," says Jenny Toomey. "Dave has such a sweet voice in it. And it's complex, the way he reveals and doesn't reveal things in that song. It's also very, very simple. I've always wanted to cover that song."

Barrett was impressed with his friend's efficiency at the session. "The songs were always completely worked out when he came in," he says. "Everything was first take. He was never like: maybe I should do it this way, or let's try this. He knew exactly what he was doing, always. That's what always just shocked me, how he could do that. I was envious of that."

Four additional songs were recorded at a July 27 1991 session that Barrett didn't produce (he also feels there were more than these two sessions, but recalls no precise dates). By now Jenny Toomey had heard the material and offered to put it out on her Simple Machines label. "My label was releasing a series of cassettes that focused on music that was either unfinished and imperfect, or finished and perfect by bands that no longer played out – Geek, My New

Boyfriend, Saturnine, The Hated, The Mommyheads, Slack, Tuff School," she explains. "It made perfect sense to ask Dave to add his solo tape to the list." Dave agreed – as long as the release didn't bear his name. And so *Pocketwatch*, the fourth tape in Simple Machines' Tool Cassette series, was released in 1992 under the name Late!, with Dave's involvement largely unknown at first. The tapes were manufactured on an as-needed basis, dubbed from a master cassette as orders came in. Once word spread about the true identity of Late!, orders increased, and Jenny suggested that an updated version be made available. "We were talking with Dave about getting good copies of the masters and adding some obscure tracks and releasing it on CD," she says. "He went back and forth with the idea and then it fell off the face of the earth. I know he also thinks it's cooler to have it this way." When the tape finally wore out, *Pocketwatch* was deleted from the label's catalogue; it has since been bootlegged extensively. Two songs were later released in re-recorded versions. 'Color Pictures Of A Marigold' was recorded during the *In Utero* sessions and released as a bonus track on the 'Heart-Shaped Box' single, under the shortened title 'Marigold'; 'Friend Of A Friend' was recorded for Foo Fighters' 2005 album *In Your Honor*.

"I really love *Pocketwatch* because it's a very human record," says Jenny. "You can't listen to it without feeling the humor and feeling the sort of sweetness of it, so I'm really proud that we played a role in putting it out." Even some of those who'd known Dave for years were surprised at his multi-instrumental abilities. "I remember when I heard *Pocketwatch*, I was like: wow, that's interesting. I had no idea that Dave wrote songs and played guitar," says Mark Andersen. "Now, of course, if you go way back before Mission Impossible to Freak Baby, he was actually a guitar player there, but I didn't know that until years later. Anyway, I remember hearing some of this stuff and thinking: you know, he's pretty good! And that was all I thought about it. Until years later when I saw Foo Fighters, and I was like: Jesus fucking Christ! Who knew? This guy behind the drums is like a renaissance man!" Although Dave would continue to downplay his solo efforts for some time ("I wouldn't give people tapes," he admitted), *Pocketwatch* effectively laid the groundwork for a solo career before he'd even started to think about having one.

Some accounts have Fugazi's Ian MacKaye saying he heard a rough mix of 'Smells Like Teen Spirit' during Dave's December 1990 visit, and telling Dave: "This is going to be really popular." He's most likely mistaken about the chronology, and probably referring to a later visit by Dave. The first known recording of 'Teen Spirit,' from the spring of 1991, is decidedly rough, and while the song's instantly recognizable main riff is catchy, you'd be hard pressed to envision it as a potential hit. The song was unlikely to have even been written at that point; if it had been, an early version would probably have been roughed out at Nirvana's next recording session, which was less than a month away.

Dave returned to Washington State after Christmas, in time for Nirvana's final show of the year, a New Year's Eve gig at Portland's Satyricon. They were back in Seattle the very next day, for a recording session booked at the Music Source, produced by Craig Montgomery. "In my young naiveté, I thought: if this goes really great, I'll get a chance to work on the record!" he says. The band recorded early versions of 'Oh, The Guilt,' 'All Apologies,' 'On A Plain,' 'Radio Friendly Unit Shifter,' and a re-recording of 'Token Eastern Song' (all but 'Oh, The Guilt' have scratch vocals). While Craig wouldn't work on *Nevermind*, two other songs from the session, 'Aneurysm' and a re-recording of 'Even In His Youth,' would end up appearing as non-album tracks on the 'Smells Like Teen Spirit' single, this version of 'Aneurysm' featuring a particularly bloodcurdling scream from Kurt. 'On A Plain' was the only song to be re-recorded for *Nevermind*; key tracks like 'Teen Spirit' and 'Come As You Are' had not yet been written.

The 'Teen Spirit' single would be released in nine months. In the meantime, there would be a farewell release on Sub Pop, another part of the buyout deal. Nirvana's time with Sub Pop would end as it began, with a Sub Pop Singles Club release, but in a larger run – 7,500 copies, more than seven times as many as the 'Love Buzz' pressing (with the first 4,000 on green vinyl). The cover featured a small photo from Charles Peterson's last session with the Chad Channing line-up of the band. It was also a split single, with Nirvana contributing a somewhat ragged live version of 'Molly's Lips' from the band's February 9 1990 show in Portland ("I find it embarrassing because it's just simply a bad version," Kurt later wrote), and The Fluid's 'Candy' on the flipside. Sub Pop also etched a final salvo in the run off groove on Nirvana's side: the single word 'Later.'

CHAPTER 16

Nirvana In Its Afterlife

"It's strange to see our faces on MTV."
KURT TO *GUITAR WORLD*, 1991

Work on *Nevermind* was completed in June 1991. Barrett Jones, who dropped by the sessions while the band was in Los Angeles, immediately sensed how big the album would be. "I was just absolutely blown away," he recalls. "I thought it was the best stuff I had heard in a long time, and I made a bet with Kurt that they'd be on the cover of *Rolling Stone* within months of the release – which actually happened! I just thought it was great. I remember I got shivers in the studio just listening to it, it sounded so great."

Barrett was more certain of the band's success than Nirvana's label, DGC, where expectations were relatively modest. "In the marketing meetings at the time, sales of 50,000 were what was planned, since Sonic Youth had sold 118,000 of *Goo*," John Rosenfelder, who handled radio promotion for the label, told Charles Cross. "We figured if it could sell half that, we were doing good."

Excitement began to grow over the course of the summer. Danny Goldberg finally saw his clients in performance after the *Nevermind* sessions had concluded, when Nirvana opened for Dinosaur Jr. at the Hollywood Palladium on June 14. "I felt a real epiphany that this was a remarkable band," he recalls. "Kurt had this ability to be intimate with the audience, and I don't know how he did it. I never saw anybody that made me feel that way before. He had the ability to connect with people; there was some kind of mystical connection that he made with the audience on a good night. And they were a great band, obviously; they played well together, they were bonded and all that, but there was an emotional component that he created that really took me by surprise. I remember driving home calling Rosemary [Carroll, Goldberg's wife] and telling her how amazing they were, and she was quite surprised to hear me that excited, because I was pretty jaded about things by this time."

Expectations were raised further by the band's show at the Roxy Theatre on August 15, which was set up primarily as a showcase for Geffen staff, and had those working for Nirvana thinking perhaps they could generate higher sales than they'd originally anticipated. "Kurt's thing was he wanted to do as well as the Pixies," says Danny. "That was always his thing. Then in the back of my mind, when he wasn't around, I would say: maybe they could be as big as Jane's Addiction! Because that was like the insanely high goal, that they would be as big as the vaguely alternative act that I think sold 800,000 records – the Pixies sold 350,000 and Sonic Youth sold 150,000. But Kurt's big thing was to be as big as the Pixies."

Audience members were also asked if they'd be interested in being extras in the 'Smells Like Teen Spirit' video, which was shot two days later. "Everybody had to be at the Roxy show, and it was hard to get people in," says Mark Kates. "Yet we were still worried about people showing up to the video shoot as extras, like that was a significant topic. That was something we were honestly concerned about. But I remember thinking at the Roxy show: (a) I don't think this band could be any greater, and (b) this feels like it's actually gonna go somewhere. But again: somewhere? Like, we do 200,000, and we thought these songs were more palatable, and we could probably get the [hard rock/metal] KNAC-type stations to play it, and wouldn't it be amazing if we could sell half a million? So, for a record that shipped, whatever, 35,000, that was still a very ambitious goal."

The number usually cited for the first US pressing of *Nevermind* is 46,251 copies; in the UK it was an equally restrained 6,000 copies. "The media still wouldn't take them that seriously," says Anton Brookes, who had nonetheless begun fielding requests for advance copies of the album. "I remember taking a few tapes in my bag," he says, "and I'd be going to gigs in London, and I'd see a journalist, or people I knew in bands, and everyone was coming up and going: oh, you got a tape of *Nevermind*? Like the really serious music heads, you know, people who collect bands, who were really into indie and obscure bands, and were just totally obsessed with Nirvana. When *Nevermind* came out, we couldn't get [magazine] covers. No one would give us covers. It wasn't until they started to explode, and everyone's just hanging onto that rollercoaster; then you couldn't get rid of the press."

Advance interest was building in Seattle as well. "I remember the very first time I heard *Nevermind*, before it came out," says Chad Channing, who'd remained on good terms with his former bandmates. "Ben Shepherd had come home from one of his tours, and he said: man, I got a tape of their new album, check this out, it's pretty cool. And I remember being really excited to hear it, and the first time I heard it I was thinking: fuck, that's really cool! And Ben's like: yeah, it's totally cool, but I had to scold them first for kicking you out. And I just looked at him and smiled, because he didn't know the full thing of it at all. But being such a good friend I just smiled at him anyway. And we listened to the tape and it was like: God, this is totally cool. I was totally into it. I was like: wow, this rocks. And made a copy of it. And I knew right then, for sure, that album was going to do real well."

Chad also noted that the drum arrangements on the songs that he'd originally recorded with Nirvana were largely the same. "There were a couple little things that Dave threw in to make it more 'Dave,' I guess," he says. "Like during the main melody of 'In Bloom,' he threw in an extra kick. But aside from the fact that it was totally polished, it was pretty much the same song. Which I thought was a cool compliment from Dave, playing the drum parts that I had put down. I was actually kind of shocked when I heard it. I was like: wow, these are not too far off at all, they're almost identical to the Madison ones."

Other people who knew the band also felt a change was coming. Charles Peterson recalls the band's in-store performance at Seattle's

Beehive Music And Video on September 16 drawing a large crowd that spilled from the store into the parking lot. "The place was packed," he says. "It was just the rawest show I'd ever seen them do. It was so amazing. They just had three amps and a drum kit, and it was just so raw and powerful. They were right there on the floor, not a stage."

Charles's excitement was tempered by the underlying realization that the band was about to step into a larger arena, and things would never be so intimate again. *The Rocket*'s Courtney Miller experienced a similar feeling. "I remember standing around with my brother and Jamie Brown [the store's manager] and a bunch of other people and we're just looking at each other like: oh my God!" she says. "Nirvana had been over at the Blue Moon [a tavern across the street], and they were walking back across the street and we were watching them, and I was thinking: wow, those unsuspecting kids don't even know what's going to happen. I really remember having those thoughts. And it was just such an amazing little performance, and you're like: this, is going to be huge ... but by then it's not really a prediction, because they'd already gotten a major record deal and things were well on their way."

'Teen Spirit' had been sent to radio on August 27 and officially released September 9 in the UK and September 10 in the USA. (*Nevermind* followed on September 23 UK, September 24 USA.) It was the first release to come out with Kurt's name properly spelled 'Kurt Cobain'; however much he told Azerrad he "didn't care" how his name was spelled, it was not insignificant that on his first major-label release he went back to the correct spelling (although on *Nevermind*'s CD inlay, a photo taken by him is still credited to 'Kurdt Kobain'). 'Teen Spirit' was considered to have the best chance of being a hit on alternative radio, with the subsequent planned singles, 'Come As You Are' and 'In Bloom,' more likely to be crossover hits. But 'Teen Spirit' began to take off right away.

"This happened so fast – I mean, so fast," says Mark Kates. "Even in current record terms, it's unusual. On Friday of Labor Day

Weekend [August 30], radio reports indicated that 'Teen Spirit' had gone from 'light' to 'heavy' at KDGE in Dallas, and we knew that meant a great deal. Because that's a station where the music director, George Gimarc – he was the Bruce Pavitt of Dallas – he would have championed Nirvana from day one, but his boss was a really conservative programmer that didn't move any record up unless he had to. Going from 'light' to 'medium' would have been an accomplishment at that station. So seeing it go from 'light' to 'heavy,' we knew that was really significant."

"I was sitting in a meeting at Geffen," says Danny Goldberg, "and Mark Kates was listing all the different airplay 'Teen Spirit' was getting, and then he was going through the list of the indie stores, where there were people on the waiting list to be among the first that could buy the record, and I said: have you ever seen anything like this before? And he said: this is totally unprecedented! His level of excitement got me excited."

Over the next few weeks, 'Teen Spirit' continued attracting attention from unexpected outlets. "KMEL [in San Francisco] decided they had to find a way to play that song – and they were a hip-hop station!" says Mark. "Moments like that just can't happen much, because radio is inherently reactive, not proactive. So any radio station wanting to play a record that they're not playing, just that alone is unusual. And my attorney was telling me that his brother lived in a frat house at the University of Michigan, and every bedroom in the frat house was blasting that record all day long, and I don't think he was exaggerating." Danny recalls Sonic Youth's booking agent telling John Silva that when 'Teen Spirit' was played over the PA before a Guns N' Roses show, the crowd broke into wild cheering. "And so John and I were like: holy shit! If a Guns N' Roses audience is cheering for this, that's much bigger than just the punk Sub Pop world!" (It was a decidedly ironic endorsement, considering that Kurt in particular would make disparaging comments about Guns N' Roses for the rest of his career.)

"The band was getting big enough that this LA-based Nirvana band was sending cease-and-desist letters to radio stations," says Mark. "And one of the things I had to do that week was call everybody that was playing the record and say: just ignore those. And I remember talking to somebody who told me it didn't matter – there was nothing that would stop them from playing this record. It was too good." (Nirvana eventually settled with the LA band – and, later, a UK-based prog rock band of the same name – for the right to use the name.)

"Once the video got played, I mean, it was really over," Mark continues. "The song was already huge where it was getting played, but this was that really amazing thing that occasionally happens still in our business, where something has its own energy and momentum, and it doesn't really matter what you're doing. Most of what's gonna happen is gonna happen anyway. Thank God. People liked to say: we just gotta get out of the way. All we can do is screw this up."

The 'Teen Spirit' video effectively captured the passion and mayhem of a typical Nirvana performance, the band playing in a dilapidated gymnasium with the audience driven into a frenzy of moshing and crowd-surfing, intercut with a few shots of a swaying janitor and bound-and-gagged teacher that could have come from a David Lynch film. (In a nod to his former band, Dave Grohl wore a Scream T-shirt.) During the shoot, Danny recalls, "John was a little stressed because the audience of extras had gotten more anarchic than was planned. And the director or someone was upset, and it was: this is chaos! And Kurt was just smiling, very pleased with himself, because this was what he had had in mind. He had a very exact vision of what he wanted and he wrote out every single scene. Not every scene he had thought out made the final edit, because he wrote out too many scenes for the length of the song, but there's not a single image in there that he didn't already describe in his treatment, so he knew exactly what he wanted, and he got it."

The video's authenticity resonated with those who knew the band, even as they wondered about its appeal beyond their immediate circle. "I felt like: no one is ever going to like this," says Jennifer Finch. "It's too weird and cool! What are they gonna do with it?" "The first time I saw 'Smells Like Teen Spirit' on TV I was so excited, because everybody looked like my friends," says Alice Wheeler. "In those days you never saw girls with tattoos on TV. For a while, a little window opened up from Seattle where what mattered was your talent, it didn't matter how pretty you were. And I think that that's what Nirvana came out of, because if anyone was gonna look at those guys when they put out their first single and go: oh, these guys are going to be the biggest rock stars in the world – it's like: there's no fucking way! You know?"

The video had its world premiere on September 14 on MTV's *120 Minutes*, a show sarcastically dubbed by some an 'alternative ghetto' to which videos from non-mainstream acts were relegated. But the song's strong performance on radio led to its being placed in MTV's *Buzz Bin* on October 14, where it was aired several times a day. *Nevermind* then broke into the *Billboard* Top 200 on October 12, at Number 144, with 'Teen Spirit' reaching the Top Ten in the magazine's Modern Rock chart. (Had the album's initial pressing been larger, it would have charted much sooner.) Butch Vig traveled to Chicago to see the band at the Metro that evening. "The buzz in the air was unbelievable!" he says. "Kids were screaming and crying during the show, and almost everyone already knew all the lyrics. I was thinking: wow, I might eventually have a Gold record. And of course it went Gold in a matter of weeks." It was the same night that Kurt began his relationship with Courtney Love.

When Nirvana arrived in Portland for a show at the Fox Theatre on October 29, they were informed that *Nevermind* had gone Gold and would be in the Top 40 the following week. "We're all like: what? How'd that happen?" says Dan Peters. Mudhoney, who'd been on tour themselves, were also on the bill; the plan was for the two bands to join up and play shows in Portland, Vancouver, and Seattle. "And actually Mudhoney, I believe, were going to be the headliner when this tour set off," says Dan. "But every club – I mean, seriously, I'm not kidding – every club we would go to, when we'd load in, we'd open up the doors and we'd hear: dah dah-dah ['Teen Spirit''s opening riff]. It seemed like everybody was playing that record. We'd turn on the MTV at the hotel room, and there they'd be. I think about halfway through our tour we realized they'd be opening up those shows.

"Portland sure was fun," he says. "The Seattle show was just a little too much. The crowd was great. The crowd was over-the-top – just too many people with movie cameras running around the band. If Kurt would drop to the ground, do one of his roll-around-on-the-ground moves, someone'd be running around him with a camera." The Seattle show, at the Paramount Theatre, generated similarly mixed feelings in the hometown audience. Ian Dickson, a friend from Olympia who'd been asked to be one of two go-go dancers on stage, was irritated to have John Silva come up and tell him: "I didn't spend a quarter of a million dollars on this video for you to fuck it up!" "I'm like: fuck you, John," Dickson told Everett True. "I don't work for you. Kurt asked me to do this." Charles Peterson had shot Mudhoney's set and was irked to then be informed he wouldn't be allowed to shoot Nirvana. "It was a great show," he says, "but it was frustrating to be standing there with my heavy camera bag watching it from the back while it seemed like there were at least ten cameramen with their little gizmo 16mils running all over the place, and of course none of that footage ever came out, or was used anywhere. So it was just very frustrating. It was the first taste of: oh, yeah, they've been co-opted by the industry."

Jack Endino, on tour in Europe with Skin Yard, was able to follow the rise of 'Teen Spirit' overseas. "That song followed us all over Europe," he says. "Every country, every time we did an interview with somebody at a radio station, they'd be: all right, thank you, that was Skin Yard. And now we'd like to play the new Nirvana song! And then we'd go to a record store and be browsing for records and they'd be playing it over the speakers. We'd go to a club – we went to a club in

Norway, where the record hadn't even been released yet, and the guy behind the PA at the club, in Bergen, which is the farthest north we ever played, he had already somehow gotten a cassette of it, and he was playing it. Everybody everywhere was playing this damn song, all through Europe, and we started to get kind of freaked out. It was like it was chasing us. We couldn't get away from this damn Nirvana song. It was obvious that this phenomenon was beginning to happen, because all that Sub Pop stuff was being heard all over Europe. I could go anywhere in Europe, walk into a club for soundcheck, and I would hear stuff on their PA that I had recorded. I would hear Screaming Trees, I would hear Cat Butt, I would hear Swallow, I would hear Mudhoney, I would hear Green River, I would hear Soundgarden – usually all of them in any given evening. It was very weird. It was sort of funny, but it was weird. And then this Nirvana song came out and just eclipsed everything. So I knew that something was going on back home. And Ben [McMillan, Skin Yard's singer] started calling people up back home and he'd come in and say Nirvana has sold 250,000, or they've sold 500,000. Just in the space of a few weeks it went Gold. So we were quite floored, because it was like this amazing thing going on." With sales exploding, Butch asked John Silva if *Nevermind* might reach Number One. "And he said no way, not a chance," Butch recalls. "The next week it was Number One."

On January 11 1992, *Nevermind* reached the top of the album charts in *Billboard* (with 'Teen Spirit' peaking at Number Six), displacing Michael Jackson's album *Dangerous* from the top spot (in the UK, surprisingly, the album and single did less well, both peaking at Number Seven). Back catalogue sales of *Bleach* pushed it into the charts, giving Sub Pop its first entry in the *Billboard* Top 100, where it peaked at Number 89 on the way to its becoming the label's biggest seller. The attention Nirvana received quickly expanded into interest in other acts from the Northwest. New albums by Pearl Jam (*Ten*) and Alice In Chains (*Dirt*) soared into the Top Ten, and Soundgarden, whose major-label debut had languished at Number 108, had their first Top 40 hit with *Badmotorfinger*. *Temple Of The Dog*, a one off album by members of Soundgarden and Pearl Jam to commemorate the memory of Andrew Wood, had been released in 1991 to little notice; now it too reached the Top Ten. The film *Singles*, Cameron Crowe's romantic comedy about young Seattleites, had been completed in 1991, but the studio, uncertain of the film's commercial appeal, had kept its release on hold. But when the studio execs realized that not only did members of Pearl Jam, Soundgarden, and Alice In Chains appear in the film, there was also a soundtrack featuring these same bands, the film and soundtrack were hurriedly released, with the soundtrack reaching Number Six. Bands that Nirvana promoted in interviews benefitted as well; the Melvins secured a deal with Atlantic, and *The Way Of The Vaselines: A Complete History* was released on Sub Pop.

Stories about the bands were often accompanied by stories of a perceived Northwest "lifestyle," which involved copious consumption of coffee and micro-brewed beer (the *New York Times* adding heroin to that list), with the thrift-store clothing and the T-shirt and flannel shirt apparel favored by the area's residents tagged as "grunge fashion." Even *The Rocket* was cannibalized for grunge signifiers. In September 1991, then-art director Art Chantry had redesigned the magazine's column headings with a malfunctioning label-embosser, with the letters misaligned and sometimes facing the wrong way. Innumerable magazines, posters, and record covers now made use of label-embosser lettering as a visual reference to something being 'alternative' – albeit in a more sanitized version, with the letters now properly aligned and facing the right direction. The style later became a formal typeface, called Recycle-Reverse.

"It was really weird," says Dawn Anderson of the intensity of the media spotlight on Seattle and the Northwest. "It was like I woke up and I was in a different city. It was like science fiction. That's how weird it was." The typical Seattle response was to poke fun at the sudden attention. The most legendary prank was when once-and-future Sub Pop employee Megan Jasper, then freelancing for Caroline

Records, fed a list of 'grunge slang' terms she made up on the spot to a gullible *New York Times* reporter, who then duly assured readers of the newspaper of record that the phrase "swingin' on the flippity-flop" was indeed Seattle speak for "hanging out," in a piece entitled 'Lexicon Of Grunge: Breaking The Code.' Mudhoney's contribution to the *Singles* soundtrack was equally wry; 'Overblown' took shots at the area's new rock stars, while at same time bemoaning their own lowly status: instead of a sack of candy, "All I got was a rock."

For others, watching an underground culture getting consumed by the mainstream generated more mixed feelings for those caught up in the sudden collision of art and commerce. "It was surreal," says Mark Andersen. "When I refer to the years of the punk rock wars, that's what it felt like to us – like we were fighting the guerrilla war in our subterranean world, and we were building something that was by no means perfect, but we were proud as fuck of it. You don't see this in a lot of the punk rock documentaries; they talk about New York's CBGB's and the London punk explosion and so forth, and then about the beginning of the 80s everything disappears until suddenly Nirvana appears and it's like: out of nowhere this band comes! And those of us who were in the trenches during those years know what a load of crap that is. Because what happened was, yes, the commercial rock world lost interest in punk rock, but kids – like me at the time – never gave up that vision. We were trying to make it happen in our own lives and our own communities, and this incredible underground network grew up, certainly throughout the United States, and also elsewhere. And we were putting our lives on the line! That's how it felt; it seemed like everybody thought this was fucking stupid, but it mattered to us, so we did it.

"And then when Nirvana breaks through, it's like the hordes of hell have invaded. You couldn't go to a show without bumping into an A&R man. And Nirvana's on the cover of *Rolling Stone*! *Rolling Stone* didn't give a fuck about us for a decade! I mean, I was glad, I was happy to see Dave up there, and actually Cobain did the nice thing with the 'Corporate Magazines Still Suck' T-shirt [which he wore on the cover of the magazine]. But on the other hand, it blew our minds and sometimes out hearts apart because we just – all of a sudden it seems like the world is being offered to you on a platter, and of course there are some catches. There are some asterisks on this offer.

"People are turning on each other," he continues. "Because some people say: OK, well, why not? Why shouldn't I be able to make my music and make a living out of it? I don't want to run my band. I don't want to put my records out myself. I just want to play my music! And there's nothing wrong with that, really – there's a legitimate point of view there. And then you've got the people who are saying: no, do not consort with the enemy. We don't have anything to do with them. And if you have something to do with them, we don't have anything to do with you, either.

"And then there's a whole bunch of us in the middle who are not sure what to do. And Nirvana breaks through, the riot grrrl stuff went crazy, people like Ahmet Ertegun [co-founder and president of Atlantic Records] are offering Fugazi the deal that they offered The Rolling Stones – millions of dollars and your own label, you do with it whatever you want. It was like the world had turned upside down. And more to the point, it's like we had built this sometimes, perhaps, comfortably complacent, but still pretty vibrant underground, and some big giant came and ripped the roof off, and the daylight came streaming in, and we were like the ants running every which way. And it was an extraordinary moment and I honestly look back at it with some pride, and a great deal of pain. Because I think most of us – myself included – wished we had dealt with it better. And certainly what you saw happen with Nirvana was an example of that extraordinary pressure that became concentrated on – in the case of Cobain – some pretty conflicted and ultimately too-weak shoulders."

Certainly, some of those who knew Kurt felt an underlying sense of disquiet even as Nirvana's star was in its ascendancy. "When I first saw him on MTV I cried," says Mari Earl. "Because it was like: this is too much! It was just like: wow, to know somebody that makes it big like that is really a very strange feeling. Because you feel – what I felt was fear for him. I don't know what it was. It was all these mixed emotions. I felt happy for him, I felt afraid for him, just a lot of different things. Because I knew that he wasn't the most stable person in the world. But it wasn't like I consciously thought of that. I was just really excited for him and very happy for him in the beginning. But it was quite a lot for him, I really think."

Jack Endino had similar thoughts about the band as a whole. "I sort of intuitively had a hunch that they weren't really psychologically prepared for success if it happened," he says. "I didn't really know what would happen if that came about. They were just these nice guys from Aberdeen that seemed an awful long way from *the biz*, if you know what I mean. They were very far removed from the biz, and all the nasty stuff that goes on, and I didn't think they would enjoy that part of it particularly, if they ever got to see it. Which turned out to be true."

Jack saw firsthand the negative repercussions of the band's newfound success. Skin Yard had opened for Nirvana at a show in Vienna on November 14. "Kurt was OK in Vienna," he says. "They seemed to be having fun. And it was a pretty good show. It was fun all around." But 11 days later, at a show at the Paradiso in Amsterdam, which was being filmed for TV, the mood was more downcast. "Kurt was looking pretty stressed out," says Jack. "And it was a really weird show, because he was really pissed off. There were all these people with cameras on the stage, and he was a little out of tune, and he was very angry at these cameras – 'get the hell off my stage!' – and backstage he was really uneasy. He looked really pale and sort of sick, and everybody seemed to be really uneasy and very unhappy. Like suddenly the success was starting to bother them, because people were starting to come at them. Suddenly people wouldn't leave them alone. And they could sort of see what was coming. And they didn't look entirely happy about it."

Kurt in particular found it hard to adjust to the new demands on his time. Even before *Nevermind*'s release he was already complaining in interviews about his promotional duties, which paled in comparison with what was to come. "We're just now coming into doing so many interviews that we're becoming exhausted by it – at least I am," he told *The Rocket*. "I mean, every waking day of my life is Nirvana now. Phone interviews and just constantly being tooled around." Having worked so hard for his success, he now seemed to disavow it. During the record release party for *Nevermind* at Seattle club Re-bar, he'd allowed the album to be played just once. Then, when it was put on a second time, he climbed into the club's DJ booth, took it off, and put on a Cars record, announcing into the club's microphone: "I don't want to hear my record anymore."

"The fact that he wanted success didn't mean that he liked all the things he got when it happened," said Danny Goldberg. "He loved the integrity of the punk culture and never wanted to betray it, and it pained him when he thought he was betraying it." He was especially bothered when people focused on his celebrity at the expense of his work. "I can't stand it when people come up to me and say: congratulations on your success!" he told journalist Jerry McCulley before a show in LA on December 27. "I want to ask them: do you like the songs? Do you like the album? Selling two million records isn't successful to me unless it's good." McCulley's article carried a litany of other complaints from Kurt ("I want to quit when I'm not having fun anymore"; "I hope to destroy my career before it's too late"), but the story became more notorious for its allusions to Kurt's drug use ("the pinned pupils; sunken cheeks; and scabbed, sallow skin suggest something more serious than mere fatigue," McCulley wrote of Kurt's appearance).

More surprising were Kurt's frequent references in interviews to his feelings of guilt. "I'm constantly feeling guilty in ways," he told one interviewer. "Our music, especially this album, is so slick-sounding. It's not that I'm totally unsatisfied with the production, but it still makes me feel like I've probably offended my own beliefs as a self-proclaimed punk rocker. A few years ago, I would have hated our band, to tell you the truth." He also mentioned guilt when talking to Everett True about having to do interviews at Top 40 radio stations. "You're there for the purpose of exposing your band when at the same time I didn't really want to expose our band any more," he said. "I felt we were getting too big. I felt guilty about that and I also felt guilty we're supporting this crap radio station that has nothing to offer anyone except commercial music" – including, of course, Nirvana's music. "There was that punk-rock guilt," Dave Grohl later told *Rolling Stone*. "Kurt felt, in some way, guilty that he had done something that so many people had latched onto."

Some of this guilt undoubtedly sprang from Kurt's own contrary feelings about his success. It was easy to downplay his ambitions when Nirvana wasn't expected to be a hit act, but now they were, which put him in the uncomfortable position of having to deny that he enjoyed any of it. He tried having it both ways. "It's never been a desire of ours to be on MTV, we've always been totally anti-MTV," he told Keith Cameron, while at the same time, according to Danny Goldberg, he kept careful track of how often Nirvana's videos were played on the station. "He was proud of his music," Everett True observed. "He wanted it to be heard by as many people as possible, but he was also conflicted ... He wanted to sell. He just didn't want to sell out." The band poked fun at their fear at having done just that on their new T-shirts; the 'Fudge Packin, Crack Smokin, Satan Worshippin Mother Fucker' slogan from 1989 had been replaced with a more sarcastic observation: 'Flower Sniffin, Kitty Pettin, Baby Kissin Corporate Rock Whores.'

Kurt's aunt feels that Nirvana's sudden fame also changed what music meant to Kurt. "Music was for Kurt – as it was for me at one time – an escape," she says. "It was an understanding friend, predictable and comforting. When he became famous, music was no longer an escape for him – it was a nightmare of scheduled 'creativity' and harried performances. It was almost as if he became a caricature of himself and the whole grunge movement. Kurt's success only reinforced my suspicions of how the music business operates. By that, I mean the artist becomes a commodity, a can of beans, if you will, merely a saleable product. Can anything drain the human spirit more?"

Adding to this burden was Kurt's gradual retreat into heroin addiction. He later wrote of becoming a regular heroin user in September 1991, the same month *Nevermind* was released, and suffered what may have been his first overdose that December, much as he insisted otherwise to his biographer. "I *didn't* OD," he told Azerrad about the incident, during which he had passed out. "I had just stood up too fast and fell down. She [the woman who'd given him the drugs] was giving me mouth-to-mouth and said I was turning blue but I wasn't out for very long at all – maybe half a minute. It was just kind of scary to her. She over exaggerated on it." Because of his drug problems, a US arena tour planned for the spring of 1992 was cancelled, and Kurt went through the first of many rehabs. He also married Courtney Love in February 1992, and the birth of their daughter, Frances Bean Cobain, that August was surrounded by rumors of the parents' purported drug use (all hotly denied by the couple).

The result was that Nirvana's career stalled at the very moment it was peaking. "That's when everything changed," Krist said. "Things progressively got worse, like the relationships. But the musical relationship – at least we'd play together and have fun playing. But it was like the classic story, once the band makes it big and everything just gets screwy."

"For me, the regrettable thing was that I just saw it as unrealized potential," says Craig Montgomery. "The band could be doing so much great stuff, but Kurt's got his Drug Problem and his They're Having The Baby Problem and there's all this stuff in the way of what they could be doing musically. Because these people can't keep their lives functioning on a personal level, you know? Like when *Nevermind* was at its hugest, we were supposed to go out and do a tour, as would befit the band with the Number One Album In The Fricking World. And we can't do it, because a guy in the band is a junkie who can't get out of bed. I don't mean that to sound mean, but at the time it was frustrating, you know? For me, as a sound guy, that's my chance to really go and do my thing, at a big level, and I can't do it. It also means I'm not working. Even though I was Nirvana's soundman for however many years, if you look at the number of shows that we did, it's not that many. The most time we spent on tour in any given year was probably 12 weeks. Not very busy."

For the next two years, Nirvana would play only one more major US arena tour, and one partial tour of Europe. They would play England just one more time, when they headlined the Reading Festival on August 30 1992. "There was a phrase that Mudhoney talked about: in a perfect world, Nirvana would be Number One," says Dan Peters. "Then we had to add: well, I guess it happened – but the world was not perfect."

Nirvana's final album, *In Utero*, recorded and released in 1993, featured a number of songs that predated *Nevermind*: 'Pennyroyal Tea,' 'Radio Friendly Unit Shifter,' 'All Apologies,' and 'Rape Me.' The album topped the charts and generated a good critical response, but it didn't help to alleviate Kurt's pervasive self-doubt. In an interview with *Impact*, he admitted to having become "lazy" after the release of *Nevermind*. "I don't have quite as much fire in me," he said. "It still comes, but in stages. I used to write all the time – every day I picked up my guitar. And now I find myself not even playing for an entire month." He told *Rolling Stone* he felt the band's music had become formulaic, and he had no clear idea which direction to go in. "Krist, Dave, and I have been working on this formula – this thing of going from quiet to loud – for so long that it's literally becoming boring for us," he said. "We've gone to the point where things are getting repetitive. There's not something you can move up toward, there's not something you can look forward to."

It was a thought that Kurt had wrestled with even before fame had swept him up. "That's one of the things I remember Kurt was always worried about," says Chad Channing. "What if I can't make another good album? What if I can't write any more good songs? How long am I going to be able to keep this up and do that?"

"Here's what I think, based on my conversations with him," says Craig. "I don't think he would have been one of those guys who kept turning out the hits; I think he would have grown bored with that really quickly. And there are signs that he already was. I got some of this feeling from Kurt, like, as great as Nirvana's music was, it's pretty simplistic stuff, and it's pretty limited, harmonically. And I just don't think it was holding his interest. Even on the In Utero tour, he really didn't enjoy playing *Nevermind* stuff. I wasn't on the In Utero tour, but based on my conversations with him, from even before that, I don't think he was that thrilled with the music he was making.

"It would have been really interesting to see what he would have done," he continues. "I really don't think it would have been some kind of conventional career arc. It would have been something other than that. I would have loved to hear what his next thing would have been. I do specifically remember one conversation I had with him, I don't remember who we were talking about, it was an older artist, and I said something like: someday when you're like that, I would love to still do sound for you, and hear what you're coming up with. And he said something like: oh, I'm not going to be doing music – something to the effect that I won't be doing this, at that age. I don't think he was really interested in a long career in music, mainly because he was disillusioned with all the other obligations that come with it. He really had so little interest in all that stuff. All the unintended consequences. And things that are out of your control."

Nirvana found themselves back in the studio in January 1994. But it was quite different from their first professional recording session in January 1988, when they'd laid down ten tracks in four hours at Reciprocal Recording with Jack Endino. Krist and Dave spent most of January 28 and 29 waiting for Kurt to show up at Robert Lang Studios in Shoreline, a suburb of Seattle, passing the time by recording a number of instrumentals and jams. (Dave would re-record some of this material later: 'Exhausted,' 'Big Me,' and 'Butterflies' appeared on the first Foo Fighters demo, 'Dave/Acoustic + Voc' became 'February Stars' on Foo Fighters' *The Colour And The Shape* album, and 'New Wave Groove' became 'Bill Hill Theme' and 'Final Miracle' in the score Dave wrote for the 1997 film *Touch*.) When Kurt finally turned up, the band recorded one song, initially simply entitled 'Kurt's Tune #1,' and later named 'You Know You're Right' when it was finally released in 2002. There's an air of defeatism about the song, which melodically has some of the sinuous Eastern pull of the band's first single, 'Love Buzz.' Lyrically, it's a song of another troubled relationship, perhaps referring to the woman mentioned in the second verse, Kurt sounding alternately wounded, bitter, and sarcastic, finally breaking out in a sustained, ravaged cry of "Hey!" during the chorus (as the isolated vocal track on the game *Guitar Hero* reveals, he's not singing "Pain," as other accounts have it). While warming up, the band also played two jams, one of which, interestingly, revived the main riff from 'Verse Chorus Verse,' which hadn't been played since the April 17 1991 show when they'd debuted 'Smells Like Teen Spirit.'

Nirvana began a European tour on February 6 1994. The band was now a foursome, with former Germs guitarist Pat Smear having been added as a second guitarist when touring in support of *In Utero* began. The tour's first leg was scheduled to end on March 3 in Offenbach, but after a March 1 performance in Munich, the remaining two dates were cancelled, and the second leg (which was to have begun March 11 in Prague) was postponed. The official reason was that Kurt was suffering from bronchitis and laryngitis, and a recording of the final show does show his voice to be noticeably rough. But he'd also become increasingly depressed during the tour and had been asking for it to be cancelled for the past week.

Nirvana's mentors, the Melvins, were also on the bill. "That tour was just a fiasco, a nightmarish fiasco," Buzz Osborne remembered. "Almost none of it was good. Some nights they played well, other nights it was just horrible – it was just kind of depressing. The last night that we played with them, in Munich, Cobain was in a massively huge fight on the phone with his wife. And I talked to him in the hallway a little bit, and he was just: I don't know how I'm going to get out of this. And my advice to him was give her everything. Get through this whole thing, get yourself off drugs, and then take it from there, even if you have to start over, even if it means you have to go on tour playing acoustic guitar, who cares. It was more complicated than that, but that's the gist of the last time I talked to him. He was certainly not happy with where he was, but he wasn't capable of getting out of it. Doing nothing's the easiest thing you can do, you know.

"And then right before they went on, the last thing he said to me was: I should just be doing this solo. That was the last thing he said, and I just walked outside. And I was just like: this is just horrible. He's surrounded by people who are draining every drop out of him and don't care about anything else. Because he's heavily under the lash of drugs, a drug addiction that's making it impossible for him to make the right life choices. And that really is where it all ended."

Kurt flew to Rome on March 2, Courtney joining him on March 3. On the morning of March 4, he was rushed to the hospital, having fallen into a coma due to an overdose of Rohypnol sleeping pills. Although reported as an accidental overdose, it was later described as a suicide attempt. And by the time Kurt returned to Seattle on March 12, Nirvana was effectively over. He spent much of his time during the following weeks on drugs, increasingly estranged from those around him. He apparently didn't see Dave Grohl again, although he spoke to him on the phone, assuring him the Rome incident had been an accident. At one point, Krist begged his old friend to come away with him to a farm that Krist owned in southwest Washington, but Kurt refused. Following an intervention on March 25, Kurt agreed to go back into rehab in LA, and Krist drove Kurt to the airport on

March 29. But at the airport the two got into a physical fight and Kurt ran away. It was the last time Krist saw or spoke to Kurt.

Kurt agreed to go to rehab again the next day, arriving in LA on the evening of March 30 and checking into the Exodus Recovery Center. One of his fellow patients was Gibby Haynes of Butthole Surfers, whom Nirvana had opened for back in 1988 at Union Station in Seattle, which probably felt like a lifetime ago to Kurt; more recently, the band had also opened for Nirvana on some dates the previous December and January. But Kurt only stayed at Exodus two days, climbing the facility's back wall on April 1 and flying back to Seattle.

There were sporadic sightings of Kurt over the next few days, but he largely avoided contact with people who knew him. A missing persons report was filed, and Courtney hired a private detective to try and locate him. But he was found almost by accident on April 8, when an electrician, hired to wire the house for a new security system, discovered Kurt's body in a room over the garage. Dr Nikolas Hartshorne, who as an aspiring medical student had booked one of Nirvana's shows at the Central in 1988, did the autopsy, determining that Kurt had died of a self-inflicted gunshot wound, putting the date of death as April 5.

The first report, aired on Seattle rock radio station KXRX around 9:30 am, said only that the body of an unidentified white male in his twenties had been found at the Cobain residence. News quickly reached *The Rocket* offices, where Courtney Miller, who'd been Nikolas' girlfriend in 1988, was still working, although April 8 happened to be her last day at the magazine. "There had been all those false alarms," she says of hearing the first reports. "You know, Rome, or you'd hear he's dead and this, that and the other, it always kept coming out. So when things started trickling out that morning I was dismissing it, like: here it goes again.

"We used to get phone messages written on little pink slips, headed 'While You Were Out,'" she continues. "And I got one of those that Nik had called. And as soon as I saw that pink slip, and I saw that it was from Nik, I was like: oh, this is real. This isn't a false alarm. I knew that was why he was calling, because he wouldn't have called otherwise. I talked to him later that day – I think they had just walked out of the post-op. And then of course Nik was on the front page. That was all surreal. And that's when I decided that truth was truly stranger than fiction. That was very bizarre."

Chad Channing also heard the news over the radio. "It was around 9:30 to 10 in the morning," he recalls. "I was driving my girlfriend to work, and I was driving back alone. I was just a couple miles from my house, listening to the radio, flipping around the dials and I stopped when I heard someone say '… has not been confirmed yet.' That's one of the few phrases on the radio that I'll give attention to; that usually means something, whether it's bombs dropping or what. Then it went to a quick little commercial break, came back, and said apparently there is a body with a self-inflicted gunshot wound … and right there I knew it was him. That was the first thing that popped in my head: my God, Kurt fucking killed himself! And I just listened to the radio intently, just listening to see who the heck they were talking about. And, sure enough: 'It appears that Kurt Cobain has been identified …' And I just got a weird blood hot rush, right over my body, like: wow, I was right! It was weird. It was almost funny to me, because it was so expected. For some reason I expected that to happen one day."

Most people had expected Kurt would probably die as the result of an overdose, so the news that his death was a suicide came as an additional shock. Charles Peterson had run into Kurt shortly before he left for rehab, and the two exchanged phone numbers. "I remember waking up that morning and going: oh, I should call Kurt. He gave me his phone number. I really should call Kurt," he says. "And then it's like: oh, it's 11 o'clock, it's probably too early for Kurt. And then the phone rang and it was *Entertainment Weekly*: we need pictures of Kurt Cobain. He's died. I didn't ask how he'd died – I just immediately assumed that it was an overdose. And while I was on the phone to them, *Rolling Stone* was on call waiting. And it just went like that for the next several days. It wasn't until I got out on the street, and I ran into my friend Kathy who lived next door, and she's like: did you hear that Kurt died? I was like: oh, yeah, stupid overdose. She was like: no, no, no, he killed himself. And I was like: oh, *man*."

Earnie Bailey got a call from Krist, who'd gone to his farm for a few days, while Shelli remained in Seattle: "Hey, guess what? Kurt's dead. Do you want to go up to the house and hang out with Shelli until I get home?" "When you first hear that somebody's dead, it really does take a while to process it," says Earnie. "I think I didn't actually believe it to be true, in a weird way. Because it seemed like he had died before a couple times. And I knew that the band was kind of over at that point, so everything was in this weird state of: what's going on? I thought: well, OK. Let's see if that's still the case this evening, if it's really true. And it was. Brenda [Earnie's wife] and I went up to Krist and Shelli's house, and we turned on the television, and I think we first saw [MTV's] Kurt Loder talking about it. And that seemed like: well, he must have gotten a call from the management. They would never let it get this far, unless it was in fact true. But it could *only* be an OD. That was the one thing that you prepared yourself for – that you had been through already before. And then came the reports of suicide. And that was a whole different thing. I mean, that was like – I think, between Brenda, Shelli, and I, there was this strange sensation of like the floor had just dropped, like you're in an elevator that has just lost all of its cables and you're falling. It was really a difficult thing to process. People aren't born with talent, they dedicate themselves to their craft, and they master it. So for somebody who I think was at the top, who was just so good at what he did – how can you process that, that somebody would build something, and then destroy it? Meaning themselves."

Butch Vig was in London, meeting with Shirley Manson to see if she was interested in working on a music project that eventually became the band Garbage. "Afterward, I was really looking forward to going to dinner and gossiping and stuff," he says. "And I got there and everybody was staring at me. And somebody pulled me aside and said: hey, did you hear Kurt Cobain's dead? He committed suicide. I was like: oh, fuck. It's something you think might happen but you never really can be prepared for it. So I just said: I really wish I could stay here, but I have to go call some people. So I went back to the hotel and I called everybody I could. I was sort of frantic because I felt so isolated. I booked a flight and I flew out early that next morning. I remember how freaky it was when I landed at New York at Kennedy [airport]; in just 24 hours, all the tabloids had Kurt's face ... I mean, it was freaky. Just walking down through the airport and looking at the stands and it's just Kurt's face everywhere. It was so weird. It was terrible, really. I felt like I was in some fucked up movie, like this isn't really happening."

Shirley Carlson, who had first played Nirvana on the radio on KCMU, telephoned Dawn Anderson at home with the news. Dawn was out, so Shirley spoke with Dawn's husband, Jack Endino. "And then Kim Thayil called me not long after that," he says. "The phone was ringing all day. As far as interviews, I don't think I talked with anyone. I think I talked to one person, finally – it was somebody I vaguely knew. But I was no comment, no comment, for the most part. People were trying to get comments from basically anybody they could talk to, because nobody wanted to talk. So the writers would just go down their list of anybody who had anything to do with Nirvana, ever: we need a quote, we need a quote. I was the completely objective outsider. And I'm the Godfather of Grunge, I might add," he notes wryly.

Jack broke the news to Dawn when she returned home. "It was really upsetting but – I hate to say it – maybe not that surprising," she says. Jack was distressed enough he later considered leaving the music business altogether. "It was the day the music died, you know? To paraphrase a certain other person," he says. "It was tough to take. I was shocked. It was like a huge black hole emotionally. I was just crushed."

The funeral was held on April 10 at Seattle's Unity Church of

Truth, while less than a mile away a public vigil was held at the Seattle Center. Kurt's suicide note was read aloud at both events. Much of the note concerned his loss of interest in music: "I haven't felt the excitement of listening to as well as creating music along with reading and writing for too many years now. I feel guilty beyond words about these things." Guilt also came up in another passage, where he wrote: "I still can't get over the frustration, the guilt and empathy I have for everyone." He later berated himself for becoming a "miserable self-destructive, death rocker." It was a note from a man who was deeply confused, engulfed in self-hatred, and could see no way out of his situation.

With Kurt's death, the race was on both to cover the story and to define Nirvana's legacy. Charles Peterson spent much of the week in the darkroom; his shot of Kurt seemingly levitating at the Motor Sports show in September 1990 was chosen for the cover of *The Rocket*'s memorial issue. "It is difficult, and Kurt's not the only dead person that I have photographs of in my collection," he says. "He's certainly the one that people want the most, you know? I don't get that many calls for Landrew [Andrew Wood] or Jesse Bernstein [a Seattle poet and writer who committed suicide in 1991], or Mia Zapata [lead singer of Seattle band The Gits, who was murdered in 1993] or whoever, but I have in the past. After a while, it's like sometimes I'm not even looking at them, really. I'm looking at them in more of an artistic or conceptual way: well, this captures the moment, or the composition on this one is great, or the autofocus is off on this one. It's not even thinking about: oh, this is a person here, who took his life, and was an acquaintance and a living breathing human being. When he died, I got all these requests, and it was like: go into the darkroom, make these prints, sort them all out in the packages, and go off to FedEx. I'd try to hit FedEx by 5:00pm. Now it's just: click, send. But then it was like a real process. And I felt: well, Kurt would have wanted to be remembered by my photos. He liked what I did. He wanted to be remembered. And probably more so in a live sense."

Kurt's death unexpectedly gave new life to the portrait Martyn Goodacre had taken of him on October 24 1990. His shot of Kurt staring into the camera lens had first appeared on the cover of *Select*'s July 1993 issue. Now he was told it was being considered for the cover of *NME*'s April 16 issue. "I didn't know until the day the magazine came out," he says. "I had been with an editor the night before it was published at a Primal Scream gig but he wouldn't tell me if it had made the cover – probably in case something else turned up. I wasn't even sure the *NME* were aware of the photo. I counted about 17 covers in the first two weeks [with the shot]. Mainly rock mags. Pretty much a dream come true for any photographer. I'm very proud of it. I set out to get a defining image in rock'n'roll history, and to my surprise I did. Then, of course, there is the story behind the image – the rock tragedy. The shot wouldn't be so famous if he was still alive.

"It's been a bit of a trip since then. Oasis and U2 have both used it as an image flashed up on their backdrops, as well as the Queen musical *We Will Rock You*. I have only just partially managed to get control of the way the image is used. Flogging it as merchandise was not the done thing for a rock photographer to engage in at the time, so I didn't and everybody else did. I should have made a million from the image but it was bootlegged a lot and I didn't set up any licensing for it until it was far too late. But I'm still proud of it. It's a nice buzz when you see someone wearing a shirt with the image on, even if it is a bootleg. I recently found it on a matchbox."

DGC was anxious to not be seen as cashing in on the tragedy, and quickly cancelled the release of 'Pennyroyal Tea' as a third single from *In Utero*. (Complicating the single's release was the fact that one of the B-sides was unfortunately titled 'I Hate Myself And Want To Die.') But they went ahead with the July 1994 release of *DGC Rarities Vol. 1*, which featured the 1990 recording of 'Pay To Play.' Since then, most releases have been live recordings: the album *MTV Unplugged In New York* and the *Live! Tonight! Sold Out!!* video (both 1994, and both also later released on DVD), the *From The Muddy Banks Of The Wishkah* album (1996), and the DVDs *Live At Reading* (2009) and *Live At The Paramount* (2011). A notable exception was the 2004 boxed set *With The Lights Out*, three CDs and a DVD of Nirvana rarities, including the first known recording of 'Teen Spirit,' and 2005's *Sliver: The Best Of The Box*, which added the Fecal Matter version of 'Spank Thru.' The 20th anniversary edition of *Nevermind* featured all the songs from the April 1990 session, as well the rehearsal where the band first worked on 'Teen Spirit.'

But Nirvana's breakthrough in 1991, and their legacy, was about more than just their music. "I think that the band definitely redefined what rock'n'roll was culturally," says Danny Goldberg. "Kurt certainly changed the concept of what masculinity was, in the context of the rock culture of the time. You know, this was the time when you had a lot of guys on MTV with big bulging biceps and macho kind of lyrics; the so-called 'hair bands' had a kind of a macho cast to them that Nirvana were really very different from. It was just a restatement of certain values of that generation: feeling socially conscious, sensitive to gays and women, and supportive of a certain kind of artist, the kind of people that he would have open to him, Captain America [Eugene Kelly's post-Vaselines band] or the Melvins. In general, I think there was a set of values associated with what they did. They redefined what was cool."

Certainly, Nirvana tried to expose their audiences to some of their favorite musicians, and open their minds to new ideas, whether it was each band-member wearing a Melvins, Flipper, or L7 T-shirt on Nirvana's first *Saturday Night Live* appearance or playing a 1993 benefit for the Tresnjevka Women's Group (a group that assisted Bosnian rape victims). "We used to refer to it as exploiting our celebrity," says Krist. "We were exploiting it. It was also kind of a good way to make excuses for where we were: we're doing something good with it!"

"You harken back to The Beatles, they weren't just writing songs – people were looking at how they looked, how they influenced fashion, design, political issues," Bruce Pavitt observed. "Nirvana had a tremendous impact and really bridged the gap between the developing alternative/indie/punk underground and the mainstream." It was a lesson people like Mark Andersen came to appreciate. "Nirvana changed things immensely, not always for the good," he says. "The thing that they could have changed, and if Kurt Cobain is somewhere in some form he's probably wincing from this, if punk was out to do anything it was to change the narrative of rock. And the narrative of rock had become kind of a boring and somewhat tragic one, maybe more pathetic than tragic, and that was: you start out, you're idealistic, you get money, you get drugs, you get boring and old and/or dead. And it's just the same old story, you know. It's the same old story. I mean, if you look at it from the outside, it's like: drug addicted rock star dies young. That was old in the 70s. That was 20 years ago. And Cobain became a cliché in that regard. And again, if he's out there somewhere, he's probably wincing as I say that, because clearly he didn't want to be that.

"But on the other hand, and it's interesting for me, years afterward I would talk to friends of mine who weren't part of that punk underground – which, on the one hand was a beautiful thing and very empowering for us; it was kind of an exclusive in-club. But when I talk to friends who were not part of that, they would talk about how much inspiration they took from Nirvana and some of the other bands that came out around then, and that it actually did put forward, in its way, ironically, a vision of independence and possibility, albeit using corporate channels. You could say that it even pushed forward a vision of revolution. It did it inconsistently, it did it imperfectly, but it did it nonetheless. And I know because I encountered for years people who were inspired to push forward in pursuit of their own vision – often radical vision – for their lives, and for the world, as a result of this, this struggle. Because basically, if we're talking about these punk rock wars, Nirvana fought them too. You can say they ended up consorting with the enemy at different points, but I don't think they ever totally lost sight of what they had actually started out to fight for. I wish Cobain hadn't died in such a clichéd way, but the art they created, the ideas they put out there, it still moves people, it still has the power to transform lives, it still has the power to bring people to an understanding and appreciation of the underground. Which is to say: to an appreciation and understanding of our own power, to revolutionize our lives and our world. So, in the final assessment, I'm proud of that."

Almost 20 years to the day after Nirvana debuted 'Smells Like Teen Spirit' at the OK Hotel, the exhibit *Nirvana: Taking Punk To The Masses* opened at Seattle's Experience Music Project museum on April 16 2011. The exhibit was two years in the making, drawing not only on EMP's substantial collection, but also on artifacts provided by Krist, family members, and friends of the band. "To me, that changed the whole focus of the exhibition," says Jacob McMurray, the exhibit's curator. "Everybody knows that sort of rock star mythologized story of Nirvana, and that certainly has a big presence in the exhibit. I mean, there are giant beautiful mythologized Charles Peterson murals and broken guitars and stuff like that, but on the other side of things, there's just lots of really candid shots of them goofing around, and the band having fun. There's about 200 objects on display, and without reading any text or anything, you can see the evolution of the band from before they even were a band – '83 and '85 are the earliest photos and materials we have – all the way up to the end."

As you enter the gallery, one of the first things you see is Kurt's Mosrite Gospel guitar, the very instrument he played at the OK Hotel show. You'd expect to see guitars in an exhibit about a rock band, but when Kurt dreamed of being a rock star, he certainly couldn't have imagined that the pink suitcase he used as an improvised drum on his *Organized Confusion* tape and later carried his guitar parts and cables in would ever end up as a museum piece. His aunt's four-track tape deck that he used to record the *Organized Confusion* and Fecal Matter's *Illiteracy Will Prevail* tapes is there too, along with Buzz Osborne's letter in which he raved about Kurt's songwriting: "Some of his songs are *real* killer! … I think he could have some kind of a future in music if he keeps at it." Jack Endino's copy of Nirvana's first demo, credited to 'Kurt Kovain and Dale Crover.' Chad Channing's North 'Formula' drum kit, with its large flared shells that drew Kurt's attention. The Univox Hi-Flyer that Kurt smashed at the gig held in Phil Buffington's dorm room on Halloween 1988. The simple hand-drawn poster advertising Dave's first show with Nirvana in October 1990. The sweater Kurt wore in the 'Teen Spirit' video and the MTV award for 'Best Alternative Music Video,' which misspells the song's title as "Smells Like *Team* Spirit." Krist's red, white, and blue Buck Owens American acoustic guitar that Pat Smear played during Nirvana's *MTV Unplugged* appearance in November 1993. A ticket for Nirvana's last show, at Flughafen Riem Terminal 1 in Munich on March 1 1994. The last song the band played that night was 'Heart-Shaped Box.'

Keith Cameron, who was covering the opening for the *Guardian*, was surprised to see the *Sounds* T-shirt he'd given to Kurt in 1990 in one of the exhibit's display cases. "My initial thought was that it looked amazingly clean!" he says. "As with so many things when it comes to Nirvana, I have mixed feelings. It's sublime and ridiculous. I'm a little bit proud that a shirt I gave to a guy whose band I loved so much should mean enough to him that he wore it out a few times so that the world would see it. I was amazed at the time that he ever wore it at all, and ascribed that at least partly to the fact that he simply didn't have many clothes. But I daresay it's obvious that he did so also as an acknowledgment of the underdog, as *Sounds* undoubtedly was. The team spirit on that magazine was quite profound, and seeing Kurt flying the flag in posthumous tribute at the 1991 Reading Festival was very special to those of us who'd worked for it. And now it's a museum piece, which is of course insane. I should ask for it back; it's probably worth a few quid now."

Along with the artifacts are items that give the show a more personal touch, such as the candid snapshots of the band loading or unloading the van on some anonymous street; the Moore Theatre's marquee with Nirvana's name on it, which Chad Channing's mother later framed and hung in the family home; a bleary-eyed Kurt in a restaurant somewhere in Europe on the band's first European tour in 1989; Kurt, Krist, and Dave crammed into a four-pictures-for-a-dollar photo booth at Re-bar, the Seattle club where the *Nevermind* record-release party was held; Kurt playing with his beloved daughter, Frances. It's the offstage side of Nirvana, a reminder that behind the iconic imagery were young men not much different from their fans, brought together by the simple desire to make music, to create something new and different, and have fun while doing it.

Screens display oral histories from EMP's archives, with Krist, Chad, Buzz Osborne, Jack Endino, Jonathan Poneman, Earnie Bailey, Charles Peterson, and many others sharing their stories. The background music you hear as you walk through the exhibit is a specially commissioned piece by Steve Fisk. One wall has 20 records from Krist's own collection that he cites as being especially influential on Nirvana, including *Led Zeppelin*, Black Sabbath's *Born Again*, The Stooges' *Fun House*, *Generic Flipper*, Black Flag's *My War*, Hüsker Dü's *Metal Circus*, Soundgarden's *Screaming Life*, The Smithereens' *Green Thoughts*, and Leadbelly's *Recorded In Concert, University Of Texas, Austin, June 15 1949*. In the corner of the last room in the exhibit, where a screen plays a constantly shuffling array of live Nirvana clips, is a selection from one of Kurt's more eccentric collecting obsessions: canned meat: Grant's Scotch Haggis, Gerber Chicken Sticks, Hormel Pigs Feet, Prairie Belt Smoked Sausage, and Armour's appetizingly named Potted Meat Food Product. It's a playful touch that's particularly welcome in that it lightens the gravitas that inevitably accompanies the Nirvana story, given how that story ends.

There was a bittersweet quality in the air on the night of the exhibit's preview. It was like a surreal high-school reunion, with three of Nirvana's six drummers (Aaron Burckhard, Dave Foster, Dan Peters), Bruce Pavitt, Screaming Trees (and Jury side project) drummer Mark Pickerel, Mark Arm, Kim Thayil, Tracy Marander, Aberdeen friend Ryan Aigner, Krist's former wife Shelli Hyrkas, Kurt's mother Wendy, his sister Kim, and his aunt Mari all in attendance along with other friends and family, each of them remembering a time when the idea of a Nirvana exhibition attracting international attention would've seemed like one of Sub Pop's farfetched 'world domination' schemes.

When EMP's CEO and director Christina Orr-Cahall made her opening remarks on a stage featuring the exhibit's logo as well as logos of corporate sponsors like Qwest, Boeing, and Wells Fargo, Aaron Burckhard unexpectedly got on stage and shouted: "Corporate America still sucks!" Orr-Cahall was momentarily nonplussed, but Krist neatly defused the moment with a jocular "shut up, Aaron!" and Burckhard good-naturedly left. Then Krist spoke, talking with affection about his bandmates. "Dave Grohl. I love Dave, and he released a new record this week [*Wasting Light*] and it rocks. Dave is out there and he works hard, he's never lost focus, and he's carrying the flame, the torch, he's out there packing the arenas, just speaking to people.

"Kurt Cobain. Here's a man who, he would never have, like, cleaned his kitchen, or taken out the garbage, or do those kind of chores, you know? But Kurt Cobain was not a lazy person ... he wrote so much music. And he was compelled to be an artist – he was a true artist. He had a natural talent, and that's what compelled him to share so many things with so many people. I walk down the street, even tonight, people walk up to me and say: Nirvana changed my life. And I think that's a testament to Kurt Cobain, and the vision that he was channeling, and what he put out there. And he spoke to so many people, and I owe him so much, that I can't even start."

The exhibit especially touches a nerve for those who knew the band. "To me, it's more about the real Kurt," says Alice Wheeler. "I mean, the real experience of how it was to be friends with them, and go to their shows, watch them get famous, and all that stuff. That's what that EMP show feels like to me with these guys. But," she adds sadly, "the other thing that I found, part of what bothered me about the opening, and it took me a couple of weeks to realize what was really bothering me was: the best part about Nirvana wasn't there. Kurt wasn't there."

Those who worked with or knew Nirvana have become used to being sought out by the media whenever an anniversary approaches, prevailed upon to call up a new memory of a period that's slowly receding into the past. "I guess I call it Nirvana In Its Afterlife," says Earnie Bailey. "Because whenever there's a new release, and there's a new attention to it all, in some ways it brings back a lot of things, and in other ways it makes it really apparent how long ago it was. Because there's kind of this, I don't know if you want to call it a homogenization, but there's – you know, it's just a long ways away from the HUB Ballroom.

"Why do they live on?" he muses. "Well, I hate to say it, but it's like Hendrix. He died young, and he died on top of his game and he left a perfect legacy. Nirvana really only released a small number of albums. They were all good. They never got around to putting out the bad one. And they never got around to having to play the Emerald Queen Casino and things like that. Or maybe they're like an artist who painted three paintings, and all you've got is three, and so you can never really get too much of them. They came and went in a time before computers and YouTube and all this stuff; they existed in this time when there was a lot of mystery, and a lot of patience required for being involved in music. You had to wait forever for albums to come out. You had to wait forever for a video – if they even chose to release them. So I think that part of it continues on because you're still dealing with a kind of limited exposure.

"And I think that Kurt Cobain, as a person, or as an entity, has just enough mystery that he is open for interpretation and also remains interesting. I think he also understands the importance of mysteries. That's what makes anything really interesting. I mean, once you have the answers, then you move on to something else. So I think he was just one of those guys that ultimately ask more questions than he'll give you answers."

In 2010, Dave Grohl asked Butch Vig to produce Foo Fighters' seventh album, *Wasting Light* (released in 2011). He also asked Krist Novoselic to participate; Krist ended up contributing bass and accordion to 'I Should Have Known.' "Krist is really no stranger to the Foo Fighters," Dave said. "He's recorded with us in the studio before, he's played with us live. But you put Krist and Butch and me in the studio for the first time in 20 fucking years it becomes more than just a guest appearance and a day in the studio. There's a lot more weight to it, which I totally understand. But to me, having Krist come down and play on the record was more of a personal opportunity. I just thought: what a trip, to sit with Krist and Butch and Pat [Smear] in the studio together. Because that was never supposed to happen again."

What transpired during the sessions was also not expected to happen again. On completing the album in December 2010, Foo Fighters were planning to play a surprise club gig. For the encore, Dave and Pat were going to play 'Marigold' with Krist, which Nirvana had never played live (although Dave had performed it with Foo Fighters). Dave, Krist, and Pat held a rehearsal the day before the show, and during a break Krist suddenly asked: "You want to play any moldy oldies?" "And I went: err, OK," Dave recalled. "Because we'd never done that. Ever." Krist surprised them further by announcing: "Fuck it. Let's play 'Teen Spirit.'" And so, 19 years after Kurt had first brought the song with its "ridiculous" riff into rehearsal, and 16 years after Nirvana had last performed it in concert, Nirvana's surviving members played the number that had transformed all of their lives, Kurt's most of all.

"Kurt had the best luck and the worse luck – both at the same time," Kurt Danielson once observed. "He was the most gifted and cursed." It was an echo of a sentiment Kurt had expressed himself in 'Teen Spirit,' about being "worse at what I do best."

Krist played bass, Dave played drums, and Pat played guitar. No one sang, nor was a recording made. "It felt pretty weird," Dave admitted. "I never thought that would happen. But it happened. It was just right. The perfect way for it to happen." And perhaps it was something that had to happen. Although Dave has gone on to great success in Foo Fighters and myriad other musical projects, and Krist is increasingly involved with politics, as well as his own bands (including a two-year stint with one of the bands that inspired him, Flipper), they both know they will never eclipse the work they did with Nirvana, a legacy that hovers like an unseen presence in their lives. "It's always there," Dave said. "When I see Butch or Krist, it's always right above my head – Nirvana ... It's still huge with all of us ... it's there and it's undeniable."

Everyone who loved Nirvana's music felt a keen sense of loss at the band's sudden, violent end. Kurt's career was cut short in mid-flight. In his last interview with *Rolling Stone* he'd spoken of pursuing new musical directions; now those avenues would be left unexplored. He also spoke of quitting music and concentrating on his visual art; now those ideas would not come to fruition. But for those who were closest to him, the loss was felt in more personal, poignant ways, when small actions suddenly take on a larger significance. "For years after Kurt died, I had this habit," Krist said. "If I'd walk by a pawn shop, I'd look in the window and I'd always look for a left-handed guitar. One day it was like: oh, I don't need to do that anymore, y'know?"

End Notes

All interviews, unless otherwise specified in the text or below, are by the author.

Prologue: Here We Are Now

17   "I just thought that" *Nevermind: It's An Interview* promo CD, 1992

17   "The most culturally important" 'The 20 Greatest Grunge Albums Of All Time,' *Spin*, April 2004

17   "The better part of" Michael Azerrad, *Come As You Are*

17   "That is so ridiculous" David Fricke, 'Kurt Cobain: The Rolling Stone Interview,' *Rolling Stone*, January 27 1994

17   "The simple guitar lines" Paul Brannigan, *This Is A Call*

18   "There's this thing you wrote" 'Our Hit Parade: Kathleen Hanna – Smells Like Teen Spirit,' youtube.com

18   "Teen revolution" Michael Azerrad, *Come As You Are*

18   "I thought she was saying" Kurt St. Thomas, 'Kurt Cobain,' *Fader*, April 2004

19   "Unannounced"/"We only heard" Everett True, *Nirvana: The True Story*

20   "Record companies are flocking" David DiMartino, 'A Seattle Slew,' *Rolling Stone*, September 20 1990

20   "When it started" Everett True, *Nirvana: The True Story*

21   "Break the ice"/"A lot of times" David Fricke, 'Kurt Cobain: The Rolling Stone Interview,' *Rolling Stone*, January 27 1994

22   "Hmm, that was kind of cool" *Classic Albums: Nirvana Nevermind*, Eagle Vision DVD

23   "About a dozen" Charles R. Cross, *Heavier Than Heaven*

24   "My generation's apathy" *Nevermind* press release

24   "It's a typical teenage" Ned Hammad, 'About A Band,' *Pulse*, October 1991

24   "Seeing Kurt write" Michael Azerrad, *Come As You Are*

24   "I've always felt" Novoselic, *Of Grunge And Government*

25   "I would tell him" John Mulvey, 'Nevermind The Sell-Out,' *Uncut Legends #2*, 2004

26   "I thought 'Teen Spirit'" Paul Brannigan, *This Is A Call*

Chapter 1: In The Pines

38   "When I was really young" Jerry McCulley, 'Spontaneous Combustion,' *BAM*, January 10 1992

38   "I was now in a different" John Hughes, 'Krist Novoselic: Of Grunge And Grange,' Washington State Legacy Project, 2009

38   "School was very demanding" John Hughes, 'Krist Novoselic: Of Grunge And Grange,' Washington State Legacy Project, 2009

39   "I played Krist" Mark Yarm, *Everybody Loves Our Town*

39   "Ah that punk rock stuff" Gina Arnold, *Route 666*

39   "Doing Iron Maiden" Experience Music Project oral history

39   "That's really all there was" Greg Prato, *Grunge Is Dead*

39   "He was more into" Experience Music Project oral history

40   "His parents were finished"/"They were open minded" Experience Music Project oral history

40   "Porno, biker[s], and gore"/"So we'd spend all this time" Kory Grow, 'Kurt Cobain Remembered: Outtakes From Revolver's Buzz Osborne Interview,' Revolvermag.com, April 5 2011

40   "Buzz was kind of like"/ "The third time I heard it" John Hughes, 'Krist Novoselic: Of Grunge And Grange,' Washington State Legacy Project, 2009

41   "I didn't see a lot" Experience Music Project oral history

42   "I just remember him saying" *Revolver*, January/February 2011

43   "I remember him showing" Experience Music Project oral history

44   "He was much more confident" Experience Music Project oral history

44   "I think I may have grown" *Incesticide* press release

44   "It sounded exactly like" Gina Arnold, *Route 666*

44   "I was looking through the lyrics" Experience Music Project oral history

45   "I have no real reason" Michael Azerrad, *Come As You Are*

46   "People talk about that demo" Greg Prato, *Grunge Is Dead*

46   "Totally wasted" Michael Azerrad, *Come As You Are*

46   "Just jumping around" nirvanaguide.com

46   "I had a splendid" Joe Preston, "Nirvana," *Matt Lukin's Legs*, 1989

47   "I like Big Black"/"And he said it" Experience Music Project oral history

47   "That says to me" Experience Music Project oral history

48   "All those Republicans" Michael Azerrad, *Come As You Are*

Chapter 2: First Steps

Chapter 3: Bright Lights, Big City

80   "It makes things a little heavier" Mark Yarm, *Everybody Loves Our Town*

80   "We didn't have a lot" Experience Music Project oral history

81   "Was like having" Mark Yarm, *Everybody Loves Our Town*

84   "Grunge was an adjective" Mark Yarm, *Everybody Loves Our Town*

84   "Imagine being harassed" Charles Peterson, *Screaming Life*

88   "The Seattle music scene"/"Under the circumstances" Greg Prato, *Grunge Is Dead*

88   "Seattle's gonna take over"/ "It was a bit tongue-in-cheek" Mark Yarm, *Everybody Loves Our Town*

89   "We did a few mildly" Mike Rubin, 'Swingin' On The Flippity Flop With Sub Pop,' *Spin*, April 1995

90   "It was the first time" Mark Yarm, *Everybody Loves Our Town*

Chapter 4: Underground Attitude

93   "I just can't believe" Gina Arnold, *Route 666*

93   "We got really serious" Gina Arnold, *Route 666*

95   "Sickening and dumb" Kurt Cobain, *Journals*

95   "He's a powerhouse" John Hughes, 'Krist Novoselic: Of Grunge And Grange,' Washington State Legacy Project, 2009

100   "It had this bridge" John Robb, "Nirvana," *Q*, June 1996

100   "By-the-numbers alternative" Charles R. Cross, *Heavier Than Heaven*

101   "Ohhhh yeah so much romance" Michael Alan Goldberg, 'Buzz Saw,' pitch.com, September 2 2004

101   "Just hit 'em hard" Michael Azerrad, *Come As You Are*

102   "We needed something rough" Joe Preston, 'Nirvana,' *Matt Lukin's Legs*, 1989

102   "There's no reason at all" Tina Caruso, 'Nirvana,' *Submerge*, 1991

102   "None of their original material" Everett True, *Nirvana: The True Story*

103   "All in all folks came away"/ "The band rock heavily" Charles R. Cross, 'Eyewitness: The First Gig In Seattle,' *Q*, April 2004

103   "We didn't play too bad" Charles R. Cross, 'Eyewitness: The First Gig In Seattle,' *Q*, April 2004

105   "Gosh, drummers from Aberdeen" Michael Azerrad, *Come As You Are*

107   "Messed up dark New Age stuff" Everett True, *Nirvana: The True Story*

108   "Sparkle purple 70s flared" *Kurt Cobain: The Early Life Of A Legend*, MVD Visual DVD

Chapter 5: Happening Olympia Combo

Chapter 6: The Distant Roar

145   "We purposely made"/"The wimpiest recording" Michael Azerrad, *Come As You Are*

Chapter 7: The Real Thing

149   "We met [Jason] maybe a couple months" Laura Begley, Anne Filson, 'Long Haired
       Nirvana Guy Shaves Head!,' *Dirt*, Fall 1990

150   "It's our big chance" Gillian G. Gaar 'Screaming North,' *Calendar*, February 1 1989

150   "played some smoken shows" Michael Azerrad, *Come As You Are*

152   "Nirvana are beauty incarnate" Everett True, *Melody Maker*, February 18 1989

154   "In awe"/"A real live British" Everett True, *Nirvana: The True Story*

155   "Suddenly Seattle is the centre"/"Britain is currently held," Everett True, 'Mudhoney:
       Sub Pop, Sub Normal, Subversion,' *Melody Maker*, March 11 1989

155   "Basically, this is the real thing" Everett True, 'Sub Pop: Rock City,' *Melody Maker*,
       March 18 1989

156   "These guys were ugly"/"It was just obvious" Michael Azerrad, *Come As You Are*

157   "I think he liked" Greg Prato, *Grunge Is Dead*

157   "Big burly unshaven logger" Michael Azerrad, *Come As You Are*

158   "The Go Team was about process" Everett True, *Nirvana: The True Story*

162   "Yet another re-write" *Incesticide* press release

Chapter 8: Lost In America

167   "In 1989, it was inconceivable" Krist Novoselic, *Of Grunge And Government*

167   "Which sounds absolutely insane" Mark Yarm, *Everybody Loves Our Town*

168   "It was very scary" Mark Yarm, *Everybody Loves Our Town*

169   "I remember thinking" Michael Azerrad, *Come As You Are*

169   "It was a definite turning point" Keith Cameron, 'Spirit Of 88,' *Mojo*, August 2008

169   "Like hotcakes" Ralph Heibutzki, 'The Last Word On Kurt Cobain,' *Discoveries*, June
       1994

169   "In his own little world" Keith Cameron, 'Spirit Of 88,' *Mojo*, August 2008

171   "Totally intense" Tony Schoengart, 'Lamefest '89,' *Backlash*, July 1989

171   "The war between the slam dancers" Paul de Barros, 'War Upstages Music At
       Lamefest '89 Concert,' *The Seattle Times*, June 12 1989

171   "Occasionally suffers" Robert Allen, 'Welcome To Nirvana's Nightmare,' *Backlash*,
       June 1989

171   "Slightly top-heavy" Edwin Pouncey, *NME*, July 8 1989

171   "Crafted around a firm base" Everett True, 'Bleached Wails,' *Melody Maker*, October 21 1989

171   "Giving a nod" Gillian G. Gaar, *The Rocket*, July 1989

172   "Don't wear that" Johnny Black, 'Nirvana's First European Tour,' *Q*, May 1999

172   "They are one of the only things" Al Kawalewski, Krk Dominguez, 'Nirvana,' *Flipside*, Fall 1989

173   "We were a hardy bunch" Chris Morris, 'Nirvana: The Year's Hottest New Band Can't Stand Still,' *Musician*, January 1992

175   "Burning, nauseous" Michael Azerrad, *Come As You Are*

175   "And once he got sick" Charles R. Cross, *Heavier Than Heaven*

175   "These guys were like" David Fricke, 'Through Feedback: The Rolling Stone Interview With Sonic Youth's Thurston Moore,' *Rolling Stone*, September 24 1994

176   "Catacylsmic" John Robb, 'White Heat,' *Sounds*, October 21 1989

177   "How am I going to explain" Everett True, *Nirvana: The True Story*

177   "It's an awesome demolition" John Robb, 'White Heat,' *Sounds*, October 21 1989

179   "The burned-out look" John Robb, 'Help Me I'm Hungry,' *Mojo Classic: Nirvana And The Story Of Grunge*, 2005

180   "We were just maladjusted" Michael Azerrad, *Come As You Are*

181   "[Jason] just wasn't into" Nils Bernstein, 'Berlin Is Just A State Of Mind,' *The Rocket*, December 1989

181   "We kicked him out" Laura Begley, Anne Filson, 'Long Haired Nirvana Guy Shaves Head!,' *Dirt*, Fall 1990

Chapter 9: Marking Time

184   "We're moving towards simplicity" Everett True, 'Bleached Wails,' *Melody Maker*, October 21 1989

184   "Totally obsessed" Michael Azerrad, *Come As You Are*

187   "One of Kurt's greatest" Michael Azerrad, *Come As You Are*

188   "We're writing a lot more pop songs" Nils Bernstein, "Berlin Is Just A State Of Mind," *The Rocket*, December 1989

196   "Really didn't do anything" Everett True, *Nirvana: The True Story*

196   "You guys didn't play" Everett True, *Nirvana: The True Story*

197   "Simple songcraft" Experience Music Project oral history

197   "My favorite group ever" Gina Arnold, *Route 666*

197   "Crap food" John Hughes, 'Krist Novoselic: Of Grunge And Grange,' Washington
        State Legacy Project, 2009

Chapter 10: Innocents Abroad

200   "The good God grunge," John Robb, 'White Noise,' *Sounds*, October 21 1989

200   "The first big grunge" ocf.berkeley.edu/~ptn/mudhoney/

201   "By the time they tour Europe" Edwin Pouncey, 'Kills All Known Germs,' *NME*,
        September 2 1989

202   "I couldn't believe that we'd" Ian Winwood, 'Overdoses,' *Kerrang*, March 30 2002

202   "Seattle's biggest bulk export"/ 'Tad & Nirvana' *Sounds*, October 21 1989

202   "Brilliant" and all quotes in this paragraph, Johnny Black, 'Nirvana's First European
        Tour,' *Q*, May 1999

205   "All too often" livenirvana.com

206   "I need to do something"/"More energetic" Johnny Black, 'Nirvana's First European
        Tour,' *Q*, May 1999

206   "Nirvana were superb" Neil Perry, 'A Tad Unruly,' *Melody Maker*, November 4 1989

206   "All the loyalties started shifting" Johnny Black, 'Nirvana's First European Tour,' *Q*,
        May 1999

207   "It never seemed like a big deal" Michael Azerrad, *Come As You Are*

208   "We had loads of bands" livenirvana.com

209   "There's a certain frequency" Everett True, *Nirvana: The True Story*

210   "It was amazing" John Hughes, 'Krist Novoselic: Of Grunge And Grange,' Washington
        State Legacy Project, 2009

216   "I was ready to die" Jon Savage, 'Howl,' *Guitar World*, October 1996

217   "I can see them thinking" Michael Azerrad, *Come As You Are*

218   "Now it's broken" Michael Azerrad, *Come As You Are*

218   "I see all these people"/ "That was the first time" Carrie Borzillo, *Nirvana: The Day
        By Day Eyewitness Chronicle*

219   "It stunk" Michael Azerrad, *Come As You Are*

220   "It was the most amazing band" Michael Azerrad, *Come As You Are*

221   "The biggest band"/ "It wasn't a boast" Paul Brannigan, *This Is A Call*

Chapter 11: A Full Phenomenon

Chapter 12: On The Road Again

255   "An orgy of frustrated violence"/ "I just felt we were playing" Sam King, 'Down On The Bleach,' *Sounds*, June 9 1990

255   "Hopped around like a muppet" Iggy Pop, 'A Fan's Notes,' *Spin*, April 1995

255   "Nirvana are astonishing" Sam King, 'Down On The Bleach,' *Sounds*, June 9 1990

256   "A mixture of white trash" Bob Gulla, cdnow.com, May 18-28 1999

257   "It just wasn't good" Michael Azerrad, *Come As You Are*

Chapter 13: The Turning Point

260   "Naïve but ambitious" Charles R. Cross, *Heavier Than Heaven*

262   "I decided I wanted to write" Michael Azerrad, *Come As You Are*

264   "An experiment in dynamics" *Incesticide* press release

264   "I just don't understand" Michael Azerrad, *Come As You Are*

264   "It really fucked with my head" Michael Azerrad, *Come As You Are*

265   "My intention was to essentially" Mark Yarm, *Everybody Loves Our Town*

265   "We felt we deserved" Michael Azerrad, *Come As You Are*

265   "We weren't being promoted" Dawn Anderson, 'Nirvana: Signin' On The Dotted Line And Other Tales Of Terror,' *Backlash*, March 1991

265   "I felt that [Kurt]" Mark Yarm, *Everybody Loves Our Town*

265   "They hit rock bottom" Michael Azerrad, *Come As You Are*

268   "A big echoey sounding garage" Experience Music Project oral history

270   "It seemed to blur" Experience Music Project oral history

271   "Should I take it" Javier Espinoza, 'Kurt Cobain Was A Shy Guy,' ohmynews.com

271   "Prophetic"/ "Floored in anguish" Carl Stanley, 'Ian Tilton: The Man Who Shot The Stone Roses,' sabotagetimes.com

271   "He had just trashed his gear" Ian Tilton, iantilton.net

273   "It's really not hard" and all quotes in this paragraph, Keith Cameron, 'Take The Money And Run,' *Sounds*, October 27 1990

273   "It's been pretty obvious" Keith Cameron, 'Take The Money And Run,' *Sounds*, October 27 1990

274   "Nah, don't worry" Mark Yarm, *Everybody Loves Our Town*

274   "Mudhoney's Dan Peters" Keith Cameron, 'Take The Money And Run,' *Sounds*, October 27 1990

Chapter 14: True Hardcore Drummer

276 "All I really had" Chris Morris, 'Nirvana: The Year's Hottest New Band Can't Stand Still,' *Musician*, January 1992

276 "He kept saying" Paul Brannigan, *This Is A Call*

277 "It changed my fucking life" Jeff Apter, *The Dave Grohl Story*

278 "I remember that moment" Paul Brannigan, *This Is A Call*

278 "It was the most fucking awesome" Jeff Apter, *The Dave Grohl Story*

278 "I had learned my basic three chords" Mark Andersen, *Dance Of Days*

278 "It was the first time I'd heard" Wes Orshoski, 'Honor Role,' *Harp*, September/October 2005

279 "That's when I said" Paul Brannigan, *This Is A Call*

282 "Man, I want to try that," Jeff Apter, *The Dave Grohl Story*

282 "This coincided nicely" "Rebellious Jukebox," *Melody Maker*, 1997

282 "They were the perfect combination" '100 Greatest Artists Of All Time,' *Rolling Stone*, April 15 2004

283 "It was like watching" Paul Brannigan, *This Is A Call*

284 "I'd never been past Chicago," Austin Scaggs, 'On An Honor Roll,' *Rolling Stone*, July 28 2005

285 "I thought: here's another hardcore" Lois Wilson, 'Last Night A Record Changed My Life,' *Mojo*, February 2004

287 "I was starting to question" Paul Brannigan, *This Is A Call*

287 "Totally exuberant" Jeff Apter, *The Dave Grohl Story*

287 "Dave, you should join Nirvana" Experience Music Project oral history

288 "I thought Dave was a great drummer" Experience Music Project oral history

288 "Rocker dudes" Michael Azerrad, *Come As You Are*

288 "Almost like a metal band" Apter, *The Dave Grohl Story*

288 "It wasn't that we were unhappy," Push, 'Heaven Can Wait,' *Melody Maker*, December 15 1990

289 "You can't pass up an opportunity" Michael Azerrad, *Come As You Are*

289 "I don't know if I have the gig" and all quotes in this paragraph, Paul Brannigan, *This Is A Call*

289 "They must have sold" Michael Azerrad, *Come As You Are*

290 "Kurt and I just messed around" Krist Novoselic, 'How I Met Dave Grohl, The Biggest

Guy In Rock And Roll,' seattleweekly.com, November 17 2009

291   "I had to do" Paul Brannigan, *This Is A Call*

292   "Rather good" livenirvana.com

292   "His name is Dave" Michael Azerrad, *Come As You Are*

292   "Better than the Melvins" Dawn Anderson, 'It May Be The Devil,' *Backlash*, August/September 1988

Chapter 15: The Crest Of The Wave

293   "In our [record] contract" Dawn Anderson, 'Nirvana: Signin' On The Dotted Line And Other Tales Of Terror," *Backlash*, March 1991

293   "I was amazed" Paul Brannigan, *This Is A Call*

293   "Our second favorite Vaselines song" *Incesticide* press release

295   "Perched on a cliff" and all quotes in this paragraph, liner notes to *A Bureaucratic Desire For Extra-Capsular Extraction* CD, 2010

296   "A love song" liner notes to *A Bureaucratic Desire For Extra-Capsular Extraction* CD, 2010

296   "When I was in Scream" Dave Everly, 'I Was A Teenage Punk Rocker,' *Kerrang*, 1997

298   "Shockingly good" and all quotes in this paragraph, Steve Lamacq, 'Nirvanarama,' *Melody Maker*, January 26 1991

300   "One hell of a pop song" and all quotes in this paragraph, Push, 'Heaven Can Wait,' *Melody Maker*, December 15 1990

300   "In less than a year" Keith Cameron, 'Breathe,' *Mojo*, January 2003

301   "Wild" and all quotes in this paragraph, Tina Caruso, 'Nirvana,' *Submerge*, 1991

301   "We were incredibly obscure" Everett True, *Nirvana: The True Story*

301   "Kurt was quite introverted" Fiona Shepherd, 'The Vaselines Interview: Success In Seattle,' *The Scotsman*, December 6 2008

302   "When I finally got to see them" 'Rebellious Jukebox,' *Melody Maker*, August 29 1992

302   "Finally we found" Joe, 'Nirvana,' *Sleep*, 1991

302   "I'm so glad"/ "I was like: wow" Austin Scaggs, 'On An Honor Roll,' *Rolling Stone*, July 28 2005

303   "All he wanted to do" Kyle Anderson, 'Nirvana Celebrate 20 Years Of *Nevermind*,' *Entertainment Weekly*, September 21 2011

303   "The sun, if there's any at all" Kyle Anderson, 'Nirvana Celebrate 20 Years Of *Nevermind*,' *Entertainment Weekly*, September 21 2011

303   "The soundtrack to my first six months" Austin Scaggs, 'On An Honor Roll,' *Rolling Stone*, July 28 2005

305   "It starts with Kurt" Ned MacDonald, 'Nirvana: *Nevermind*,' *InPress Magazine*, January 15 1992

306   "We just started experimenting" Alan di Perna, 'Absolutely Foobulous,' *Guitar World*, August 1997

306   "Like he was playing drums" David Fricke, "Dave Grohl," *Rolling Stone*, September 13 2001

306   "[Kurt] really downplayed" Clark Collins, 'Dave Grohl Q&A,' *Entertainment Weekly*, April 15 2011

308   "The song's not about me" The Stud Brothers, 'Dark Side Of The Womb,' *NME*, August 21 1993

308   "Bad evil spirits" Michael Azerrad, *Come As You Are*

308   "The song is about a person" Jennie Punter, 'In Womb,' *Impact*, October 1993

309   "Hey Krist" and all quotes in this paragraph, Michael Azerrad, *Come As You Are*

309   "The minimal pop songs"/ "Kurt had a lot of cool ideas" Everett True, *Nirvana: The True Story*

309   "A wreck" Michael Azerrad, *Come As You Are*

309   "The punk rock scene" Paul Rees, 'Let's Go To Work,' *Q*, May 2011

310   "Really close" Michael Azerrad, *Come As You Are*

311   "That's the hit" Charles R. Cross, *Heavier Than Heaven*

312   "Barely minimum wage" Michael Azerrad, *Come As You Are*

313   "In awe" and all quotes in this paragraph, Wes Orshoski, 'Honor Roll,' *Harp*, September/October 2005

313   "I just wanted to see" David Daley, 'Feels Like The First Time,' *Alternative Press*, 1996

316   "This is going to be" Paul Brannigan, *This Is A Call*

317   "I find it embarrassing" Kurt Cobain, *Journals*

Chapter 16: Nirvana In Its Afterlife

318   "It's strange to see our faces" Jeff Gilbert, 'Smells Like Teen Idol,' *Guitar World*, February 1992

318   "In the marketing meetings" Charles R. Cross, *Heavier Than Heaven*

325   "I didn't spent a quarter of a million"/ "I'm like: fuck you, John" Everett True, *Nirvana: The True Story*

328   "Swingin' on the flippity-flop" Rick Marin, 'Lexicon Of Grunge: Breaking The Code,' *New York Times*, November 15 1992

331   "We're just now coming" Jennifer Boddy, 'Oh Gawd Part II,' *The Rocket*, October 1991

331   "The fact that he wanted" Patrick MacDonald, 'Nirvana Manager's Book Tells Of Life In The Rock 'N' Roll Trenches,' *Seattle Times*, October 7 2008

331   "I can't stand it" Jerry McCulley, 'Spontaneous Combustion,' *BAM*, January 10 1992

331   "I'm constantly feeling guilty" Michael Deeds, 'Nirvana,' *New Route*, December 1991

332   "You're there for the purpose" Everett True, *Nirvana: The True Story*

332   "There was that punk-rock guilt" David Fricke, 'Dave Grohl,' *Rolling Stone*, September 13 2001

332   "It's never been a desire" Keith Cameron, 'Nirvana Be In Our Gang,' *NME*, September 21 1991

332   "He was proud of his music" Everett True, 'Ten Myths About Grunge, Nirvana, And Kurt Cobain,' guardian.co.uk, August 24 2011

333   "I *didn't* OD" Michael Azerrad, *Come As You Are*

334   "I don't have quite as much fire" Jennie Punter, 'In Womb,' *Impact*, October 1993

334   "Krist, Dave, and I" David Fricke, 'Kurt Cobain: The Rolling Stone Interview' *Rolling Stone*, January 27 1994

336   "That tour was just a fiasco" Experience Music Project oral history

340   "Hey, guess what?" Everett True, *Nirvana: The True Story*

344   "You harken back to the Beatles" Experience Music Project oral history

351   "Krist is really no stranger" Clark Collis, 'Dave Grohl Q&A,' *Entertainment Weekly*, April 15 2011

351   "You want to play"/"And I went"/"Fuck it" Cameron Adams, 'Grohl Goes Back To The Foo-ture,' thetelegraph.com.au, April 13 2011

351   "Kurt had the best luck" Greg Prato, *Grunge Is Dead*

352   "It felt pretty weird" Cameron Adams, 'Grohl Goes Back To The Foo-ture,' thetelegraph.com.au, April 13 2011

352   "It's always there" Paul Rees, 'Let's Go To Work,' *Q*, 2011

352   "For years after Kurt died" Jacob McMurray, *Taking Punk To The Masses*

Bibliography

Mark Andersen and Mark Jenkins *Dance of Days: Two Decades Of Punk In The Nation's Capital* (Akashic 2009)

Jeff Apter *The Dave Grohl Story* (Omnibus 2006)

Gina Arnold *Route 666: On The Road To Nirvana* (St. Martin's 1993)

Michael Azerrad *Come As You Are: The Story Of Nirvana* (Main Street 1994)

Michael Azerrad *Our Band Could Be Your Life: Scenes From The American Indie Underground* (Little Brown 2001)

Jim Berkenstadt and Charles R. Cross *Nevermind: Nirvana* (Schirmer Trade 1998)

Carrie Borzillo *Nirvana: The Day By Day Eyewitness Chronicle* (Carlton 2000)

Paul Brannigan *This Is A Call: The Life And Times Of Dave Grohl* (Da Capo 2011)

David Browne *Goodbye 20th Century: A Biography Of Sonic Youth* (Da Capo 2008)

Jeff Burlingame *Kurt Cobain: Oh Well, Whatever, Nevermind* (Enslow 2006)

James Bush (ed.) *Encyclopedia Of Northwest Music* (Sasquatch 1999)

Art Chantry *Instant Litter: Concert Posters From Seattle Punk Culture* (The Real Comet Press 1985)

Kurt Cobain *Journals* (Riverhead 2002)

Chuck Crisafulli *Nirvana: The Stories Behind Every Song* (Thunder's Mouth 2006)

Charles R. Cross *Heavier Than Heaven: A Biography Of Kurt Cobain* (Hyperion 2001)

Charles R. Cross *Cobain Unseen* (Little Brown 2008)

Gillian G. Gaar *In Utero* (Continuum 2006)

Gillian G. Gaar *The Rough Guide To Nirvana* (Rough Guides 2009)

Holly George-Warren (ed.) *Cobain By The Editors Of Rolling Stone* (Little Brown 1994)

Danny Goldberg *Bumping Into Geniuses: My Life Inside The Rock And Roll Business* (Gotham 2008)

James Hector *Nirvana: The Complete Guide To Their Music* (Omnibus 2004)

Clark Humphrey *Loser: The Real Seattle Music Story* (MISCMedia 1999)

Jeff Kitts, Brad Tolinski, Harold Steinblatt (eds.) *Nirvana And The Grunge Revolution* (Hal Leonard 1998)

Jeff Kitts (ed.) *The Complete History Of Guitar World: 30 Years Of Music, Magic & Six-String Mayhem* (Backbeat 2010)

Jacob McMurray *Taking Punk To The Masses: From Nowhere To Nevermind* (Fantagraphics 2011)

Kim Neely *Five Against One: The Pearl Jam Story* (Penguin 1998)

Chris Nickson *Soundgarden: New Metal Crown* (St. Martin's Griffin 1995)

Krist Novoselic *Of Grunge And Government: Let's Fix This Broken Democracy!* (RDV/Akashic 2004)

Charles Peterson *Screaming Life: A Chronicle Of The Seattle Music Scene* (HarperCollins West 1995)

Charles Peterson *Touch Me I'm Sick* (powerHouse 2003)

Greg Prato *Grunge Is Dead: The Oral History Of Seattle Rock Music* (ECW 2009)

John Rocco, John (ed.) *The Nirvana Companion: Two Decades Of Commentary* (Schirmer 1998)

Stephen Tow *The Strangest Tribe: How A Group Of Seattle Rock Bands Invented Grunge* (Sasquatch 2011)

Everett True *Nirvana: The True Story* (Omnibus 2006)

Mark Yarm *Everybody Loves Our Town: An Oral History Of Grunge* (Crown Archetype 2011)

WEBSITES

livenirvana.com
nirvanaguide.com
sliver.it

Selected Discography

Releases featuring songs recorded between 1986 and 1990

1988
SINGLES
'Love Buzz'/'Big Cheese' (Sub Pop)
COMPILATIONS
Sub Pop 200 ('Spank Thru') (Sub Pop)

1989
EPs
Teriyaki Asthma Vol. 1 ('Mexican Seafood') (C/Z)
Blew (Tupelo)
ALBUMS
Bleach (Sub Pop)

1990
SINGLES
'Sliver'/ 'Dive' (12-inch single and CD have additional live tracks) (Sub Pop)
COMPILATIONS
Hard To Believe ('Do You Love Me') (C/Z)
Heaven And Hell ('Here She Comes Now') (Imaginary)

1991
SINGLES
'Molly's Lips'/'Candy' (by The Fluid) (Sub Pop)
COMPILATIONS
Kill Rock Stars ('Beeswax') (Kill Rock Stars)
ALBUMS
Nevermind ('Polly') (DGC)

1992
EPs
Hormoaning (BBC session tracks) (Geffen)
ALBUMS
Pocketwatch (Dave Grohl cassette, under the name "Late!") (Simple Machines)
Incesticide (DGC)

1994
DGC Rarities Vol. 1 ('Pay To Play') (DGC)

1996
From The Muddy Banks Of The Wishkah (live album) (DGC)

2004
With The Lights Out (boxed set) (DGC)

2005
Sliver: The Best Of The Box (Geffen)

2009
Bleach: 20th Anniversary Deluxe Edition (Sub Pop)

2011
Nevermind: 20th Anniversary Super Deluxe Edition (Smart Studios 1990 sessions) (Geffen/UME)

Selected Live Performances 1984–90

This listing was assembled with the help of Mike Ziegler and Kris Sproul of nirvanaguide.com and Chad Channing.

1984

May 4 D&R Theater, Aberdeen, Washington (Krist Novoselic guesting with The Melvins)

1986

May 6 GESCCO, Olympia, Washington (Kurt Cobain, Buzz Osborne, Dale Crover as one-off group Brown Towel)

1987

March 7 17 Nussbaum Road (house party), Raymond, Washington

April 18 Community World Theatre, Tacoma, Washington

May 1 GESCCO, Olympia, Washington

June 27 Community World Theater, Tacoma, Washington

August 9 Community World Theater, Tacoma, Washington

1988

January 23 Community World Theater, Tacoma, Washington

March 19 Community World Theater, Tacoma, Washington

April 24 The Vogue, Seattle, Washington

May 14 The Glass House (house party), Olympia, Washington

May 21 The Evergreen State College (soccer field), Olympia, Washington

June 5 The Central Tavern, Seattle, Washington (possibly cancelled)

June 15 The Vogue, Seattle, Washington (possibly cancelled)

June 17 Hal Holmes Community Center, Ellensburg, Washington

July 3 The Vogue, Seattle, Washington

July 23 The Central Tavern, Seattle, Washington

July 30 Squid Row, Seattle, Washington

August 20 Capitol Lake Jam, Capitol Lake Park, Olympia, Washington

August 29 The Vogue, Seattle, Washington

October 28 Union Station, Seattle, Washington

October 30 Dorm K208, The Evergreen State College, Olympia, Washington

November 23 Speedy O'Tubbs Rhythmic Underground, Bellingham, Washington

December 1 The Underground, Seattle, Washington

December 21 Eagles Hall, Hoquiam, Washington

December 28 The Underground (*Sub Pop 200* record release party), Seattle, Washington

1989

January 6 Satyricon, Portland, Oregon

January 21 Satyricon, Portland, Oregon

February 10 Covered Wagon Saloon, San Francisco, California

February 11 Marsugi's, San Jose, California

February 25 East Ballroom, Husky Union Building, University of Washington, Seattle, Washington

April 1 Reko/Muse Gallery, Olympia, Washington

April 7 Annex Theatre, Seattle, Washington

April 14 Hal Holmes Community center, Ellensburg, Washington

April 26 The Vogue, Seattle, Washington

May 9 The Central Tavern, Seattle, Washington

May 26 Lindbloom Student Center, Green River Community College, Auburn, Washington

June 9 Moore Theatre (Lame Fest), Seattle, Washington

June 10 The Blue Gallery, Portland, Oregon

June 16 Reko/Muse Gallery, Olympia, Washington

June 21 The Vogue, Seattle, Washington

June 22 Covered Wagon Saloon, San Francisco, California

June 23 Rhino Records (in-store performance), Los Angeles, California

June 23 Bogart's, Long Beach, California

June 24 Al's Bar, Los Angeles, California

June 25 Sun Club, Tempe, Arizona

June 27 Rockin' T.P., Santa Fe, New Mexico

June 30 Happy Dogs, San Antonio, Texas

July 1 Axiom, Houston, Texas

July 2 The Axis, Fort Worth, Texas

July 3 The Electric Jungle, Dallas, Texas

July 5 Gabe's Oasis, Iowa City, Iowa

July 6 Uptown Bar, Minneapolis, Minnesota

July 7 O'Cayz Corral, Madison, Wisconsin

July 8 Club Dreamerz, Chicago, Illinois

July 9 The Sonic Temple, Wilkinsburg, Pennsylvania

July 12 J.C. Dobbs, Philadelphia, Pennsylvania

July 13 Maxwell's, Hoboken, New Jersey

July 15 Green Street Station, Jamaica Plain, Massachusetts

July 18 Pyramid Club, New York City, New York

August 26 Center On Contemporary Art, Seattle, Washington

September 26 The Vogue, Seattle, Washington

September 28 Uptown Bar, Minneapolis, Minnesota

September 30 Cabaret Metro, Chicago, Illinois

October 1 Trito's Uptown, Champaign, Illinois

October 2 The Club Sosa, Kalamazoo, Michigan

October 3 Bling Pig, Ann Arbor, Illinois

October 6 Murphy's Pub, Cincinnati, Ohio

October 7 The Outhouse, Lawrence, Kansas

October 8 Lifticket Lounge, Omaha, Nebraska

October 11 The Garage,

Denver, Colorado

October 13 Penny Lane Coffeehouse, Boulder, Colorado

October 23 Riverside, Newcastle Upon Tyne, United Kingdom

October 24 Mandela Building, Manchester Polytechnic, Manchester, United Kingdom

October 25 Duchess Of York, Leeds, United Kingdom

October 27 Students' Union, School of Oriental and African Studies, London, United Kingdom

October 28 Ents Hall, Portsmouth Polytechnic, Portsmouth, United Kingdom

October 29 Edward's No. 8, Birmingham, United Kingdom

October 30 The Wilde Club, Norwich Arts Centre, Norwich, United Kingdom

November 1 Nighttown, Rotterdam, The Netherlands

November 2 Vera, Groningen, The Netherlands

November 3 Tivoli, Utrecht, The Netherlands

November 4 Gigant, Apeldoorn, The Netherlands

November 5 Melkweg, Amsterdam, The Netherlands

November 7 B-52, Mönchengladbach, West Germany

November 8 Rose Club, Cologne, West Germany

November 9 Bad, Hanover, West Germany

November 10 Forum Enger, Enger, West Germany

November 11 Ecstasy, Berlin, West Germany

November 12 Kulturzentrum, Oldenburg, West Germany

November 13 Fabrik, Hamburg, West Germany

November 15 Schwimmbad Musik-Club, Heidelberg, West Germany

November 16 Trust, Nuremberg, West Germany

November 17 Circus, Gammelsdorf, West Germany

November 18 Kultur-Basar, Hanau, West Germany

November 20 Kapu, Linz, Austria

November 21 Petöfi Csarnok, Budapest, Hungary

November 22 U4, Vienna, Austria

November 23 Cafe Pi, Graz, Austria

November 24 Konkret, Hohenems, Austria

November 25 Fri-Son, Fribourg, Switzerland

November 26 Bloom, Mezzago, Italy

November 27 Piper Club, Rome, Italy

November 29 L'Usine, Geneva, Switzerland

November 30 Rote Fabrik, Zurich, Switzerland

December 1 Fahrenheit, MJC Espace Icare, Issy-les-Moulineaux, France

December 2 Democrazy, Ghent, Belgium

December 3 Astoria Theatre (Lame Fest), London, United Kingdom

1990

January 6 East Ballroom, Husky Union Building, University of Washington, Seattle, Washington

January 12 Satyricon, Portland, Oregon

January 19 Rignall Hall, Olympia, Washington

January 20 Legends, Tacoma, Washington

February 9 Pine Street Theatre, Portland, Oregon

February 11 Cactus Club, San Jose, California

February 12 Cattle Club, Sacramento, California

February 14 Rough Trade Records (in-store performance), San Francisco, California

February 14 Kennel Club, San Francisco, California

February 15 Raji's, Hollywood, California

February 16 Bogart's, Long Beach, California

February 17 Iguana's, Tijuana, Mexico

February 19 The Mason Jar, Phoenix, Arizona

February 21 Blue Max, Chico, California

March 12 Town Pump, Vancouver, British Columbia, Canada

April 1 Cabaret Metro, Chicago, Illinois

April 6 Club Underground, Madison, Wisconsin

April 8 The Unicorn, Milwaukee, Wisconsin

April 9 7th Street Entry, Minneapolis, Minnesota

April 10 Blind Pig, Ann Arbor, Michigan

April 14 Shorty's Underground, Cincinnati, Ohio

April 16 Lee's Palace, Toronto, Ontario, Canada

April 17 Foufounes Electriques, Montreal, Quebec, Canada

April 18 ManRay Nightclub, Cambridge, Massachusetts

April 20 Olde Club, Swarthmore College, Swarthmore, Pennsylvania

April 21 Senior House, Massachusetts Institute of Technology, Cambridge, Massachusetts

April 26 Pyramid Club, New York, New York

April 27 SAGA, Hampshire College, Amherst, Massachusetts

April 28 Maxwell's, Hoboken, New Jersey

April 29 9:30 Club, Washington DC

April 30 J.C. Dobbs, Philadelphia, Pennsylvania

May 1 Cat's Cradle, Chapel Hill, North Carolina

May 2 The Milestone, Charlotte, North Carolina

May 4 The Masquerade, Tampa, Florida

May 5 Einstein a Go-Go, Jacksonville Beach, Florida

May 6 The Masquerade, Atlanta, Georgia

May 9 Stache's, Columbus, Ohio

May 10 Shorty's Underground, Cincinnati, Ohio

May 11 Tulsa Theatre, Tulsa, Oklahoma

May 13 Duffy's Tavern, Lincoln, Nebraska

May 14 The Garage, Denver, Colorado

May 17 The Zoo, Boise, Idaho

August 16 Calamity Jayne's Nashville Nevada, Las Vegas, Nevada

August 17 Hollywood Palladium, Hollywood, California

August 19 The Casbah, San Diego, California

August 29 Crest Theatre, Sacramento, California

August 21 Warfield Theatre, San Francisco, California

August 23 Melody Ballroom, Portland, Oregon

August 24 Moore Theatre, Seattle, Washington

August 25 New York Theatre, Vancouver British Columbia, Canada

September 22 Motor Sports International Garage, Seattle, Washington

October 11 North Shore Surf Club, Olympia, Washington

October 17 The Mods (dorm party), The Evergreen State College, Olympia, Washington

October 23 Goldwyn's Suite, Birmingham, United Kingdom

October 24 Astoria Theatre, London, United Kingdom

October 25 Students Union, Leeds Polytechnic, Leeds, United Kingdom

October 26 Calton Studios, Edinburgh, United Kingdom

October 27 Byron Building, Trent Polytechnic, Nottingham, United Kingdom

October 29 The Waterfront, Norwich, United Kingdom

November 25 The Off Ramp Café, Seattle, Washington

December 31 Satyricon, Portland, Oregon

Index

Words in *italics* indicate album titles unless otherwise stated. Words in quotes indicate song titles. Page numbers in **bold** refer to illustrations.

Acknowledgements

I first typed Nirvana's name in March 1988, when I was preparing calendar listings for the April 1988 issue of *The Rocket* magazine (The Vogue: 'Sub Pop with Nirvana 4/24'), little suspecting that writing about the band would occupy much of my future work for the next quarter of a century. During that time I've interviewed many people about the Northwest music scene, Nirvana, and other bands, giving me a wealth of information to draw from.

Thanks to all my interviewees over the years: Ryan Aigner, Grant Alden, Mark Andersen, Dawn Anderson, Mark Arm, Greg Babior, Earnie Bailey, Maria Braganza, Anton Brookes, Phil Buffingon, Aaron Burckhard, Jeff Burlingame, Keith Cameron, Kurt Danielson, Mari Earl, Jason Everman, Jennifer Finch, Steve Fisk, Erik 4-A, Danny Goldberg, J.J. Gonson, John Goodmanson, Dave Grohl, Nikolas Hartshorne, Greg Hokanson, Daniel House, Mark Kates, Tom Kipp, Alex Kostelnik, Jacob McMurray, Courtney Miller, Craig Montgomery, Rob Nyberg, Bruce Pavitt, Candice Pederson, Dan Peters, Charles Peterson, Mark Pickerel, Jonathan Poneman, Tony Poukkula, Alan Pruzan, John Robb, Jon Snyder, Kim Thayil, Ian Tilton, Jenny Toomey, Everett True, Kurdt Vanderhoof, Butch Vig, Alice Wheeler.

Extra thanks are due to Jacob McMurray, Chad Channing, and Jack Endino, for their accessibility (and, in Jacob's case, access to the Experience Music Project's oral history archives), and always being willing to answer yet another question (Wait, I forgot to ask you about …).

When I interviewed Krist Novoselic in 1997, he mentioned that a Nirvana boxed set was being planned, and I said I'd like to work on it. Had he not said yes, my life (and this book) would've taken quite a different path. Thanks, Krist.

More thanks also to: Kris Sproul and Mike Ziegler of nirvanaguide.com for all our discussions, as well as their help and advice; Mitch Holmquist for serving as a willing driver, and for his assistance in other areas; Alex Roberts of livenirvana.com for fielding various questions; Matt 'The Tube' Crowley for help with transportation; William Clark for access to his collection; Andrew Hamlin for help with transcription; everyone who contributed photographs to this book (Mark Andersen, James Bush, Kevin Estrada, Martyn Goodacre, Tracy Marander, Charles Peterson, J.J. Gonson, Alice Wheeler); Tom Jerome Seabrook of Jawbone Press for giving this project the go-ahead; Nigel Osborne at Jawbone Press; and of course my mother.

This book is dedicated to William Kennedy, who went above and beyond the call of duty in helping with the transcription. And to the memories of Charles Lawson (a victim of the American health care system) and his beloved cat Mingus. I miss them both.

Picture credits

The pictures used in this book came from the following sources, and we are grateful for their help. **Jacket front** Kevin Estrada; **spine** Charles Peterson; **jacket rear** Tracy Marander; **2–3** Alice Wheeler; **6** Tracy Marander (2), Alice Wheeler; **7** Alice Wheeler; **8** Tracy Marander, Charles Peterson; **9** Alice Wheeler; **10** Charles Peterson (2); **11** J.J. Gonson (2); **12** Charles Peterson, J.J. Gonson/Getty Images; **13** J.J. Gonson/Getty Images, Charles Peterson; **14** Alice Wheeler, Amanda MacKaye; **15** Charles Peterson, James Bush; **16** Martyn Goodacre.